Fodor's

LOS ANGELES

Contents

Welcome to Los Angeles

Drive for miles between towering palm trees, bodega-lined streets, and Downtown's skyscrapers, and you'll still never discover all of L.A.'s hidden gems. Scratch the surface to find people-watching on Rodeo Drive, historic bars on the Sunset Strip, and the glitz and grime of Hollywood Boulevard. From the trendy East Side to beachy Santa Monica, experience everything in the city's year-round idyllic weather. This book was produced in the middle of the COVID-19 pandemic. As you plan your upcoming travels to Los Angeles, please confirm that places are still open and let us know when we need to make updates by writing to us at editors@fodors.com.

TOP REASONS TO GO

★ **Seeing Stars:** Both through the telescope atop Griffith Park and among the residents of Beverly Hills.

★ **Eating:** From food trucks to fine dining, an unparalleled meal awaits your palate.

★ **Beaches and Boardwalks:** The dream of '80s Venice is alive in California.

★ **Shopping:** Peruse eclectic boutiques or window-shop on Rodeo Drive.

★ **Architecture:** Art deco wonders to Frank Gehry masterpieces abound.

★ **Scenic Drives:** You haven't seen the sunset until you've seen it from a winding L.A. road.

Fodor's Features

MAPS

Chapter 1

EXPERIENCE LOS ANGELES

20 ULTIMATE EXPERIENCES

Los Angeles offers terrific experiences that should be on every traveler's list. Here are Fodor's top picks for a memorable trip.

1 Walt Disney Concert Hall

Designed by Frank Gehry, the curves of this stainless steel-clad masterpiece are a signature of the modern metropolis. The 2,265-seat Disney Hall is home to the Los Angeles Philharmonic. *(Ch. 8)*

2 Disneyland

"The Happiest Place on Earth" continues to delight children and all but the most cynical adults. *(Ch. 12)*

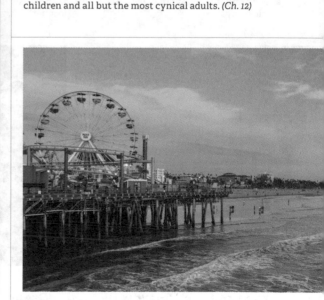

3 Santa Monica Pier

Spend a sunny day beside the Pacific Ocean riding the Ferris wheel and playing dozens of games for prizes at this popular family destination. *(Ch. 3)*

4 Universal Studios Hollywood

Universal is more of a theme park with lots of roller coasters and thrill rides than a backstage pass, though its tour provides a good firsthand look at familiar TV and movie sets. *(Ch. 6)*

5 Los Angeles County Museum of Art

LACMA is the focal point of the museum district along Wilshire Boulevard. Chris Burden's *Urban Light* sculpture, with more than 220 cast-iron street lamps, marks the location. *(Ch. 7)*

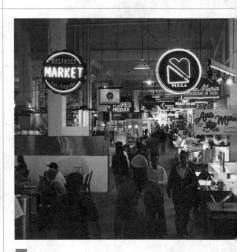

6 Venice Beach Boardwalk

The bohemian vibe of this famous boardwalk is constantly threatened by gentrification. Still, the magicians, fortune-tellers, and Muscle Beach weight lifters survive. *(Ch. 3)*

7 Grand Central Market

In continuous operation since 1917, this market is a hub for fresh produce, deli staples, and dozens of restaurant vendors that attracts hungry lunch crowds. *(Ch. 8)*

8 Pacific Coast Highway

Nothing epitomizes L.A. more than a drive down the scenic PCH. After taking in the sweeping views, stop at a seafood shack for ahi burgers or fish-and-chips. *(Ch. 11)*

9 The Broad Museum

Philanthropists Eli and Edythe Broad built this striking museum to house their stunning art collection, which features work from Jean-Michel Basquiat and Kara Walker. *(Ch. 8)*

10 TCL Chinese Theatre and the Walk of Fame

When this theater opened in 1927, the tradition of stars imprinting their hands or feet into the cement began. Today, the Walk of Fame runs a mile along Hollywood Boulevard. *(Ch. 6)*

11 Mexican Food

Whether you're searching for authentic Oaxacan mole, fresh ceviche, cheap tacos, or bottomless margaritas, L.A. has unbeatable choices for every type of Mexican food experience. *(Ch. 3–11)*

12 Sunset Boulevard

This avenue began humbly in the 18th century as a route from El Pueblo de Los Angeles to the Pacific. Today, as it passes through West Hollywood, it becomes the sexy and seductive Sunset Strip. *(Ch. 5)*

13 Rodeo Drive

Dominated by exclusive fashion brands, Rodeo Drive is a shoppers' paradise. Along the cobblestoned Via Rodeo, you can drop $1,000 on python pumps or splurge on a $500 sushi dinner. *(Ch. 4)*

14 The Hollywood Sign

It's actually illegal to get up close to one of the city's most iconic images, but there are multiple hiking trails in and around Griffith Park to help you get the perfect pic. *(Ch. 9)*

15 Malibu

The white-sand beaches of Malibu are magnets for surfers, sunbathers, swimmers, and whale-watchers. Spots like Point Dume and Zuma Beach also beckon. *(Ch. 11)*

16 Hollywood Bowl

Nothing compares to spending a summer evening at the Hollywood Bowl. For a true local experience, pack a picnic and don't be afraid to share with your neighbors. *(Ch. 6)*

17 Paramount Pictures

This is the only surviving major studio from Hollywood's golden age. Paramount offers probably the most authentic studio tour, giving you a real sense of the film industry's history. *(Ch. 6)*

18 Koreatown

As the biggest (and many claim best) Koreatown in the country, this L.A. neighborhood wows with its collection of authentic and delicious restaurants, many focusing on Korean BBQ. *(Ch. 7)*

19 Getty Center

On a hillside above Brentwood, the Getty Center houses airy galleries filled with impressionist canvases, Greek antiquities, and French decorative arts. *(Ch. 3)*

20 Griffith Park and Observatory

The country's largest municipal park has plenty of hiking and biking trails, along with its famed observatory offering breathtaking city views. *(Ch. 9)*

WHAT'S WHERE

1 Santa Monica and Venice. In Santa Monica, a lively beach scene plays out daily. Venice is a more raffish mix of artists, beach punks, and yuppies, most of whom you can see on the Venice Boardwalk.

2 Beverly Hills. Go for the glamour, the restaurants, and the scene. Rodeo Drive is particularly good for a look at wretched or ravishing excess.

3 West Hollywood and Fairfax. West Hollywood is an area for urban indulgences—shopping, restaurants, nightlife—rather than sightseeing. The Fairfax District within WeHo offers loads of shopping options and a wide array of restaurants.

4 Hollywood and the Studios. Glitzy and tarnished, good and bad—Hollywood is just like the entertainment business itself. The Walk of Fame, TCL Chinese Theatre, Paramount Pictures studio, and the Hollywood Bowl keep the romantic past alive.

5 Mid-Wilshire and Koreatown. Mid-Wilshire is a glorious hodgepodge of manicured lawns and art deco high-rises. Here you can also peruse art along Museum Row. Just east is Koreatown, which boasts some of the best bars and restaurants in the city.

6 Downtown Los Angeles. One of the oldest parts of the city, DTLA shows off spectacular modern architecture. The MOCA and the Broad anchor a world-class art scene, while El Pueblo de Los Angeles, Chinatown, and Little Tokyo reflect the city's diversity.

7 Los Feliz, Silver Lake, and the Eastside. If you've come to L.A. in search of everything young, cool, and hip, then head east. This is a land of good eats and better booze.

8 Pasadena. Parts of Pasadena are even older than Downtown. It's a quiet, genteel area to visit, with outstanding Arts and Crafts homes and a pair of exceptional museums.

9 Malibu and the Beaches. Drive up the Pacific Coast Highway to Malibu, where the rich and famous reside, or plop down on the white-sand beaches along the way to spy on sunbathing sea lions and migrating whales deep in the Pacific.

Los Angeles Today

Starstruck. Excessive. Smoggy. Superficial? There's a modicum of truth to each of the adjectives regularly applied to L.A., but the locals dismiss their prevalence as envy from those who aren't as blessed with year-round sunshine. Pop culture does permeate life here, its massive economy employing millions of Southern Californians, but the city where dreams are made accommodates those from all avenues of life.

POLITICS

L.A.'s political scene is completely dominated by Democrats; so much so, that 15 of the county's 18 congressional seats are typically held by the Democratic Party. Locally, the biggest hotbed issue the city faces surrounds housing, or a lack thereof. The latest homeless numbers in Los Angeles have reached apocalyptic levels with more than 60,000 people sleeping on the streets. The city is constantly trying to solve the issue with new shelters, tax hikes, and ordinances, but it's a problem that has only gotten worse throughout the past decade.

DEMOGRAPHICS

Officially, Los Angeles is home to more than 10 million people. Unofficial estimates put the number somewhere between 12 and 15 million. Regardless of the count, the city is one of the most diverse in the country. Nearly half the population is Hispanic or Latinx, the Asian population is more than 15%, and 10% of residents are Black or African American.

WILDFIRES

Every year, wildfires rip through California causing people to lose their lives and their homes. Stories of harrowing escapes are becoming more common than ever. Fortunately, the city of Los Angeles has mostly been spared from massive fire damage (air quality aside), though the dried foliage in Griffith Park and the Santa Monica Mountains keep residents on high alert. Make sure to check local news reports when hiking on hot summer days.

PUBLIC TRANSIT

Though it's nowhere near perfect (or completed), L.A. has been slowly adding Metro lines that run throughout the entire city. Expanding like spider legs from Union Station Downtown, routes can take you deep into Hollywood, down to Santa Monica, and will eventually reach the Los Angeles International Airport.

HOLLYWOOD

Hollywood may disappoint tourists looking to overdose on glitz; after all, most of its moviemakers departed for the San Fernando Valley decades ago, leaving the area to languish. Even after the much-hyped debut of the Hollywood & Highland Center, the area remains more gritty than glamorous, but that's part of its charm.

Tourists continue to flock to the region, trodding over the stars on the Hollywood Walk of Fame or seeing how the size of their hand compares to celebrities both living and dead at the TCL Chinese Theatre. It's truly the Times Square of the city, but it's still a must for any first-time visitor to experience.

SCOOTERS AND AIRBNBS

It's no secret that L.A. is a hard town to maneuver without a car, but competing scooter companies—Bird, Lime, and Uber—have popped up throughout the city, especially in tourist-heavy areas on the Westside and in Hollywood. The scooter invasion may have some residents griping that they're discarded on sidewalks like trash, but it's heavenly for the out-of-towner who doesn't want to hoof it along the long stretches between Metro stops.

Meanwhile, another tech solution for tourists is being heavily limited: the Los Angeles City Council has restricted Airbnb rentals. Since 2019, property owners have only been able to list their primary residence (as opposed to one owner renting out multiple properties through the website) and only homes that are not under rent control.

HIP HOODS

First, it was Los Feliz. Then it was Silver Lake. Then it was Echo Park. Now it's Highland Park, Glassell Park, Cypress Park. The cool kids keep going farther and farther northeast. So, if you want to find the best bars in town, you'll have to keep venturing farther afield.

THE FOOD SCENE

Star chefs continue to make their mark in every pocket of Los Angeles. You can head to Chinatown for David Chang's eclectic spot Majordomo or dine in style at Wolfgang Puck's famous Beverly Hills hub, Spago. Get carnivorous at chef Curtis Stone's meat-lovers' den Gwen in Hollywood. Or slurp up spaghetti at Top Chef alum Antonia Lofaso's Scopa Italian Roots in Venice.

Eating in L.A. remains relatively egalitarian. Even posh places seldom require jackets, so the dress code is casual. Ditto for the menu. (In the city that invented fast food, it's no coincidence that Govind Armstrong flips gourmet burgers at LAX or that Nancy Silverton built her reputation on pizza.) If you want to go budget, you can easily justify chowing down at McDonald's, Carl's Jr., and In-N-Out Burger since they qualify as true local cuisine; they all originated in the Five-County Area.

WHAT'S NEW

After a few delays, the Academy Museum of Motion Pictures finally opened in fall 2021. The 300,000-square-foot Renzo Piano–designed museum will unveil *Where Dreams Are Made,* a permanent exhibit that takes visitors inside *The Wizard of Oz, 2001: A Space Odyssey,* and the films of Charlie Chaplin. The first temporary exhibit will be a tribute to Japanese filmmaker Hayao Miyazaki and will include production materials from *Spirited Away* and *My Neighbor Totoro.*

You'll also be able to step inside another eagerly awaited cinematic wonder: Star Wars: Galaxy's Edge at Disneyland opened in 2019. Here you can pilot the Millennium Falcon, join the resistance, and go to the far, far away planet of Batuu.

A long time ago, L.A. lost both the Rams and the Raiders. The Rams came back, but the Raiders stayed away, replaced by the Chargers. The only problem was they had nowhere to play. In 2021, a brand-spankin'-new stadium will be open for business in Inglewood, hosting both teams.

Helping to ferry people to Inglewood in 2021 will be the newly opened Crenshaw/LAX line of the Metro, which connects the Expo Line in the north to the Green Line in the south. Commuters will be able to access Leimert Park and Hyde Park, and eventually, LAX. A few years later, in 2023, the Purple Line is scheduled to expand into Mid-City, connecting it with Downtown.

What to Eat and Drink in Los Angeles

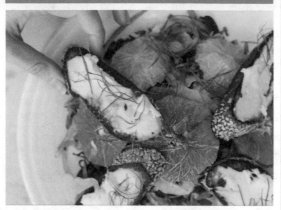

VEGAN FARE
Los Angeles is one of the best places in the country to eat healthy, and for anyone trying to eat less meat, it's overflowing with restaurants catering to vegans. Places like Café Gratitude and Pura Vita are excellent plant-based dining stops.

L.A. HOTDOGS
While every major city in the country has their own take on street hot dogs, L.A.'s Mexican-inspired version is arguably the best. Wrapped in bacon and topped with grilled onions, bell peppers, ketchup, mustard, mayo, and jalapeños, it's practically a ritual for anyone stumbling home drunk to grab one. By the way, you should probably be drunk while eating them. Look for street carts in areas with a lot of bars—Spring Street and Staples Center in Downtown, Sunset Boulevard in Echo Park, and Normandie Avenue in Koreatown.

KOREAN BBQ
Los Angeles claims to have the biggest (and best) Koreatown in the world. So if there's one place you should feast on Korean BBQ—outside of South Korea, that is—it's here. There are so many Korean BBQ joints in the city, in fact, that it's hard to pick the best ones, though Park's BBQ and Magal certainly have our votes. If you like Korean BBQ and you enjoyed those street tacos, then you might be ready for Korean BBQ tacos, which is one of the few culinary creations that originated in La La Land. They're exactly what it sounds like—tacos but with Korean BBQ meats, and the best place to get them is from one of Roy Choi's legendary Kogi food trucks. To find a location, go to kogibbq.com.

ORGANIC JUICE AND SMOOTHIES
Make fun of L.A.'s healthy juice obsession all you want, but they're actually surprisingly delicious, not to mention nutritious. Don't knock it until you try it. Naturewell and Vitalist Food are good, popular spots to sample them.

STREET TACOS
This is a beautifully simple dish: grilled meat (al pastor, chorizo, or carne asada) with chopped cilantro and onion, wrapped in corn or flour tortillas, drizzled with lime and salsa. They're not only delicious, but cheap at $1 to $3 a piece. Every Angeleno has their own go-to spot, usually a stand or a truck, so ask your favorite local for recommendations. Guisados is always a good choice, with multiple locations, including West Hollywood and Boyle Heights.

ELOTE
This Mexican corn concoction is essentially just grilled corn smothered with butter, crema fresca (or mayo), cotija, chile powder, and lime then served on a cob or in a cup. But it's a delightful assault on your taste buds and a favorite Los Angelenos snack. Keep an eye out for street carts that tout it or take a chance at one of L.A.'s many farmers' markets.

Experience Los Angeles WHAT TO EAT AND DRINK IN LOS ANGELES

Korean BBQ

FILIPINO FOOD

The city is teeming with Filipino food joints that either champion traditional Filipino dishes like Pork Adobo, Kare-Kare and Pinakbet, or boast modern takes. For a traditional take, go to Max's in Glendale. For a modern twist, Petite Peso in Downtown is a good spot. Regardless of your choice, leave room for dessert, as they're to die for.

IN-N-OUT

No L.A. food list is complete without the legendary In-N-Out. "Where's the closest In-N-Out" is asked by just about every tourist the moment they arrive. Not that we blame them— In-N-Out burgers and fries are made fresh and made to order, which is why they're so good in the first place. But which location should you go to? Any of them! Whether it's the one near LAX as soon as you leave the airport or in Hollywood, which gets a lot of traffic.

FRENCH DIP SANDWICH

There's an ever-present debate about where the legendary French Dip sandwich was created. But whether you're a fan of Cole's French Dip in the middle of Downtown or Philippe the Original in Chinatown, know that both have over 100 years of history and make savory versions that make the debate moot.

CHICKEN AND WAFFLES

Angelenos are in love with the magical combo of chicken and waffles. The craze really took off in the 1970s when Roscoe's House of Chicken and Waffles opened in Hollywood. Today, you can find the tasty mix at multiple restaurants like the Broad-adjacent Otium in Downtown or at Brite Spot Diner in Echo Park.

SUSHI

People understandably think of L.A. as a Mexican-food city, but the sushi here is also world-class. There are hundreds and hundreds of options to choose from, such as counter spots Hide or Sushi Gen, the omakase magicians at Q or Sushi Ginza Onodera, or sceney joints like Katsuya and Izaka-ya.

CRAFT BEER

As one of the most creative cities in the world, it shouldn't be shocking that L.A. artisans have been doling out incredibly unique craft beers. There are respectable spots all over the city—check out Highland Park Brewery, Monkish Brewing Co., and Brouwerij West for some of the tastiest.

The Best Beaches in Los Angeles

HERMOSA BEACH

Blazing orange sunsets draw sunning crowds and shutterbugs, but this is, without a doubt, a surfing beach. Even its famous landmark—the statue of Tim Kelly riding a swell—is a declaration of this fact.

SURFRIDER BEACH

There are two sets of people who frequent the sandy Malibu outpost—the surf nuts (hence, the name) and the anglers.

WILL ROGERS STATE BEACH

This stretch in Pacific Palisades is known for its epic sunsets. Out of L.A.'s top beaches, Will Rogers is also probably the quietest.

EL MATADOR BEACH

Throngs of people flock to Malibu's worst-kept secret, from selfie-taking tourists to locals hoping for quiet spots to call their own. But don't worry about the crowds. El Matador's sweeping, sea-meets-land panoramas make up for it.

ZUMA BEACH

On summer weekends, you'll be hard-pressed to find a good place to lay your blanket, but this popular Malibu beach is 2 miles of gorgeous zigzagging shore.

VENICE BEACH

Even though Venice is now shockingly expensive, a colorful, artistic past still lingers. Along the boardwalk, vibrant street art adorn the modern retail and gastronomic spaces. Watch out for the tech bros that have taken over the neighborhood.

POINT DUME

Walk along the trail that meanders through this state beach and nature reserve, and you'll often see waves crashing against the wind-carved bluff, tide pools, the occasional migrating whale, and one of the most epic panoramas in Southern California.

Manhattan Beach

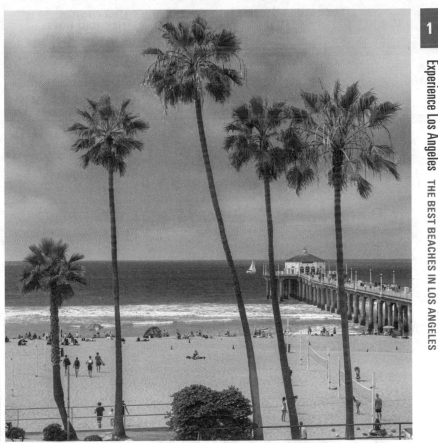

LEO CARRILLO STATE PARK

This is a tale of two beaches. When the tide is in, it's a serene spot to gaze at the sea. When out, it's for those seeking exploration—that's when the tide pools and caves are unveiled. Camping is allowed, so pitch a tent and stay a while.

MANHATTAN BEACH

A day at this beach might involve taking your cruiser for a spin along the bike trail, a bit of retail therapy, and a nosh at a restaurant serving freshly caught seafood.

DOCKWEILER STATE BEACH

Is there a dreamier way of topping off your day at the beach than a bonfire at twilight? Beach bonfires are largely illegal in L.A., but at Dockweiler's 3.7-mile stretch, lighting up isn't just permitted, it's practically encouraged. It's for this reason that the beach is almost always a scene where twenty- and thirty-somethings roast marshmallows and guzzle beer.

The Best Famous Film Locations in Los Angeles

GRIFFITH PARK OBSERVATORY

Movie buffs will recognize this building in countless films like *Rebel Without a Cause* with James Dean (there's even a James Dean bust outside), *Charlie's Angels: Full Throttle*, and recent (almost) best picture Oscar winner, *La La Land*.

MILLENNIUM BILTMORE HOTEL

A grande dame of L.A.'s Downtown hospitality scene, the hotel was opened in 1923 and was once the home of the Academy Awards ceremony. It's also made appearances in movies like *Ghostbusters*, *Beverly Hills Cop*, and *Cruel Intentions*.

CIRCUS LIQUOR

If you happen to be hanging out in Burbank after a tour at the Warner Bros. lot, head over to Circus Liquor, which is known for its 32-foot clown sign. More famously, however, it's the parking lot where Cher Horowitz was mugged in *Clueless*. "It's an Alaïa!"

BEVERLY WILSHIRE HOTEL

This iconic hotel was built in 1928 and has hosted the likes of Elvis, John Lennon, and Barack Obama. But it's mostly known as the setting for *Pretty Woman*, starring Julia Roberts. Fans of the movie can book the "Pretty Woman for a Day" experience at the hotel.

POINT DUME

Point Dume and Westward Beach are constantly in the movies. There's a good chance on any given weekday that you may spot a film crew here. It's been used in *The Big Lebowski* and *Iron Man*. But it's most famous claim to fame: the iconic ending of the original *Planet of the Apes*.

THE WESTIN BONAVENTURE HOTEL

Another behemoth Downtown hotel, the Bonaventure is actually the biggest in L.A. with more than 1,300 rooms. Its unique cylindrical towers have starred in a bevy of films. California's former governor, Arnold Schwarzenegger, rode a horse into the glass elevator in *True Lies*.

Bradbury Building

GAMBLE HOUSE

Head up to Pasadena and check out Doc Brown's house, a stunning example of American Craftsman style. Close your eyes, and you can picture Michael J. Fox wearing an orange windbreaker vest as he runs up to the front door in *Back to the Future.*

USC CAMPUS

The University of Southern California is a private school known for its football team and stunning campus that also houses one of the best film schools in the country. So it shouldn't come as a surprise that a number of its graduates and wannabe attendees have taken time to film here in movies like *Legally Blonde* and *The Graduate.*

BRADBURY BUILDING

Built in 1893, this DTLA architectural marvel is like an M.C. Escher painting come to life. With a series of interlocking wrought iron stairs and caged elevators, the Bradbury Building has been featured in *500 Days of Summer, Double Indemnity, D.O.A.,* and most famously, *Blade Runner.*

The Best Celebrity Hangouts in Los Angeles

CAFÉ GRATITUDE LARCHMONT

Round out your L.A. vacation with a plant-based meal at local chain Café Gratitude. For a celeb sighting, head to their Larchmont Boulevard location where Jake Gyllenhaal and Beyoncé obligingly declare what they're grateful for before digging in.

THE HOLLYWOOD ROOSEVELT

The Hollywood Roosevelt is one of L.A.'s oldest hotels, and has hosted numerous celebrities and dignitaries in its Spanish Colonial Revival rooms. Set in the heart of Hollywood, it offers a convenient location as well as a number of watering holes, including Tropicana Pool & Café.

THE GROVE

L.A. may be strewn with outdoor malls, but it's The Grove that gets the highest billing, not just for its collection of mid- to high-end shops and restaurants, but also for its next-door neighbor, the Farmers Market. It's also one of the best places to see stars like Lena Headey, Zendaya, and Mario Lopez.

PINZ BOWLING CENTER

For a bit of family-friendly fun, head to Pinz in Studio City, where bowling is more than just a game, it's also a neon- and black-light party. Celebrities often pop in here for bowling night, from A-listers like Vin Diesel and Jessica Alba to performers like Bruno Mars and Missy Elliott.

NOBU MALIBU

Nobu is a known A-list hot spot that's hosted everyone from Keanu Reeves to Kendall Jenner. Even if you don't spot a star, it's still worth the trip for its impeccable sushi and sashimi. Be warned, though: mingling with A-listers doesn't come cheap.

TOSCANA

Upscale Brentwood is home to many celebrities, and rustic trattoria Toscana is one of their neighborhood haunts. It may not be L.A.'s best Italian restaurant—for that, check out Osteria Mozza—but for star sightings, it's your best bet.

CHATEAU MARMONT

The Chateau Marmont is possibly L.A.'s best-known celebrity haunt. Come for brunch in the garden terrace or drop in at night for the Hollywood-inspired cocktails. Photos are not allowed.

Catch

CRAIG'S

A West Hollywood dining staple, Craig's plain facade provides a safe haven for the movie industry's most important names and well-known faces like John Legend and Chrissy Teigen. Just keep in mind this joint is always busy, so you might not even get a table. It's a good thing the food is worth the effort.

CATCH

Secure a table at the flora-cluttered Catch in West Hollywood and rub elbows with the likes of David Beckham and the Jenner-Kardashian clan. This eatery is as L.A. as you can get, with its alfresco setting, vegan and gluten-free offerings, and locally and sustainably grown ingredients.

RUNYON CANYON

Out of L.A.'s numerous beautiful hiking spots, Runyon Canyon gets the biggest share of celebrity regulars, probably because it's strategically tucked between the Hollywood Hills, where many stars live, and the Sunset Strip. It's also a great venue for getting some fresh air, not to mention an ideal spot to take panoramic sunset photos.

Best Historic Restaurants in Los Angeles

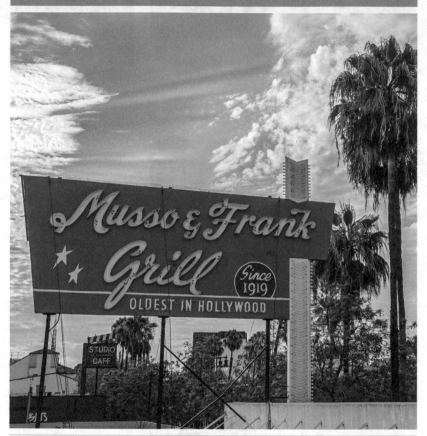

COLE'S

There's a fight in Los Angeles over who created the French Dip sandwich. The first contender is Cole's, whose sign on the door says they're the originator of the salty, juicy, melt-in-your-mouth meats. The restaurant opened in 1908 and today is still going strong with dark lighting, delicious sandwiches, and a secret speakeasy called the Varnish hidden in the back.

PHILLIPE'S

Also opened in 1908, Phillipe's is the second restaurant to claim ownership of the French Dip. Owner Philippe Mathieu claims that the sandwich was invented in 1918 when he accidentally dropped the roll into a vat of hot jus and the customer said he didn't care. It was so good, he came back the next day for more. The French Dip sandwich was coined because of the dipping into the jus and because of Mathieu's French heritage or possibly because the customer was French. No one actually knows, but their sandwiches are incredible.

THE MUSSO & FRANK GRILL

This classic steak house opened in 1919 by Frank Toulet, Joseph Musso, and French chef Jean Rue. The

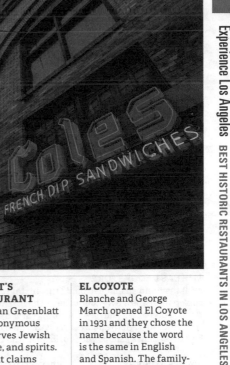

eatery quickly became a hot spot for A-list guests like Charlie Chaplin, Gary Cooper, Marilyn Monroe, Elizabeth Taylor, and even F. Scott Fitzgerald who allegedly proofread his novels in the booths. Today the restaurant is known for perfect martinis, red tux–wearing waiters, leather booths, and sizzling steaks.

ORIGINAL PANTRY CAFÉ

Opened in 1924 by Dewey Logan, this classic diner claims to have never closed in the entirety of its run and is currently owned by former L.A. mayor Richard Riordan. Open 24/7, the diner serves American food for breakfast, lunch, and dinner, and is known for cakes, pies, steaks, and chops. The cash-only establishment is also a Los Angeles historic cultural monument.

GREENBLATT'S DELI-RESTAURANT

In 1926, Herman Greenblatt opened his eponymous deli, which serves Jewish deli food, wine, and spirits. The restaurant claims to have the rarest roast beef in town—and they're probably right. The deli also boasts a famous clientele that included Marlon Brando, Lenny Bruce, Rita Hayworth, and John Belushi.

CANTER'S

Opened in 1931, Canter's is your classic Jewish deli, through and through. In front you can buy freshly baked breads and pastries, while the enormous restaurant offers everything from giant sandwiches to matzo ball soup 24 hours a day. In addition to the food, there's also the Kibbitz Room, which features live music and comedy throughout the week.

EL COYOTE

Blanche and George March opened El Coyote in 1931 and they chose the name because the word is the same in English and Spanish. The family-friendly Mexican restaurant is one of the oldest in town and offers up all the standard nachos, burritos, and enchiladas. If it's on the menu, make sure you get the Ostrich tacos—they're one of a kind.

PINK'S HOT DOGS

Since it opened in 1939 by Paul and Betty Pink, this ultrafamous hot dog stand has had lines around the block filled with Angelenos and tourists alike. Pink's is most-known for their chili dogs as well as being open until 3 am on weekends.

Under the Radar Los Angeles

THE LAST BOOKSTORE

Built inside an abandoned bank, this Instagram-worthy book paradise is a two-floor behemoth with more than 250,000 books, old and new, including rare first editions. As you wind through the maze of shelves, you'll be surprised to find tucked-away shops with curios, art, and even yarn.

WATTS TOWERS

It's probably not on most tourists' top lists, but that's a mistake considering the Watts Towers is on the U.S. National Register of Historic Places, a U.S. National Historic Landmark, a California Historical Landmark, and a Los Angeles Historic-Cultural Monument. The towers were built over 33 years ago by Italian immigrant Simon Rodia between 1921 and 1954 and consist of 17 interlaced iron spirals with mosaics and other architectural features.

BRONSON CAVES

Located in the southwest section of Griffith Park, the Bronson Caves are the remnants of an old quarry that was used in the early 1900s. Fans of the original '60s *Batman* TV show might recognize this spot as the Batcave.

THE MAGIC CASTLE

Up on a hill, just north of Hollywood Boulevard is a Victorian mansion that is home to the Academy of Magical Arts. Inside this secret spot is a magician's Shangri-La filled with multiple bars and stages. In order to get in, you need to be invited by a member, but there is a work-around. If you stay at the Magic Castle Hotel next door, they can get you inside without any hocus-pocus.

THE CECIL HOTEL

Fans of the macabre will find lots to love when they learn about the history of Downtown L.A.'s most notorious hotel. Originally built in 1924, the hotel was once home to multiple serial killers, including the Night Stalker, and the spot of many mysterious deaths, including suicides and unsolved murders. The most recent occurred only a few years ago when they found the remains of a tourist inside the hotel's water tower.

MARILYN MONROE'S GRAVE

The world's fascination with Marilyn Monroe, the most famous blonde bombshell in Hollywood history, continues decades after her death. That fascination even carries over to Monroe's final resting place, which is in a hallway of aboveground crypts at the Pierce Brothers Westwood Village Memorial Park and Mortuary. While you're there, you can also find other luminaries like Truman Capote, Billy Wilder, Rodney Dangerfield, Jack Lemmon, and many others.

BINOCULARS BUILDING

Frank Gehry is known around the world for his architectural masterpieces. In L.A. alone he's responsible for multiple houses and buildings like the Gehry Residence, Loyola

Spadena House

Law School, and Walt Disney Hall. But one of his most interesting creations is the Binoculars Building, a quirky Venice spot that is exactly as advertised: a giant set of binoculars. The project was originally designed for the Chiat/Day advertising agency and today is home to Google's main L.A. office.

BARNSDALL ART PARK
In East Hollywood is a hidden-away park that happens to be a Los Angeles Historic-Cultural Monument and National Historic Landmark that features the Hollyhock House, a Frank Lloyd Wright masterpiece. Named after Aline Barnsdall, an oil heiress who commissioned the Wright work in 1915, the park today is a destination for art, architecture, and a city getaway. During summer months, the park hosts a Friday night wine tasting event where Angeleno's can picnic on the lawn with glasses of Chardonnay while watching the setting sun.

PETERSEN AUTOMOTIVE MUSEUM
Car lovers will salivate over the insane collection at this museum set right on Museum Row in the Miracle Mile section of L.A. But what tourists may not know is that beyond the standard museum exhibitions, there's a secret vault that has more than 250 additional vehicles that are some of the coolest and most-rare automotive treasures in the world.

HOLLYWOOD FOREVER CEMETERY
The most famous celebrity burial ground around is without question the Hollywood Forever Cemetery. Built in 1899, the cemetery is home to Judy Garland, Bugsy Siegel, Cecil B. DeMille, and many others. There are tours of the space that last around two hours where you can discover lots of history and a few mysteries. The cemetery is also known for movie screenings and concerts.

SPADENA HOUSE
Otherwise known as the Witch's House in Beverly Hills, the Spadena House has an interesting history. First built on the Willat Studios lot in 1920, the house was physically moved to its current ritzy location in 1924. The house is not open for tourists, but the fairy tale–like appearance is viewable from the street for onlookers to snap pics. Movie buffs will also recognize it from a background shot in the film *Clueless*.

Los Angeles with Kids

With seemingly endless sunny days, Angeleno kids almost never have to play indoors. There are a few things to keep in mind, however, when navigating the city with little ones: if possible, avoid the freeways by exploring no more than one neighborhood each day, and remember that you can never have too much sunscreen—L.A. parents don't leave home without the stuff.

Of course, the top reason many families come to the L.A. area is to visit Disneyland. Experience all the classic attractions that you may recall from your own childhood visit, such as the "It's a Small World" ride, a meet-and-greet with Tinkerbell, or a Mickey Mouse home tour, who, unlike less amenable celebrities, makes a daily appearance for fans. But there's plenty more to see and do.

HEAD UNDER THE SEA
Head down to the **Aquarium of the Pacific** in Long Beach to learn tons of interesting facts about the Pacific Ocean. On display are shimmering schools of fish, a swaying kelp forest, a shark lagoon featuring more than 150 varieties, and a tropical reef habitat filled with zebra sharks, porcupine puffers, and a large blue Napoleon wrasse.

COMMUNE WITH NATURE
Don't miss your chance to see the retired space shuttle *Endeavour* or catch a film at the seven-story IMAX theater at the **California Science Center.** Just down the road is the **Natural History Museum,** where kids can explore everything from diamonds to the vast dinosaur hall. In spring, there's the outdoor butterfly habitat, fittingly named the Pavilion of Wings, which makes way for the Spider Pavilion come fall.

WALK IN THE PARK
Griffith Park is the largest municipal park and urban wilderness area in the United States, and the kids will go wild for the pony rides and the classic 1926 merry-go-round. But the pièce de résistance is the Griffith Park and Southern Railroad, a circa-1940s miniature train that travels through an old Western town and a Native American village. Other highlights are the Los Angeles Zoo and the Griffith Observatory, an L.A. icon in its own right.

LEARN BY DOING
Little ones can pan for gold in a small creek, play Spider-Man on a weblike climber, or race around a trike track at the **Kidspace Children's Museum.** Indoor activities include a walk-through kaleidoscope, two climbing towers—one mimicking raindrops, the other modeled after a wisteria vine, a bug diner (think banana worm bread and roasted cricket pizza), and a contraption that lets kids generate their very own earthquake.

HIT THE BEACH
The best way to check out **Santa Monica Beach** is by renting bikes or roller skates at any one of the shacks on the Strand (a stretch of concrete boardwalk that snakes along the beach toward Venice). Some must-sees along the way: the roller dancers of Venice Beach, the bodybuilders of Muscle Beach, and the Santa Monica Pier, a 100-year-old structure that's home to a vintage 1920s carousel, an oversize Ferris wheel, and old-time amusement park games. After hitting the beach, drive over to the pedestrian-only Third Street Promenade to grab a bite and do some shopping.

Sports in Los Angeles

BASEBALL

Los Angeles Angels of Anaheim. The Angels often contend for the top slot in the Western Division of pro baseball's American League. ⊠ *Angel Stadium of Anaheim, 2000 E. Gene Autry Way, Anaheim* ☎ *714/940–2000* ⊕ *www.angelsbaseball. com.*

Los Angeles Dodgers. The Dodgers take on their National League rivals at one of major league baseball's most comfortable ballparks, Dodger Stadium. ⊠ *Dodger Stadium, 1000 Elysian Park Ave., Echo Park ✛ Exit off I–110, Pasadena Fwy.* ☎ *323/224–1507* ⊕ *www.dodgers.com.*

BASKETBALL

Los Angeles Clippers. L.A.'s "other" pro basketball team, the Clippers, was formerly an easy ticket, but these days the club routinely sells out its home games. ⊠ *Staples Center, 1111 S. Figueroa St., Downtown* ☎ *213/742–7100* ⊕ *www.nba. com/clippers* Ⓜ *Pico.*

Los Angeles Lakers. The team of pro-basketball champions Magic, Kareem, Shaq, and Kobe had slipped in recent years, but thanks to LeBron's arrival, excitement has been renewed, championships restored, and seats are packed. ⊠ *Staples Center, 1111 S. Figueroa St., Downtown* ☎ *310/426–6000* ⊕ *www.nba.com/lakers* Ⓜ *Pico.*

Los Angeles Sparks. The women's pro basketball team has made it to the WNBA playoffs more than a dozen times in the past two decades. ⊠ *Staples Center, 1111 S. Figueroa St., Downtown* ☎ *310/426–6031* ⊕ *www.wnba.com/sparks* Ⓜ *Pico.*

University of California at Los Angeles. The University of California at Los Angeles Bruins play at Pauley Pavilion on the UCLA campus. ⊠ *Pauley Pavilion, 301 Westwood Plaza, Westwood* ☎ *310/825–2101* ⊕ *www.uclabruins.com.*

University of Southern California. The Trojans of the University of Southern California play at the Galen Center. ⊠ *Galen Center, 3400 S. Figueroa St., Downtown* ☎ *213/740–4672* ⊕ *www.usctrojans.com.*

FOOTBALL

The Los Angeles Rams began playing home games at the L.A. Memorial Coliseum in 2016, and the Los Angeles Chargers joined them in town in 2018, although they claimed the Dignity Health Sports Park as their home field. Both will be calling the brand-new SoFi Stadium in Inglewood home sweet home starting in 2021.

UCLA Bruins. The UCLA Bruins pack 'em in at the Rose Bowl. ⊠ *Rose Bowl, 1001 Rose Bowl Dr., Pasadena* ☎ *626/577–3100* ⊕ *www.uclabruins.com.*

USC Trojans. The USC Trojans play at the L.A. Memorial Coliseum, both a state and federal historic landmark. ⊠ *L.A. Memorial Coliseum, 3911 S. Figueroa St., Downtown* ☎ *213/740–4672* ⊕ *wwwl. usctrojans.com* Ⓜ *Expo/Vermont.*

HOCKEY

Anaheim Ducks. The Anaheim Ducks push the puck at Honda Center. They became the first Southern California team to win the Stanley Cup, in 2007. ⊠ *Honda Center, 2695 E. Katella Ave., Anaheim* ☎ *877/945–3946* ⊕ *www.nhl.com/ducks.*

L.A. Kings. The National Hockey League's L.A. Kings clinched the Stanley Cup for the first time in 2012, and in 2014 they won it again against the New York Rangers. ⊠ *Staples Center, 1111 S. Figueroa St., Downtown* ☎ *213/742–7100* ⊕ *www. lakings.com* Ⓜ *Pico.*

What to Watch and Read Before You Go

AMERICAN CRIME STORY: THE PEOPLE VERSUS OJ SIMPSON

With the backdrop of race relations and police brutality in L.A. in the 1990s, *American Crime Story: The People Versus OJ Simpson* retells the cultural phenomenon that was the trial of OJ Simpson for the murder of his wife Nicole Brown Simpson and her friend Ron Goldman. The series won multiple Emmy awards, including Outstanding Lead Actress for Sarah Paulson's portrayal of Marcia Clark and Outstanding Lead Actor for Courtney B. Vance's portrayal of Johnnie Cochran.

BEVERLY HILLS 90210

For the more glamorous side of L.A. life, this 1990s teen drama is the reason everyone knows at least one Los Angeles zip code. It centers around a group of high school friends as they grow up, grow apart, and come back together.

THE BIG LEBOWSKI

A Coen Brothers masterpiece, *The Big Lebowski* is a tale of mistaken identity. The Dude (Jeff Bridges) is an L.A. slacker who gets mixed up in a tale of murder, pornography, nihilists, and more when people think he's a millionaire. The tale winds through Los Angeles and into Malibu, where The Dude is no longer welcome.

BOJACK HORSEMAN

This Netflix animated show is about a washed-up TV star from the '80s and '90s suffering from depression and addiction in Hollywood. The surreal animation imagines humans and animals living and working together (Bojack is actually a horse), and yet the show does a fantastic job tackling myriad social issues like depression, anxiety, and addiction, while also critiquing L.A. culture and the entertainment industry as a whole.

BOYZ N THE HOOD

A striking look at South Central Los Angeles, *Boyz n the Hood* follows the exploits of a group of high schoolers as they deal with the temptations of sex and drugs, gang violence, and family dynamics. The movie, starring Cuba Gooding Jr., Ice Cube, Angela Bassett, and Lawrence Fishburn shows another side of L.A. rarely seen in movies before.

CHINATOWN

In this classic film noir, a young private eye (Jack Nicholson) in Depression-era Los Angeles gets in over his head with a client's case involving her husband's death and the city's sketchy water rights dealings. Incorporating fictionalized details of L.A.'s historic water wars, it's a tale of corruption and mystery.

THE FRESH PRINCE OF BEL-AIR

The ultimate fish-out-of-water comedy, *The Fresh Prince of Bel-Air* is about Will (Will Smith) who moves from the rough streets of Philadelphia to the stunning confines of Bel-Air. The classic comedy deals with issues of family dynamics, class warfare, racism, and more in a very light-hearted yet warm-hearted way (and with one of the best sitcom theme songs of all-time).

GENTEFIED

This L.A.-based TV show is about three Latino cousins who run their grandfather's taco shop in Boyle Heights as the neighborhood goes through rapid gentrification. The show's satire focuses on how L.A. neighborhoods can change on a dime while also exploring the Latinx experience in the city.

INSECURE

Starring stand-out performer Issa Rae, *Insecure* follows the life of Issa and Molly, two Black, single women trying to navigate their careers and love lives in

Los Angeles. The biting comedy tackles issue of race, class, and more through the eyes of young women in the biggest city in America.

LA LA LAND

An ode to classic Hollywood tales like *Singin' in the Rain, La La Land* idealizes the entertainment industry and reveals the Faustian bargains many actors are forced to make in order to succeed. The film centers around a love story of two up-and-comers: Ryan Gosling playing jazz musician, and Emma Stone as a wannabe movie star, both of whom are forced to grapple with the ultimate question of "What if?"

MULHOLLAND DRIVE

Surreal, psychotic, and artsy, David Lynch's *Mulholland Drive* paints L.A. as a city of scary fun house turns that blur the lines between reality and cuts from a movie. Such dichotomies exist as well in the two main characters: Betty (Naomi Watts), the blond Midwesterner fresh to L.A. and full of dreams, and Rita, an amnesiac whose life seems to be shrouded in violence and mystery.

ONCE UPON A TIME IN HOLLYWOOD

Quentin Tarantino writes and directs this retelling of the Charles Manson murders through the eyes of a washed-up movie star played by Leonardo DiCaprio and his stunt double played by Brad Pitt. Like in other films by Tarantino, it's a reimagining of history that lets viewers ponder what would have happened if certain events during the end of Hollywood's golden age took place in a slightly different way.

SINGIN' IN THE RAIN

In this classic film, two stars of the silent film era, Don Lockwood (Gene Kelly) and Lina Lamont (Jean Hagen), have to confront the advent of talkies. Through

the help of his friend Cosmo (Donald O'Connor) and love interest Kathy Selden (Debbie Reynolds), Lockwood embraces the new format and sings and dances his way into the future, with Selden along for the ride. It's the perfect film to capture Hollywood's golden age.

SUNSET BOULEVARD

This 1950s Billy Wilder classic is a wild ride and entertaining glimpse into the film business and its eccentric characters. A has-been star and a young screenwriter hope to use each other in some way, while things get more complicated—proving that what happens behind the scenes in Hollywood isn't the same as what appears on the big screen.

TANGERINE

Shot entirely with an iPhone camera, this indie film explores the streets of Hollywood with a close lens on a few characters. Recently out of prison, a transgender sex worker tries to track down her pimp and his new girlfriend with the help of a friend. It's hard to explain just how much light, humor, and beauty fills this film—you just have to see it for yourself.

THE BIG SLEEP BY RAYMOND CHANDLER

In this classic noir crime novel, L.A.-based detective Philip Marlowe is hired to solve a blackmail case, but gets entwined with double-crosses, surprises, and disappearances. The book has been adapted for film and TV multiple times including the 1946 version starring Humphrey Bogart and a 1978 version starring Robert Mitchum.

HELTER SKELTER BY VINCENT BUGLIOSI

Vincent Bugliosi was the prosecutor in the trial of Charles Manson and this book is his firsthand account of the entire story. The Manson murders took place in 1969 in Los Angeles and have been recounted by multiple books and movies, but Bugliosi's is the most chilling and best-selling of any true crime book in history.

IF HE HOLLERS LET HIM GO BY CHESTER HIMES

Considered to be a protest novel, the book follows an African American shipyard worker in L.A. during World War II. The novel delves into issues of racism, classism, and even communism.

INHERENT VICE BY THOMAS PYNCHON

Taking place in Los Angeles in the 1970s, this detective novel follows the exploits of Larry "Doc" Sportello with the backdrop of the Manson family trials. The story follows Doc as he tries to find his missing former girlfriend in the midst of drugs, gambling, and the city's counterculture. The book was turned into a movie starring Joaquin Phoenix and directed by Paul Thomas Anderson.

PLAY IT AS IT LAYS BY JOAN DIDION

This terse novel by author Joan Didion delves into the mental breakdown of an actress and the dichotomy of the glitz and glamour of Hollywood with the grittier side of the city in the 1960s. The book was turned into a 1972 movie starring Anthony Perkins.

THE REVOLT OF THE COCKROACH PEOPLE BY OSCAR ZETA ACOSTA

This story about Chicano radicalization in East Los Angeles is based on real events. The protagonist lawyer is based on Oscar Zeta Acosta himself, an author, activist, and lawyer/politician with his own fascinating life (and mysterious disappearance), and a key player in the Chicano movement.

THE RIOT WITHIN: MY JOURNEY FROM REBELLION TO REDEMPTION BY RODNEY KING AND LAWRENCE J. SPAGNOLA

In Los Angeles in 1992, the world was appalled by the video of police officers beating Rodney King on the side of the road. The beating was followed by the infamous L.A. riots that ravaged the city, but also brought media attention to the realities of police violence against Black men and women. Rodney King's autobiography not only recounts the incident, but also his life leading up to that pivotal moment and his role as a civil rights figure afterward.

SHANGHAI GIRLS BY LISA SEE

Two sisters from Shanghai begin the novel as young women celebrated for their beauty in a sophisticated, international city—but all this works against them when they are forced into marriage by their father and must leave a now war-torn Shanghai for new life in L.A. Set in the late 1930s, at the brink of change and revolution, this novel mixes historical events, revolution, and culture clashes with themes about womanhood and friendship.

THE WHITE BOY SHUFFLE BY PAUL BEATTY

Dealing with issues of race, identity, and sexuality, The White Boy Shuffle is a coming-of-age novel about an African American poet who recounts his personal history, taking place in Santa Monica. The satirical novel focuses on the idea of the Black Messiah and Black representation.

Chapter 2

TRAVEL SMART

Updated by
Paul Feinstein

★ **STATE CAPITAL:**
Sacramento

♦ **POPULATION:**
4 million in the city; 10 million countywide

💬 **LANGUAGE:**
English

$ **CURRENCY:**
U.S. dollar

☎ **AREA CODES:**
310, 323, 213, 424

⚠ **EMERGENCIES:**
911

🚗 **DRIVING:**
On the right

⚡ **ELECTRICITY:**
120–240 v/60 cycles; plugs have two or three rectangular prongs

🕐 **TIME:**
Three hours behind New York

🌐 **WEB RESOURCES:**
www.discoverlosangeles.com
www.lacity.org

Know Before You Go

As one of the country's most-visited cities, Los Angeles has dozens of notable attractions and can even be a little overwhelming for a first-time visitor. Here are some key tips to help you navigate your trip, whether it's your first time visiting or your twentieth.

THIS CITY IS BIG.

Oh, you wanted to do Malibu and Disneyland on the same day? That's cute. Here's some perspective— that drive is 77 miles and, depending on traffic, can take more than three hours from end to end. It's best to picture L.A. in pieces, and to think about visiting one neighborhood or a collection of nearby neighborhoods a day. There's the Westside, consisting of Malibu, Santa Monica, and Venice. The middle: Beverly Hills, West Hollywood, and Hollywood. The Eastside: Downtown, Silver Lake, and Pasadena. Stick to these on individual days or else risk spending most of your day in traffic.

TRANSPORTATION IS ANNOYING.

You have a lot of options, so choose wisely. You can rent a car, ride a bus, take the Metro, use a ride-sharing app, or scoot. Lesson 1: The bus lines can be challenging to navigate, even for locals, and traffic still exists for buses; chances are as a tourist, taking the bus will be more trouble than it's worth. Lesson 2: The Metro doesn't go everywhere, so pick your routes carefully. Lesson 3: Ride-sharing apps are infinitely cheaper than taxis. Lesson 4: If you must, scooter. The newest transpo kids on the block are Lime and Bird, electric scooters that make it easy to get around individual neighborhoods. Just be careful because bike lanes are scarce and L.A. drivers don't look.

TRAFFIC IS BAD.

Knowing how L.A. traffic works is the difference between a sweet vacation and hell on earth. Here are some rules to live by: first, only get in a car before 7 am, after 10 am, before 3 pm, or after 7 pm. If you must drive at any other times, find routes that don't involve L.A.'s maze of freeways. Side streets are your friends and give you lots of alternatives. If you get stuck on the 405 at 5:30, you will miss your dinner reservation.

PARKING IS COMPLICATED AND EXPENSIVE.

If you've seen L.A.'s draconian signage, you know how confusing things can be. But to avoid a ticket, stick to the meters (which take credit cards). If they're blinking red/green, you'll generally know you're in a place that works. If you rent a car, hotel parking can be obnoxiously expensive. We're talking $40–$50 per night. To avoid all these pratfalls, use ride-sharing apps and save yourself the hassle.

THE HOUSING CRISIS IS REAL.

This is probably the most shocking thing that newcomers to L.A. will experience. The homeless population has exploded in the last decade and rough estimates put it at 60,000 people on the streets. It's a big problem that the government is struggling to find a solution to fix. Just don't be surprised and, most important, don't be rude. People are people, and everyone deserves respect and kindness.

CELEBRITIES LIVE HERE, TOO.

If you want to see celebs, you need to know where to find them. But this isn't a safari and they're not animals—so be cool. If you want some guarantees, go to lunch at the Chateau Marmont or Polo Lounge. Hit up dinner at Craig's or Catch LA. If you're more into movie stuff than movie people, head over to the Warner Bros. and Universal

Studios lots, where you can tour soundstages and movie sets and maybe, just maybe, see an A-lister eating lunch at the commissary—again, be cool.

MARIJUANA IS LEGAL.

OK, stoners, this is what you've been waiting for. L.A. has legalized marijuana and you want to know where to get high. First off, think of the marijuana rules like the alcohol rules. You need to be 21. You can't consume in public. You can't smoke and drive (and you absolutely shouldn't). Fines can be as high (not a pun) as $250 just for driving with an open container. So, if you need a pick-me-up or take-me-down, look for the green crosses on storefronts.

THERE ARE A LOT OF BEACHES.

No trip to L.A. would be complete without lounging on one of the city's many beaches. Whether you're a surfer, skater, or volleyball player, there's a beach for you. Malibu is worth hitting for the drive alone along the Pacific Coast Highway, but it is far away. Santa Monica and Venice are closer, though less serene. Head a little farther south and you'll get your top surf spots: Manhattan, Hermosa, and Redondo.

THIS IS A FOODIE'S PARADISE.

New Yorkers can disagree all they want—L.A. is one of the best food cities in America. The food truck was practically invented here, and you'll find a

rolling restaurant for any cuisine imaginable. Beyond the trucks, L.A. has dozens of farmers' markets and near-weekly food festivals celebrating the melting pot that is this city. Lastly, you'll find more celebrity chefs in L.A. than just about any other city as cheap(er) rents have ushered in an experimental wave of food not seen elsewhere. Whether it's tacos, Italian, Ethiopian, Korean, or burgers, L.A. is a primo city for any traveling foodie.

THERE IS SUCH A THING AS AWARDS SEASON.

Los Angeles's weather is so ideal that most locals shrug off the high cost of living as a "sunshine tax." But it does get chilly (read: highs in the 50s). January and February tend to be the coldest and rainiest months; however, occasionally the rain begins in December and ends in March.

Springtime in Los Angeles is typically from mid-March to May, when the temperatures fluctuate between the low 70s and mid-80s. Nights tend to be in the 50s. Jacaranda trees bloom across the city and purple flowers litter the sidewalks. It's no cherry blossoms in Japan, but it's still pretty. September is usually the hottest and driest month. It's also when the Santa Ana winds begin—the hot "devil winds" that usher in fire season and fray everyone's nerves. They usually blow on out of here in December.

Awards Season in Los Angeles can be mildly annoying. From January

through February, L.A. hosts the Golden Globes, the Academy Awards, the Grammys (sometimes), and a slew of other ceremonies. This creates two problems: hotel prices tend to go up on the weekends of events, especially in Beverly Hills, West Hollywood, and Downtown; and traffic is even worse—Hollywood Boulevard is closed around Hollywood & Highland, the Oscars venue, for a week.

The peak season runs from June through August. Beaches are packed every weekend, so plan to go early and expect traffic, especially en route to Malibu. June is usually cooler, especially in the mornings and evenings when the fog rolls in—they don't call it "June gloom" for nothing. But temperatures in July and August hover in the 80s and can spike to triple digits. The coasts are usually between 5 and 10 degrees cooler than Downtown.

Getting Here and Around

The Los Angeles metro area has more than 13 million residents, so be prepared to rent a car and fight for space on the freeway (especially at rush hour) to make your way along the array of destinations that span from the carefree beaches of the coastline to the glitz and glamour of Beverly Hills shops, the nightlife of Hollywood, and the film studio action of the Valley. It's worth it. Nowhere else in the country can you spot celebrities over breakfast or sunbathe on the beach and head to the slopes for skiing on the same day.

Air

Nonstop flights from New York to Los Angeles take about six hours; with the three-hour time change, you can leave JFK by 8 am and be in L.A. by 11 am. Some flights may require a midway stop, making the total excursion between 7½ and 8½ hours. Flight times are three hours from Dallas, four hours from Chicago, and 11½ hours from London.

AIRPORTS

The fourth-largest airport in the world in terms of passenger traffic, Los Angeles International Airport (LAX) is served by more than 65 major airlines. Because of heavy traffic around the airport (not to mention the city's extended rush hours), you should allow yourself plenty of extra time. All departures are from the upper level, while arrivals are on the lower level. There's no Metro in or out of the airport, but it's coming in the not-too-distant-future.

Several secondary airports serve the city. Hollywood Burbank Airport in Burbank is close to Downtown L.A., so it's definitely worth checking out. Long Beach Airport is equally convenient. Flights to Orange County's John Wayne Airport are often more expensive than those to the other secondary airports. Also check out L.A./Ontario International Airport.

Driving times from LAX to different parts of the city vary considerably: it will take you 20 minutes to get to Santa Monica, 30 minutes to Beverly Hills, and at least 45 minutes to Downtown L.A. In heavy traffic it can take much longer. From Hollywood Burbank Airport, it's 30 minutes to Downtown. Plan on at least 45 minutes for the drive from Long Beach Airport, and an hour from John Wayne Airport or L.A./Ontario International Airport.

GROUND TRANSPORTATION

If you're not renting a car, a taxi is the most convenient way to get to and from the airport. There's a flat rate between LAX and Downtown for $50.50. Getting Downtown from Hollywood Burbank Airport costs $40 to $50. Taxis to and from L.A./Ontario International Airport run on a meter and cost $60 and $70, depending on traffic. From Long Beach Airport, trips to Downtown L.A. are metered and cost roughly $72.

For two or three passengers, shuttles can be an economical option at $17 to $35. These big vans typically circle the airport, departing when they're full. Your travel time depends on how many other travelers are dropped off before you. At LAX, SuperShuttle allows walk-on shuttle passengers without prior reservations; if you're headed to the airport, call at least 24 hours in advance.

Operated by Los Angeles World Airports, FlyAway buses travel between LAX and Van Nuys, Westwood, La Brea, and Union Station in Downtown L.A. The cost is $8 to $10 and is payable only by credit or debit card. With departure at least every hour, buses run 24 hours a day.

Most Angelenos use ride-share apps like Lyft, which you can download to your smartphone. The app will estimate the cost before you accept the ride. A ride from the airport (drivers pick you up at a dedicated lot) to the Eastside could cost as much as $40 or less if you pick up another passenger along the way.

FLIGHTS

Delta, United, Southwest, and American have the most nonstop flights to LAX. JetBlue and Alaska also have numerous daily flights to airports in and around Los Angeles.

🚌 Bus

Inadequate public transportation has plagued L.A. for decades. That said, many local trips can be made, with time and patience, by buses run by the Los Angeles County Metropolitan Transit Authority. In certain cases—visiting the Getty Center, for instance, or Universal Studios—buses may be your best option. There's a special Dodger Stadium Express that shuttles passengers between Union Station and the world-famous ballpark for home games. It's free if you have a ticket in hand and saves you parking-related stress.

Metro Buses cost $1.75, plus 50¢ for each transfer to another bus or to the subway. A one-day pass costs $7, and a weekly pass is $25 for unlimited travel on all buses and trains. Passes are valid from Sunday through Saturday. For the fastest service, look for the red-and-white Metro Rapid buses; these stop less frequently and are able to extend green lights. There are 25 Metro Rapid

routes, including along Wilshire and Vermont boulevards.

Other bus services make it possible to explore the entire metropolitan area. DASH minibuses cover six different circular routes in Hollywood, Mid-Wilshire, and Downtown. You pay 50¢ every time you get on. The Santa Monica Municipal Bus Line, also known as the Big Blue Bus, is a pleasant and inexpensive way to move around the Westside. Trips cost $1.

You can pay your fare in cash on MTA, Santa Monica, and Culver City buses, but you must have exact change. You can buy MTA TAP cards at Metro Rail stations, customer centers throughout the city, and some convenience and grocery stores.

🚗 Car

If you're used to urban driving, you shouldn't have too much trouble navigating the streets of Los Angeles. If not, L.A. can be unnerving. However, the city has evolved with drivers in mind. Streets are wide and parking garages abound, so it's more car-friendly than many older big cities.

If you get discombobulated while on the freeway, remember this rule of thumb: even-numbered freeways run east and west, odd-numbered freeways run north and south.

GASOLINE

As of this writing, gasoline costs around $3 a gallon. Most stations are self-service; the few remaining full-service stations are mostly in and around the Westside. There are plenty of stations everywhere. Most stay open late, and many are open 24 hours.

Getting Here and Around

GETTING AROUND

There are plenty of identical or similarly named streets in L.A. (Beverly Boulevard and Beverly Drive, for example), so be as specific as you can when asking directions or inputting into a map app. Expect sudden changes in addresses as streets pass through neighborhoods, then incorporated cities, then back into neighborhoods. This can be most bewildering on Robertson Boulevard, an otherwise useful north–south artery that, by crossing through L.A., West Hollywood, and Beverly Hills, dips in and out of several such numbering shifts in a matter of miles.

PARKING

Parking rules are strictly enforced in Los Angeles, so make sure you check for signs and read them carefully. Illegally parked cars are ticketed or towed quickly. Parking prices vary from 25¢ (in public lots and at meters) to $2 per half hour (in private lots). Downtown and Century City rates may be as high as $25 an hour.

Parking in Downtown L.A. can be tough, especially on weekdays. Try the garage at the FIG at 7th retail complex (⊠ 725 S. Figueroa St.), which is spacious, reasonably priced, and visitor-friendly.

In Hollywood, the underground facility at the Hollywood & Highland shopping complex (⊠ 6801 Hollywood Blvd.) charges $3 for the first four hours with validation. In Beverly Hills, the first two hours are free at several lots on or around Rodeo Drive. The Westside Pavilion (⊠ 10800 Pico Blvd.) offers three hours of free parking at its garage.

At some shops, most restaurants, and hotels in Los Angeles, valet parking is virtually assumed. The cost is usually $6 to $16 for restaurants, but can be as high as $60 for hotels. Keep small bills on hand to tip the valets.

ROAD CONDITIONS

Beware of weekday rush-hour traffic, which is heaviest from 8 to 10 am and 3 to 7 pm. Go511.com and the Waze app offer real-time traffic information, and the California Highway Patrol has a road-conditions hotline. To encourage carpooling, some crowded freeways reserve an express lane for cars carrying more than one passenger.

Parallel streets can often provide viable alternatives to jam-packed freeways, notably Sepulveda Boulevard for I-405; Venice and Washington boulevards for I-10 from Mid-Wilshire west to the beach; and Ventura Boulevard, Moorpark Street, or Riverside Drive for U.S. 101 through the San Fernando Valley.

ROADSIDE EMERGENCIES

For minor problems faced by motorists (running out of gas, blowing a tire, needing a tow to the nearest phone), California's Department of Transportation has a Metro Freeway Service Patrol. More than 145 tow trucks patrol the freeways offering free aid to stranded drivers. Reach them on your cell phone by calling 511.

If your car breaks down on an interstate, pull over onto the shoulder and call the state police from your cell phone or walk to the nearest emergency roadside phone. When calling for help, note your location according to the small green mileage markers posted along the highway.

RULES OF THE ROAD

Seat belts are required for all passengers in California, as is the use of federally approved car seats for children under nine or less than 4 feet, 9 inches tall. California law requires that drivers use hands-free devices when talking on cell phones. Texting and driving is illegal and results in a hefty fine.

The speed limit is 25 to 35 mph on city streets and 65 mph on freeways unless otherwise posted. Some towns, including Beverly Hills and Culver City, use cameras at traffic lights to reduce speeding. Speeding can earn you fines starting at $266. It is illegal to drive in California with a blood alcohol content of 0.08% or above (0.01% if you're under 21). There are strict penalties for first offenders. Checkpoints are set up on weekends and holidays across the county.

Parking infractions can result in penalties starting at $63. Having your vehicle towed and impounded will cost nearly $300 even if you pay up immediately, and more if you don't. LAX is notorious for handing out tickets to drivers circling its busy terminals; avoid the no-parking zones and keep loading or unloading to a minimum.

Turning right on red after a complete stop is legal unless otherwise posted. Many streets in Downtown L.A. are one-way, and a left turn from one one-way street onto another is allowed. On some major arteries, left turns are illegal during rush hour. Certain carpool lanes, designated by signage and a white diamond, are reserved for cars with more than one passenger. Freeway on-ramps often have stop-and-go signals to regulate the flow of traffic, but cars in high-occupancy-vehicle (HOV) lanes can pass the signal without stopping.

Keep in mind that pedestrians always have the right of way in California; not yielding to them, even if they're jaywalkers, may result in a $200 ticket.

RENTALS

In Los Angeles, a car is a necessity. Keep in mind that you'll likely be spending a lot of time in it, and options like a plug for your cell phone could make a significant difference in your day-to-day comfort.

Major-chain rates in L.A. begin at $38 a day and $300 a week, plus sales tax and concession fees. Luxury vehicles start at $75 a day. Open-top convertibles are a popular choice for visitors wanting to make the most of the sun. Note that the major agencies offer services for travelers with disabilities, such as hand controls, for little or no extra cost.

In California you must be 21 and have a valid credit card to rent a car. Some agencies won't rent to those under 25, and those that do may charge extra.

Ⓜ Metro/Public Transport

Metro Rail covers only a small part of L.A.'s vast expanse, but it's convenient, frequent, and inexpensive. Most popular with visitors is the underground Red Line, which runs from Downtown's Union Station through Mid-Wilshire, Hollywood, and Universal City on its way to North Hollywood, stopping at the most popular tourist destinations along the way.

The light-rail Green Line stretches from Redondo Beach to Norwalk, while the partially underground Blue Line travels from Downtown to the South Bay. The monorail-like Gold Line extends from Union Station to Pasadena and out to the deep San Gabriel Valley and Azusa. The Orange Line, a 14-mile bus corridor, connects the North Hollywood subway station with the western San Fernando Valley.

Most recently extended was the Expo Line, which connects Downtown to the Westside, and terminates in Santa Monica, two blocks from the Pacific Ocean.

Getting Here and Around

Daily service is offered from about 4:30 am to 12:30 am, with departures every 5 to 15 minutes. On weekends trains run until 2 am. Buy tickets from station vending machines; fares are $1.75, or $7 for an all-day pass. Bicycles are allowed on Metro Rail trains at all times.

🚗 Ride-Sharing

Request a ride using apps like Lyft or Uber, and a driver will usually arrive within minutes. Fares increase during busy times, but it's often the most affordable option, especially for the convenience.

🚕 Taxi

Instead of trying to hail a taxi on the street, phone one of the many taxi companies. The Curb Taxi app allows for online hailing of L.A. taxis. The metered rate is $2.70 per mile, plus a $2.85 per-fare charge and an additional $2 curb fee. Taxi rides from LAX have an additional $4 surcharge. Be aware that distances are greater than they might appear on the map so fares add up quickly.

On the other end of the price spectrum, limousines come equipped with everything from full bars to night-club-style sound-and-light systems. Most charge by the hour, minimum hours sometimes required.

🚈 Train

Downtown's Union Station is one of the great American railroad terminals. The interior includes comfortable seating, restaurants, and several bars. As the city's rail hub, it's the place to catch an Amtrak, Metrolink commuter train, or the Red, Gold, or Purple lines. Among Amtrak's Southern California routes are 11 daily trips to San Diego and 6 to Santa Barbara. Amtrak's luxury *Coast Starlight* travels along the spectacular coastline from Seattle to Los Angeles in just a day and a half (though it's often a little late). The *Sunset Limited* arrives from New Orleans, and the *Southwest Chief* comes from Chicago.

Essentials

🍴 Dining

Los Angeles may be known for its beach living and celebrity-infused backdrop, but it was once a farm town. The hillsides were covered in citrus orchards and dairy farms, and agriculture was a major industry. Today, even as L.A. is urbanized, the city's culinary landscape has reembraced a local, sustainable, and seasonal philosophy at many levels—from fine dining to street snacks.

With a growing interest in farm-to-fork, the city's farmers' market scene has exploded, becoming popular at big-name restaurants and small eateries alike. In Hollywood and Santa Monica you can often find high-profile chefs scouring farm stands for fresh produce.

The status of the celebrity chef carries weight around this town. People follow the culinary zeitgeist with the same fervor as celebrity gossip. You can queue up with the hungry hordes at Nancy Silverton's **Mozza,** or try and snag a reservation at Ludo Lefebvre's ever-popular **Petit Trois** or David Chang's L.A. outpost, **Majordomo.**

International eats continue to be a backbone of the L.A. dining scene. People head to Koreatown for epic Korean cooking and late-night coffeehouses and to West L.A. for phenomenal sushi. Latin food is well represented in the city, making it tough to choose between Guatemalan eateries, Peruvian restaurants, nouveau Mexican bistros, and Tijuana-style taco trucks. With so many dining options, sometimes the best strategy is simply to drive and explore.

CHILDREN
Although it's unusual to see children in the dining rooms of L.A.'s most elite restaurants, dining with youngsters here does not have to mean culinary exile.

SMOKING
Smokers should keep in mind that California law forbids smoking in all enclosed areas, including bars.

RESERVATIONS
You'll be happy to hear it's getting easier to snag a desired reservation, but it's still a good idea to plan ahead. Some renowned restaurants are booked weeks or even months in advance. If that's the case, you can get lucky at the last minute if you're flexible—and friendly. Most restaurants keep a few tables open for walk-ins and VIPs. Show up for dinner early (6 pm) or late (after 9 pm) and politely inquire about any last-minute vacancies or cancellations. Try booking apps like Open Table and Resy. Most places, except small mom-and-pop establishments, provide valet parking at dinner for semi-reasonable rates (often around $10, plus tip).

DINING HOURS
Despite its veneer of decadence, L.A. is not a particularly late-night city for eating. (The reenergized Hollywood dining scene is emerging as a notable exception.) The peak dinner times are from 7 to 9, and most restaurants won't take reservations after 10. Unless otherwise noted, the restaurants listed in this guide are open daily for lunch and dinner. Generally speaking, restaurants are closed either Sunday or Monday; a few are shuttered both days. Most places—even the upscale spots—are open for lunch on weekdays, since many Hollywood mega-deals are conceived at that time.

Essentials

WHAT TO WEAR

Dining out in Los Angeles tends to be a casual affair, and even at some of the most expensive restaurants you're likely to see customers in jeans (although this is not necessarily considered in good taste). It's extremely rare for L.A. restaurants to actually require a jacket and tie, but all of the city's more formal establishments appreciate a gentleman who dons a jacket—let your good judgment be your guide.

TIPPING AND TAXES

In most restaurants, tip the waiter 16%–20%. (To figure out a 20% tip quickly, just move the decimal point one place to the left on your total and double that amount.) Note that checks for parties of six or more sometimes include the tip already. Tip at least $1 per drink at the bar, and $1 for each coat checked. Never tip the maître d' unless you're out to impress your guests or expect to pay another visit soon. Also, be prepared for a sales tax of around 9.5% to appear on your bill.

PRICES

If you're watching your budget, be sure to ask the price of daily specials recited by the waiter. The charge for specials at some restaurants is noticeably out of line with the other prices on the menu. Beware of the $10 bottle of water; ask for tap water instead.

If you eat early or late, you may be able to take advantage of a prix-fixe deal not offered at peak hours. Most upscale restaurants are offering great lunch deals with special menus at cut-rate prices designed to give customers a true taste of the place.

Credit cards are accepted unless otherwise noted in the review. While many restaurants do accept credit cards, some smaller places accept only cash. If you plan to use a credit card it's a good idea to double-check its acceptability when making reservations or before sitting down to eat.

Restaurant reviews have been shortened. For full information, visit Fodors.com. Prices in the restaurant reviews are the average cost of a main course at dinner or, if dinner is not served, at lunch.

What It Costs in U.S. Dollars			
$	$$	$$$	$$$$
RESTAURANTS			
under $14	$14–$22	$23–$31	over $31

🛏 Lodging

When it comes to finding a place to stay, travelers have never been more spoiled for choice than in today's Los Angeles. From luxurious digs in Beverly Hills and along the coast to budget boutiques in Hollywood, hotels are stepping up service, upgrading amenities, and trying all-new concepts, like upscale hostels and retro-chic motels. Hotels in Los Angeles today are more than just a place to rest your head; they're a key part of the experience.

RESERVATIONS

Hotel reservations are an absolute necessity when planning your trip to Los Angeles—although rooms are easier to come by these days. Competition for clients also means properties undergo frequent improvements, so when booking ask about any renovations, lest you get a room within earshot of construction. In this ever-changing city, travelers can find themselves without amenities like room service or spa access if their hotel is upgrading.

SERVICES

Most hotels have air-conditioning and flat-screen cable TV. Those in the moderate and expensive price ranges often have coffeemakers, bathrobes, and hair dryers. Most also have high-speed Internet access in guest rooms, with a 24-hour use fee (though at a number of hotels, it's free). Wi-Fi is common even at budget properties. Southern California's emphasis on being in shape means most hotels have fitness facilities; if the one on-site is not to your liking, ask for a reference to a nearby sports club or gym.

STAYING WITH KIDS

From Disneyland to the beach cities, laid-back Los Angeles definitely has a reputation as a family-friendly destination. Resorts and hotels along the coast, in particular, attract plenty of beach-going family vacationers looking for sun and sand castles. Some properties provide such diversions as in-room movies, toys, and video games; others have suites with kitchenettes and fold-out sofa beds. Hotels often provide cribs, rollaway beds, and references for babysitting services, but make arrangements when booking the room, not when you arrive. *Properties that are especially kid-friendly are marked FAMILY throughout the chapter.*

PARKING

Exploring Los Angeles, a sprawling city of wide boulevards and five-lane freeways, requires a car. Though you might stroll Rodeo Drive on foot or amble along the Hollywood Walk of Fame, to get from one part of town to another, you'll need wheels. Thankfully, there's street parking in most areas (read signs carefully as some neighborhoods are by permit only), and many public parking lots are free for the first hour or two. Though a few hotels have free parking, most charge for the privilege, and some resorts only have valet parking, with fees as high as $50 per night.

PRICES

Tax rates for the area will add 10%–14% to your bill depending on where in Los Angeles County you stay; some hoteliers tack on energy, service, or occupancy surcharges—ask about customary charges when you book your room.

When looking for a hotel, don't write off the pricier establishments immediately. Price categories here are determined by "rack rates"—the list price of a hotel room—which are often higher than those you'll find online or by calling the hotel directly. Specials abound, particularly in Downtown on the weekends. Many hotels have packages that include breakfast, theater tickets, spa services, or luxury rental cars. Pricing is competitive, so always check with the hotel for current special offers.

When making reservations, don't forget to check the hotel's website for exclusive online specials.

Hotel reviews have been shortened. For full information, visit Fodors.com. Prices in the hotel reviews are the lowest cost of a standard double room in high season.

What It Costs in U.S. Dollars			
$	$$	$$$	$$$$
HOTELS			
under $200	$200–$300	$301–$400	over $400

Essentials

ⓨ Nightlife

Los Angeles is not the city that never sleeps—instead it parties until 2 am (save for the secret after-hours parties at private clubs, Hollywood Hills mansions, and warehouses) and wakes up to imbibe green juices and breakfast burritos as hangover cures or to sweat it out in a yoga class. Whether you plan to test your limit at historic establishments Downtown or take advantage of a cheap happy hour at a Hollywood dive, this city's nightlife has something for you.

A night out in Los Angeles can simultaneously surprise and impress. Seeing an unscheduled set by an A-list comedian at a comedy club, being talked into singing karaoke at the diviest place you've ever seen, dancing at a bar with no dance floor because, well, the DJ is just too good at his job—going out isn't always what you expect, but it certainly is never boring.

The focus of nightlife once centered on the Sunset Strip, with its multitude of bars, rock clubs, and dance spots, but more neighborhoods are competing with each other and forcing the nightlife scene to evolve. Although the Strip can be a worthwhile trip, other areas of the city are catching people's attention. Downtown Los Angeles, for instance, is a destination in its own right. Other areas foster more of a neighborhood vibe. Silver Lake and Los Feliz have both cultivated a relaxed environment.

So if you find yourself disappointed with a rude bouncer, or drinks that are too watery, or a cover charge that just isn't worth it, try again. Eventually you'll find that perfect place where each time is the best time. If not, at least you'll walk away with a good story.

ⓣ Performing Arts

The arts scene in Los Angeles extends beyond the screen and onto the stage. A place of artistic innovation and history, one can discover new and challenging theatrical works across L.A. stages, while the city still maintains a respect for tradition with its restored theaters and classic plays. See live music at impeccably designed amphitheaters like the Hollywood Bowl or listen in on captivating lectures by authors and directors at various intimate spaces. In homage to the city's roots as a filmmaking mecca, there are also retrospectives and rare screenings in movie theaters all over the city, often followed by Q&As with the cast.

L.A.'s arts scene is varied and caters to all budgets and tastes. East West Players at the David Henry Hwang Theatre focuses on Asian American–themed plays, and if an opera at the Dorothy Chandler Pavilion seems out of your price range, Actors' Gang in Culver City offers a free Shakespeare play in Media Park in the summer. The Independent Shakespeare Co. hosts a free Shakespeare festival in Griffith Park, also during summer.

Temperate weather allows for an extended season of outdoor events. Enjoy a classic summer picnic listening to the L.A. Philharmonic at the Hollywood Bowl or watching a play outdoors at the John Anson Ford Amphitheater.

American Cinematheque, showing classic and independent films, operates out of the Aero Theatre in Santa Monica, as well as the historic Egyptian Theatre on Hollywood Boulevard.

⊕ Health

The air pollution in L.A. may affect sensitive people in different ways. When pollution levels are high, it's a good idea to plan a day indoors or on a windy beach. The sun can burn even on overcast days, and the dry heat can dehydrate, so wear hats, sunglasses, and sunblock, and carry water with you.

COVID-19

COVID-19 brought travel to a virtual standstill for most of 2020 and into 2021, but vaccinations have made travel possible and safe again. However, each destination (and each business within that destination) may have its own requirements and regulations. Travelers should expect to continue to wear a mask in some places and obey any other rules. Given how abruptly travel was curtailed at the onset of the pandemic, it is wise to consider protecting yourself by purchasing a travel insurance policy that will reimburse you for cancellation costs related to COVID-19. Not all travel insurance policies protect against pandemic-related cancellations, so always read the fine print.

⊕ Safety

Very minor earthquakes occur frequently in Southern California; most of the time they're so slight that you won't notice them. If you feel a stronger tremor, follow basic safety precautions. If you're indoors, take cover in a doorway or under a table or desk—whichever is closest. Protect your head with your arms. Stay clear of windows, mirrors, or anything that might fall from the walls. Do not use elevators. If you're in an open space, move away from buildings, trees, and power lines. If you're outdoors near buildings, duck into a doorway. If you're

driving, pull over to the side of the road, avoiding overpasses, bridges, and power lines, and stay inside the car. Expect aftershocks, and take cover again if they are strong.

Of the Metro lines, the Red, Green, and Expo lines are the safest and are more regularly patrolled. The Blue Line can be sketchy after dark. Avoid riding in empty cars, and move with the crowd when going from the station to the street.

💲 Taxes

The sales tax in L.A. is 9.5%, one of the highest in California. There's none on most groceries, but there is on newspapers and magazines. The tax on hotel rooms ranges from 13% to 15.5%. Food tax varies, but expect to pay around 9.5%.

💵 Tipping

The customary tip rate is 15%–20% for waiters, taxi drivers, hairdressers, and barbers. Bellhops and baggage handlers receive $1–$2 per bag; parking valets and hotel housekeepers are usually tipped $2–$3. Bartenders get about $1 per drink, but tip your mixologists like you would a waiter.

📍 Visitor Information

Discover Los Angeles, the official tourism site, has an annually updated general information packet that includes suggestions for entertainment, lodging, and dining and a list of special events. There are two visitor information centers, both accessible to Metro stops: the Hollywood & Highland Center and Union Station.

Great Itineraries

The Perfect Week in Los Angeles

The trick to having a decent quality of life in Los Angeles, claims one longtime Angeleno, is to live near where you work. The same adage holds true for visitors in that staying put in a single area of the city—being in a car for as short a time as possible—is a good rule of thumb. The best way to explore is one neighborhood at a time. Here's how to spend the perfect week in L.A. doing just that.

DAY 1: DOWNTOWN LOS ANGELES

Formerly an unwelcoming neighborhood dominated by the glass-and-steel office buildings of Bunker Hill on one side and the poverty and despair of Skid Row on the other, Downtown Los Angeles has staged a major comeback.

Start your first day with some culture on Grand Avenue: the Walt Disney Concert Hall, the Broad Museum, and the Museum of Contemporary Art are all next to each other and are home to priceless works of art and stunning architecture. At the concert hall, be sure to take the hour-long self-guided audio tour, which includes a walk through the venue's second-story hidden garden. It can be tough, but not impossible to see all three in one morning/afternoon trip.

After feasting on culture, grab lunch at one of the many stalls of Grand Central Market. Then Uber over to the art deco icon, Union Station, to admire the heavy wood-beam ceilings, leather-upholstered chairs, and inlaid marble floors. You can also stay for a happy hour drink or snack at one of the many restaurant and bar options now open inside.

For more L.A. history, walk across Alameda Street to stroll past the shops and restaurants of historic Olvera Street, where you'll find traditional Mexican fare. For dinner, venture into Little Tokyo for a wide variety of Japanese cuisine or head to Chinatown for authentic eats. With a full belly, head back into the historic core of Downtown, where you'll find a large concentration of bars on Spring Street between 5th and 7th streets, and on 6th between Main and Los Angeles streets.

DAY 2: HOLLYWOOD

On your second day, you can join the tourists who flock to Hollywood Boulevard to see old movie palaces such as TCL Chinese Theatre, where movie stars have left their mark, literally, in the concrete courtyard of the theater since 1927. These days the theater's entrance is also graced by dozens of impersonators—from Marilyn Monroe to Spiderman—who are more than happy to pose for photos with visitors (they do expect to be paid, however).

To avoid the heaviest crowds, go to Hollywood & Highland Center in the morning, followed by a tour of the Kodak Theatre, which hosts the annual Academy Awards ceremony.

Wander the Walk of Fame, a 1.3-mile stretch of bronze stars embedded in pink terrazzo that lines Hollywood Boulevard, to pay homage to your favorite movie stars. For lunch, head into the famous Roosevelt Hotel and grab a spot by the pool. Look up and you'll see the Marilyn Monroe suite hovering over the sunbathers.

Pre-dinner, you should take part in a Hollywood rite of passage and see a movie in the town that made them famous. Some of the historic movie palaces, including TCL, still show films, but the real movie buffs should opt to see a movie at the ArcLight, a state-of-the-art theater on Sunset Boulevard that features gourmet food and reserved seating. Though all the theaters at the ArcLight are great, opt to see something at the iconic Cinerama Dome. The ArcLight also boasts an in-house café bar that is perfect for a quick meal before a film or an après-show martini.

Post-dinner, check out Hollywood's famous food scene and then make the night truly epic at one of the neighborhood's clubs, music venues, or dive bars.

DAY 3: WEST HOLLYWOOD

Thanks to its central location, West Hollywood is the ideal place to spend a couple of hours without committing an entire day—not that there isn't a day's worth of things to do in this neighborhood.

Like most things in L.A., the early bird gets the worm. For shoppers, that means going to stores when they open and are less crowded. A shopping hub in its own right, West Hollywood has multiple indoor and outdoor shopping options like The Grove and the mammoth indoor Beverly Center. There are also countless small boutiques and specialty shops lining Beverly Boulevard, 3rd Street, and Melrose Avenue.

For lunch, grab a corned beef sandwich or some matzo ball soup at Canter's Delicatessen, a Los Angeles landmark since 1931, or head to the Farmers Market for a collection of ethnic food stalls and local products.

If you haven't had your shopping fill, tack Robertson Boulevard onto your agenda to find boutiques ranging from Chanel to Kitson. Swing by the picket-fenced Ivy, a restaurant which had its celebrity heyday in the mid-aughts, but you still may see a star or two.

Finally, West Hollywood is known for its buzzing nightlife, so afterward choose from hundreds of small restaurants for dinner, then follow up with a drink from one of the area's many bars.

DAY 4: BEVERLY HILLS AND MID-WILSHIRE

Depending on how hardcore of a shopper you are, you can easily check out the boutiques of Beverly Hills in a couple of hours. In fact, with all of the designer flagships and tony department stores, it might be dangerous to spend too much time (translation: too much money) in this ritzy neighborhood.

Hit Rodeo Drive in the morning for all the runway names, such as Chanel, Christian Dior, Dolce & Gabbana, Fendi, Gucci, Prada, Valentino, and Versace.

Of course, not all the action is on Rodeo; don't forget to wander the side streets for more high fashion. The department stores—Neiman Marcus and Saks Fifth Avenue—are located nearby on Wilshire Boulevard. After you finish shopping, refuel with a dose of sugar at local dessert favorite Sprinkles Cupcakes.

After all that shopping, jump in the car to get some culture by heading east to the Miracle Mile in Mid-Wilshire, a stretch of Wilshire Boulevard that's home to the mammoth Los Angeles County Museum of Art, the Petersen Automotive Museum, and the Academy Museum of Motion Pictures. Depending on your preference of cuisine, have dinner in either Little Ethiopia or Koreatown.

DAY 5: SANTA MONICA AND VENICE

With a couple of hours on your hands, it's a quick trip (if there's no traffic) to the beaches of Santa Monica or Venice. While they may not offer quite as much

Great Itineraries

in the natural beauty department as their Malibu counterparts, they have plenty of sights of a different variety.

Start the day at Santa Monica Pier, where you can enjoy the old-school amusement park. Then walk (or bike ride) down the Strand, which eventually takes you to Venice Beach. Take your time browsing (and stopping for lunch) at the many beachside restaurants and quirky shops; you can even enjoy a few hours on the beach itself if you like.

Then end the day with a walk over the Venice Canals and a meal at any of the increasingly hip restaurants in Venice; don't miss sunset over the beach.

DAY 6: MALIBU

The ideal way to see Los Angeles's most beautiful beaches is to set aside an entire day for Malibu. Driving up the scenic Pacific Coast Highway is a treat in and of itself with sheer cliffs on one side of the road and ocean views on the other.

Stop at the Malibu Country Mart along the way for a seafood-laden lunch and gawk at the high-end shoppers and possible celebrity or two.

As you drive, you'll hit Topanga State Beach, Malibu Lagoon State Beach, and Malibu Surfrider Beach, which are all beautiful and popular spots to pass the day, but it's worth the extra drive time to see Point Dume State Beach, which is nestled away from the hustle and bustle of the highway.

Be sure to seek out the single-track trail that winds its way up a nearby coastal bluff revealing breathtaking views of Santa Monica Bay, the Malibu Coast, and Catalina Island. Stop for dinner at any of the seafood shacks that line PCH and catch an epic California sunset.

DAY 7: ORANGE COUNTY AND CATALINA ISLAND

If you want the California coastline all to yourself, head out in the early morning to one of the seemingly endless strings of beaches along this stretch of shoreline, extending from Long Beach to San Juan Capistrano. There's plenty to do besides sit in the sand: check out one of the fascinating aquariums, explore a nature preserve, or take in some impressive art at the area's surprisingly good museums.

Finding somewhere to eat lunch won't be a problem, as this area is a major foodie destination. There are also plenty of reasonably priced family eateries.

If you're traveling with kids, you're going to end up at one of the classic theme parks, either Disneyland or Knott's Berry Farm (plan an entire day around Disneyland). Grown-ups, though, will be drawn to the natural beauty of Catalina Island, and it's worth spending a whole day exploring. There's a tiny town with its fair share of attractions, but make sure you see the unspoiled coastline.

On the Calendar

Spring

Knotts's Boysenberry Festival. Known as the birthplace of the boysenberry, the Knotts's festival celebrates all things purple with live shows, plenty of boysenberry-inspired food, and no shortage of wine for adults.

Los Angeles Marathon. Starting at Dodger Stadium and ending in Santa Monica, the L.A. Marathon is the biggest running event in the city, and various streets are shut down to give runners free reign on a Sunday morning in March.

Los Angeles Times **Festival of Books.** Taking place on the USC campus in April, the *L.A. Times* Festival of Books celebrates authors and readers alike with new releases, lectures, celebrity signings, and food trucks.

Summer

Los Angeles Pride Festival and Parade. West Hollywood is home to the largest LGBTQ+ population in the city and hosts one of the biggest Pride festivals and parades in America. The festivities usually happen in June.

Nisei Week Japanese Festival. Over eight days in August in the Little Tokyo neighborhood of Downtown Los Angeles, Japanese culture is on full display with tea ceremonies, food stalls, parades, and the coronation of the Nisei Week Queen.

U.S. Open of Surfing. Every late July/early August, the best surfers on the planet (and their thousands of fans) congregate on Huntington Beach for the most prestigious surf competition in the country.

Fall

Abbot Kinney Festival. Every October, the entire stretch of the city's famous Venice Street Abbot Kinney is turned into a free community festival with food trucks, concerts, art booths, and all the weird and wonderful quirks of the neighborhood.

Dia de los Muertos (Day of the Dead). Head down to Olvera Street on November 1 for food, dancing, and more to celebrate the Day of the Dead and remember loved ones we've lost.

West Hollywood Halloween Carnaval. One of the craziest, flashiest, and most fun parties in L.A., the WeHo Halloween Carnaval is a costumed extravaganza in the heart of the city's LGBTQ+ neighborhood.

Winter

Chinese New Year. Head down to Chinatown for the annual Golden Dragon Parade along Hill and Temple streets. The festivities include fireworks, a lantern procession, food stalls, and more.

Hollywood Christmas Parade. More than a million people flock to Hollywood and Sunset boulevards to watch celebrities, floats, antique cars, and marching bands roll through Hollywood in this annual holiday celebration.

Tournament of Roses Parade. Since 1890, every New Year's Day in Pasadena is filled with the spectacular Tournament of Roses Parade. Elaborate floats roll through the streets and draw in millions of spectators. Following the parade is always the big Rose Bowl college football game inside Rose Bowl Stadium.

The Best Tours in Los Angeles

BUS TOURS

Guideline Tours. This offers sightseeing trips all around L.A., including Downtown, Universal Studios, and Hollywood. ⊠ *Los Angeles* ☎ *323/465–3004, 213/385–3004* ⊕ *www.tourslosangeles. com* ⊠ *From $70.*

Starline Tours. Operating double-decker and open-roof-van tours, Starline Tours offers hop-on/off tours around town and to Disneyland, Universal Studios, and Six Flags Magic Mountain. Passengers are picked up from the TCL Chinese Theatre and in Santa Monica. ⊠ *6801 Hollywood Blvd., Hollywood* ☎ *323/463–3333* ⊕ *www.starlinetours.com* ⊠ *From $50* Ⓜ *Hollywood/Highland.*

TMZ Celebrity Tour. If you want to feel like a paparazzi for a day, then check out the slightly tawdry TMZ Celebrity Tour of reputed celebrity hot spots that leaves from two locations: in front of the Hard Rock in Hollywood or The Grove. ⊠ *Los Angeles* ☎ *844/869–8687* ⊕ *www.tmz-tour.com* ⊠ *From $50.*

SCOOTER TOURS

Segwow. For an unusual perspective on L.A.'s attractions, you can take a tour of the city on a Segway electric scooter. Segwow tours might include the UCLA campus, Santa Monica, Rodeo Drive, or Downtown. The guided rides range from over an hour to four hours. ⊠ *Los Angeles* ☎ *310/358–5900* ⊕ *www.segwow. com* ⊠ *From $59 per person.*

SPECIAL-INTEREST TOURS

Access Hollywood Celebrity Homes Tours. This company takes groups in an open-air van through the glitzy streets of Beverly Hills where you can see homes belonging to the likes of A-listers like Mick Jagger, Tom Cruise, Katy Perry, and many more. ⊠ *Los Angeles* ☎ *323/472–7938* ⊕ *www.accesshollywoodtours.com* ⊠ *From $39.*

Architecture Tours L.A. With Architecture Tours L.A., you can zip all over the city in a comfortable minivan on a private tour with a historian. See famous buildings and homes designed by luminaries like Frank Lloyd Wright, Frank Gehry, and more. ⊠ *Los Angeles* ☎ *323/464–7868* ⊕ *www.architecturetoursla.com* ⊠ *From $80.*

Beverly Hills Trolley Tours. Beverly Hills operates year-round trolley tours focused on art and architecture. They last 40 minutes and depart from 11 am to 4 pm every weekend throughout the year, as well as Tuesday to Friday in the summer. ⊠ *Dayton Way and Rodeo Dr., Beverly Hills* ☎ *310/285–1000* ⊕ *www.beverly-hills.org/departments/publicworks/trans-portation/transit* ⊠ *$5.*

Esotouric. With an innovative take on the city, Esotouric's varied weekend bus tours explore historic architecture along Route 66 and the darker side of L.A. that Raymond Chandler revealed in books like *The Big Sleep* and *The Long Goodbye.* ⊠ *Los Angeles* ☎ *213/373–1947* ⊕ *www. esotouric.com* ⊠ *From $64.*

My Valley Pass Tours. This company serves as an excellent guide to the San Fernando Valley and runs one-of-a-kind tours. The San Fernando Valley Film Tour is one of their best and takes tourists on a three-hour trip to the Valley's most iconic film locations. ⊠ *Los Angeles* ☎ *818/850–3836* ⊕ *www.myvalleypass. com/tours* ⊠ *From $45.*

Neon Cruise. Soak up the glow of classic neon signs around L.A. from an open double-decker bus on tours offered by the Museum of Neon Art. There are also walking tours through different neighborhoods like Chinatown, the Broadway Theatre District, Hollywood, and more. ⊠ *Los Angeles* ☎ *818/696–2149* ⊕ *www. neonmona.org/neon-cruise* ⊠ *$55.*

Sidewalk Food Tours. For food lovers, the Sidewalk Food Tours are unique walking tours around Los Angeles that let you explore this incredible city through its many cuisines. Tours are broken up between West Hollywood and Downtown L.A., run for 2½ hours, and hit six different food outlets along the way. ⊠ *1933 Bronson Ave.* ☎ *877/568–6877* ⊕ *www.sidewalkfoodtours.com/los-ange-les* ⊠ *$75.*

Take My Mother Please. Take My Mother Please will arrange lively, thematic combination walking and driving tours; for instance, you could explore sights associated with the film *L.A. Confidential.* ⊠ *Los Angeles* ☎ *323/737–2200* ⊕ *www. takemymotherplease.com* ⊠ *From $450 for up to three people for a half day.*

WALKING TOURS

Los Angeles Conservancy. The Los Angeles Conservancy's 2½-hour-long walking tours ($10) cover the Downtown area. ⊠ *Los Angeles* ☎ *213/623–2489* ⊕ *www. laconservancy.org/tours.*

Red Line Tours. This company offers daily walking tours of behind-the-scenes Hollywood. Tours are led by docents and include headsets to block out street noise. ⊠ *6708 Hollywood Blvd., Hollywood* ☎ *323/402–1074* ⊕ *www. redlinetours.com* ⊠ *From $15.*

Universal Studio Tour. For one hour, you can get a unique look behind the scenes of one of the biggest film studios in the world. The tour covers 13 blocks as Jimmy Fallon virtually guides you through a close encounter with *Jaws*, the wreckage of a 747 from *War of the Worlds*, and much more. ⊠ *100 Universal City Plaza, Universal City* ☎ *800/864–8377* ⊕ *www. universalstudioshollywood.com/web/en/ us/things-to-do/rides-and-attractions/the-world-famous-studio-tour* ⊠ *From $70* Ⓜ *Universal City/Studio City.*

Contacts

Air

AIRPORTS Hollywood Burbank Airport. (*BUR*). ✉ *2627 N. Hollywood Way, near I–5 and U.S. 101, Burbank* ☎ *818/840–8840* ⊕ *www.hollywoodburbankairport.com.* **John Wayne Airport.** (*SNA*). ✉ *18601 Airport Way, Santa Ana* ☎ *949/252–5200* ⊕ *www.ocair.com.* **L.A./ Ontario International Airport.** (*ONT*). ✉ *2500 E. Airport Dr., off I–10, Ontario* ☎ *909/544–5300* ⊕ *www.flyontario.com.* **Long Beach Airport.** (*LGB*). ✉ *4100 Donald Douglas Dr., Long Beach* ☎ *562/570–2600* ⊕ *www.lgb.org.* **Los Angeles International Airport.** (*LAX*). ✉ *1 World Way, off Hwy. 1* ☎ *855/463–5252* ⊕ *www.flylax.com.*

AIRPORT TRANSPORT FlyAway. ☎ *714/507–1170* ⊕ *www.flylax.com/en/ flyaway-bus.* **SuperShuttle.** ☎ *323/775–6600, 800/258–3826* ⊕ *www. supershuttle.com.*

🚌 Bus

CONTACTS Culver CityBus. ☎ *310/253–6510* ⊕ *www. culvercitybus.com.* **DASH.** ☎ *310/808–2273* ⊕ *www. ladottransit.com.* **Los Angeles County Metropolitan Transit Authority.** ☎ *323/466–3876* ⊕ *www.metro.net.*

Santa Monica Municipal Bus Line. ☎ *310/451–5444* ⊕ *www.bigbluebus.com.*

Ⓜ Metro/ Public Transport

CONTACTS Los Angeles County Metropolitan Transit Authority. ☎ *323/466–3876* ⊕ *www.metro.net.*

🚕 Taxi

TAXI COMPANIES Beverly Hills Cab Co. ☎ *800/273–6611* ⊕ *www.beverlyhillscabco.com.* **Independent Cab Co..** ☎ *800/521–8294* ⊕ *www.lataxi.com/ new.* **LA Checker Cab.** ☎ *800/300–5007* ⊕ *www. ineedtaxi.com.* **United Independent Taxi.** ☎ *800/822–8294, 323/653–5050 text to order taxi* ⊕ *www.unitedtaxi.com.* **Yellow Cab Los Angeles.** ☎ *424/222–2222* ⊕ *www.layellowcab.com.*

🚆 Train

CONTACTS Amtrak. ☎ *800/872–7245* ⊕ *www. amtrak.com.* **Metrolink.** ☎ *800/371–5465* ⊕ *www. metrolinktrains.com.* **Union Station.** ✉ *800 N. Alameda St., Downtown* ☎ *213/683–6979* ⊕ *www. unionstationla.com* Ⓜ *Union Station.*

📍 Visitor Information

CONTACTS Beverly Hills Conference and Visitors Bureau. ✉ *Beverly Hills* ☎ *310/248–1015, 800/345–2210* ⊕ *www.lovebeverlyhills.com.* **Discover Los Angeles.** ☎ *213/624–7300* ⊕ *www.discoverlosangeles.com.* **Hollywood Chamber of Commerce.** ✉ *Hollywood* ☎ *323/469–8311* ⊕ *www.hollywoodchamber.net.* **Long Beach Area Convention and Visitors Bureau.** ✉ *301 E. Ocean Blvd., Suite 1900, Long Beach* ☎ *562/436–3645* ⊕ *www.visitlongbeach. com.* **Pasadena Convention and Visitor Bureau.** ✉ *300 E. Green St., Pasadena* ☎ *800/307–7977* ⊕ *www. visitpasadena.com.* **Santa Monica Travel and Tourism.** ✉ *2427 Main St., Santa Monica* ☎ *800/544–5319* ⊕ *www.santamonica.com.* **Visit California.** ✉ *555 Capitol Mall, Suite 1100, Sacramento* ☎ *916/444–4429, 800/862–2543* ⊕ *www.visitcalifornia.com.* **Visit West Hollywood.** ✉ *1017 N. La Cienega Blvd., West Hollywood* ☎ *310/289–2525, 800/368–6020* ⊕ *www. visitwesthollywood.com.*

Chapter 3

SANTA MONICA AND VENICE

WITH BRENTWOOD AND SAWTELLE JAPANTOWN

Updated by
Candice Yacono

3

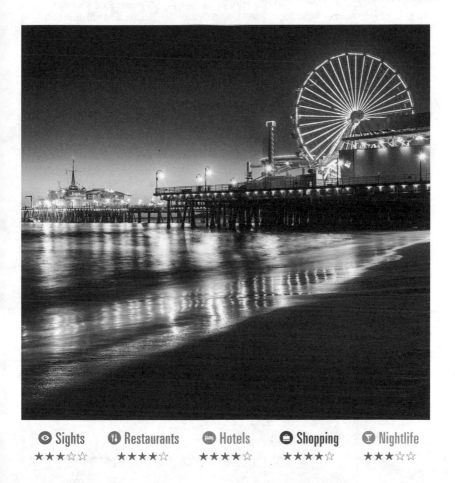

⊙ Sights	🍴 Restaurants	🛏 Hotels	🛍 Shopping	🍸 Nightlife
★★★☆☆	★★★★☆	★★★★☆	★★★★☆	★★★☆☆

NEIGHBORHOOD SNAPSHOT

TOP EXPERIENCES

■ **Bike along the Strand:** Spend the day on this 22-mile paved path, also known as the South Bay Bike Trail, which stretches from Santa Monica to Redondo Beach.

■ **Spend the day at Santa Monica Pier:** See concerts here in the summer, or bring your family for a stroll during the day and enjoy classic fair food and carnival attractions; you can even try your hand at aerial trapeze work.

■ **Catch the mellow vibes in Venice Beach:** Walk along the canals, shop, and grab an all-organic lunch on Abbot Kinney, or watch tanned locals in tie-dye toting longboards.

■ **Dine at a Michelin-starred eatery:** Santa Monica is the happy home to multiple Michelin-honored restaurants; one, Rustic Canyon, even has a coveted star. Act quick to get a reservation, then prepare your taste-buds for paradise.

■ **View some art:** Rise up into the hills of Brentwood where the architecturally striking Getty Center towers over the city and houses priceless works of art.

QUICK BITES

The Cow's End Cafe. Stop at this two-story locals' favorite for coffee and pastries, or choose from a long list of sandwiches for something more substantial. ✉ *34 Washington Blvd.* ⊕ *www.thecowsend-cafe.com*

Mariasol Cocina Mexican. Soak up the atmosphere inside this fun-loving eatery at the very end of Santa Monica Pier. The fajitas reign as the most popular item. ✉ *401 Santa Monica Pier* ⊕ *www.mariasol. com*

Venice Whaler. This beachfront bar has been the local watering hole for musicians like the Doors and the Beach Boys since 1944. It boasts an amazing view and serves tasty California pub food like fish tacos, pulled-pork sliders, and avocado toast with a basic selection of beers. ✉ *10 Washington Blvd.* ⊕ *www.venicewhaler.com*

GETTING HERE

■ From Downtown, the easiest way to hit the coast is by taking the Santa Monica Freeway (I–10) due west. Once you reach the end of the freeway, I–10 runs into Pacific Coast Highway, or PCH. Venice is just south of Santa Monica and is accessible from the PCH, too. MTA buses run from Downtown along Pico, Olympic, Santa Monica, Sunset, and Wilshire boulevards to the coast. The Metro Expo Line runs to Downtown Santa Monica. Public parking is usually available at the beach or in city parking lots, although fees can range anywhere from $8 to $20.

PLANNING YOUR TIME

■ The best way to tour Santa Monica and the adjoining Venice is to park your car and walk, cycle, or skate along the area's famed bike path, known as the Strand. Short jaunts from there will take you to noncoastal main thoroughfares like Third Street Promenade or Abbot Kinney, though some of the top Santa Monica restaurants lie a bit farther east.

Santa Monica and Venice are two of the region's most iconic destinations, but while Santa Monica has its eyes firmly on the future, Venice enjoys indulging a bit in its past.

Silicon Beach, Southern California's tech hub, is centered on the Santa Monica area, which means employees from hundreds of companies like Activision, Hulu, and Snap (of Snapchat fame) flood the area and influence the flavor of its shops and restaurants. (Silicon Beach's influence also impacts many hotel amenity lists, to your benefit.) The Santa Monica Pier, with its Ferris wheel and roller coaster, is the scene of a thousand movie and television show filmings, from *Forrest Gump* to *Iron Man,* while Venice Beach has conjured images of greased-up bodybuilders, boho hippies, and boardwalk palm readers for generations.

Santa Monica

This pedestrian-friendly little city, about 8.3 square miles, has a dynamic population of artists and writers, entertainment folks, educators, and retired people; its left-wing politics have earned it the nickname of the People's Republic of Santa Monica (just like Berkeley in Northern California). Mature trees, Mediterranean-style architecture, and strict zoning have helped create a sense of place often missing from L.A.'s residential neighborhoods, and its cooler, sometimes-foggy climate is another draw. Since it's a desirable neighborhood, real estate here isn't cheap.

◉ Sights

Annenberg Community Beach House
LOCAL INTEREST | This beachfront property was originally developed in the 1920s by William Randolph Hearst as a palatial private residence and a gathering spot for Hollywood's megastars. In 1947 it was converted into a members-only beach club; the state of California bought and renamed the club in 1959, but it took the earthquake of 2004 for the state to reconceive the property as a public place. With the help of the Annenberg Foundation, it reopened as a community beach house in 2009. Feel like a millionaire lounging by the pool on one of the beachside chairs, or lunch at the café while enjoying uninterrupted ocean views. The house's Beach=Culture event series includes a variety of classes (yoga, beach volleyball), readings, and exhibits; check the website for the calendar. Hours are subject to change, so call to confirm hours and book in advance. Book a pool reservation online in advance if possible. ✉ *415 Pacific Coast Hwy., Santa Monica* ☎ *310/458–4904* ⊕ *www.annenbergbeachhouse.com* ⌖ *Free; pool $10.*

Bergamot Station
ARTS VENUE | Named after a stop on the Air Line trolley that once shuttled between Downtown and the Santa Monica Pier, Bergamot Station is now a depot for intriguing art. The industrial facades house more than 30 art galleries, shops, a café, a theater, and a museum. The galleries cover many kinds of media:

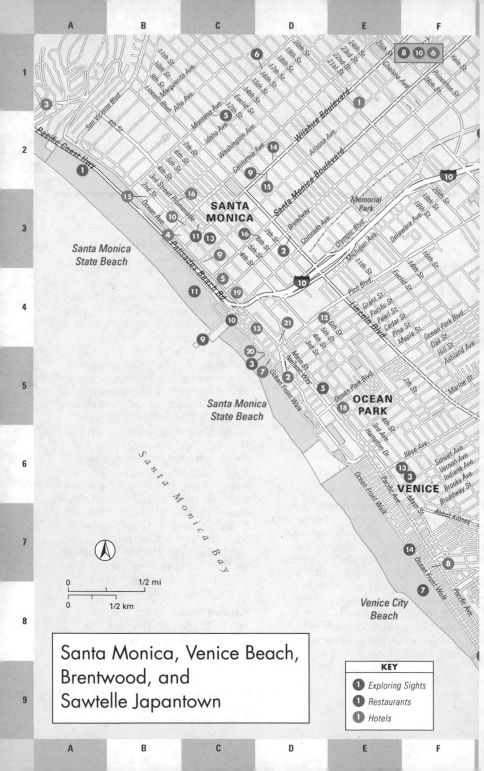

Santa Monica, Venice Beach, Brentwood, and Sawtelle Japantown

Santa Monica State Beach

Santa Monica State Beach

Santa Monica Bay

SANTA MONICA

OCEAN PARK

VENICE

Venice City Beach

Pacific Coast Hwy
San Vicente Blvd.
11th St.
10th St.
9th St.
Marguerita Ave.
Lincoln Blvd.
Alta Ave.
4th St.
Montana Ave.
12th St.
Euclid St.
14th St.
15th St.
16th St.
17th St.
18th St.
19th St.
20th St.
21st St.
23rd St.
24th St.
25th St.
Chelsea Ave.
Yale St.
Princeton St.
Harvard St.
Wilshire Boulevard
Arizona Ave.
Santa Monica Boulevard
Idaho Ave.
Washington Ave.
California Ave.
7th St.
6th St.
5th St.
4th St.
3rd St.
2nd St.
Ocean Ave.
3rd Street Promenade
Palisades Beach Rd.
Broadway
Colorado Ave.
Olympic Blvd.
Michigan Ave.
Delaware Ave.
19th St.
18th St.
17th St.
14th St.
16th St.
Euclid St.
Memorial Park
Pico Blvd.
11th Blvd.
Lincoln Blvd.
Grant St.
Pacific St.
Pearl St.
Cedar St.
Pine St.
Maple St.
Ocean Park Blvd.
Oak St.
Hill St.
Ashland Ave.
7th St.
Marine St.
Main St.
Neilson Way
Ocean Front Walk
4th St.
5th St.
3rd St.
Ocean Park Blvd.
3rd Ave.
Hampton Dr.
Rose Ave.
Sunset Ave.
Vernon Ave.
Indiana Ave.
Brooks Ave.
Broadway St.
Abbot Kinner
Main St.
Pacific Ave.
Ocean Front Walk

0   1/2 mi
0   1/2 km

KEY
1 Exploring Sights
1 Restaurants
1 Hotels

Sights ▼

1 Annenberg Community Beach House............. **A2**
2 Bergamot Station........ **D2**
3 Binoculars Building **F6**
4 The Getty Center.......... **I1**
5 Main Street.............. **D5**
6 Marina del Rey............ **I9**
7 Muscle Beach **F8**
8 Pierce Brothers Westwood Village Memorial Park and Mortuary............. **F1**
9 Santa Monica Pier....... **C4**
10 Santa Monica Pier Aquarium **C4**
11 Santa Monica State Beach..................... **C4**
12 Skirball Cultural Center..................... **I1**
13 Third Street Promenade and Santa Monica Place..... **C3**
14 Venice Beach Boardwalk................ **F7**

Restaurants ▼

1 Baltaire Restaurant....... **I1**
2 Bay Cities Italian Deli... **D3**
3 Coach **D5**
4 The Cow's End Cafe **G8**
5 Father's Office **C2**
6 Forma Restaurant and Cheese Bar.............. **D1**
7 Gjelina.................... **G7**
8 Hide Sushi **H1**
9 Huckleberry Bakery and Cafe **D2**
10 Lady Chocolatt........... **F1**
11 Michael's Santa Monica............. **C3**
12 Pizzana..................... **I1**
13 Rose Cafe................. **E6**
14 Rustic Canyon........... **D2**
15 Santa Monica Seafood.................. **D2**
16 Tar and Roses........... **D3**
17 Toscana.................... **I1**
18 Tsujita L.A. Artisan Noodles.................. **H1**
19 Venice Whaler **G8**

Hotels ▼

1 The Ambrose............. **E1**
2 Bayside Hotel **D5**
3 Channel Road Inn....... **A1**
4 Fairmont Miramar Hotel and Bungalows Santa Monica............ **C3**
5 The Georgian Hotel...... **C4**
6 Hotel Bel-Air **F1**
7 Hotel Casa del Mar..... **D5**
8 Hotel Erwin **F7**
9 Hotel Shangri-La......... **C3**
10 Huntley Santa Monica Beach..................... **C3**
11 The Kinney.............. **H7**
12 Le Meridien Delfina Santa Monica........... **D4**
13 Loews Santa Monica Beach Hotel............. **D4**
14 Marina del Rey Marriott.................. **G8**
15 Oceana Beach Club Hotel..................... **B3**
16 Palihouse Santa Monica.................. **B3**
17 The Ritz-Carlton Marina del Rey............ **I8**
18 Sea Shore Motel......... **E5**
19 Shore Hotel............... **C4**
20 Shutters on the Beach.................... **D5**
21 Viceroy Santa Monica........... **D4**

The three-block Third Street Promenade is great for shopping and is for pedestrians only.

photography, jewelry, and paintings from somber to lurid. Leashed, tame dogs are welcome and admission is free. ✉ *2525 Michigan Ave., Santa Monica* ☎ *310/453–7535* ⊕ *www.bergamotstation.com* ⊘ *Closed Sun. and Mon.*

Main Street

COMMERCIAL CENTER | FAMILY | This thoroughfare is a great spot for star sightings or for strolling among the laid-back California crowd. Streets are lined with old-fashioned, colorful, and cozy boutiques that stock everything from high-end garments to bohemian favorites. There's also a standard crop of shopping mall outposts plus a good selection of casual restaurants and cafés. If you're in town on the last Saturday of the month, check out the sidewalk sale. ✉ *Between Pacific St. and Rose Ave., and Santa Monica and Venice Blvds., Santa Monica* ⊕ *www.mainstreetsm.com.*

★ Santa Monica Pier

CAROUSEL | FAMILY | Souvenir shops, carnival games, arcades, eateries, an outdoor trapeze school, a small amusement park, and an aquarium all contribute to the festive atmosphere of this truncated pier at the foot of Colorado Boulevard below Palisades Park. The pier's trademark 46-horse Looff Carousel, built in 1922, has appeared in several films, including *The Sting.* The Soda Jerks ice-cream fountain (named for the motion the attendant makes when pulling the machine's arm) inside the carousel building is a pier staple. Free concerts are held on the pier in the summer. ✉ *Colorado Ave., Santa Monica* ☎ *310/458–8901* ⊕ *www.santamonicapier.org.*

Santa Monica Pier Aquarium

ZOO | FAMILY | Run by beach conservation group Heal the Bay, this live marine life menagerie contains more than 100 species of marine animals and plants, all found in Santa Monica Bay. The Dorothy Green Room features live and interactive exhibits about local watersheds and short educational films on the weekends. The Kid's Corner provides books, games, and a puppet show. Don't miss this chance to learn about the area's ecology and staggering evidence of how pollution is affecting ocean life. The aquarium can be tricky to find—look for it tucked under the eastern end of the Santa Monica Pier bridge along Ocean Front Walk. Follow the colorful seascape murals that cover the outside walls. ■ TIP➔ **Kids ages 12 and under receive free admission.** ✉ *1600 Ocean Front Walk, Santa Monica* ☎ *310/393–6149* ⊕ *www.healthebay.org/ aquarium* ☞ *$7.*

Santa Monica State Beach

BEACH—SIGHT | The first beach you'll hit after the Santa Monica Freeway (Interstate 10) runs into the Pacific Coast Highway, wide and sandy Santa Monica is *the* place for sunning and socializing. The Strand, which runs across the beach and for 22 miles in total, is popular among walkers, joggers, and bicyclists. Be prepared for a mob scene on summer weekends, when parking becomes an expensive ordeal. Swimming is fine (with the usual poststorm-pollution caveat); for surfing, go elsewhere. For a memorable view, climb up the stairway over PCH to Palisades Park, at the top of the bluffs. Free summer concerts are held on the pier on Thursday evening. **Amenities:** parking; lifeguards; toilets; food and drink; showers; water sports. **Best for:** partiers; sunset; surfing; swimming; walking. ✉ *1642 Promenade, PCH at California Incline, Santa Monica* ☎ *310/458–8573* ⊕ *www.smgov.net/portals/beach* ☞ *Parking from $7.*

★ Third Street Promenade and Santa Monica Place

COMMERCIAL CENTER | Stretch your legs along this pedestrian-only, three-block stretch of 3rd Street, close to the Pacific, lined with jacaranda trees, ivy-topiary dinosaur fountains, strings of lights, and branches of nearly every major U.S. retail chain; indeed, it always seems to house the most-coveted brands for each generation of teens. Outdoor cafés, street vendors, movie theaters, and a rich nightlife make this a main gathering spot for locals, visitors, street artists and musicians, and performance artists. Plan a night just to take it all in or take an afternoon for a long people-watching stroll. There's plenty of parking in city structures on the streets flanking the promenade. **Santa Monica Place,** at the south end of the promenade, is a sleek outdoor mall and foodie haven. Its three stories are home to Nordstrom, Louis Vuitton, Coach, and other upscale retailers. Don't miss the ocean views from the rooftop food court. ✉ *3rd St., between Colorado and Wilshire Blvds., Santa Monica* ⊕ *www.downtownsm.com.*

🍴 Restaurants

This idyllic seaside town is a hotbed of culinary activity, with a dynamic farmers' market that attracts chefs from all over Los Angeles and local restaurants that celebrate farm-to-table, seasonal dining.

★ Bay Cities Italian Deli

$ | **DELI** | Part deli, part market, Bay Cities has been home to incredible Italian subs since 1925. This renowned counter-service spot is always crowded (best to order ahead), but monster subs run the gamut from the mighty meatball to the signature Godmother, made with prosciutto, ham, capicola, mortadella, Genoa salami, and provolone. **Known for:** market with rare imports; old-school, deli-style service; huge sandwiches. $ *Average main: $10* ✉ *1517 Lincoln Blvd., Santa Monica* ☎ *310/395–8279* ⊕ *www.baycitiesitaliandeli.com* ⊗ *Closed Mon.*

Coach

$$$ | **AMERICAN** | Escape busy Santa Monica State Beach to dine at this casual café and bar within the unfussy oceanfront hotel Shutters on the Beach. Head here at sunset for sophisticated, fruity cocktails and fresh seafood, like oysters and Dungeness crab, one block from Santa Monica Pier. **Known for:** great sunset drinks and dining; casual beachside atmosphere; California-inspired

Santa Monica Pier has several classic amusement park rides, including the Looff Carousel, built in 1922.

cuisine. [$] *Average main: $25* ✉ *Shutters on the Beach, 1 Pico Blvd., Santa Monica* ☎ *310/458–0030* ⊕ *www.shuttersonthe-beach.com.*

Father's Office
$$ | AMERICAN | Distinguished by its vintage neon sign, this gastropub is famous for handcrafted beers and a brilliant signature burger. Topped with Gruyère and Maytag blue cheeses, arugula, caramelized onions, and applewood-smoked bacon compote, the Office Burger is a guilty pleasure worth waiting in line for, which is usually required. **Known for:** addictive sweet potato fries; strict no-substitutions policy; 36 craft beers on tap. [$] *Average main: $15* ✉ *1018 Montana Ave., Santa Monica* ☎ *310/736–2224* ⊕ *www.fathersoffice.com* ☉ *No lunch weekdays.*

Forma Restaurant and Cheese Bar
$$$ | ITALIAN | Pasta is served here *dalla forma,* meaning it's cooked, then dipped into a cheese wheel and stirred up until it's coated with melted cheese before serving. Catering to a higher-end crowd, Forma specializes in cheeses, pastas, and pizzas. **Known for:** amazing pasta stirred in a cheese wheel; fresh mozzarella knots; Roman-style crispy artichokes. [$] *Average main: $28* ✉ *1610 Montana Ave., Santa Monica* ☎ *424/231–2868* ⊕ *www.formarestaurant.com.*

Huckleberry Bakery and Cafe
$$ | AMERICANAMERICAN | FAMILY | Founded by Santa Monica natives, Huckleberry brings together the best ingredients from local farmers and growers to craft diner-style comfort food with a chic twist. Everything is made on-site, even the hot sauce and almond milk. **Known for:** from-scratch diner-style breakfast options; delectable pastries; green eggs and Niman Ranch ham. [$] *Average main: $14* ✉ *1014 Wilshire Blvd., Santa Monica* ☎ *310/451–2311* ⊕ *www.huckleberryca-fe.com.*

Michael's Santa Monica
$$$ | MODERN AMERICAN | Michael's is a Santa Monica institution, and its new American shared-plates menu runs the gamut from peruviana beans to branzino

with pomegranate to sunchoke gnocchi. Tie it all together with a whipped deconstructed cheesecake (insane). **Known for:** stunning patio; incredible cheesecake; incredible happy hour with a cocktail for only $1.79. $ *Average main: $30 ⊠ 1147 3rd St., Santa Monica ☎ 310/451–0843* ⊕ *www.michaelssantamonica.com* ☾ *Closed Sun. No lunch.*

★ Rustic Canyon

$$$$ | **MODERN AMERICAN** | A Santa Monica mainstay, the seasonally changing menu at this farm-to-table restaurant consistently upends norms and has even earned a Michelin star. The homey, minimalist space offers sweeping views of Wilshire Boulevard, and on any given night the menu of California cuisine may include Channel Island rockfish with shelling beans and Sun Gold tomatoes, or buttered ricotta dumplings with golden chanterelles and Coolea cheese. **Known for:** never-ending wine list; knowledgeable staff; everything is made in-house. $ *Average main: $35 ⊠ 1119 Wilshire Blvd., Santa Monica ☎ 310/393–7050* ⊕ *www.rusticcanyonrestaurant.com.*

Santa Monica Seafood

$$ | **SEAFOOD** | **FAMILY** | A Southern California favorite that seems like a tourist trap at first blush but decidedly isn't, this Italian seafood haven has been serving up fresh fish since 1939. This freshness comes from its pedigree as the largest seafood distributor in the Southwest. **Known for:** deliciously seasoned rainbow trout; oyster bar; historic fish market. $ *Average main: $20 ⊠ 1000 Wilshire Blvd., Santa Monica ☎ 310/393–5244* ⊕ *www.santamonicaseafood.com.*

★ Tar and Roses

$$$ | **MODERN AMERICAN** | This small and dimly lit romantic spot in Santa Monica is full of adventurous global options, like octopus skewers and venison loin. The new American cuisine, which is centered on the restaurant's wood-fired oven, also features standouts like braised lamb belly with minted apple chutney and

drool-worthy strawberry ricotta crostata with honeycomb ice cream for dessert. **Known for:** phenomenal oxtail dumplings; delicious hanger steak; ever-changing menu. $ *Average main: $30 ⊠ 602 Santa Monica Blvd., Santa Monica ☎ 310/587–0700* ⊕ *www.tarandroses.com.*

🛏 Hotels

The Ambrose

$$$ | **HOTEL** | Tranquillity pervades the airy, California Craftsman–style, four-story Ambrose, which blends right into its mostly residential Santa Monica neighborhood. **Pros:** "green" practices like nontoxic cleaners and recycling bins; partial ocean views; nice amenities (like car service and wine reception) for a $25 extra fee. **Cons:** quiet, residential area of Santa Monica; parking fee ($27); not walking distance to beach. $ *Rooms from: $359 ⊠ 1255 20th St., Santa Monica ☎ 310/315–1555, 877/262–7673* ⊕ *www.ambrosehotel.com* 🛏 *77 rooms* ⧖ *Free breakfast.*

Bayside Hotel

$ | **HOTEL** | Tucked snugly into a narrow corner lot, the supremely casual Bayside's greatest asset is its prime spot directly across from the beach, within walkable blocks from the Third Street Promenade and Santa Monica Pier. **Pros:** cheaper weeknight stays; beach access and views; dog-friendly rooms and rooms with kitchens available. **Cons:** no lobby and expensive parking; basic bedding; thin walls and street noise. $ *Rooms from: $199 ⊠ 2001 Ocean Ave., Santa Monica ☎ 310/396–6000, 800/525–4447* ⊕ *baysidehotel.com* 🛏 *45 rooms* ⧖ *No meals.*

★ Channel Road Inn

$$ | **B&B/INN** | A quaint surprise in Southern California, the Channel Road Inn is every bit the country retreat bed-and-breakfast lovers adore, with four-poster beds, fluffy duvets, and a cozy living room with a fireplace. **Pros:** free wine

and cheese "minipicnic" each afternoon; home-cooked breakfast included; meditative rose garden on-site. **Cons:** no pool; need a car (or Uber) to get around; decidedly non-L.A. decor not for everyone. ⑤ *Rooms from: $225* ✉ *219 W. Channel Rd., Santa Monica* ☎ *310/459–1920* ⊕ *www.channelroadinn.com* ↩ *15 rooms* ⦿ *Free breakfast.*

Fairmont Miramar Hotel and Bungalows Santa Monica

$$$$ | **HOTEL** | A mammoth Moreton Bay fig tree dwarfs the main entrance of the 5-acre, beach-adjacent Santa Monica wellness retreat and lends its name to the inviting on-site Mediterranean-inspired restaurant, FIG, which focuses on local ingredients and frequently refreshes its menu. **Pros:** guests can play games on the heated patio; swanky open-air cocktail spot, the Bungalow, on-site; retrofitted '20s and '40s bungalows. **Cons:** all this luxury comes at a big price; standard rooms are on the small side; breakfast not included. ⑤ *Rooms from: $599* ✉ *101 Wilshire Blvd., Santa Monica* ☎ *310/576–7777, 866/540–4470* ⊕ *www. fairmont.com/santamonica* ↩ *334 rooms* ⦿ *No meals.*

The Georgian Hotel

$$$$ | **HOTEL** | Driving by, you can't miss the Georgian, built in 1933: the art deco exterior is aqua, with ornate bronze grillwork and a charming oceanfront veranda. **Pros:** many ocean-view rooms; front terrace is a great people-watching spot; free Wi-Fi. **Cons:** $38 parking; some rooms have unremarkable views; decor a bit tired in places. ⑤ *Rooms from: $409* ✉ *1415 Ocean Ave., Santa Monica* ☎ *310/395–9945, 800/538–8147* ⊕ *www. georgianhotel.com* ↩ *84 rooms* ⦿ *No meals.*

Hotel Casa del Mar

$$$$ | **HOTEL** | In the 1920s it was a posh beach club catering to the city's elite; now the Casa del Mar is one of SoCal's most luxurious and pricey beachfront hotels with a heavenly lobby, three

extravagant two-story penthouses, a raised deck and pool, an indulgent spa, and an elegant ballroom facing the sand. **Pros:** excellent dining at Catch; modern amenities; gorgeous beachfront rooms. **Cons:** no room balconies; without a doubt, one of L.A.'s priciest beach stays; atmosphere can be a bit stuffy. ⑤ *Rooms from: $700* ✉ *1910 Ocean Way, Santa Monica* ☎ *310/581–5533, 800/898–6999* ⊕ *www.hotelcasadelmar.com* ↩ *129 rooms* ⦿ *No meals.*

Hotel Shangri-La

$$$ | **HOTEL** | Across from Santa Monica's oceanfront Palisades Park, the 1939-built art deco, ocean-liner-inspired Hotel Shangri-La is firmly in tune with the 21st century. **Pros:** sunken Jacuzzis in bathrooms; ONYX rooftop bar is the place to be; active pool scene in the summer. **Cons:** some rooms have tight, cruise-ship-like quarters; pricey parking rates ($49); some furnishings are a little tired. ⑤ *Rooms from: $385* ✉ *301 Ocean Ave., Santa Monica* ☎ *310/394–2791* ⊕ *www. shangrila-hotel.com* ↩ *70 rooms* ⦿ *No meals.*

Huntley Santa Monica Beach

$$$$ | **HOTEL** | This sleek, tech-savvy property keeps the Silicon Beach business traveler in mind. **Pros:** great ocean views; fun social scene; great views (and drinks) at the Penthouse, the hotel's top-floor restaurant. **Cons:** no pool; noise from the restaurant and bar; tech bro vibe not for everyone. ⑤ *Rooms from: $459* ✉ *1111 2nd St., Santa Monica* ☎ *310/394–5454* ⊕ *www.thehuntleyhotel.com* ↩ *204 rooms* ⦿ *No meals.*

Le Meridien Delfina Santa Monica

$$$ | **HOTEL** | **FAMILY** | Not far from I–10 and four blocks from the Expo Line, this hotel appeals to business travelers and jet-setting leisure travelers who fancy the sleek interiors and close proximity to beaches and restaurants. **Pros:** casual and upscale eateries on property; retro designer touches; cabanas and pool on ground floor. **Cons:** not as centrally located

as some Santa Monica hotels, not all rooms have balconies; pool on the small side. [$] *Rooms from: $319* ⊠ *530 Pico Blvd., Santa Monica* ☎ *310/399–9344, 888/627–8532* ⊕ *www.lemeridiendelfina. com* ⤴ *310 rooms* ❌ *No meals.*

Loews Santa Monica Beach Hotel

$$$$ | HOTEL | FAMILY | Walk to the ocean side of the soaring atrium at this family- and pet-friendly hotel, and you feel like you're on a cruise ship: massive windows give way to the expansive sea below, sunny staff seems content to assist with your needs, and a massive photo screen behind reception intuits a sense of place. **Pros:** resort vibe with three restaurants; walk to beach; wonderful spa and fitness center. **Cons:** small pool; parking is pricey ($55); large size can be overwhelming. [$] *Rooms from: $600* ⊠ *1700 Ocean Ave., Santa Monica* ☎ *310/458–6700, 800/235–6397* ⊕ *www.loewshotels.com* ⤴ *347 rooms* ❌ *No meals.*

Oceana Beach Club Hotel

$$$ | HOTEL | Following an ultraswank refresh, the suites-only Oceana manages to achieve a low-key vibe while still dripping in luxury. **Pros:** walk to prime shopping districts; gorgeous Sandpiper restaurant with stunning ocean views; bubbly at check-in. **Cons:** small pool; breakfast not included; no coffeemakers in rooms. [$] *Rooms from: $365* ⊠ *849 Ocean Ave., Santa Monica* ☎ *310/393–0486, 800/777–0758* ⊕ *www.hoteloceanasantamonica. com* ⤴ *70 suites* ❌ *No meals.*

Palihouse Santa Monica

$$$ | HOTEL | Tucked in a posh residential area three blocks from the sea and lively Third Street Promenade, Palihouse Santa Monica caters to design-minded world travelers, with spacious rooms and suites decked out in whimsical antiques. **Pros:** Apple TV in rooms; walking distance to Santa Monica attractions; fully equipped kitchens. **Cons:** no pool; decor might not appeal to more traditional travelers; parking fee ($45). [$] *Rooms from: $355* ⊠ *1001 3rd St., Santa Monica*

☎ *310/394–1279* ⊕ *www.palihousesanta-monica.com* ⤴ *38 rooms* ❌ *No meals.*

Sea Shore Motel

$ | HOTEL | On Santa Monica's busy Main Street, the Sea Shore (family-owned for almost 50 years) is a charming throwback to Route 66 and to '60s-style roadside motels in an ultratrendy neighborhood. **Pros:** close to beach and restaurants; free Wi-Fi, parking, and use of beach equipment; popular rooftop deck. **Cons:** street noise; motel-style decor and beds; not the Santa Monica style a lot of people are looking for. [$] *Rooms from: $159* ⊠ *2637 Main St., Santa Monica* ☎ *310/392–2787* ⊕ *www.seashoremotel.com* ⤴ *25 rooms* ❌ *No meals.*

Shore Hotel

$$$$ | HOTEL | With views of the Santa Monica Pier, this hotel with a friendly staff offers eco-minded travelers stylish rooms with a modern design, just steps from the sand and sea. **Pros:** near beach and Third Street Promenade; rainfall showerheads; solar-heated pool and hot tub. **Cons:** expensive rooms and parking fees; fronting busy Ocean Avenue; some sharing a room may be wary of the see-through shower. [$] *Rooms from: $432* ⊠ *1515 Ocean Ave., Santa Monica* ☎ *310/458–1515* ⊕ *shorehotel.com* ⤴ *164 rooms* ❌ *No meals.*

★ Shutters on the Beach

$$$$ | HOTEL | FAMILY | Set right on the sand, this inn has become synonymous with staycations, with the beachfront location and show-house decor making it one of SoCal's most popular luxury hotels. **Pros:** built-in cabinets filled with art books and curios; rooms designed by Michael Smith; bathrooms come with whirlpool tubs. **Cons:** have to pay for extras like beach chairs; very expensive; breakfast not included. [$] *Rooms from: $675* ⊠ *1 Pico Blvd., Santa Monica* ☎ *310/458–0030, 800/334–9000* ⊕ *www. shuttersonthebeach.com* ⤴ *198 rooms* ❌ *No meals.*

3

Santa Monica and Venice SANTA MONICA

Viceroy Santa Monica

$$$$ | HOTEL | Tropical casual meets urbane at this stylized, airy seaside escape, where the cozy rooms, which all have French balconies, draw quite the upscale clientele. **Pros:** hip lobby and restaurant/lounge; chic lounge and poolside socializing; pedestrian-friendly area. **Cons:** super-pricey bar and dining; pool for dipping, not laps; sometimes snooty ambience. ⑤ *Rooms from: $510* ✉ *1819 Ocean Ave., Santa Monica* ☎ *310/260–7500, 800/622–8711* ⊕ *www.viceroysantamonica.com* ⤳ *162 rooms* ❌ *No meals.*

ⓨ Nightlife

In Santa Monica, the focus of nightlife shifts toward live music, historic dives, and any space that has a view of the ocean.

★ Chez Jay

BARS/PUBS | Around since 1959, this dive bar continues to be a well-loved place in Santa Monica. Everyone from the young to the old (including families) frequents this historical landmark. It's a charming place, from the well-worn booths with their red checkered tablecloths to the ship's wheel near the door. The backyard lounge is perfect for warm low-key days. ✉ *1657 Ocean Ave., Santa Monica* ☎ *310/395–1741* ⊕ *www.chezjays.com.*

The Galley

BARS/PUBS | Nostalgia reigns at this true neighborhood fixture, which has had the same owner for more than 30 years. As Santa Monica's oldest restaurant and bar, the Galley has a consistent nautical theme inside and out: the boatlike exterior features wavy blue neon lights and porthole windows; inside, fishing nets and anchors adorn the walls, and the whole place is aglow with colorful string lights. Most patrons tend to crowd the center bar, with the more dinner-oriented folks frequenting the booths. Prices are a good deal during "most hours" and a

steal during "happy hours." And strangely enough, the secret-recipe salad dressing is justifiably famous. ✉ *2442 Main St., Santa Monica* ☎ *310/452–1934.*

Performing Arts

Aero Theatre

FILM | This Santa Monica–based American Cinematheque theater first opened in 1940 and shows movies on a big screen. ✉ *1328 Montana Ave., Santa Monica* ☎ *323/466–3456* ⊕ *www.aerotheatre.com.*

Nuart

FILM | Foreign, indie, documentaries, classics, recent releases, Oscar short-film screenings—there's not much the Nuart doesn't show. Midnight showings, like the long-running *Rocky Horror Picture Show* with a live "shadow cast" on Saturday night, continue to bring in locals. Q&A sessions with directors and actors also happen here frequently. ✉ *11272 Santa Monica Blvd., West L.A.* ☎ *310/473–8530* ⊕ *www.landmarktheatres.com/los-angeles/nuart-theatre.*

Santa Monica Playhouse

THEATER | FAMILY | Housing three theaters, this venue brings a number of original plays, touring companies, poetry readings, spoken word events, and revival shows to the stage. The Family Theatre Musical Matinee Series features family-friendly reworked classic plays. A number of educational programs and workshops are available for all ages. ✉ *1211 4th St., Santa Monica* ☎ *310/394–9779* ⊕ *www.santamonicaplayhouse.com.*

🛍 Shopping

The breezy beachside communities of Santa Monica and Venice are ideal for leisurely shopping. Scores of tourists (and many locals) gravitate to the Third Street Promenade, a popular pedestrian-only shopping area that's within walking range of the beach and historic Santa Monica

Pier. But there's more to the area than trendy chain stores; there's also a treasure trove of vintage goods and antiques to be found on Main Street and Ocean Park Boulevard, and Montana Avenue is home to retailers specializing in indie and artisanal wares.

In Venice, Abbot Kinney Boulevard is abuzz with spots to shop for chic clothing, accessories, and housewares—including plenty of upscale outposts. The strip also has some of the city's best eateries, so it's easy to kill two birds with one stone. Nearby Lincoln and Rose avenues have also gained retail momentum in recent years, with many emerging brands choosing the area to open their first-ever storefronts. For those looking for the next big thing, this just might be the place to find it.

The Acorn Store
TOYS | FAMILY | Remember when toys didn't require computer programming? This old-fashioned shop (for ages 10 and under) sparks children's imaginations with dress-up clothes, picture books, and hand-painted wooden toys by brands like Poan and Haba. ⊠ *1220 5th St., near Wilshire Blvd., Santa Monica* ☎ *310/451–5845* ⊕ *www.theacornstore.com.*

The Levi's Store
CLOTHING | The beachside brick-and-mortar for America's classic denim brand is always a popular stop for those strolling down the Third Street Promenade. Besides stocking loads of the signature 501s and 511s, the store offers a slew of slim, slouchy, and stretchy styles of jeans, plus casual essentials like tees, sweats, and jackets for men, women, and little ones. ⊠ *1409 Third St. Promenade, Santa Monica* ☎ *310/393–4899* ⊕ *www.levi.com.*

Limonaia
GIFTS/SOUVENIRS | This charming and cozy neighborhood boutique has something for every kind of gift recipient. Ben's Garden goods (pillows, coasters, trays, etc.)

Parking Tip   👁

Parking in Santa Monica is next to impossible on Wednesday, when some streets are blocked off for the Farmers Market, but there are several parking structures with free one-to-two-hour parking.

decorated with inspirational words, lovely cards for all occasions, beaded jewelry, cookbooks, and an extensive puzzle selection are just a few things shoppers can find here. ⊠ *1325 Montana Ave., Santa Monica* ☎ *310/458–1858* ⊕ *www.shoplimonaia.com.*

Quinnie and B
TOYS | FAMILY | This self-described "tiny toy shop" fails to mention that it is also a beautifully curated jewel box of a tiny toy shop. Along with traditional toys like L.O.L. Surprise, this sunny, well-organized space offers a wide range of kids' books, plushies, accessories, musical instruments, science and craft kits, puzzles, art, holiday cookie kits and seasonal decorations, and more. ⊠ *1632 Ocean Park Blvd., Santa Monica* ☎ *310/398–8814.*

Third Street Promenade
SHOPPING CENTERS/MALLS | There is no shortage of spots to shop everything from sporting goods to trendy fashions on this pedestrian-friendly strip. Outposts here are mainly of the chain variety, and in between splurging on books, clothing, sneakers, and more, shoppers can pop into one of the many eateries to stay satiated or even catch a movie at one of the theaters. Additionally, the chef-approved Farmers Market takes over twice a week, and with the beach just a few steps away, the destination is a quintessential California stop. ⊠ *3rd St., between Broadway and Wilshire Blvd., Santa Monica.*

⚡ Activities

Legends Beach Bike Tours

TOUR—SIGHT | Those who like a little history with their vacations should take a guided tour with Legends, part of Perry's Café and Rentals. A tour takes you through the unique enclaves of Santa Monica and Venice Beach, and you can learn their role in the history of surf and skate in Southern California. Bike tours are offered daily at 11 am, last two hours (plus one hour of free riding), and cost $69 per adult, $35 for kids under 12, and $60 for students with ID and seniors. ⊠ 930 Palisades Beach Rd., Santa Monica ☎ 310/939–0000 ⊕ www.perryscafe.com.

Trapeze School New York

PROMENADE | Get a different view of the energetic scene by taking a trapeze class right on the Santa Monica Pier. Launch off from a platform 23 feet high and sail above the crowds and waves. Beginners are welcome. Classes are held daily, but times vary, so check the website and make reservations in advance. ⊠ 370 Santa Monica Pier, Santa Monica ☎ 310/394–5800 ⊕ www.losangeles.trapezeschool.com.

Venice

From the resident musicians and roving hippies of the boardwalk to the boho boutiques and farm-to-table cafés of Abbot Kinney Boulevard, Venice is not easily defined—which is what makes this creative-minded neighborhood so fun to explore.

Considering all of the dreamers who flock here today, it makes sense that Venice was a turn-of-the-20th-century fantasy that never quite came to be. Abbot Kinney, a wealthy Los Angeles businessman, envisioned this little piece of real estate as a romantic replica of Venice, Italy. He developed an incredible 16 miles of canals, floated gondolas on them, and built scaled-down versions of the Doge's Palace and other Venetian landmarks.

Ever since Kinney first planned his project, it was plagued by ongoing engineering problems and drifted into disrepair. Today only a few small canals and bridges remain. Some canals were rebuilt in 1996, but they don't reflect the old-world connection quite as well as they could (although they are still fun to wander around). On nearby **Abbot Kinney Boulevard** there's a wealth of fashion, design, and home decor shops and chic cafés—plus great people-watching.

◉ Sights

Binoculars Building

BUILDING | Frank Gehry is known around the world for his architectural master-pieces. In L.A. alone he's responsible for multiple houses and buildings like the Gehry Residence, Loyola Law School, and Walt Disney Hall. But one of his most interesting creations is the Binoculars Building, a quirky Venice spot that is exactly as advertised—a giant set of binoculars. The project was originally designed for the Chiat/Day advertising agency and today is home to one of Google's Silicon Beach offices. While you can't tour the building, you can take a clever Instagram shot out front. ⊠ 340 Main St., Venice.

Marina del Rey

MARINA | Just south of Venice, this con-do-laden, chain restaurant–lined development is a good place to grab brunch (but watch for price gougers), walk, or ride bikes along the waterfront. A number of places, such as **Hornblower Cruises and Events** in Fisherman's Village, rent boats for romantic dinner or party cruises around the marina. There are a few man-made beaches, but you're better off hit-ting the larger (and cleaner) beaches up the coast. ⊠ Fisherman's Village, 13755

The boardwalk of Venice Beach offers some of Los Angeles's best people-watching.

Fiji Way, Los Angeles ☎ *888/467–6256* ⊕ *www.hornblower.com/port/category/ mdr+diningcruises.*

Muscle Beach

LOCAL INTEREST | Bronzed young men bench-pressing five girls at once, weightlifters doing tricks on the sand—the Muscle Beach facility fired up the country's imagination from the get-go. There are actually two spots known as Muscle Beach. The original Muscle Beach, just south of the Santa Monica Pier, is where bodybuilders Jack LaLanne and Vic and Armand Tanny used to work out in the 1950s. When it was closed in 1959, the bodybuilders moved south along the beach to Venice, to a city-run facility known as "the Pen," and the Venice Beach spot inherited the Muscle Beach moniker. The spot is probably best known now as a place where a young Arnold Schwarzenegger first came to flex his muscles in the late '60s and began his rise to fame. The area now hosts a variety of sports and gymnastics events and the occasional "beach babe" beauty contests that always draw a crowd. But stop by any time during daylight for an eye-popping array of beefcakes (and would-be beefcakes). ⊠ *1800 Ocean Front Walk, Venice* ⊕ *www.musclebeach. net.*

★ Venice Beach Boardwalk

PROMENADE | The surf and sand of Venice are fine, but the main attraction here is the boardwalk scene, which is a cosmos all its own. Go on weekend afternoons for the best people-watching experience. You can also swim, fish, surf, and skateboard, or play racquetball, handball, shuffleboard, and basketball (the boardwalk is the site of hotly contested pickup games). Or you can rent a bike or in-line skates and hit the Strand bike path, then pull up a seat at a sidewalk café and watch the action unfold. ⊠ *1800 Ocean Front Walk, west of Pacific Ave., Venice* ☎ *310/392–4687* ⊕ *www.venicebeach. com.*

The Venice Skatepark brings skateboarders, roller skaters, and drum circles.

🍴 Restaurants

A bit rough around the edges, this urban beach town is home to many of L.A.'s artists, skaters, and surfers. The dining scene continues to grow but remains true to its cool and casual roots.

The Cow's End Cafe

$ | CAFÉ | Stop at this two-story locals' favorite for coffee and pastries, or choose from a long list of sandwiches for something more substantial. Sit out front and watch the crowds drifting in off the beach, or get cozy upstairs in one of the comfortable reading chairs. **Known for:** coffee; pastries; sandwiches. [$] *Average main: $5* ⊠ *34 Washington Blvd., Venice* ☎ *310/574–1080* ⊕ *www.thecowsendca-fe.com.*

★ Gjelina

$$ | AMERICAN | This spot comes alive the moment you walk through the rustic wooden door and into a softly lit dining room with long communal tables. The menu is seasonal, with outstanding small plates, charcuterie, pastas, and pizza. **Known for:** lively crowd on the patio; late-night menu; Michelin-approved dishes like crispy duck leg confit. [$] *Average main: $22* ⊠ *1429 Abbot Kinney Blvd., Venice* ☎ *310/450–1429* ⊕ *www.gjelina. com.*

Rose Cafe

$$$ | MODERN AMERICAN | FAMILY | This indoor-outdoor restaurant has served Venice for decades but constantly reinvents itself, serving mouthwatering California cuisines with multiple patios, a full bar, and a bakery. Creative types loiter under the macramé chandeliers for the Wi-Fi and sip espressos, while young families gather out back to snack on smoked radiatore carbonara and crispy brussels sprouts. **Known for:** sophisticated but unpretentious vibe; location in the heart of Venice; lively patio seating. [$] *Average main: $25* ⊠ *220 Rose Ave., Venice* ☎ *310/399–0711* ⊕ *www.rosecafevenice.com.*

Venice Whaler

$$ | AMERICAN | This beachfront bar that's been the local watering hole for musicians like the Doors and the Beach Boys since 1944 boasts an amazing view and serves tasty California pub food like fish tacos, pulled-pork sliders, and avocado toast with a basic selection of beers. The Whaler Double Burger is an institution in itself. **Known for:** rock-n-roll history; great pub food; fun brunch. $ *Average main: $15* ⊠ *10 W. Washington Blvd., Venice* ☎ *310/821–8737* ⊕ *www.venicewhaler. com.*

 ## Hotels

Hotel Erwin

$$$ | HOTEL | A boutique hotel a block off the Venice Beach Boardwalk, the Erwin will make you feel like a hipper version of yourself. **Pros:** dining emphasizing fresh ingredients; playful design in guest rooms; free Wi-Fi and use of hotel bikes. **Cons:** some rooms face a noisy alley; no pool; breakfast not included. $ *Rooms from: $369* ⊠ *1697 Pacific Ave., Venice* ☎ *310/452–1111, 800/786–7789* ⊕ *www. hotelerwin.com* ⇥ *119 rooms* ⏹ *No meals.*

★ The Kinney

$$ | HOTEL | Walking distance to Venice Beach and Abbot Kinney's artsy commercial strip, this playful hotel announces itself boldly with wall murals by Melissa Scrivner before you even enter the lobby. **Pros:** affordable, artistic rooms; Ping-Pong area; Jacuzzi bar. **Cons:** valet parking is a must ($15); hotel can get loud; some hipper-than-thou vibes. $ *Rooms from: $239* ⊠ *737 Washington Blvd., Venice* ☎ *310/821–4455* ⊕ *www.thekinneyvenicebeach.com* ⇥ *68 rooms* ⏹ *No meals.*

Marina del Rey Marriott

$$$ | HOTEL | FAMILY | Just across from the protected waters of the marina and a short jaunt to Venice, this hotel has across-the-board appeal for families, business travelers, couples, and more. **Pros:** outdoor lounge for nighttime socializing; quiet beach across the street; 15 minutes to LAX. **Cons:** traffic and noise from busy Admiralty Way; predominantly corporate aesthetic; expensive for what it is. $ *Rooms from: $329* ⊠ *4100 Admiralty Way, Marina del Rey* ☎ *310/301–3000, 800/228–9290* ⊕ *www.marriott.com/ hotels/travel/laxmb-marina-del-rey-marriott/* ⇥ *370 rooms* ⏹ *No meals.*

★ The Ritz-Carlton Marina del Rey

$$$$ | HOTEL | FAMILY | You might have a sense of déjà vu here—this resort, overlooking L.A.'s largest marina's boats, is a favorite location of dozens of TV and film productions. Traditionally styled rooms are decked out in warm, gold tones with French doors, marble baths, and feather beds. **Pros:** sparkling gym and large, kid-friendly, chlorine-free pool; chic restaurant Cast and Plow on-site; feather beds and marble baths in rooms. **Cons:** formal dining only when seasonal poolside bar and grill isn't open; $42 valet parking; quite pricey. $ *Rooms from: $549* ⊠ *4375 Admiralty Way, Marina del Rey* ☎ *310/823–1700, 800/241–3333* ⊕ *www.ritzcarlton.com* ⇥ *304 rooms* ⏹ *No meals.*

 ## Nightlife

The Brig

BARS/PUBS | This charming bar has its pluses (interesting drinks, talented DJs) and minuses (ugh, parking) but is worth a look if you're in the area. There's always a food truck around, and the bar's fine with you bringing in outside food. ⊠ *1515 Abbot Kinney Blvd., Venice* ☎ *310/399– 7537* ⊕ *www.thebrig.com.*

Continued on page 77

ALONG THE STRAND

L.A.'S COASTAL BIKE PATH

Cycling along the Strand

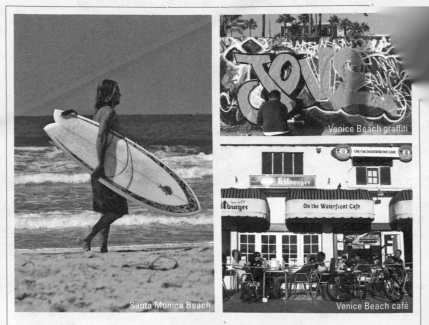

Venice Beach graffiti

On the Waterfront Cafe

Santa Monica Beach

Venice Beach café

When L.A. wants to get out and play by the water, people hit the Strand for the afternoon. This paved 22-mile path hugs the coastline and loops through tourist-packed stretches and sleepy beach towns. Quirky cafés, loads of souvenir stands, a family-packed amusement park on a pier, and spots for gazing at the Pacific are just a few things to see along the way.

The path extends from Santa Monica's Will Rogers State Beach to Torrance County Beach in South Redondo. It's primarily flat—aside from a few hills you encounter as you head toward Playa del Rey—and it's a terrific way for people of all fitness levels to experience L.A.'s beaches not far from Hollywood or Beverly Hills. You can explore at your own pace.

The hardest part of the journey isn't tackling the path itself—it's trying to get through it all without being distracted by the surrounding activity. With colorful graffitied murals, surfers and sailboats, weightlifters and tattoo parlors, local characters in carnivalesque costumes, volleyball games and skateboarders, there are almost too many things to busy youself with.

Rogers State Beach 🅿 🛉

Pacific Coast Hwy.

Montana Ave.

SANTA MONICA

2

Wilshire Ave.

Santa Monica Blvd.

Santa Monica State Beach 🍴 🅿 🅿 🛉 ❶

Santa Monica Pier →

Santa Monica Amusement Park

Santa Monica Fwy. 10

Pico Blvd.

THE STRAND

Ocean Park Blvd.

1

Rose Ave.

Lincoln Blvd.

405

0 ——— 1 mi
0 ——— 1 km

KEY

🍴	Restaurants
🅿	Paid Parking
🅿	Street Parking
🛉	Food and Drink

Venice State Beach 🍴 🅿 🅿 🛉

Muscle Beach •

VENICE BEACH

❷

Venice Ave.

Venice Blvd.

Washington Blvd.

Pacific Ocean

Venice Fishing Pier •

MARINA DEL REY

Culver Blvd.

Marina del Rey Beach 🍴 🅿 ❸

90

Jefferson Blvd.

PLAYA DEL REY

Pershing Dr.

Manchester

Dockweiler State Beach 🅿 🅿 🛉

Vista del Mar

Los Angeles International Airport

1

Imperial Hwy.

El Porto Beach

THE STRAND

EL SEGUNDO

Sepulveda Blvd.

Highland Ave.

Rosecrans Ave.

Manhattan Beach 🍴 🅿 🅿 🛉 ❹

Manhattan Beach Pier •

MANHATTAN BEACH

Manhattan Beach Blvd.

Hermosa Ave.

HERMOSA BEACH

Hermosa City Beach 🍴 🅿 🅿 🛉

Hermosa Beach Pier •

Artesia Blvd.

91

PCH

REDONDO BEACH

Redondo Beach Pier •

Redondo Beach 🍴 🅿 🅿 🛉 ❺

1

GETTING HERE AND AROUND

ITINERARY BASICS

❶ **Santa Monica** is an ideal place to start your trip; if you're biking, rent here. On the way back, stop for dinner at one of the many restaurants along and near the Third Street Promenade.

Take a break when you get to Venice Beach to soak up the scene on the ❷ **Venice Ocean Boardwalk**. Grab some fresh-squeezed lemonade from a stand or snag a table at a café.

If you're dedicating only a half-day to explore the Strand, ❸ **Marina del Rey** is a good spot to turn around; with more time and energy, follow signs for the slight detour here and continue to the second half, known as the South Bay Bike Trail.

❹ **Manhattan Beach** Manhattan Beach wins for being one of the best for kids, with its wide stretch of sand and good swimming.

The pier at ❺ **Redondo Beach**, lined with restaurants and shops, makes stopping here well worthwhile.

PARKING, RENTALS & TOURS

If you're driving to any of the ocean beaches, expect to pay $5 to $12 for parking, depending on the time of year, day of week, and location.

Those who like a little history with their vacation should take a guided tour from **Legends Bike Tours** (part of Perry's Rental's) with a Santa Monica Beach Sherpa who will tour you through the unique enclaves of Santa Monica, Venice Beach, and their role in the history of surf and skate in Southern California. ✉ 930 Palisades Beach Rd., Santa Monica ☎ 310/746–5556.

🛍 Shopping

Coutula

CLOTHING | Owner Carrie Hauman of Coutula (a portmanteau of "Couture LA") travels around the globe to hand-select the clothing, accessories, jewelry, and home furnishings sold in her light-filled, airy Abbot Kinney 1930s cottage. Nab anything from a $10 bracelet to a $6,000 necklace here, along with floaty sundresses that look much more expensive than they are, handmade Cut n Paste leather handbags, and bliss-inducing Tyler candles. ✉ *1204 Abbot Kinney Blvd., Venice* ☎ *310/581–8010* ⊕ *www.coutula.com.*

General Store

GIFTS/SOUVENIRS | Right at home in the beachy, bohemian neighborhood, this well-curated shop is a decidedly contemporary take on the concept of general stores. The very definition of "California cool," General Store offers beauty and bath products loaded with organic natural ingredients, handmade ceramics, linen tea towels, and a spot-on selection of art books. Featuring an impressive number of local makers and designers, the boutique also sells modern, minimal clothing and has a kids' section that will wow even the hippest moms and dads. ✉ *1801 Lincoln Blvd., Venice* ☎ *310/751–6393* ⊕ *www.shop-generalstore.com.*

Heist

CLOTHING | Owner Nilou Ghodsi has admitted that she stocks her Westside shop like an extension of her own closet, which in her case means keeping the focus on floaty, modern-yet-classic pieces as opposed to trendy ones. The airy boutique offers elegantly edgy separates from American designers like Nili Lotan and Ulla Johnson, as well as from hard-to-find French and Italian designers like Pas de Calais. ✉ *1100 Abbot Kinney Blvd., Venice* ☎ *310/450–6531* ⊕ *www.shopheist.com.*

LCD

CLOTHING | Anyone who's looking to get a leg up on the hottest new designers will want to make this Lincoln Boulevard boutique a stop on their Venice shopping spree. The clean, modern space features cool, contemporary clothing by the likes of Ryan Roche, Sandy Liang, and Assembly New York, plus beauty loot from Verso, bags and eyewear from beloved local labels, and so much more for fashion followers to fawn over. The owner has a background in the music industry, and it shows. ✉ *1121 Abbot Kinney Blvd., Suite 2, Venice* ☎ *424/280–4132* ⊕ *www.shoplcd.co.*

Strange Invisible Perfumes

PERFUME/COSMETICS | Finding your signature fragrance at this sleek Abbot Kinney boutique won't come cheap, but perfumer Alexandra Balahoutis takes creating her scents as seriously as a seasoned winemaker—and they're just as nuanced as a well-balanced glass of vino. Essences for the perfumes are organic, wild crafted, biodynamic, and bottled locally. Highlights from SI's core collection include the cacao-spiked Dimanche and leathery Black Rosette. ✉ *1138 Abbot Kinney Blvd., Venice* ☎ *310/314–1505* ⊕ *www.siperfumes.com.*

🏃 Activities

Venice Skatepark

CITY PARK | Watch skateboarders displaying a wide range of ability levels as they careen around this concrete park, situated between the beach and the boardwalk in Venice. There's also an impressive crew of disco roller skaters, and drum circles that gravitate toward the middle of the boardwalk. ✉ *1800 Ocean Front Walk, off E. Market St., Venice* ⊕ *www.veniceskatepark.com.*

The Getty Center has stunning architecture, world-class art collections, and gorgeous views of the city.

Brentwood

This wealthy residential enclave north of Santa Monica is home to the world-class Getty Center.

◉ Sights

★ The Getty Center

MUSEUM | FAMILY | With its curving walls and isolated hilltop perch, the Getty Center resembles a pristine fortified city of its own. You may have been lured there by the beautiful views of Los Angeles—on a clear day stretching all the way to the Pacific Ocean—but the amazing architecture, uncommon gardens, and fascinating art collections will be more than enough to capture and hold your attention. When the sun is out, the complex's rough-cut travertine marble skin seems to soak up the light.

Getting to the center involves a bit of anticipatory lead-up. At the base of the hill lies the underground parking structure. From there you either walk or take a smooth, computer-driven tram up the steep slope, checking out the Bel Air estates across the humming 405 freeway. The six pavilions that house the museum surround a central courtyard and are bridged by walkways. From the courtyard, plazas, and walkways, you can survey the city from the San Gabriel Mountains to the ocean.

In a ravine separating the museum and the Getty Research Institute, conceptual artist Robert Irwin created the playful Central Garden in stark contrast to Richard Meier's mathematical architectural geometry. The garden's design is what Hollywood feuds are made of: Meier couldn't control Irwin's vision, and the two men sniped at each other during construction, with Irwin stirring the pot with every loose twist his garden path took. The result is a refreshing garden walk whose focal point is an azalea maze (some insist the Mickey Mouse shape is on purpose) in a reflecting pool.

Inside the pavilions are the galleries for the permanent collections of European paintings, drawings, sculpture, illuminated manuscripts, and decorative arts, as well as world-class temporary exhibitions and photographs gathered internationally. The Getty's collection of French furniture and decorative arts, especially from the early years of Louis XIV (1643–1715) to the end of the reign of Louis XVI (1774–92), is renowned for its quality and condition; you can even see a pair of completely reconstructed salons. In the paintings galleries, a computerized system of louvered skylights allows natural light to filter in, creating a closer approximation of the conditions in which the artists painted. Notable among the paintings are Rembrandt's *The Abduction of Europa,* Van Gogh's *Irises,* Monet's *Wheatstacks, Snow Effects,* and *Morning,* and James Ensor's *Christ's Entry into Brussels.*

If you want to start with a quick overview, pick up the brochure in the entrance hall that guides you to collection highlights. There's also an instructive audio tour (free, but you have to leave your ID) with commentaries by art historians and other experts. The Getty also presents lectures, films, concerts, art workshops, and special programs for kids, families, and all-around culture lovers. The complex includes an upscale restaurant and downstairs cafeteria with panoramic window views. There are also outdoor coffee carts. ■TIP➜ **On-site parking is subject to availability and can fill up by midday on holidays and in the summer, so try to come early in the day or after lunch.** A tram takes you from the street-level entrance to the top of the hill. Public buses (Metro Rapid Line 734) also serve the center and link to the Expo Rail extension. ⊠ *1200 Getty Center Dr., Brentwood* 🕾 *310/440–7300* ⊕ *www.getty.edu* 🚊 *Free; parking $15* ⊙ *Closed Mon.*

Pierce Brothers Westw... Memorial Park and Mortu...

CEMETERY | The who's who departed can all be found at ful, though unremarkable, cer. Notable residents include Marily roe and Joe DiMaggio; authors Tru Capote, Ray Bradbury, and Jackie C actors Natalie Wood, Rodney Dangerf, Farrah Fawcett, Jack Lemmon, and Dea. Martin; and directors Billy Wilder and John Cassavetes. ⊠ *1218 Glendon Ave., Westwood* 🕾 *310/474–1579* ⊕ *www. dignitymemorial.com.*

Skirball Cultural Center

MUSEUM | The mission of this Jewish cultural institution in the beautiful Santa Monica Mountains is to explore the connections "between 4,000 years of Jewish heritage and the vitality of American democratic ideals." The extraordinary museum, featuring exhibits like *Visions and Values: Jewish Life from Antiquity to America,* has a massive collection of Judaica—the third largest in the world. A big draw is the Noah's Ark interactive exhibition, where children are invited to re-create the famous tale using their own imagination. ⊠ *2701 N. Sepulveda Blvd., north of Brentwood, Los Angeles* 🕾 *310/440–4500* ⊕ *www.skirball.org* 🚊 *$12; free Thurs.* ⊙ *Closed Mon.*

🍴 Restaurants

★ Baltaire Restaurant

$$$$ | STEAKHOUSE | The chicest and buzziest nighttime spot in the neighborhood, Baltaire attracts both well-heeled Brentwood denizens on dressed-up dates and single sippers looking for late-night rendezvous. The meat-heavy menu features giant slabs of porterhouse steaks as well as special A5 Wagyu straight from Japan. **Known for:** sizzling steaks; buzzing bar scene; classic cocktails. ⑤ *Average main: $50* ⊠ *11647 San Vicente Blvd., Los Angeles* 🕾 *424/273–1660* ⊕ *www. baltaire.com.*

urveyor of the finest ... e in all of Los Angeles, ... t is the perfect answer ... d question of what to gift ... cial occasion. The ornate ... ase is filled with dark chocolate ... s, hazelnut pralines, Grand Marnier ... ches, and so much more. **Known** ...: Belgian chocolate; Italian espresso; ... tasty sandwiches. ⑤ *Average main: $5* ✉ *12008 Wilshire Blvd., Los Angeles* ☎ *310/442-2245* ⊕ *www.chocolatt.com.*

Pizzana

$$ | PIZZA | Certainly on any short list for the best pizza in Los Angeles, chef Daniele Uditi utlizes his family's over 65-year-old sourdough starter to make the sizzling pies here with crackling crusts and inventive toppings. In addition to the perfect pizzas, the shop offers weekly sandwich specials and a bevy of healthier salad-loving sides. **Known for:** excellent Neapolitan pizza; sandwich specials; laid-back atmosphere. ⑤ *Average main: $18* ✉ *11712 San Vicente Blvd., Los Angeles* ☎ *310/481-7108* ⊕ *www.pizzana.com.*

Toscana

$$$$ | ITALIAN | This rustic trattoria along San Vicente is a favorite celebrity haunt. Expect elevated sensory offerings, from its cozy atmosphere to its mouthwatering Tuscan fare and excellent wine list. **Known for:** excellent wine list; seasonal menu items like truffle sliders; great celeb-spotting. ⑤ *Average main: $35* ✉ *11633 San Vicente Blvd., Brentwood* ☎ *310/820-2448* ⊕ *www.toscanabrentwood.com.*

Hotels

★ Hotel Bel-Air

$$$$ | HOTEL | This Spanish Mission–style icon has been a discreet hillside retreat for celebrities and society types since 1946 and was given a face-lift by star designers Alexandra Champalimaud and David Rockwell. **Pros:** shuttle available within 3 mile radius of hotel; perfect for the privacy minded; alfresco dining at Wolfgang Puck restaurant. **Cons:** not walking distance to restaurants or shops; hefty price tag; controversial ownership by the Sultan of Brunei. ⑤ *Rooms from: $645* ✉ *701 Stone Canyon Rd., Bel Air* ☎ *310/472-1211* ⊕ *www.dorchestercollection.com/en/los-angeles/hotel-bel-air* ➥ *103 rooms* ⦿ *No meals.*

🛍 Shopping

Brentwood Country Mart

SHOPPING CENTERS/MALLS | FAMILY | Among the dozens of stores within this family-friendly faux country market are Goop (Gwyneth Paltrow's lifestyle brand's gorgeous first brick-and-mortar store), Turpan (for luxury home goods), James Perse (for laid-back cotton knits), Jenni Kayne (for a curated mix of modern clothing, housewares, and gifts), and Malia Mills (for American-made swimwear separates). Grab a chicken basket at Reddi Chick and chow down on the open-air patio. ✉ *225 26th St., at San Vicente Blvd., Brentwood* ☎ *310/458-6682* ⊕ *www.brentwoodcountrymart.com.*

Sawtelle Japantown

The four blocks on Sawtelle Boulevard between Olympic Boulevard and Missouri Avenue are filled with predominantly Japanese specialty stores, restaurants, and plant nurseries. A trip here makes for an interesting, out-of-the-ordinary jaunt from Santa Monica.

In the 1920s, after a wave of Japanese immigrants arrived in L.A., Sawtelle began to resemble an authentic Japanese main street rather than a touristy Little Tokyo. Although most establishments remain Japanese, the area also encompasses Chinese, Taiwanese, and Malaysian businesses.

🍴 Restaurants

Hide Sushi

$ | JAPANESE | Some of the best sushi spots in Los Angeles are the most hidden and most discreet and come with zero fanfare, and Hide (pronounced hee-day) is one of those restaurants. Walking through a curtained entryway, diners will find a smattering of tables and a sushi counter (which is where you should sit) where master sushi chefs slice raw cuts of the freshest fish in town. **Known for:** counter sushi; quiet atmosphere; cash-only policy. ⑤ *Average main: $13* ✉ *2040 Sawtelle Blvd., West L.A.* ☎ *310/477–7242* ⊕ *www.hidesushi.com* ☉ *Closed Mon.* ⊟ *No credit cards.*

★ Tsujita L.A. Artisan Noodles

$ | JAPANESE | Ramen lovers have no shortage of choices across Los Angeles, but if you want the best, head over to this Sawtelle Japantown hot spot. Lines typically bend around the corner as hungry Angelenos drive from far and wide to have Tsujita's signature *tsukemen* (a type of ramen where the noodles are served to the side of the broth and you dip each bite individually). **Known for:** signature tsukemen ramen; lots of ramen options, including vegan ramen; long lines. ⑤ *Average main: $12* ✉ *2057 Sawtelle Blvd., West L.A.* ☎ *310/231–7373* ⊕ *www.tsujita-la.com.*

🛍 Shopping

Nijiya Market

FOOD/CANDY | If you're looking for an authentic Japanese supermarket, you'll find everything you could ever want at Nijiya. Inside, you'll discover fresh fish for make-it-at-home sushi, baked Japanese delicacies, daily-made take-away bento boxes, and every Japanese candy treat imaginable. On weekends, there is a giant skillet set up outside the entrance where employees fry up sizzling and savory *okonomiyaki* (Japanese pancake). ✉ *2130 Sawtelle Blvd., #105, West L.A.* ☎ *310/575–3300* ⊕ *www.nijiya.com.*

Chapter 4

BEVERLY HILLS

WITH CULVER CITY

Updated by
Paul Feinstein

◉ Sights	🍴 Restaurants	🛏 Hotels	💼 Shopping	🍸 Nightlife
★★☆☆☆	★★★★☆	★★★★☆	★★★★★	★★☆☆☆

NEIGHBORHOOD SNAPSHOT

TOP EXPERIENCES

■ **Shop on Rodeo Drive:** Even if it's window-shopping, it's a one-of-a-kind experience to watch the parade of diamonds, couture gowns, and Ferraris being fetishized.

■ **Stroll the Beverly Gardens Park:** Pose for photos in front of the world famous 40-foot Beverly Hills sign or meander along the nearly 2-mile-long park to awe at the stunning foliage, calming water features, and one-of-a-kind sculptures.

■ **Watch a concert:** Every summer, the Beverly Canon Gardens near the Maybourne Beverly Hills Hotel features a free concert series.

■ **See the stars:** Celeb spotting is practically an art form in this city, and the streets of Beverly Hills hide them in plain sight. Head to the area's many five-star hotel bars and swanky eateries to catch glimpses of your A-list favorites.

QUICK BITES

Nate 'n' Al's: A longtime refuge from California's lean cuisine, Nate 'n' Al serves up steaming pastrami, matzo ball soup, and potato latkes. ⊠ *414 N. Beverly Dr.* ⊕ *www.natenals.com*

Pizzana: It would be hard to crown a winner of the best pizza in L.A., but any list would have to include the chef Daniele Uditi–helmed Pizzana made with a 65-year-old sourdough starter. ⊠ *11712 San Vicente Blvd.* ⊕ *www.pizzana.com*

Sprinkles Cupcakes: Home of the cupcake ATM machine, Sprinkles serves up an afternoon sugar rush with red velvet, salty caramel, and triple cinnamon cupcakes right in the heart of Beverly Hills. ⊠ *9635 S. Santa Monica Blvd.* ⊕ *www.sprinkles. com*

SUGARFISH: With set boxes labeled "Trust Me," SUGARFISH takes the decision-making out of lunchtime, with its quick sushi meals filled with perfect cuts of albacore, yellowtail, and more. ⊠ *212 N. Canon Dr.* ⊕ *www.sugarfishsushi.com*

GETTING HERE

■ All main west–east roads in the city will get you toward Beverly Hills; Wilshire Boulevard is the easiest. It starts in Santa Monica, heads into Brentwood and continues east right into the heart of Beverly Hills. But traffic can be a nightmare, as it can be for L.A.'s other main artery, Santa Monica Boulevard, which also hits Beverly Hills and runs just south of Brentwood. For a smoother ride, try Pico or Olympic Boulevard, which both run roughly parallel a bit farther south.

■ In Beverly Hills, you can park your car in one of several municipal lots (often free for the first hour or two), and spend as long as you like strolling along Rodeo Drive. For street parking, bring quarters for the meter, or pay with a credit card. Parking on residential streets is often by permit only.

PLANNING YOUR TIME

■ Let's be honest—in Beverly Hills, you're probably here to shop and do lunch, and this can easily take a whole day. Once you're all shopped out, you'll find a lively nightlife scene in the bars of the high-end hotels that are peppered throughout the neighborhood.

The rumors are true: Beverly Hills delivers on a dramatic, cinematic scale of wealth and excess. A known celebrity haunt, come here to daydream or to live like the rich and famous for a day. Window-shop or splurge at tony stores, and keep an eye out for filming locales; just walking around here will make you feel like you're on a movie set.

South of Beverly Hills, Culver City is a fast-growing neighborhood that's known for a mix of high-end and experimental restaurants, an up-and-coming shopping scene, and the Sony Pictures studio lot. An explosion of growth has coincided with the opening of the Metro Expo Line that runs from downtown through Culver and all the way to Santa Monica.

Beverly Hills

When visiting Beverly Hills for the first time, many people head for the boutiques and restaurants that line the palm tree–fringed sidewalks of **Rodeo Drive.** People tend to stroll, not rush. Shopping ranges from the accessible and familiar (Pottery Barn) to the unique, expensive, and architecturally stunning (Prada).

Sights

Fox Plaza
BUILDING | Towering over the 20th Century Fox studio lot in Century City is Fox Plaza, a 34-story skyscraper where former president Ronald Reagan once had an office. Savvy screen watchers will undoubtedly know it by its more famous name—Nakatomi Plaza. Starring in the blockbusting juggernaut *Die Hard*, the building is shot at, blown apart, and set on fire as Bruce Willis takes down a German terrorist cell. It can be fun to see if you're a fan of the movie, but be aware this is just an office building, so there's not a whole lot to do but look at it. ✉ *2121 Ave. of the Stars, Century City.*

Gagosian Gallery
ART GALLERIES—ARTS | This contemporary art gallery, owned and directed by the legendary Larry Gagosian, features cutting-edge artists in a minimalist-styled space. It's free to enter, exhibits rotate every six weeks, and the gallery has displayed everyone from Richard Avedon and Takashi Murakami to Frank Gehry and Jeff Koons. During Oscar season the gallery is known for its celeb-filled openings. ✉ *456 N. Camden Dr., Beverly Hills* ☎ *310/271–9400* ⊕ *www.gagosian.com.*

Greystone Mansion
HOUSE | Built in 1928, this stunning mansion resides in a discreet residential part of Beverly Hills, surrounded by 18 acres of manicured grounds that are open to the public. The historic house was built

Sights ▼

1 Culver Hotel **E9**
2 Culver Studios...., ... **E9**
3 Fox Plaza................. **B5**
4 Gagosian Gallery **D2**
5 Greystone Mansion **D1**
6 Museum of Jurassic
   Technology **E9**
7 Museum of Tolerance.. **D5**
8 Rodeo Drive **D2**
9 Sony Pictures Studios... **E9**
10 Spadena House..........**C2**
11 Virginia Robinson
   Gardens................ .. **B1**
12 Wallis Annenberg
   Center for the
   Performing Arts......... **D2**

Restaurants ▼

1 Crustacean...............**C2**
2 CUT...................... **D3**
3 Guccio Osteria da
   Massimo Rottura **D2**
4 Jean-Georges
   Beverly Hills............ **B3**
5 Lodge Bread
   Company................. **A9**
6 Margot.................... **F9**
7 Nate 'n' Al's.............. **D2**
8 n/naka.................... **B9**
9 Nozawa Bar............. **D2**
10 Polo Lounge **B1**
11 Spago Beverly Hills...... **E2**
12 Sprinkles Cupcakes **C2**
13 Vespertine **G9**

Hotels ▼

1 Beverly Hills Hotel...., **B1**
2 Beverly Wilshire,
   a Four Seasons
   Hotel...................... **D3**
3 The Crescent
   Beverly Hills **D2**
4 Four Seasons Hotel,
   Los Angeles at
   Beverly Hills **F2**
5 The Maybourne
   Beverly Hills............. **D2**
6 Mr. C Beverly Hills **D4**
7 Peninsula
   Beverly Hills..............**C3**
8 SLS Hotel
   Beverly Hills.............. **G2**
9 Viceroy L'Ermitage
   Beverly Hills.............. **E2**
10 Waldorf Astoria
   Beverly Hills **C3**

KEY

1 *Exploring Sights*
1 *Restaurants*
1 *Hotels*

Beverly Hills and Culver City

One of L.A.'s most photographed homes is the Spadena House aka the Witch's House.

by oil magnate Ned Doheny (inspiration for the Daniel Day-Lewis character in *There Will Be Blood*) and has been featured in a number of films like *The Big Lebowski*, *Spider-Man*, *The Social Network*, and *X-Men*. Park rangers offer tours for $20 where you can gawk at the 46,000-square-foot estate with a bowling alley, secret panels for liquor, and even a screening room. ⊠ *905 Loma Vista Dr., Beverly Hills* ☎ *310/286–0119* ⊕ *www.greystonemansion.org.*

Museum of Tolerance

MUSEUM | FAMILY | A museum that unflinchingly confronts bigotry and racism, one of its most affecting sections covers the Holocaust, with film footage of deportations and concentration camps. Upon entering, you are issued a "passport" bearing the name of a child whose life was dramatically changed by the Nazis; as you go through the exhibit, you learn the fate of that child. Another exhibit called *Anne: The Life and Legacy of Anne Frank* brings her story to life through immersive environments, multimedia presentations, and interesting artifacts, while Simon Wiesenthal's Vienna office is set exactly as the famous "Nazi hunter" had it while conducting his research that brought more than 1,000 war criminals to justice.

Interactive exhibits include the Millennium Machine, which engages visitors in finding solutions to human rights abuses around the world; Globalhate.com, which examines hate on the Internet by exposing problematic sites via touch-screen computer terminals; and the Point of View Diner, a re-creation of a 1950s diner that "serves" a menu of controversial topics on video jukeboxes. ■ TIP→ **Plan to spend at least three hours touring the museum; making a reservation is especially recommended for Friday, Sunday, and holiday visits.** ⊠ *9786 W. Pico Blvd., south of Beverly Hills, Los Angeles* ☎ *310/772–2505 for reservations* ⊕ *www.museumoftolerance.com* 🎟 *From $16* ⊙ *Closed Sat.*

★ Rodeo Drive

NEIGHBORHOOD | The ultimate shopping indulgence, Rodeo Drive is one of L.A.'s bona fide tourist attractions. The art of window-shopping (and reenacting your *Pretty Woman* fantasies) is prime among the retail elite: Tiffany & Co., Gucci, Jimmy Choo, Valentino, Harry Winston, Prada—you get the picture. Near the southern end of Rodeo Drive is Via Rodeo, a curvy cobblestone street designed to resemble a European shopping area and the perfect backdrop to pose for your Instagram feed. To give your feet a rest, free trolley tours depart from the southeast corner of Rodeo Drive and Dayton Way from 11:30 to 4:30. They're a terrific way to get an overview of the neighborhood. ✉ *Rodeo Dr., Beverly Hills* ⊕ *www.rodeodrive-bh.com.*

★ Spadena House

BUILDING | Otherwise known as the Witch's House in Beverly Hills, the Spadena House has an interesting history. First built on the Willat Studios lot in 1920, the house was physically moved to its current ritzy location in 1924. The house is not open for tourists, but the fairy-tale-like appearance is viewable from the street for onlookers to snap pics. Movie buffs will also recognize it from a background shot in the film *Clueless*. ✉ *516 Walden Dr., Beverly Hills.*

Virginia Robinson Gardens

GARDEN | As an heiress to the Robinson department store dynasty, Virginia Robinson lived on what is the oldest intact estate in Beverly Hills, dating back to 1911. The house and gardens cover 6½ acres of immaculately landscaped flora with a distinct Italian villa–vibe right out of Tuscany. The beaux arts–style house includes a tennis court, pool house, and five separate gardens including a rose garden, Italian terrace, palm tree forest, and more. ✉ *1008 Elden Way, Beverly Hills* 🕿 *310/550–2065* ⊕ *www.robinson-gardens.org* ☾ *Closed weekends.*

Wallis Annenberg Center for the Performing Arts

THEATER | Located in the heart of Beverly Hills, the Wallis Annenberg Center for the Performing Arts is a cultural hub for a wide variety of artistic performances. A breath of fresh air, the complex is centered on the 1934 Italianate-style Beverly Hills Post Office. The interior is gorgeous, with eight Depression-era murals painted by California artist Charles Kassler depicting laborers and artisans. The building includes the 500-seat Bram Goldsmith Theater and the 150-seat Lovelace Studio Theater. Affordable parking is available underneath the space. ✉ *9390 N. Santa Monica Blvd., Beverly Hills* 🕿 *310/746–4000* ⊕ *www.thewallis.org.*

🍽 Restaurants

Dining in the 90210 is always an elegant experience, especially when you're leaving your car with the valet at one of the hot new restaurants along Wilshire Boulevard. But meals here don't always break the bank; there are plenty of casual and affordable eateries here worth a visit.

Crustacean

$$$$ | VIETNAMESE | A Euro-Vietnamese fusion gem in the heart of Beverly Hills, Crustacean allows you to walk on water above exotic fish and see the kitchen preparing your perfect garlic noodles through a glass window. Standouts (besides the noodles) include Dungeness crab, A5 Wagyu beef, tuna cigars, and hearts-of-palm crab cakes. **Known for:** sake-simmered dishes; no-grease garlic noodles; unique cocktails like artichoke old-fashioneds. ⑤ *Average main: $36* ✉ *468 N. Bedford Dr., Beverly Hills* 🕿 *310/205–8990* ⊕ *crustaceanbh.com* ☾ *Closed Mon.*

CUT

$$$$ | STEAKHOUSE | In a true collision of artistic titans, celebrity chef Wolfgang Puck presents his take on steak houses in a space designed by Getty Center

architect Richard Meier. Playful dishes like bone-marrow flan take center stage, while dry-aged and seared hunks of Nebraskan sirloin prove the Austrian-born chef understands America's love affair with beef. **Known for:** decadent dark chocolate soufflé; fantastic crab and shrimp cocktail; perfect cuts of beef. $ *Average main: $40 ⊠ Beverly Wilshire (a Four Seasons Hotel), 9500 Wilshire Blvd., Beverly Hills ☎ 310/276–8500 ⊕ www. wolfgangpuck.com/dining/cut-beverly-hills ☾ Closed Sun. No lunch.*

★ Gucci Osteria da Massimo Bottura

$$$$ | ITALIAN | Legendary Italian chef Massimo Bottura opened this spot, his first L.A. eatery, to loads of fanfare and celebrity sightings. The restaurant mirrors the Florence, Italy, location of the same name with a menu filled with favorites like a mouthwatering tortellini in brodo. **Known for:** excellent pastas; great people-watching; avant-garde design. $ *Average main: $80 ⊠ 347 N. Rodeo Dr., Beverly Hills ☎ 424/600–7490 ⊕ www.gucci.com/us/en/st/capsule/ gucci-osteria-beverly-hills.*

Jean-Georges Beverly Hills

$$$$ | FRENCH FUSION | Fine dining is hard to come by in L.A. (even in Beverly Hills), so when it's actually done well, it's worth applauding. World-famous chef Jean-Georges Vongerichten's elaborate menu inside the Waldorf Astoria isn't just fine dining, it's a tasting wonderland filled with delights like toasted egg yolk and caviar, Icelandic cod, and Wagyu beef tenderloin from a wood-burning grill. **Known for:** fine-dining date nights; endless wine list; romantic ambience. $ *Average main: $50 ⊠ Waldorf Astoria Beverly Hills, 9850 Wilshire Blvd., Beverly Hills ☎ 310/860–6566 ⊕ www.jean-georges.com ☾ Closed Mon.–Thurs.*

Nate 'n' Al's

$$ | DELI | A longtime refuge from California's lean cuisine, Nate 'n' Al's serves up steaming pastrami, matzo ball soup, and potato latkes. Big time media and entertainment insiders are often seen kibbitzing at this old-time East Coast–style establishment. **Known for:** matzo ball soup; killer pastrami; long waits. $ *Average main: $15 ⊠ 414 N. Beverly Dr., Beverly Hills ☎ 310/274–0101 ⊕ www. natenals.com.*

Nozawa Bar

$$$$ | JAPANESE | Tucked into the back of Sugarfish (a popular sushi chain) in the middle of Beverly Hills, this secret *omakase* (chef's choice) sushi spot has only 10 seats, where master chef Osamu Fujita slices up the freshest cuts of raw fish from a 20-course tasting menu. If you ever wanted to get a one-on-one with a culinary wizard, this is your chance as you sit a foot away from the chef while he prepares your perfect portions. **Known for:** omakase sushi; bluefin tuna hand rolls; hard-to-get reservations needed. $ *Average main: $175 ⊠ 212 N. Canon Dr., Beverly Hills ☎ 424/216–6158 ⊕ www.nozawabar.com ☾ Closed Sun.*

Polo Lounge

$$$$ | AMERICAN | Nothing says Beverly Hills quite like the Polo Lounge inside the Beverly Hills Hotel. This classic, monied spot is home to Hollywood royalty and entertainment luminaries noshing on lobster Nicoise or the famed Wagyu burger during power lunches. **Known for:** celebrity sightings; mouthwatering Wagyu burgers; dress code of no ripped jeans or baseball caps. $ *Average main: $35 ⊠ The Beverly Hills Hotel, 9641 Sunset Blvd., Beverly Hills ☎ 310/887–2777 ⊕ www.dorchestercollection.com/ en/los-angeles/the-beverly-hills-hotel/ restaurants-bars/the-polo-lounge.*

★ Spago Beverly Hills

$$$$ | MODERN AMERICAN | Wolfgang Puck's flagship restaurant is a modern L.A. classic. Spago centers on a buzzing redbrick outdoor courtyard (with retractable roof) shaded by 100-year-old olive trees, and a daily-changing menu that offers dishes like smoked salmon pizza or off-menu schnitzel. **Known for:** great people-watching; off-menu schnitzel; sizzling smoked salmon pizza. $ *Average main: $35* ✉ *176 N. Canon Dr., Beverly Hills* ☎ *310/385–0880* ⊕ *www.wolfgangpuck.com* ⊗ *Closed Mon. and Tues.*

Sprinkles Cupcakes

$ | BAKERY | The haute cupcake craze isn't going away, so expect lines that extend out the door and down the block here. If you need an after-hours fix, not to worry: Sprinkles also has the world's first cupcake (and cookie) ATM, open round the clock. **Known for:** red velvet cupcakes; banana peanut butter cupcakes; long lines. $ *Average main: $5* ✉ *9635 S. Santa Monica Blvd., Beverly Hills* ☎ *310/274–8765* ⊕ *www.sprinkles.com.*

🛏 Hotels

Beverly Hills Hotel

$$$$ | HOTEL | FAMILY | Nicknamed the "Pink Palace," this luxury spot with giant marble bathrooms continues to attract Hollywood's elite after more than 100 years. **Pros:** iconic Polo Lounge; swanky spa and pool; ultraluxurious private bungalows. **Cons:** pricey fare at the Polo Lounge; expensive valet parking ($50); controversial ownership by the Sultan of Brunei. $ *Rooms from: $645* ✉ *9641 Sunset Blvd., Beverly Hills* ☎ *310/276–2251, 800/283–8885* ⊕ *www.beverlyhillshotel.com* ⬅ *210 rooms, 23 bungalows* ⦿ *No meals.*

Beverly Wilshire, a Four Seasons Hotel

$$$$ | HOTEL | Built in 1928, this Rodeo Drive–adjacent hotel is part Italian Renaissance (with elegant details like crystal chandeliers) and part contemporary. **Pros:** complimentary car service; Wolfgang Puck restaurant on-site; first-rate spa. **Cons:** small lobby; valet parking is expensive; might be too sceney for some. $ *Rooms from: $545* ✉ *9500 Wilshire Blvd., Beverly Hills* ☎ *310/275–5200, 800/427–4354* ⊕ *www.fourseasons.com/beverlywilshire* ⬅ *395 rooms* ⦿ *No meals.*

The Crescent Beverly Hills

$$ | HOTEL | Built in 1927 as a dorm for silent-film actors, the Crescent is now a fanciful boutique hotel with a great location—within the Beverly Hills shopping triangle—and with an even better price (for the area). **Pros:** indoor/outdoor fireplace; lively on-site restaurant, Crescent Bar and Terrace; economic room available for $148. **Cons:** $30 resort fee is not optional; no elevator; rooms on the small side. $ *Rooms from: $245* ✉ *403 N. Crescent Dr., Beverly Hills* ☎ *310/247–0505* ⊕ *www.crescentbh.com* ⬅ *35 rooms* ⦿ *Free breakfast.*

Four Seasons Hotel, Los Angeles at Beverly Hills

$$$$ | HOTEL | High hedges and patio gardens make this hotel a secluded retreat that even the hum of traffic can't permeate—one reason it's a favorite of Hollywood's elite, whom you might spot at the pool and espresso bar. **Pros:** tropical terrace with pool; high-end Italian eatery, Culina, on-site; great massages and nail salon. **Cons:** Hollywood scene in bar and restaurant means high prices; sometimes snooty atmosphere; breakfast not included. $ *Rooms from: $545* ✉ *300 S. Doheny Dr., Beverly Hills* ☎ *310/273–2222, 800/819–5053* ⊕ *www.fourseasons.com/losangeles* ⬅ *285 rooms* ⦿ *No meals.*

★ The Maybourne Beverly Hills

$$$$ | HOTEL | The nine-story, Mediterranean-style palazzo is dedicated to welcoming those who relish luxury, providing classic style and exemplary service. **Pros:** secret whiskey bar tucked upstairs; obliging, highly trained staff; lots of activities and amenities for kids. **Cons:** hefty tab for all this finery; not all rooms have balconies; pricey valet parking. $ *Rooms from: $550* ✉ *225 N. Canon Dr., Beverly Hills* ☎ *310/860–7800* ⊕ *www.maybournebeverlyhills.com* ⬅ *201 rooms* ⦿ *No meals.*

Mr. C Beverly Hills

$$ | **HOTEL** | An Italian getaway in the middle of Los Angeles, Mr. C Beverly Hills of the famed Cipriani family welcomes guests to their European home. **Pros:** free shuttle with a 3-mile radius including Beverly Hills and Century City; Italian restaurant serving classic Cipriani dishes; welcome Bellini at check-in. **Cons:** not directly in prime Beverly Hills; views of Beverly Hills are often 15% extra; breakfast not included. $ *Rooms from: $300 ☒ 1224 Beverwil Dr., Beverly Hills ☎ 310/277–2800 ⊕ www.mrchotels. com/mrcbeverlyhills ↩ 138 rooms ◉ No meals.*

★ Peninsula Beverly Hills

$$$$ | **HOTEL** | This French Riviera–style palace overflowing with antiques and art is a favorite of boldface names, but visitors consistently describe a stay here as near perfect. **Pros:** 24-hour check-in/check-out policy; sunny pool area with cabanas; complimentary Rolls-Royce takes you to nearby Beverly Hills. **Cons:** very expensive; room decor might feel too ornate for some; exclusive vibe can be intimidating. $ *Rooms from: $600 ☒ 9882 S. Santa Monica Blvd., Beverly Hills ☎ 310/551–2888, 800/462–7899 ⊕ www.peninsula.com/en/beverly-hills/5-star-luxury-hotel-beverly-hills ↩ 195 rooms ◉ No meals.*

SLS Hotel Beverly Hills

$$$ | **HOTEL** | From the sleek, Philippe Starck–designed lobby and lounge with fireplaces, hidden nooks, and a communal table to luxurious poolside cabanas, this hotel offers a cushy, dreamlike stay. **Pros:** great cocktails at lobby bar; complimentary house car for use within 3-mile radius; dreamy Ciel spa. **Cons:** standard rooms are compact; pricey dining and parking; on a busy intersection outside Beverly Hills. $ *Rooms from: $365 ☒ 465 S. La Cienega Blvd., Beverly Hills ☎ 310/247–0400 ⊕ slshotels.com/beverlyhills ↩ 297 rooms ◉ No meals.*

★ Viceroy L'Ermitage Beverly Hills

$$$$ | **HOTEL** | This all-suite hotel is the picture of luxury: French doors open to a mini-balcony with views of the Hollywood sign; inside the very large rooms you'll find soaking tubs and oversize bath towels. **Pros:** traditional French cuisine at Avec Nous on-site; free shuttle service within 2-mile radius; all rooms are large suites. **Cons:** small spa and pool; very expensive; a bit of a trek to Beverly Hills shopping. $ *Rooms from: $495 ☒ 9291 Burton Way, Beverly Hills ☎ 310/278–3344 ⊕ www.viceroyhotelsandresorts. com/beverly-hills ↩ 116 rooms ◉ No meals.*

Waldorf Astoria Beverly Hills

$$$$ | **HOTEL** | The belle of Beverly Hills, this Pierre-Yves Rochon–designed five-star property impresses with a top-notch spa, rooftop pool with VIP cabanas, a restaurant program created by Jean-Georges Vongerichten, and state-of-the-art amenities. **Pros:** impeccable service; free shuttle within 5-mile radius; excellent La Prairie Spa. **Cons:** one of L.A.'s priciest rooms; on the busy corner of Wilshire and Santa Monica; restaurants and spa are expensive, too. $ *Rooms from: $815 ☒ 9850 Wilshire Blvd., Beverly Hills ☎ 310/860–6666 ⊕ www.waldorfastoriabeverlyhills.com ↩ 170 rooms ◉ No meals.*

🛍 Shopping

Agent Provocateur

CLOTHING | Garter belts, corsets, and pasties—oh my! Shoppers will find a playful mix of naughty and nice at this Beverly Hills outpost of the beloved lingerie brand. Yes, the boudoir items here range from lovely and lacy (slinky slips and plunging bras) to downright racy (handcuffs and body chains), but everything in the shop is without question beautifully made, which makes it a desirable shopping destination even for the shy set. ☒ *242 N. Rodeo Dr., Beverly*

Hills ☎ 310/888–0050 ⊕ www.agent-provocateur.com.

AllSaints Spitalfields

CLOTHING | The British store invaded Beverly Drive, bringing with it a rock-and-roll edge mixed with a dash of Downton Abbey. Look for leather biker jackets, tough shoes, edgy prints, and long sweaters and cardigans, which, worn correctly, let them know you're with the band. ✉ 328–330 N. Beverly Dr., Beverly Hills ☎ 310/499–0970 ⊕ www.us.all-saints.com.

Alo Yoga

CLOTHING | In a city that takes its yoga seriously, it only makes sense that this locally designed activewear brand would take its very first Los Angeles storefront to the next level. For Alo Yoga's flagship, that means an 8,000-square-foot space complete with an organic coffee bar, kombucha on tap, and a rooftop deck that hosts daily sweat-and-stretch sessions. As for the clothing, the model-favorite line offers stylish leggings, sports bras, tanks, and more pieces that look as cool outside the fitness studio as they do during downward dog. ✉ 370 N. Canon Dr., Beverly Hills ☎ 310/295–1860 ⊕ www.aloyoga.com.

Anto Distinctive Shirtmaker

CLOTHING | A who's who of Hollywood's leading men, including Ryan Gosling and Tom Cruise, have been wearing Anto's bespoke shirts both on- and offscreen since 1955. An expertly tailored, customized shirt from this iconic showroom is decidedly an investment piece (you'll need to make an appointment for that service ahead of time), but you can also shop ready-made ties and button-downs here if you're just dropping by. If you know your measurements, take a look at their website, where you can build custom shirts from scratch. ✉ 258 N. Beverly Dr., Beverly Hills ☎ 310/278–4500 ⊕ www.antoshirt.com.

Bijan

CLOTHING | The House of Bijan is hard to miss with its trademark canary yellow Bugatti or Rolls-Royce always parked right out front. Inside, a Mediterranean palazzo welcomes high-end menswear shoppers into what is billed as the most expensive store in the world (by appointment only, of course). Some of the famous clientele includes George W. Bush, Bill Clinton, Barack Obama, and, infamously, Paul Manafort. ✉ 443 N. Rodeo Dr., Beverly Hills ☎ 310/273–6544 ⊕ bijan.com.

Cartier

JEWELRY/ACCESSORIES | Cartier has a bridal collection to sigh for in its chandeliered and respectfully hushed showroom, along with more playful pieces (chunky, diamond-encrusted panther cocktail rings, for example), watches, and accessories. The stop itself feels like the ultimate playground for A-list clientele, complete with a red-carpeted spiral staircase. ✉ 370 N. Rodeo Dr., Beverly Hills ☎ 310/275–4272 ⊕ www.cartier.com.

Céline

CLOTHING | Under designer Hedi Slimane's creative direction, the Parisian brand has entered a new chapter. At the Beverly Hills brick-and-mortar, fashion lovers looking for French Cool Girl clothing will love the selection of the label's leather handbags, heels, and chic ready-to-wear clothing. ✉ 456 N. Rodeo Dr., Beverly Hills ☎ 310/888–0120 ⊕ www.celine.com.

Chanel

CLOTHING | Fans of the French luxury retailer will be happy to find that the Beverly Hills flagship store stocks the brand's trademark pieces, like quilted leather bags, tweed jackets, and jewelry designed with the signature double C logo. Beyond those essentials are plenty of other pieces from Chanel's ready-to-wear collection. ✉ 9560 Wilshire Blvd., Beverly Hills ☎ 310/278–5500 ⊕ www.chanel.com.

Gearys of Beverly Hills

GIFTS/SOUVENIRS | Since 1930, this has been the ultimate destination for those seeking the most exquisite fine china, crystal, silver, and jewelry, mostly from classic sources like Christofle, Baccarat, and Waterford. No wonder it's a favorite for registries of the rich and famous. ⊠ *351 N. Beverly Dr., Beverly Hills* ☎ *310/273–4741* ⊕ *www.gearys.com.*

Harry Winston

JEWELRY/ACCESSORIES | Perhaps the most locally famous jeweler is Harry Winston, *the* source for Oscar-night jewelry. The three-level space, with a bronze sculptural facade, velvet-panel walls, private salons, and a rooftop patio, is as glamorous as the gems. ⊠ *310 N. Rodeo Dr., Beverly Hills* ☎ *310/271–8554* ⊕ *www. harrywinston.com.*

Jimmy Choo

SHOES/LUGGAGE/LEATHER GOODS | This footwear designer is practically synonymous with flat-out sexy, sky-high stilettos. But there's also plenty more eye candy for fashionistas within the Rodeo Drive location's posh, monochromatic interior. ⊠ *240 N. Rodeo Dr., Beverly Hills* ☎ *310/860–9045* ⊕ *www.jimmychoo. com.*

Louis Vuitton

JEWELRY/ACCESSORIES | Holding court on a prominent corner, Louis Vuitton carries its sought-after monogram (the ultimate symbol of luxury for many) on all manner of accessories and leather goods. ⊠ *295 N. Rodeo Dr., Beverly Hills* ☎ *310/859– 0457* ⊕ *www.louisvuitton.com.*

Neiman Marcus

DEPARTMENT STORES | Luxury shopping at its finest, this couture salon frequently trots out designer trunk shows, and most locals go right for the shoe department, which features high-end footwear favorites like Giuseppe Zanotti and Christian Louboutin. A café on the third floor keeps your blood sugar high during multiple wardrobe changes, while a bar on

the fourth is for celebrating those perfect finds with a glass of champagne. ⊠ *9700 Wilshire Blvd., Beverly Hills* ☎ *310/550– 5900* ⊕ *www.neimanmarcus.com.*

Prada

CLOTHING | Prada's Rodeo Drive haven sits inside the incredibly cool Rem Koolhaas–designed Italian showcase space, which features 20-foot-wide staircases and funhouse curves. ⊠ *343 N. Rodeo Dr., Beverly Hills* ☎ *310/278–8661* ⊕ *www. prada.com.*

Saint Laurent

CLOTHING | Celebrities with the coolest, edgiest styles know they can head to the slick storefront to score the label's signature pieces, like moto jackets, skinny jeans, and platform pumps. A men's store with equally rock star–worthy clothing and accessories is just down the street. ⊠ *326 N. Rodeo Dr., Beverly Hills* ☎ *310/271–5051* ⊕ *www.ysl.com.*

Taschen

BOOKS/STATIONERY | Philippe Starck designed the Taschen space to evoke a cool 1920s Parisian salon—a perfect showcase for the publisher's design-forward coffee-table books about architecture, travel, culture, and photography. A suspended glass cube gallery in back hosts art exhibits and features limited-edition books. ⊠ *354 N. Beverly Dr., Beverly Hills* ☎ *310/274–4300* ⊕ *www. taschen.com.*

Tiffany & Co.

JEWELRY/ACCESSORIES | Who can resist a gift that comes in those iconic blue boxes? Discover three floors of classic and contemporary jewelry (including plenty of sparklers perfect for popping the question) as well as watches, crystal, and china. ⊠ *210 N. Rodeo Dr., Beverly Hills* ☎ *310/273–8880* ⊕ *www.tiffany.com.*

Versace

CLOTHING | With its columned facade, temple dome ceiling, and recherché design, this is just the place for a dramatic red-carpet gown, bold bags, sunglasses, and accessories. It also stocks sleek menswear for fashion-forward fellows. ✉ *248 N. Rodeo Dr., Beverly Hills* ☎ *310/205–3921* ⊕ *www.versace.com/us.*

Westfield Century City

SHOPPING CENTERS/MALLS | FAMILY | This mall that sits between Beverly Hills and Brentwood is home to dozens of great stores, restaurants, and a massive movie theater. The best options here include L.A.'s iteration of Eataly, the ultimate Italian market; Din Tai Fung, an award-winning dumpling house; and Shake Shack, the famous East Coast burger joint. Some unique stores include a Tesla showroom, a Pelaton shop, and Amazon Books. ✉ *10250 Santa Monica Blvd., Century City* ☎ *310/277–3898* ⊕ *www.westfield.com/centurycity.*

Culver City

Located about halfway between Hollywood and the coast, Culver City has a glamorous history of its own. The area boasts two film studios, Sony (formerly MGM) Studios and the Culver Studios. Culver City itself has seen revitalization in recent years as visitors discover the charming district of the area's "downtown." The Metro's new Expo Line has a Culver City Station stop, making it an easy subway and light rail trip from Hollywood or Downtown Los Angeles. The Culver Hotel is in the heart of Culver City, and the surrounding area is loaded with shops, cafés, the art deco–style ArcLight Cinemas, and a vibrant art gallery scene. A place for adventurous eaters, you can also find cuisines spanning the globe.

Sights

Culver Hotel

HISTORIC SITE | In the heart of Culver City is the Culver Hotel, built in 1924 and now preserved as a historical landmark. It will catch your eye with its old-world glory

and lobby entrance with its sweeping dark wood and high ceiling that's as seductive as the many classic film stars that took up residency here over the years, including Greta Garbo, Joan Crawford, John Wayne, Clark Gable, Buster Keaton, Ronald Reagan, and cast members from *Wizard of Oz* and *Gone with the Wind* as they filmed in the nearby studio. ✉ *9400 Culver Blvd., Culver City* ☎ *310/558–9400* ⊕ *www.culverhotel.com* Ⓜ *Culver City.*

Culver Studios

FILM STUDIO | The Culver Studios are best known as the location where *Gone with the Wind* was filmed in addition to classics including *Citizen Kane* and the Desilu Productions TV hits of the '50s–'60s, including *The Andy Griffith Show, Lassie,* and *Batman.* Amazon Studio currently occupies the space and is further developing it. This studio currently does not offer tours to the public. ✉ *9336 W. Washington Blvd., Culver City* ☎ *310/202–1234* ⊕ *www.theculverstudios.com* Ⓜ *Culver City.*

★ Museum of Jurassic Technology

MUSEUM | One museum with its own unique spin is the Museum of Jurassic Technology, with an oddball assortment of natural (and partly fictional) "art" pieces such as fruit stone carvings, theater models, string figures, and finds from mobile home parks, and a tribute room filled with paintings of dogs from the Soviet Space Program. All are housed in a low-lighted haunted house–style atmosphere that makes you feel as if the *Addams Family* butler will come to greet you at any moment. ✉ *9341 Venice Blvd., Culver City* ☎ *310/836–6131* ⊕ *www.mjt.org* ▣ *$10* Ⓜ *Culver City.*

Sony Pictures Studios

FILM STUDIO | Sony Pictures Studios (former the MGM studios), where movie magic from *Wizard of Oz* to *Spiderman* was made, offers two-hour walking tours ($50, reservation required) to dive into their rich TV and blockbuster film history.

In addition to movies and television shows, Sony Picture Studios is also where game shows like *Jeopardy* are filmed.

If game shows are your thing, you can also be a part of the studio audience for *Jeopardy!* or *Wheel of Fortune.* ✉ 10202 W. Washington, Culver City ☎ 310/244–8687 ⊕ www.sonypicturesstudios.com 🎫 Tours $50 Ⓜ Culver City.

🍴 Restaurants

Lodge Bread Company
$$ | **BAKERY** | Part restaurant, part bakery, and part learning annex, Lodge Bread Company beckons customers with freshly baked sourdough that wafts over the entire neighborhood. Inside, guests can enjoy fermented pizzas, savory sandwiches, and crisp morning toasts. **Known for:** incredible sourdough bread; fluffy pizzas; bakery items and bread-making classes. $ *Average main: $15* ✉ 11918 W. Washington Blvd., Culver City ☎ 424/384–5097 ⊕ www.lodgebread.com.

Margot
$$$ | **MEDITERRANEAN** | Boasting one of the most stunning rooftops in L.A., Margot is a fresh face and hopping hot spot for the Culver City dining and drinking scene. The expansive space gives off a Moroccan Casbah vibe with just as many hints of Southern California for good measure. **Known for:** fresh fish and lots of shared plates; epic views; fun happy hour. $ *Average main: $25* ✉ 8820 Washington Blvd., #301, Culver City ☎ 310/643–5853 ⊕ www.margot.la ⊘ No lunch weekdays Ⓜ Culver City.

★ n/naka
$$$$ | **JAPANESE** | *Chef's Table* star Niki Nakayama helms this two-Michelin-starred *omakase* (chef-selected) fine-dining establishment. Small and intimate, any given night will feature sashimi with *kanpachi*, sea bass with *uni* butter, or Myazaki Wagyu beef. **Known for:** decadent three-hour meals worth every penny; excellent sake pairings; romantic atmosphere. $ *Average main: $185* ✉ 3455 Overland Ave., Culver City ☎ 310/836–6252 ⊕ www.n-naka.com ⊘ Closed Sun. and Mon.

Vespertine

$$$$ | **AMERICAN** | Vespertine isn't just a two-Michelin-starred restaurant, but a multisensory event and a space-age dining experience that is nothing short of unique. Chef Jordan Kahn and architect Eric Owen Moss created a one-of-a-kind space with a menu that's as artistic as it is delicious. **Known for:** elaborate tasting menu; modern design; unique everything. ⑤ *Average main: $250* ⊠ *3599 Hayden Ave., Culver City* ☎ *323/320–4023* ⊕ *www.vespertine.la* ⊘ *Closed Sun. and Mon.* Ⓜ *Culver City.*

 ## Shopping

Platform

SHOPPING CENTERS/MALLS | **FAMILY** | Culver City's revitalization has created hot spots like Platform, a design-forward space filled with independent restaurants, boutiques, coffee shops, and spas. Standouts include Italian bakery Bianca, New York pizza transplant Roberta's, Paris-meets-Tokyo fashion brand Maison Kitsuné, and massage haven Lifehood. Weekly events include food and fashion pop-ups in addition to outdoor fitness classes. ⊠ *8850 Washington Blvd., Culver City* ☎ *310/558–0415* ⊕ *www. platformlosangeles.com* Ⓜ *Culver City.*

Chapter 5

WEST HOLLYWOOD AND FAIRFAX

Updated by
Paul Feinstein

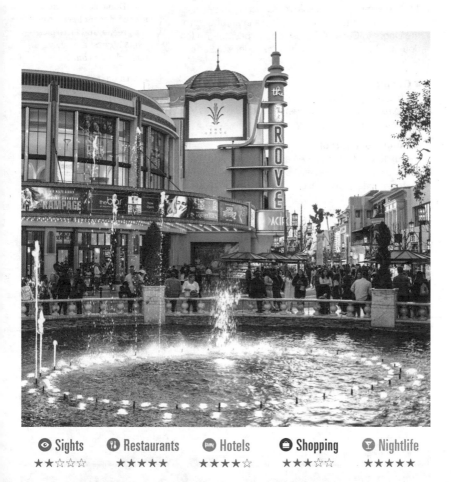

👁 Sights	🍴 Restaurants	🛏 Hotels	🛍 Shopping	🍸 Nightlife
★★☆☆☆	★★★★★	★★★★☆	★★★☆☆	★★★★★

NEIGHBORHOOD SNAPSHOT

TOP EXPERIENCES

■ **Wander the Grove and feast at the Farmers Market:** Visit for a shopping respite or to take in and appreciate the Farmers Market's over 75-year-old history and atmosphere.

■ **Drive down Sunset Boulevard to the Ocean:** The quintessential Los Angeles experience, it's best to start at La Cienega headed west on Sunset, which will take you through the Sunset Strip. Now may be a good time to test-drive that convertible.

■ **Experience the '60s, '70s, and '80s all over again:** To truly experience the L.A. music scene of decades past, wander into the venues where everyone from the Doors to Guns N' Roses used to pay: the Troubadour, the Whisky A Go Go, and the Rainbow Bar and Grill.

■ **Get proud:** Since you're in L.A.'s bastion of LGBTQ+ culture, visit the ONE Gallery, part of the ONE Archives, home to the largest repository of LGBTQ+ materials in the world.

■ **Laugh your butt off:** West Hollywood is home to the Hollywood Improv, the Laugh Factory, and the Comedy Store, where A-list comedians test out new material and headline epically funny shows.

GETTING HERE

All main west–east roads will get you toward West Hollywood and the Fairfax District. Santa Monica Boulevard is the easiest. It starts in Santa Monica, heads straight into West Hollywood; and intersects with Fairfax. But traffic can be a nightmare, as it can be for another one of L.A.'s main arteries, Sunset Boulevard, which also hits West Hollywood. Secret streets that can be easier to zip around on include San Vicente, which cuts diagonally from Sunset down to West 3rd Street, or Fountain, which will take you from La Cienega to La Brea and beyond.

QUICK BITES

■ **Milk Bar LA.** This place is so popular that lines often spill out the door and onto the sidewalk. Suffer through them for the crack pie and cereal-milk soft serve. ⊠ *7150 Melrose Ave.* ⊕ *www.milkbarstore.com*

■ **Slab Barbecue.** It's nearly impossible to understand how brisket can taste this good. Don't sleep on the sides of mac n' cheese, collard greens, and Frito pies. ⊠ *8136 W. 3rd St.* ⊕ *www. slabbarbecue.com*

■ **Urth Caffé Melrose.** Join the beautiful people at this ultratrendy café to refuel on organic coffee and tea along with a range of health-conscious sandwiches, salads, and juices. ⊠ *8565 Melrose Ave.* ⊕ *www. urthcaffe.com/melrose*

■ **Vito's Pizza.** Who says you can't get a New York slice in L.A.? Come to Vito's for a taste of the East Coast, from perfect pies to melt-in-your-mouth sandwiches. ⊠ *846 N. La Cienega Blvd.* ⊕ *www.vitopizza.com*

West Hollywood is not a place to see things (like museums or movie studios) as much as it is a place to do things—like go to a nightclub, eat at a world-famous restaurant, or attend an art gallery opening. Since the end of Prohibition, the Sunset Strip has been Hollywood's nighttime playground, where stars headed to such glamorous nightclubs as the Trocadero, the Mocambo, and Ciro's.

It's still going strong, with crowds still filing into well-established spots like Whisky A Go Go and paparazzi staking out the members-only Soho House. But hedonism isn't all that drives West Hollywood. Also thriving is an important interior design and art gallery trade exemplified by the Cesar Pelli–designed Pacific Design Center.

West Hollywood has also emerged as one of the most progressive cities in Southern California. It's one of the most gay-friendly cities anywhere, with a large LGBTQ+ community. Its annual Gay Pride Parade is one of the largest in the nation, drawing tens of thousands of participants each June.

The historic Farmers Market and The Grove shopping mall are both great places to people-watch over breakfast.

 ## Sights

★ The Grove
STORE/MALL | Come to this popular outdoor mall for familiar names like Apple, Nike, and Nordstrom; stay for the central fountain with "dancing" water and light shows, people-watching from the trolley, and, during the holiday season, artificial snowfall and a winter wonderland. Feel-good pop blasting over the loudspeakers aims to boost your mood while you spend, and a giant cineplex gives shoppers a needed break with the latest box office blockbusters. ⊠ *189 The Grove Dr., Fairfax District* 🕾 *323/900–8080* ⊕ *www. thegrovela.com.*

Los Angeles Museum of the Holocaust
MUSEUM | A museum dedicated solely to the Holocaust, it uses its extensive collections of photos and artifacts as well as award-winning audio tours and interactive tools to evoke European Jewish life in the 20th century. The mission is to commemorate the lives of those who perished and those who survived the Holocaust. The building is itself a marvel, having won two awards from the American Institute of Architects. Every Sunday, the museum hosts talks given by Holocaust survivors, while other events include a lecture series, educational programs, and concerts. ⊠ *100 The*

Sights ▼

Restaurants ▼

Hotels ▼

Grove Dr., Los Angeles ☎ *323/651–3704* ⊕ *www.holocaustmuseumla.org* ✉ *Free.*

Melrose Avenue

NEIGHBORHOOD | Melrose Avenue is a tale of two streets: west of Fairfax Avenue is a haven of high-end boutique shopping, chichi restaurants, and avant-garde galleries while east of Fairfax is much grittier, where street style is more in vogue, with sneaker stores, head shops, fast casual food, and vintage boutiques. Fans of *Melrose Place* will be excited to learn that the eponymous street actually exists and is home to upscale shops and restaurants. Instagram junkies will recognize a number of photo hot spots like the shockingly pink Paul Smith store or graffitied angel wings along numerous storefronts. ⊠ *Melrose Ave., West Hollywood* ⊕ *www.melrose-avenue.com.*

★ The Original Farmers Market

MARKET | FAMILY | Called the Original Farmers Market for a reason, this special piece of land brought out farmers to sell their wares starting in 1934. Today, the market has more permanent residences, but fresh produce still abounds among the dozens of vendors. Some purveyor standouts include gourmet market Monsieur Marcel, Bob's Coffee & Doughnuts, and Patsy D'Amore's Pizzeria, which has been serving slices since 1949. The market is adjacent to The Grove shopping center, and locals and tourists flock to both in droves. ⊠ *6333 W. 3rd St., Fairfax District* ☎ *323/933–9211* ⊕ *www.farmersmarketla.com.*

Pacific Design Center

BUILDING | World-renowned architect Cesar Pelli's original vision for the Pacific Design Center was three buildings that together housed designer showrooms, office buildings, parking, and more—a sleek shrine to design. These architecturally intriguing buildings were built years apart: the building sheathed in blue glass (known as the Blue Whale) opened in 1975; the green building

opened in 1988. The final "Red" building opened in 2013, completing Pelli's grand vision many years later. All together the 1.6-million-square-foot complex covers more than 14 acres, housing more than 100 design showrooms as well as 2,200 interior product lines. ⊠ *8687 Melrose Ave., West Hollywood* ☎ *310/657–0800* ⊕ *www.pacificdesigncenter.com.*

Santa Monica Boulevard

NEIGHBORHOOD | From Fairfax Avenue in the east to Doheny Drive in the west, Santa Monica Boulevard is the commercial core of West Hollywood's gay community, with restaurants and cafés, bars and clubs, bookstores and galleries, and other establishments catering largely to the LGBTQ scene. Twice a year—during June's L.A. Pride and on Halloween—the boulevard becomes an open-air festival. ⊠ *Santa Monica Blvd. between Fairfax Ave. and Doheny Dr., West Hollywood* ☎ *323/848-6400* ⊕ *weho.org.*

Sunset Boulevard

NEIGHBORHOOD | One of the most fabled avenues in the world, Sunset Boulevard began humbly enough in the 18th century as a route from El Pueblo de Los Angeles to the Pacific Ocean. Today, as it passes through West Hollywood, it becomes the sexy and seductive Sunset Strip, where rock and roll had its heyday and cocktail bars charge a premium for the views. It slips quietly into the tony environs of Beverly Hills and Bel-Air, twisting and winding past gated estates and undulating vistas. ⊠ *Sunset Blvd., West Hollywood* ⊕ *www.weho.org.*

Sunset Plaza

NEIGHBORHOOD | With a profusion of sidewalk cafés, Sunset Plaza is one of the best people-watching spots in town. Sunny weekends reach the highest pitch, when people flock to this stretch of Sunset Boulevard for brunch or lunch and to browse in the trendy shops that offer a range of price points. There's free parking in the lot behind the shops. ⊠ *8623 W.*

Sunset Blvd., West Hollywood ⊕ www. sunsetplaza.com.

West Hollywood Design District

STORE/MALL | More than 200 businesses—art galleries, antiques shops, fashion outlets (including Rag & Bone and James Perse), and interior design stores—are found in the design district. There are also about 30 restaurants, including the famous paparazzi magnet, the Ivy. All are clustered within walking distance of each other—rare for L.A. ⊠ Melrose Ave. and Robertson and Beverly Blvds., West Hollywood ☎ 310/289–2534 ⊕ westhollywooddesigndistrict.com.

West Hollywood Library

LIBRARY | Across from the Pacific Design Center, this library, designed by architects Steve Johnson and James Favaro, is a charming part of the city. Replete with floor-to-ceiling glass, a modern and airy interior, a huge mural by Shepard Fairey, and other art by Kenny Scharf and Retna, the three-story building and the adjoining park are a great place to take a break from your tour of the city. They also have an impressive LGBTQ+ book collection. There's inexpensive parking and a café below. ⊠ 625 N. San Vicente Blvd., West Hollywood ☎ 310/652–5340 ⊕ lacountylibrary.org/west-hollywood-library.

🍴 Restaurants

Lively, stylish, and surrounded by the best restaurants and nightlife in Los Angeles, WeHo (as locals call it) is a magnet for celebrity sightings. There are great bakeries, well-regarded burger joints, and upscale bars serving couture cocktails.

★ Angelini Osteria

$$$$ | ITALIAN | Despite its modest, rather congested dining room, this is one of L.A.'s most celebrated Italian restaurants. The keys are chef-owner Gino Angelini's consistently impressive dishes, like whole branzino, tagliolini al limone, veal chop alla Milanese, as well as lasagna oozing with besciamella (Italian béchamel sauce). Known for: large Italian wine selection; bold flavors; savory pastas. ⑤ Average main: $40 ⊠ 7313 Beverly Blvd., Beverly–La Brea ☎ 323/297–0070 ⊕ www.angelinirestaurantgroup.com.

Animal

$$$ | AMERICAN | Owned by Jon Shook and Vinny Dotolo of Iron Chef fame, this oft-packed James Beard Award–winning restaurant offers shareable plates with a focus on meat. Highlights include barbecue pork belly sandwiches, poutine with oxtail gravy, and braised rabbit legs with mushrooms. Known for: bacon-chocolate crunch bar for dessert; reputation as a must for foodies; menu that is carnivore heaven. ⑤ Average main: $30 ⊠ 435 N. Fairfax Ave., Fairfax District ☎ 323/782–9225 ⊕ www.animalrestaurant.com ⊗ No lunch.

A.O.C.

$$$ | MEDITERRANEAN | Not to be confused with the congresswoman from New York, the acronym here stands for Appellation d'Origine Contrôlée, the regulatory system that ensures the quality of local wines and cheeses in France. Fittingly, A.O.C. upholds this standard of excellence in its shared plates and perfect wine pairings in the stunning exposed-brick and vine-laden courtyard. Known for: amazing cocktail hour; quaint outdoor courtyard; charming indoor fireplaces. ⑤ Average main: $25 ⊠ 8700 W. 3rd St., West Hollywood ☎ 310/859–9859 ⊕ www.aocwinebar.com.

BOA Steakhouse

$$$$ | STEAKHOUSE | The ultimate in steak-house dining, this sceney spot on the border of West Hollywood and Beverly Hills is an indoor/outdoor gem with perfectly prepared cuts of prime rib. Every night has a packed crowd of

Continued on page 113

CRUISING THE SUNSET STRIP

For more than half a century, Hollywood's night owls have headed for the 1¾-mile stretch of Sunset Boulevard between Crescent Heights Boulevard on the east and Doheny Drive on the west, known as the Sunset Strip. The experience of driving it from end to end gives you a sampling of everything that makes L.A. what it is, with all its glamour and grit, and its history of those who rose fast and fell faster.

Left and top right, two views of Sunset Boulevard. Bottom right, Mel's Drive-in Diner.

In the 1930s and '40s, stars such as Errol Flynn and Rita Hayworth came for wild evenings of dancing and drinking at nightclubs like Trocadero, Ciro's, and Mocambo.

The Strip's image as Tinseltown's glamorous nighttime playground began to die in the '50s, and by the mid-'60s it was the center of L.A.'s raucous music-and-nightlife scene. Bands like the Doors and the Byrds played the Whisky a Go Go, and the city's counterculture clashed with police in the famous Sunset Strip curfew riots in the summer of 1966.

In the '70s, the Strip was all about glam rock, with David Bowie, T. Rex, and Queen hitting the venues. But this was when it began a decline that would last almost two decades, until it became a seedy section of the city where hookers hung out on every corner.

It's only been in the last decade that the Strip has seen a true revitalization, with new hotels, restaurants, and bars opening that have become haunts for celebs and A-listers. It retains its rough-and-tumble image in some sections but overall is a much classier spot to spend a night out.

A CLASSIC DRIVE THROUGH L.A.

Depending on the time of day, driving the Strip is a different experience. In the afternoon grab lunch at a hotel and hobnob with industry types. At night, drive with the top down and come to hear music, hit a club, or have cocktails at a rooftop bar. Either way, it's good to park the car and walk (yes, walk!).

WHERE TO EAT & DRINK

See and be seen at **Sky-bar at the Mondrian Hotel** (✉ 8440 Sunset Blvd. ☎ 323/848–6025), the luxe outdoor lounge and pool deck. The bar opens to the public at 8 pm daily. Come early to enjoy sweeping views of the city before turning your gaze inward to the beautiful people milling around. Go to **Greenblatt's Deli** (✉ 8017 Sunset Blvd. ☎ 323/656-0606) for some of the best roast beef you'll ever have. Around since 1926, this casual deli has free parking in the back, and you can order picnic basket dinners to take to the Hollywood Bowl.

Stop in for a burger and shake at **Mel's Drive-In** (✉ 8585 Sunset Blvd. ☎ 310/854–7201), open 24 hours a day. The iconic

Whisky a Go Go

The Roxy

The Chateau Marmont

Andaz West Hollywood

Map labels:
Selma Ave.
N. Fairfax Ave.
Laurel Canyon Blvd.
Selma Dr.
N. Crescent Heights Blvd.
N. Havenhurst Dr.
Greenblatt's Deli
The Chateau Marmont
Sunset Blvd.
Andaz West Hollywood ("Riot Hyatt")
Carney's
Standard Hotel's Cactus Lounge
N. Kings Rd.
N. Harper Ave.
Queens Way
Comedy Store
Saddle Ranch Chop House
Sunset Tower Hotel
The House of Blues
De Longpre Ave.
Olive Dr.
Skybar at the Mondrian Hotel
Fountain Ave.

1950s-inspired diner in the heart of the Strip is a fun place to people-watch, day or night.

For the city's best hot dogs, chili fries, and frozen chocolate-dipped bananas, head to **Carney's** (✉ 8351 Sunset Blvd. ☎ 323/654-8300), a popular spot for a quick bite. You can't miss it—look for the yellow railcar.

SIGHTS TO SEE
The Chateau Marmont
(✉ 8221 West Sunset Boulevard). Greta Garbo once called this castle-like hotel home. It's also where John Belushi died.

Comedy Store (✉ 8433 Sunset Boulevard). David Letterman and Robin Williams rose to fame here.

Andaz West Hollywood ("Riot Hyatt") (✉ 8401 Sunset Boulevard). Led Zeppelin, the Rolling Stones, and the Who stayed and played here when they hit town.

Rainbow Bar & Grill (✉ 9015 Sunset Boulevard). Jimi Hendrix and Bob Marley began their climb to the top of the charts here.

The Roxy (✉ 9009 Sunset Boulevard). Neil Young was the opening act here in 1973; it's been a Strip anchor and front-runner in revitalization.

The Viper Room (✉ 8852 Sunset Blvd.) This always popular, always booked venue was where River Phoenix OD'd in 1993.

Saddle Ranch Chop House (✉ 8371 Sunset Boulevard). Originally the Thunder Roadhouse (co-owned by Dennis Hopper and Peter Fonda), this raucous steakhouse has a mechanical bull featured on many a TV show, including *Sex and the City*.

A DRIVE BEYOND THE STRIP

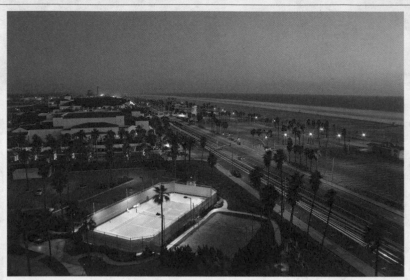

California's Pacific Coast Highway at dusk

There's more to see along Sunset Boulevard than just the Strip. For another classic L.A. drive, just before dusk, continue west on Sunset until you reach the Pacific Coast Highway (PCH) in Pacific Palisades, right along the ocean, and you'll understand how the boulevard got its name.

WHEN TO GO

Time it right so you can catch that famous L.A. sunset, or drive down Sunset Boulevard late morning after rush hour and arrive just in time for lunch at a waterfront restaurant or a picnic on the beach.

The PCH is also known for its fresh seafood shacks along the roadside. For a cocktail with a great view, try **Gladstone's 4 Fish** (⊠ 17300 Pacific Coast Hwy.), where Sunset Boulevard hits the PCH.

TRIP TIPS

While it's hard to tear your eyes away from sites along the way, there are hairpin turns on the Boulevard, and driving can be a challenge. Stop-and-go traffic—especially along the Strip—means lots of fender benders, so be careful and keep a safe distance.

Sunset view from Gladstone's

well-heeled carnivores looking to flirt at the backlit bar or devour slabs of sizzling steak. **Known for:** sizzling steaks; sceney bar; table-side Caesar salad. $ Average main: $50 ✉ 9200 Sunset Blvd., West Hollywood ☎ 310/278-2050 ⊕ www. innovativedining.com/locations/boa ⊗ No lunch weekends.

Canter's
$ | DELI | FAMILY | This granddaddy of L.A. delicatessens (it opened in 1931) cures its own corned beef and pastrami and features delectable desserts from the in-house bakery. It's not the best (or friendliest) deli in town, but it's a classic. **Known for:** location adjacent to Kibitz Room bar; plenty of seating and short wait times; open 24 hours. $ Average main: $12 ✉ 419 N. Fairfax Ave., Fairfax District ☎ 323/651-2030 ⊕ www.canters-deli.com.

Catch LA
$$$$ | ASIAN FUSION | Boasting the best see-and-be-seen crowd in West Hollywood, this rooftop restaurant also has some of the best views. As you enter through a pergola, you'll find an extremely good-looking crowd of well-heeled diners and drinkers flirting at the large bar or getting cozy in the teal brushed-leather booths. **Known for:** some of the city's best celeb sightings; rooftop views; excellent crab tempura. $ Average main: $40 ✉ 8715 Melrose Ave., West Hollywood ☎ 323/347-6060 ⊕ catchrestaurants. com/catchla ⊗ No brunch weekdays.

Connie and Ted's
$$$ | SEAFOOD | Inspired by the classic clam, oyster, and fish houses of New England, this beautiful space (the roof is arched like a wave) is occupied by a dressed-up crowd dipping fried calamari or spooning up Jo's wicked-good chowda. Lobster rolls are insanely good, and you can never go wrong with the catch of the day. **Known for:** buttery lobster rolls; catch of the day; classic New England seafood spot atmosphere. $ Average

main: $28 ✉ 8171 Santa Monica Blvd., West Hollywood ☎ 323/848-2722 ⊕ www.connieandteds.com ⊗ No lunch Mon. and Tues.

Craig's
$$$$ | AMERICAN | Behind the unremarkable facade is a trendy—yet decidedly old-school—den of American cuisine that doubles as a safe haven for the movie industry's most important names and well-known faces. Be aware that this joint is always busy so you might not even get a table and reservations are hard to come by. **Known for:** lots of celebrities; delicious chicken Parm; strong drinks. $ Average main: $32 ✉ 8826 Melrose Ave., West Hollywood ☎ 310/276-1900 ⊕ craigs.la.

★ Crossroads
$$$ | VEGETARIAN | From its famous Impossible Burger (you can't believe it's not meat) to its spicy meatball pizza (again, not meat), Crossroads's level of plant-based inventiveness knows no bounds. The space itself is dimly lit, with red-leather booths and a full bar illuminating its A-list clientele. **Known for:** high-end plant-based cuisine; great bar menu; popular celebrity hangout. $ Average main: $24 ✉ 8284 Melrose Ave., West Hollywood ☎ 323/782-9245 ⊕ www. crossroadskitchen.com.

Dan Tana's
$$$$ | ITALIAN | If you're looking for an Italian vibe straight out of Goodfellas, your search ends here. Checkered tablecloths cover the tightly packed tables as Hollywood players dine on the city's best chicken and veal Parm, and down Scotches by the finger. **Known for:** elbow-room-only bar; lively atmosphere; celeb spotting. $ Average main: $35 ✉ 9071 Santa Monica Blvd., West Hollywood ☎ 310/275-9444 ⊕ www.dantanasrestaurant.com.

★ El Coyote Mexican Food

$$ | MEXICAN | FAMILY | Open since 1931, this landmark spot is perfect for those on a budget or anyone after an authentic Mexican meal. The traditional fare is decadent and delicious while the margaritas are sweetened to perfection. **Known for:** affordable, quality cuisine; festive atmosphere; being an L.A. staple. ⑤ Average main: $14 ⊠ 7312 Beverly Blvd., Beverly–La Brea ☎ 323/939–2255 ⊕ www.elcoyotecafe.com ⊙ Closed Mon. and Tues.

Greenblatt's Deli

$$ | DELI | In 1926, Herman Greenblatt opened his eponymous deli which serves Jewish deli food, wine, and spirits. The restaurant claims to have the rarest roast beef in town—and they're probably right. **Known for:** matzo ball soup; pastrami sandwiches; old-school vibe. ⑤ Average main: $18 ⊠ 8017 Sunset Blvd., West Hollywood ☎ 323/656–0606 ⊕ www.greenblattsdeli.com.

Happy Ice

$ | AMERICAN | From a food truck to a brick-and-mortar space, Happy Ice is a rainbow-colored icee shop that keeps the crowds coming. Customers can combine up to three of the nine flavors, including the world-famous Rainbow Rocket, Mango Madness, Sour Apple Lush, and more. **Known for:** colorful, Instagram-worthy atmosphere; creative slushies and icees; vegan-friendly ingredients. ⑤ Average main: $5 ⊠ 7324 Melrose Ave., West Hollywood ☎ 215/800–3965 ⊕ www.happyicela.com.

★ Joan's on Third

$$ | CAFÉ | FAMILY | Part restaurant, part bakery, part market, Joan's on Third has a little bit of everything. This roadside French-style café caters to families, the occasional local celebrity, and lovers of all things wholesome. **Known for:** crispy baguettes and fresh pastries; deli sandwiches and imported cheeses; long lines (get there before 9 am). ⑤ Average main: $16 ⊠ 8350 W. 3rd St., West Hollywood ☎ 323/655–2285 ⊕ www.joansonthird.com.

Milk Bar LA

$ | BAKERY | This place is so popular that lines often spill out the door and onto the sidewalk. The Milk Bar pie and cereal-milk soft serve are favorites, but you can also take classes with owner Christina Tosi to become your own baking master. **Known for:** famous Milk Bar pie; cereal-milk soft serve; long lines. ⑤ Average main: $6 ⊠ 7150 Melrose Ave., West Hollywood ☎ 213/341–8423 ⊕ milkbarstore.com.

★ MozzaPlex

$$$ | ITALIAN | A trio of restaurants by star chef Nancy Silverton, MozzaPlex consists of Pizzeria Mozza, a casual pizza and wine spot; Osteria Mozza, an upscale Italian restaurant with incredible pastas; and chi SPACCA, an Italian steakhouse with succulent cuts of steak. The restaurant complex is one of the most beloved in the whole city and if you're craving any kind of Italian food, you'll want to get yourself inside. **Known for:** great pizzas; intimate atmosphere; the chi SPACCA burger. ⑤ Average main: $25 ⊠ 641 N. Highland Ave., Beverly–La Brea ☎ 323/297–1130 ⊕ www.mozzarestaurantgroup.com.

The Nice Guy

$$$ | ITALIAN | This dark and brooding Italian restaurant sits discretely on La Cienega Boulevard and hides one of the cooler scenes in L.A. A favorite among privacy-minded celebs (there's a no-photo policy), the Nice Guy is known for its cavatelli alla vodka and mouthwatering chicken Parm. **Known for:** mouthwatering pastas; see-and-be-seen crowd; live piano music. ⑤ Average main: $25 ⊠ 401 N. La Cienega Blvd., West Hollywood ☎ 310/360–9500 ⊕ www.theniceguyla.com.

Petty Cash Taqueria and Bar

$$ | MODERN MEXICAN | A boisterous vibe permeates PCT as groups of twenty- and thirty-somethings feast on fresh guaca mole under the graffitied walls. There are 10 or so tacos on the ever-changing menu, from grilled octopus and Baja fish to pork belly and shrimp. **Known for:** house-made tortillas; delicious mezcal cocktails; lively atmosphere. ⑤ *Average main: $15* ⊠ *7360 Beverly Blvd., Beverly–La Brea* ☎ *323/933–5300* ⊕ *www. pettycashtaqueria.com* ⊗ *Closed Sun. and Mon.*

★ Pink's Hot Dogs

$ | HOT DOG | FAMILY | Since 1939, Angelenos and tourists alike have been lining up at this roadside hot dog stand. But Pink's is more than just an institution, it's a beloved family-run joint that serves a damn good hot dog. **Known for:** the famous Brando Dog; late-night dining; chili fries. ⑤ *Average main: $6* ⊠ *709 N. La Brea Ave., Hollywood* ☎ *323/931–4223* ⊕ *www.pinkshollywood.com.*

Pura Vita

$$ | VEGETARIAN | At the first 100% plant-based Italian restaurant and wine bar in the whole country, chef Tara Punzone makes you believe her caprese has real mozzarella, her meatballs come from cows, and her cacio e pepe is filled with dairy. The food is exceptional, the atmosphere screams New York, and the best part is that no animals were harmed for any of it. **Known for:** all vegan cuisine; incredible pastas; stellar wine list. ⑤ *Average main: $17* ⊠ *8247 Santa Monica Blvd., West Hollywood* ☎ *323/688–2303* ⊕ *www.puravitalosangeles.com* ⊗ *Closed Mon.*

SUR Restaurant & Lounge

$$$ | MODERN AMERICAN | Fans of Lisa Vanderpump and the *Vanderpump Rules* reality show on Bravo will instantly recognize SUR as the backdrop for the series's endless drama, broken relationships, one-night stands, and countless drinks. The actual restaurant serves a melange of new American items that range from fried goat cheese balls to prime pork chops. **Known for:** celebrity sightings; crafty cocktails; bachelorette parties galore. ⑤ *Average main: $25* ⊠ *606 N. Robertson Blvd., West Hollywood* ☎ *310/289–2824* ⊕ *www.surrestaurant. com* ⊗ *Closed Mon. and Tues.*

Sushi Tama

$$ | JAPANESE | A calming effect comes over you as you enter this simple sushi bar on one of L.A.'s most fashionable streets. Chef Yoshimoto actually sharpened his skills inside Tokyo's Tsukiji Fish Market where he learned what the best quality fish really means, resulting in sushi that transports you to Japan. **Known for:** fresh fish; donburi bowls; traditional sushi. ⑤ *Average main: $20* ⊠ *116 N. Robertson Blvd., West Hollywood* ☎ *424/249–3009* ⊕ *www.sushitama-la. com.*

Tesse

$$$$ | FRENCH FUSION | Jaws drop upon entering this French hot spot in West Hollywood, thanks to the marvelous interior design with sloping wood ceilings, lush leather banquettes, angled mirrors, and an open kitchen. But more important, French-food fanatics will salivate over the gooey cheese plates, caviar toast, and duck leg confit. **Known for:** duck leg confit; stunning interior design; great cocktail program. ⑤ *Average main: $35* ⊠ *8500 W. Sunset Blvd., Suite B, West Hollywood* ☎ *310/360–3866* ⊕ *www. tesserestaurant.com* ⊗ *No dinner Mon. and Tues.*

Urth Caffé Melrose

$ | AMERICAN | The ultratrendy Urth Caffé is full of beautiful people refueling on organic coffee and tea with a range of health-conscious sandwiches, salads, and juices. The outdoor patio is a great place to take in the scene or spot

Celebrity hot spot Chateau Marmont is one of the most famous hotels in Los Angeles.

celebrities. **Known for:** healthy eats; organic coffee and tea; celeb spotting. ⑤ *Average main: $10* ✉ *8565 Melrose Ave., West Hollywood* ☎ *310/659–0628* ⊕ *www.urthcaffe.com.*

🛌 Hotels

ANdAZ West Hollywood
$$ | HOTEL | On the north side of the Sunset Strip, the ANdAZ is Hyatt's fun younger sister, catering to hipsters, techies, and rock stars lounging in the lobby as "hosts" check them in via tablets (there's no front desk). **Pros:** fridge stocked with healthy drinks and snacks; ambitious hotel dining and bar concepts; gym overlooks Sunset Boulevard. **Cons:** traffic congestion impedes access; Sunset Strip is wildly popular on weekends and holidays; expensive parking ($44). ⑤ *Rooms from: $299* ✉ *8401 Sunset Blvd., West Hollywood* ☎ *323/656–1234, 800/233–1234* ⊕ *www.hyatt.com/brands/andaz* ⇦ *239 rooms* ⑩ *No meals.*

Chamberlain
$$ | HOTEL | On a leafy residential side street, the Chamberlain is steps from Santa Monica Boulevard and close to the Sunset Strip, bringing in fashionable young professionals and 24-hour party people looking to roam West Hollywood. **Pros:** excellent guests-only dining room and bar; suites come with fireplace and balcony; 24-hour fitness center. **Cons:** compact bathrooms; uphill climb to the Sunset Strip; party-friendly crowds might be too noisy for some. ⑤ *Rooms from: $249* ✉ *1000 Westmount Dr., West Hollywood* ☎ *310/657–7400, 888/377–7181* ⊕ *www.chamberlainwesthollywood.com* ⇦ *114 suites* ⑩ *No meals.*

Chateau Marmont
$$$$ | HOTEL | Built in 1929 as a luxury apartment complex, the Chateau is now one of the most unique see-and-be-seen hotel hot spots in all of L.A. A remarkably good-looking, young, and super-creative crowd of artists, writers, actors, and photographers roams about this historic haunt. **Pros:** private and exclusive vibe;

famous history; beautiful pool. **Cons:** some may find it pretentious; service can be spotty; some of the rooms are underwhelming. $ *Rooms from: $450* ✉ *8221 Sunset Blvd., West Hollywood* ☎ *323/656–1010* ⊕ *www.chateaumarmont.com* ⚲ *63 rooms* ⏹ *No meals.*

★ Farmer's Daughter Hotel

$$ | **HOTEL** | A favorite of *Price Is Right* and *Dancing with the Stars* hopefuls (both TV shows tape at the CBS studios nearby), this hotel has a tongue-in-cheek country style with a hopping Sunday brunch and a little pool accented by giant rubber duckies and a living wall. **Pros:** bikes for rent; fun brunch restaurant; book lending library. **Cons:** shaded pool; no bathtubs; restaurant food is just okay. $ *Rooms from: $200* ✉ *115 S. Fairfax Ave., Fairfax District* ☎ *323/937–3930, 800/334–1658* ⊕ *www.farmersdaughterhotel.com* ⚲ *65 rooms* ⏹ *No meals.*

Kimpton La Peer Hotel

$$ | **HOTEL** | The newest boutique hotel in West Hollywood, the Kimpton La Peer sits in the West Hollywood Design District and attracts an in-crowd of creative types. **Pros:** fashionable location; chic bar scene; great outdoor pool. **Cons:** daily amenity fee is $28 plus tax; expensive parking; rooms by pool can be noisy. $ *Rooms from: $250* ✉ *627 N. La Peer Dr., West Hollywood* ☎ *213/296–3038, 800/373–6365* ⊕ *www.lapeerhotel.com/ hotels-in-west-hollywood* ⚲ *105 rooms* ⏹ *No meals.*

★ The London West Hollywood at Beverly Hills

$$$ | **HOTEL** | Cosmopolitan and chic, the London West Hollywood is known for its large suites, rooftop pool with citywide views, and luxury touches throughout. **Pros:** state-of-the-art fitness center; chef Anthony Keene oversees dining program; 110-seat screening room. **Cons:** too refined for kids to be comfortable; lower floors have mundane views; spa and restaurant are pricey. $ *Rooms from:*

$350 ✉ *1020 N. San Vicente Blvd., West Hollywood* ☎ *310/854–1111* ⊕ *www.thelondonwesthollywood.com* ⚲ *220 suites* ⏹ *No meals.*

Mondrian Los Angeles

$$$ | **HOTEL** | The Mondrian has a city club feel; socializing begins in the lobby bar and lounge and extends from the restaurant to the scenic patio and pool, where you can listen to music underwater, and the lively Skybar. **Pros:** acclaimed Skybar on property; flirty social scene; double-paned windows keep out noise. **Cons:** pricey valet parking; late-night party scene not for everyone; Alice in Wonderland theme might be too much for some. $ *Rooms from: $300* ✉ *8440 Sunset Blvd., West Hollywood* ☎ *323/650–8999, 800/606–6090* ⊕ *www.mondrianhotel. com* ⚲ *236 rooms* ⏹ *No meals.*

Palihotel Melrose Avenue

$$ | **HOTEL** | A mostly young and creative clientele flocks here, to one of the only boutique hotels on Melrose Avenue. **Pros:** great decor; walking distance to Melrose shops and restaurants; cheap bike rentals ($20/day). **Cons:** no gym, spa, or pool; neighborhood can be sketchy at night; need to request alarm clocks and phones from front desk. $ *Rooms from: $200* ✉ *7950 Melrose Ave., West Hollywood* ☎ *323/272–4588* ⊕ *www.pali-hotel.com* ⚲ *33 rooms* ⏹ *No meals.*

★ Sunset Marquis Hotel and Villas

$$$ | **HOTEL** | If you're in town to cut your new hit single, you'll appreciate this near-the-Strip hidden retreat in the heart of WeHo, with two on-site recording studios. **Pros:** favorite among rock stars; 53 villas with lavish extras like completely soundproof rooms; exclusive Bar 1200. **Cons:** rooms can feel dark; small balconies; vibe can feel too exclusive. $ *Rooms from: $365* ✉ *1200 N. Alta Loma Rd., West Hollywood* ☎ *310/657–1333, 800/858–9758* ⊕ *www.sunsetmarquis.com* ⚲ *152 rooms* ⏹ *No meals.*

Sunset Tower Hotel

$$$ | HOTEL | A 1929 art deco landmark, this boutique hotel on the Sunset Strip brings out as many locals as it does tourists. **Pros:** incredible city views; Tower Bar, a favorite of Hollywood's elite; exclusive spa favored by locals. **Cons:** wedged into the Strip, so the driveway is a challenge; small standard rooms; parts of the hotel feel dated. $ *Rooms from: $400* ✉ *8358 Sunset Blvd., West Hollywood* ☎ *323/654–7100* ⊕ *www.sunsettowerhotel.com* ⇗ *81 rooms* ⦿ *No meals.*

West Hollywood EDITION

$$$$ | HOTEL | Fans of EDITION hotels from around the world will find a lot to love at this Sunset Strip iteration, thanks to its chic space and minimalist vibe, complete with pool table and hopping bar in the lobby. **Pros:** exceptional rooftop pool; fun social scene; great location on the Sunset Strip. **Cons:** expensive parking; high room prices; might be too party-friendly for some. $ *Rooms from: $450* ✉ *9040 W. Sunset Blvd., West Hollywood* ☎ *310/953–9899* ⊕ *www.marriott.com/hotels/travel/laxeb-the-west-hollywood-edition* ⇗ *190 rooms.*

ⓨ Nightlife

Gay or straight, head to West Hollywood if you're looking for a party-loving crowd. This town has plenty of bars and clubs within walking distance, so you can hop around easily. Santa Monica Boulevard has everything from low-key sports bars to trendy clubs with raised dancing platforms.

★ The Abbey

BARS/PUBS | The Abbey in West Hollywood is one of the most famous gay bars in the world. And rightfully so. Seven days a week, a mixed and very good-looking crowd comes to eat, drink, dance, and flirt. Creative cocktails are whipped up by buff bartenders with a bevy of theme nights and parties each day. ✉ *692 N. Robertson Blvd., West Hollywood* ☎ *310/289–8410* ⊕ *www.theabbeyweho.com.*

Barney's Beanery

BARS/PUBS | Open since 1920, Barney's Beanery is an iconic spot along the original Route 66 that drew legendary regulars Janis Joplin and Jim Morrison (among others) to its doorstep. There's an extensive menu, but all anyone talks about is the famous chili and the list of more than 85 beers. There are plenty of distractions, including three pool tables, a foosball table, and arcade games. ✉ *8447 Santa Monica Blvd., West Hollywood* ☎ *323/654–2287* ⊕ *www.barneysbeanery.com.*

Comedy Store

COMEDY CLUBS | Three stages give seasoned and unseasoned comedians a place to perform and try out new material, with big-name performers dropping by just for fun. The front bar along Sunset Boulevard is a popular hangout after or between shows, oftentimes with that night's comedians mingling with fans. ✉ *8433 Sunset Blvd., West Hollywood* ☎ *323/650–6268* ⊕ *www.thecomedystore.com.*

Delilah

THEMED ENTERTAINMENT | Reservations are definitely required for this swanky, New York-style space in West Hollywood. Waiters in white coats serve a mix of upscale American cuisine, but the true reason to come happens a little later when live jazz and burlesque dancers turn the night into a sultry singles scene that's visited by the who's who of Hollywood celebrity royalty. ✉ *7969 Santa Monica Blvd., West Hollywood* ☎ *323/745–0600* ⊕ *www.delilahla.com.*

Employees Only

BARS/PUBS | If you're looking for the best cocktail program in L.A., you'll find it at Employees Only. This very chic spot is a sister of the New York original and is consistently awarded worldwide for its delicious drinks. At this iteration,

Legendary music venue the Troubadour is still a great place to see live music.

there are various themed nights with burlesque on Saturday and sporadic live music. In the back is a speakeasy called Harry's, which is a more intimate space where you can get up close and personal with the master barkeeps to tailor you the perfect drink. ☒ *7953 Santa Monica Blvd., West Hollywood* ☎ *323/536–9045* ⊕ *www.employeesonlyla.com.*

Hollywood Improv
COMEDY CLUBS | Arguably the best comedy club in the city, set apart from its competitors on the Sunset Strip, the Hollywood Improv (which is not technically in Hollywood) is known to bring in heavy-hitting A-list comics that range from Craig Robinson and Bob Saget to Maria Bamford and Whitney Cummings. Don't be surprised if major stars like Dave Chappelle pop in to try out a set. The club features theme nights throughout the week, so check the schedule online. ☒ *8162 Melrose Ave., West Hollywood* ☎ *323/651–2583* ⊕ *www.improv. com/hollywood.*

Jones
BARS/PUBS | Italian food and serious cocktails are the mainstays at Jones. Whiskey is a popular choice for the classic cocktails, but the bartenders also do up martinis properly (read: strong). The Beggar's Banquet is their version of happy hour (10 pm to 2 am, Sunday through Thursday), with specials on drinks and pizza. ☒ *7205 Santa Monica Blvd., West Hollywood* ☎ *323/850–1726* ⊕ *www. joneshollywood.com.*

Laugh Factory
COMEDY CLUBS | Top stand-up comics regularly appear at this Sunset Boulevard mainstay, often working out the kinks in new material in advance of national tours. Stars such as Tiffany Haddish and Kevin Nealon sometimes drop by unannounced, and theme nights like Midnight Madness and Chocolate Sundaes are extremely popular, with comics performing more daring sets. ☒ *8001 W. Sunset Blvd., West Hollywood* ☎ *323/656–1336* ⊕ *www.laughfactory.com.*

Rainbow Bar and Grill

BARS/PUBS | Its location next door to a long-running music venue, the Roxy, helped cement this bar and restaurant's status as a legendary watering hole for musicians (as well as their entourages and groupies). The Who, Guns N' Roses, Poison, Kiss, and many others have all passed through the doors. Expect a $5–$10 cover, but you'll get the money back in drink tickets or a food discount. ✉ *9015 W. Sunset Blvd., West Hollywood* ☎ *310/278–4232* ⊕ *www.rainbowbarand-grill.com.*

Skybar

BARS/PUBS | This beautiful poolside bar is well worth a visit, but it can be a hassle to get into if you're not staying at the hotel, on the guest list, or know someone who can pull strings. The drinks are on the pricier side, but in this part of town that's to be expected, and the views just make it all worthwhile. ✉ *Hotel Mondrian, 8440 Sunset Blvd., West Hollywood* ☎ *323/848–6025* ⊕ *www.sbe.com/nightlife/skybar/los-angeles.*

★ The Troubadour

MUSIC CLUBS | The intimate vibe of the Troubadour helps make this club a favorite with music fans. Around since 1957, this venue has a storied past where legends like Elton John and James Taylor have graced the stage. These days, the eclectic lineup is still attracting crowds, with the focus mostly on rock, indie, and folk music. Those looking for drinks can imbibe to their heart's content at the adjacent bar. ✉ *9081 Santa Monica Blvd., West Hollywood* ⊕ *www.troubadour.com.*

Whisky A Go Go

MUSIC CLUBS | The hard-core metal and rock scene is alive and well at the legendary Whisky A Go Go (the full name includes the prefix "World Famous"), where Janis Joplin, Led Zeppelin, Alice Cooper, Van Halen, the Doors (they were the house band for a short stint), and Frank Zappa have all played. On the Strip for more than five decades, the club books both underground acts and huge names in rock. ✉ *8901 W. Sunset Blvd., West Hollywood* ☎ *310/652–4202* ⊕ *www.whiskyagogo.com.*

🛍 Shopping

West Hollywood is prime shopping real estate. And as they say with real estate, it's all about location, location, location. Here you can find art, design, and antiques stores, clothing boutiques, mega music stores, and specialty book vendors.

Melrose Avenue, for instance, is part bohemian-punk shopping district (from North Highland to Sweetzer) and part upscale art and design mecca (upper Melrose Avenue and Melrose Place). Discerning locals and celebs haunt the posh boutiques around Sunset Plaza (Sunset Boulevard at Sunset Plaza Drive), on Robertson Boulevard (between Beverly Boulevard and 3rd Street), and along upper Melrose Avenue.

The huge, blue Pacific Design Center, on Melrose at San Vicente Boulevard, is the focal point for this neighborhood's art- and interior design–related stores, including many on nearby Beverly Boulevard. The Beverly–La Brea neighborhood also claims a number of trendy clothing stores. Perched between Beverly Hills and West Hollywood, 3rd Street (between La Cienega Boulevard and Fairfax Avenue) is a magnet for small, friendly designer boutiques.

Melrose Place, not to be confused with the cheaper and trendier Melrose Avenue, is an in-the-know haven to savvy Los Angeles fashionistas and a charming anecdote to the city's addiction to strip malls and mega shopping centers. This three-block-long strip, east of La Cienega and a block north of Melrose Avenue, lacks the pretentiousness of Rodeo Drive. Reminiscent of the best of West Village shopping in New York, here haute couture meets pedestrian-friendly, tree-lined walkways.

Finally, the Fairfax District, along Fairfax Avenue below Melrose Avenue, is filled with streetwear shops, trendy restaurants, the historic Farmers Market at Fairfax Avenue and 3rd Street, and the adjacent shopping extravaganza, The Grove. There are also some excellent galleries around Museum Row at Fairfax Avenue and Wilshire Boulevard.

★ American Rag Cie

CLOTHING | Half the store features new clothing from established and emerging labels, while the other side is stocked with well-preserved vintage clothing organized by color and style. You'll also find plenty of shoes and accessories being picked over by the hippest of Angelenos. ⊠ *150 S. La Brea Ave., West Hollywood* ☎ *323/935–3154* ⊕ *americanrag.com.*

Beverly Center

SHOPPING CENTERS/MALLS | This eight-level shopping center is home to luxury retailers like Gucci, Louis Vuitton, and Salvatore Ferragamo but also offers plenty of outposts for more affordable brands including Aldo, H&M, and Uniqlo. Don't miss the bevy of great dining options like Eggslut, an extraordinarily popular breakfast joint; Tocaya Organica, a modern Mexican concept with vegan, vegetarian, and gluten-free options; and Yardbird, a fried-chicken lovers' favorite, plus many, many more. ⊠ *8500 Beverly Blvd., West Hollywood* ☎ *310/854–0070* ⊕ *www.beverlycenter.com.*

Blackman Cruz

ANTIQUES/COLLECTIBLES | Not your grandmother's antiques shop, David Cruz and Adam Blackman's celebrity-loved shopping destination is known for selecting beautifully offbeat pieces (there's no shortage of ceremonial masks and

animal figurines at any given time) as well as fine European and Asian furniture from the 18th to the mid-20th century. ⊠ *836 N. Highland Ave., West Hollywood* ☎ *323/466–8600* ⊕ *www.blackmancruz. com.*

Book Soup

BOOKS/STATIONERY | One of the best independent bookstores in the country, Book Soup has been serving Angelenos since 1975. Given its Hollywood pedigree, it's especially deep in books about film, music, art, and photography. Fringe benefits include an international newsstand, a bargain-book section, and author readings several times a week. ⊠ *8818 Sunset Blvd., West Hollywood* ☎ *310/659–3110* ⊕ *www.booksoup.com.*

Boot Star

SHOES/LUGGAGE/LEATHER GOODS | This huge selection of Western-style boots is heaven for urban cowboys and cowgirls. You can find materials ranging from calfskin to alligator, and most boots are handmade in Mexico and Texas. Custom sizing is available for a guaranteed perfect fit. ⊠ *8493 Sunset Blvd., West Hollywood* ☎ *323/650–0475* ⊕ *www. bootstarusa.com.*

Decades

CLOTHING | A-listers scour these racks for dresses to wear during awards season. Owner Cameron Silver's stellar selection includes dresses by Pucci and Ossie Clark and bags by Hermès. On the street level, Decades Two resells contemporary designer and couture clothing and accessories. ⊠ *8214 Melrose Ave., West Hollywood* ☎ *323/746–0480* ⊕ *www. decadesinc.com.*

★ Fred Segal

CLOTHING | One of the most well-known boutiques in all of Los Angeles, Fred Segal is a fashion design mecca that has been clothing the rich, famous, and their acolytes since the 1960s. Since moving from its original location on Melrose, the flagship store sits atop Sunset Boulevard with more than 21,000 square feet of space that showcases innovative brands and high-end threads. Inside is also Fred Segal Café and Bakery, which offers fashionistas some fast casual fare as they peruse the merchandise. ⊠ *8500 Sunset Blvd., West Hollywood* ☎ *310/432–0560* ⊕ *www.fredsegal.com.*

Golf Wang

CLOTHING | Right in the middle of streetwear haven Fairfax Avenue, Golf Wang stands apart with its avant-garde clothes and accessories created from the mind of rapper Tyler, the Creator. Whether you're shopping for hats, beanies, socks, or even custom skateboard decks, Golf Wang will continuously keep you surprised and delighted with an ever-changing showroom. ⊠ *350 N. Fairfax Ave., Fairfax District* ☎ *No phone* ⊕ *www.golfwang.com.*

Heath Ceramics

CERAMICS/GLASSWARE | This loftlike outpost of the beloved Sausalito-based ceramics company stocks everything from the Coupe Line (created by founder Edith Heath herself in the 1940s) to glass tumblers handblown in West Virginia. Also look for table linens, bud vases, and specialty foods like artisanal jams from Pasadena. ⊠ *7525 Beverly Blvd., Beverly–La Brea* ☎ *323/965–0800* ⊕ *www. heathceramics.com.*

H. Lorenzo

CLOTHING | Funky, high-end designer clothes (Ann Demeulemeester, Walid, and Comme des Garcons, to name a few) attract a young Hollywood crowd that doesn't mind paying top dollar for such fresh finds. Next door, H. Men provides equally hot styles for guys. ⊠ *8660 Sunset Blvd., West Hollywood* ☎ *310/659–1432* ⊕ *www.hlorenzo.com.*

Isabel Marant

CLOTHING | Even before falling for the French designer's effortlessly cool clothing, footwear, and bags (think Paris meets Los Angeles), shoppers will already be enamored of the lush location on fashionable Melrose Place. Inside, the model-favorite destination has a modern rustic vibe, but the outside is a plant paradise, loaded with cacti and succulents. ⊠ *8454 Melrose Pl., West Hollywood* ☎ *323/651–1493* ⊕ *www.isabelmarant. com.*

Jonathan Adler

HOUSEHOLD ITEMS/FURNITURE | For fans of the whimsical NYC-based designer, this West Coast flagship store is the place to be. Midcentury and country-club styles get retooled in playful pottery, cheeky pillows, and graphic textiles. ⊠ *8125 Melrose Ave., West Hollywood* ☎ *323/658–8390* ⊕ *www.jonathanadler.com.*

★ Maxfield

CLOTHING | This modern concrete structure is one of L.A.'s most desirable destinations for ultimate high fashion. The space is stocked with sleek offerings from Givenchy, Saint Laurent, Valentino, and Rick Owens, plus occasional pop-ups by fashion's labels-of-the-moment. For serious shoppers (or gawkers) only. ⊠ *8825 Melrose Ave., West Hollywood* ☎ *310/274–8800* ⊕ *www.maxfieldla.com.*

MedMen

SPECIALTY STORES | The legalization of marijuana in California has led to an explosion of cannabis shops around Los Angeles. One of the most reputable is MedMen, a more refined dispensary that traffics in high-quality buds in a very welcoming environment. Here you can find edibles, vaporizers, concentrates, topical ointments, and more cannabis-laced products. A cannabis shop with a cause, MedMen is also actively involved in criminal justice reform. ⊠ *110 S. Robertson Blvd., West Hollywood* ☎ *323/579–1456* ⊕ *www.medmen.com/ stores/los-angeles-beverly-hills.*

Unique artwork abounds at Melrose Trading Post.

★ Melrose Trading Post

OUTDOOR/FLEA/GREEN MARKETS | Hollywood denizens love this hip market, where you're likely to find recycled rock t-shirts or some vinyl to complete your collection in addition to antique furniture and quirky arts and crafts. Live music and fresh munchies entertain vintage hunters and collectors. The market is held 9 to 5 every Sunday—rain or shine—in Fairfax High School's parking lot and admission is $5. ⊠ *Fairfax Ave. and Melrose Ave., Fairfax District* ☎ *323/655-7679* ⊕ *www. melrosetradingpost.org.*

OK

GIFTS/SOUVENIRS | A classy gift shop, OK stocks items such as Scandinavian stemware and vintage phones; it also specializes in architecture and design books. There's also a second Silver Lake location. ⊠ *8303 W. 3rd St., West Hollywood* ☎ *323/653-3501* ⊕ *okthestore. com.*

Paul Smith

CLOTHING | You can't miss the massive, minimalist pink box that houses Paul Smith's fantastical collection of clothing, boots, hats, luggage, and objets d'art (seriously, there will be hordes of Instagrammers shooting selfies in front of the bright facade). Photos and art line the walls above shelves of books on pop culture, art, and Hollywood. As for the clothing here, expect the British brand's signature playfully preppy style, with vibrant colors and whimsical patterns mixed in with well-tailored closet staples. ⊠ *8221 Melrose Ave., West Hollywood* ☎ *323/951-4800* ⊕ *www.paulsmith.com/ uk.*

Reformation

CLOTHING | Local trendsetters flock here for the sexy, easy-to-wear silhouettes of Reformation's dresses (including a totally affordable bridal line), jumpsuits, and separates—it's a welcome bonus that the pieces here are sustainably manufactured using recycled materials. ⊠ *8000 Melrose Ave., West Hollywood* ☎ *213/408-4154* ⊕ *www.thereformation.com.*

Restoration Hardware

HOUSEHOLD ITEMS/FURNITURE | With 40,000 square feet, this iteration of Restoration Hardware is a beacon for shoppers looking for a curated collection of furniture, rugs, lighting, textiles, bathware, and more. The stunning shop also has an outdoor rooftop park and conservatory with wicker furniture, hanging lights, tea candles, and epic views of the Hollywood Hills. ✉ *8564 Melrose Ave., West Hollywood* ☎ *310/652–0323* ⊕ *www.rh.com.*

Supreme

SHOES/LUGGAGE/LEATHER GOODS | The L.A. location for NYC's premier street-wear brand regularly sees crowds of sneakerheads and skaters, who know that this is the place to get the freshest urban gear around. When new merchandise drops in, lines can easily wrap around the block—but getting your hands on the goods (namely shoes, shirts, outerwear, hats, and backpacks) before anyone else just might be worth the trouble. ✉ *439 N. Fairfax Ave., Fairfax District* ☎ *323/655–6205* ⊕ *www.supremenewyork.com.*

The Way We Wore

CLOTHING | Beyond the over-the-top vintage store furnishings, you'll find one of the city's best selections of well-cared-for and one-of-a-kind items, with a focus on sequins and beads. Upstairs, couture from Halston, Dior, and Chanel can cost up to $20,000. ✉ *334 S. La Brea Ave., Beverly–La Brea* ☎ *323/937–0878* ⊕ *www.thewaywewore.com.*

Chapter 6

HOLLYWOOD AND THE STUDIOS

Updated by
Michelle Rae Uy

	🍽 Restaurants	🛏 Hotels	🛍 Shopping	▼ Nightlife
★★★★★	★★★☆☆	★★★☆☆	★★★☆☆	★★★☆☆

NEIGHBORHOOD SNAPSHOT

TOP EXPERIENCES

■ **See the studios:** Catch a glimpse of movie magic in action at Paramount Pictures, Warner Bros. Studios, and Universal Studios Hollywood.

■ **Walk in famous footsteps:** Outside the TCL Chinese Theatre are footprints of more than 200 of the silver screen's biggest stars. The Hollywood Walk of Fame has stars honoring more than 2,500 of the entertainment industry's most famous on its sidewalks.

■ **Picnic at the Hollywood Bowl:** Even if you don't get tickets for a show, stop at this L.A. landmark just north of Hollywood Boulevard for a great outdoor meal.

■ **Check out Hollywood memorabilia:** The Hollywood Museum has an incredible collection of Tinseltown's most glamorous costumes, photos, and more.

QUICK BITES

Luv2eat Thai Bistro. Thai food is a work of art at this Sunset Boulevard eatery. The casual spot serves the greatest hits, from Isan sausages to a soulful tom kha soup. ✉ 6660 Sunset Blvd. ⊕ www.luv2eatthai.com

Pig 'n Whistle. During Hollywood's heyday, the Pig 'n Whistle was the place to stop for a bite before or after seeing a movie in the neighboring Egyptian Theatre. You can expect overstuffed booths, dramatic paneled ceilings, and attentive service. ✉ 6714 Hollywood Blvd. ⊕ pignwhistlehollywood.com

25 Degrees. Proudly serving its signature burgers, fries, and shakes, 25 Degrees has one of the best burgers in town. Located in the Roosevelt Hotel, the round-the-clock eatery exudes a bit of the old Hollywood glamour while putting a modern spin on the classic burger joint. ✉ 7000 Hollywood Blvd. ⊕ www.thehollywoodroosevelt.com/about/food-drink/25-degrees

GETTING HERE

■ Traffic jams on the Hollywood Freeway (U.S. 101/Highway 170), San Diego Freeway (I–405), and Ventura Freeway (U.S. 101/Highway 134) can make for lengthy trips to or from the Valley. The best way to get from Hollywood to Burbank is to skip the freeways and take Hollywood Boulevard to Cahuenga Boulevard heading north, and take a right on Barham Boulevard straight into Burbank. The Metro's Red Line subway makes two stops in the heart of Hollywood: the Hollywood/Vine Station and the Hollywood/Highland Station. This is the easiest way to get to the Valley or to Downtown L.A.

PLANNING YOUR TIME

■ Plan to spend several hours exploring central Hollywood, where you can see the TCL Chinese Theatre and the Walk of Fame. Hollywood Boulevard can be a little seedy, so families might prefer a daytime walk. Later in the evening, you can return to Hollywood for a movie at El Capitan or the ArcLight, or a concert at the Hollywood Bowl. Expect to spend most of a day at Universal Studios Hollywood and CityWalk; studio tours at Paramount and Warner Bros. last up to two hours.

The Tinseltown mythology of Los Angeles was born in Hollywood, still one of the city's largest and most vibrant neighborhoods. In the Hollywood Hills to the north of Franklin Avenue sit some of the most marvelous mansions the moguls ever built; in the flats below Sunset and Santa Monica boulevards are the classic Hollywood bungalows where studio workers once resided.

Reputation aside, though, it's mostly a workaday neighborhood without the glitz and glamour of places like Beverly Hills. The only major studio still located in Hollywood is Paramount; Warner Bros., Disney, and Universal Studios Hollywood are to the north in Burbank and Universal City.

Of course, the notion of Hollywood as a center of the entertainment industry can be expanded to include more than one neighborhood: to the north is Studio City, a thriving strip at the base of the Hollywood Hills, which is home to many smaller film companies; Universal City, where you'll find Universal Studios Hollywood; and Burbank, home to several major studios.

The San Fernando Valley is only a couple of miles north of the Hollywood Bowl, yet some say it's worlds away. Over the hill from the notably trendier areas of Downtown and Hollywood, "the Valley" gets a bad rap. But all snickering aside, this area is home to many of the places that have made Los Angeles famous:

Disney Studios, Warner Bros. Studios, and **Universal Studios Hollywood.**

For newcomers, it's hard to resist the allure of the soundstages and backlots of Tinseltown's studios. Studio tours are the best way for mere mortals to get close to where celebs work. Most tours last at least a couple of hours, and allow you to see where hit television shows are filmed, spot actors on the lot, and visit movie soundstages—some directors even permit visitors on the set while shooting.

Hollywood

Sure, Hollywood's top attractions are a bit touristy—but if it's your first time, you should at least make a brief stop here. Be sure to check out the Hollywood Walk of Fame and catch a movie in one of the neighborhood's opulent movie palaces, such as the TCL Chinese Theatre or El Capitan.

Sights ▼

1 Dolby Theatre **C4**
2 Egyptian Theatre.................. **D4**
3 El Capitan Theatre................. **C4**
4 Guinness World
  Records Museum.................. **C4**
5 Hollywood Bowl **C2**
6 Hollywood Bowl Museum **C2**
7 Hollywood Forever Cemetery **G7**
8 Hollywood Heritage Museum **D2**
9 Hollywood Museum **C4**
10 Hollywood Rock Walk............. **A5**
11 Hollywood Sign **I1**
12 Hollywood Walk of Fame **E4**
13 Hollywood Wax Museum.......... **C4**
14 Pantages Theatre.................. **F4**
15 Paramount Pictures **F8**
16 Ripley's Believe It or Not.......... **C4**
17 TCL Chinese Theatre **C4**

Restaurants ▼

1 APL Restaurant **E4**
2 Cactus Taqueria #1 .... **E7**
3 Gwen............................... **D5**
4 Jitlada............................. **J5**
5 Luv2Eat Thai Bistro **D5**
6 Marouch........................... **J6**
7 Petit Trois **C8**
8 Providence **E8**
9 Roscoe's House of
  Chicken and Waffles **F5**
10 Salt's Cure **C6**
11 Stout Burgers & Beers............ **E4**

Hotels ▼

1 Dream Hollywood.................. **E4**
2 Hollywood Roosevelt Hotel....... **B4**
3 Loews Hollywood.................. **C4**
4 Magic Castle Hotel **C3**
5 Mama Shelter...................... **D4**
6 Moment Hotel..................... **A5**
7 W Hollywood....................... **E4**

Like Downtown L.A., Hollywood continues to undergo a transformation designed to lure a hip, younger crowd and big money back into the fold. New sleek clubs and restaurants seem to pop up every month drawing in celebrities, scenesters, and starry-eyed newcomers to create a colorful nighttime landscape (and some parking headaches).

Many daytime attractions can be found on foot around the home of the Academy Awards at the **Dolby Theatre,** part of the Hollywood & Highland entertainment complex. The adjacent **TCL Chinese Theatre** delivers silver-screen magic with its iconic facade and ornate interiors from a bygone era. A shining example of a successful Hollywood revival can be seen and experienced just across Hollywood Boulevard at the 1926 **El Capitan Theatre,** which offers live stage shows and a Wurlitzer organ concert before select movie engagements.

Walk the renowned **Hollywood Walk of Fame** to find your favorite celebrities, and you can encounter derelict diversions literally screaming for your attention (and dollar), numerous panhandlers, and an occasional costumed superhero not sanctioned by Marvel Comics. At Sunset and Vine, a developer-interpreted revival with sushi, stars, and swank condos promises to continue the ongoing renovations of the area. In summer, visit the crown jewel of Hollywood, the **Hollywood Bowl,** which features shows by the Los Angeles Philharmonic and many guest stars.

 ## Sights

Dolby Theatre

ARTS VENUE | More than just a prominent fixture on Hollywood Boulevard, the Dolby Theatre has a few accolades under its belt as well, most notably as home to the Academy Awards. The theater is the blend of the traditional and the modern, where an exquisite classical design inspired by the grand opera houses of Europe meets a state-of-the-art sound and technical system for an immersive, theatrical experience. Watch a concert or a show here to experience it fully, but before you do, take a tour for an informative, behind-the-scenes look and to step into the VIP lounge where celebrities rub elbows on the big night. ⊠ *6801 Hollywood Blvd., Hollywood* ☎ *323/308–6300* ⊕ *www.dolbytheatre.com* 🎟 *Tour $25.*

Egyptian Theatre

ARTS VENUE | Built by Sid Grauman, who also constructed the TCL Chinese Theatre, this Hollywood Boulevard movie house is famed not only for its Egyptian theme, complete with hieroglyphs and carvings, but also for being the venue of Hollywood's first-ever movie premiere. Currently, it hosts many of the American Cinematheque's classic film screenings. ⊠ *6712 Hollywood Blvd., Hollywood* ☎ *323/461–2020* ⊕ *www.americancinemathequecalendar.com* ☞ *Check website for tickets.*

El Capitan Theatre

ARTS VENUE | A classic movie palace built in 1926 and Los Angeles's first home of spoken drama, the El Capitan Theatre boasts two different architectural styles—the Spanish Colonial look of its facade and storm lobby, and the East Indian Revival style of its interior. Having survived several transformations, it has been restored to almost exactly how it looked in 1926 when Disney bought it in the 1980s. The theater is the grand venue for all Disney movie premieres, during which movie fans can watch celebrities walk the red carpet on Hollywood Boulevard. On a regular day, pop in to see a movie, as they always have something special in store for their showings. ⊠ *6838 Hollywood Blvd., Hollywood* ☎ *800/347–6396* ⊕ *elcapitantheatre.com.*

Guinness World Records Museum

MUSEUM | While there are several Guinness World Records Museum locations across the globe, popping into the location in Hollywood is a fun, little side trip of the record-breaking, albeit kitschy, kind. Besides its weird and interactive exhibits like those of the most tattooed lad and the world's heaviest man, it's also chock full of informative details and trivia, not to mention Hollywood-themed and movie-related facts. ⊠ *6764 Hollywood Blvd., Hollywood* ☎ *323/463–6433* ⊕ *www.guinnessmuseumhollywood.com* ☒ *$26.*

★ Hollywood Bowl

ARTS VENUE | For those seeking a quintessential Los Angeles experience, a concert on a summer night at the Bowl, the city's iconic outdoor venue, is unsurpassed. The Bowl has presented world-class performers since it opened in 1920. The L.A. Philharmonic plays here from June to September; its performances and other events draw large crowds. Parking is limited near the venue, but there are additional remote parking locations serviced by shuttles. You can bring food and drink to any event, which Angelenos often do, though you can only bring alcohol when the L.A. Phil is performing. (Bars sell alcohol at all events, and there are dining options.) It's wise to bring a jacket even if daytime temperatures have been warm—the Bowl can get quite chilly at night. ■**TIP→ Visitors can sometimes watch the L.A. Phil practice for free, usually on a weekday; call ahead for times.** ⊠ *2301 Highland Ave., Hollywood* ☎ *323/850–2000* ⊕ *www.hollywoodbowl. com.*

Hollywood Bowl Museum

MUSEUM | Originally the tearoom for the Hollywood Bowl, this unassuming, two-story museum not only recounts the history of one of L.A.'s most renowned landmarks, but also commemorates some of the major and unforgettable performances that have taken place here. While the second floor mostly touts temporary exhibits, the first floor boasts permanent displays, a few of which are interactive. A quick visit to this museum is a definite must whether you're a musicophile or you're coming to see a performance at the Hollywood Bowl. ⊠ *2301 N. Highland Ave., Hollywood* ☎ *323/850–2058* ⊕ *www.hollywoodbowl. com/visit/hollywood-bowl-museum* ☒ *Free* ☉ *Closed Sat.–Mon. during off-season.*

★ Hollywood Forever Cemetery

CEMETERY | One of the many things that makes this cemetery in the middle of Hollywood so fascinating is that it's the final resting place of many of the Hollywood greats, from directors like Cecil B. DeMille and actors like Douglas Fairbanks and Judy Garland to musicians like Johnny Ramone. Beyond its famous residents, however, the Hollywood Forever Cemetery is also frequented for its serene grounds peppered with intricately designed tombstones, not to mention by cinephiles in the summer and fall months for the outdoor movie screenings that take place under the stars on the Fairbanks Lawn. If you're looking for both tourist and local experiences while in town, this sight lets you tick off both in one visit. ⊠ *6000 Santa Monica Blvd., Hollywood* ☎ *323/706–4826* ⊕ *www.hollywoodforever.com* ☒ *Free; check online for film screenings.*

Hollywood Heritage Museum

MUSEUM | This unassuming building across from the Hollywood Bowl is a treasure trove of memorabilia from the earliest days of Hollywood filmmaking, including a thorough look back at Cecil B. DeMille's starry career. Large sections of the original stone statues from *The Ten Commandments* lay like fallen giants among smaller items in glass cases around the perimeter of this modest museum. A documentary tracking

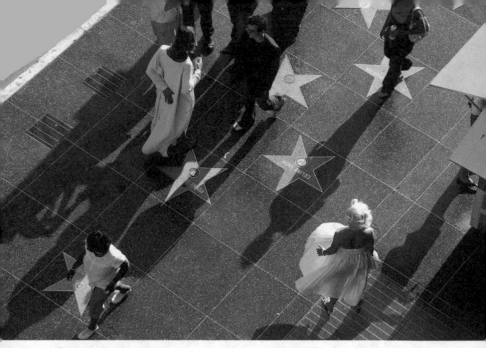

There are more than 2,500 stars honored on the Hollywood Walk of Fame.

Hollywood's golden era is worth taking in. The building itself is the restored Lasky-DeMille Barn, designated a California State Historic Landmark in 1956. ✉ *2100 N. Highland Ave., Hollywood* ☎ *323/874–2276* ⊕ *www.hollywoodheritage.org* 🖃 *$7* ⊙ *Closed weekdays.*

★ Hollywood Museum

MUSEUM | Don't let its kitschy facade turn you off: the Hollywood Museum, nestled at the busy intersection of Hollywood and Highland, is worth it, especially for film aficionados. A museum deserving of its name, it boasts an impressive collection of exhibits from the moviemaking world, spanning several film genres and eras. Start in its pink, art deco lobby where the Max Factor exhibit pays tribute to the cosmetics company's pivotal role in Hollywood, make your way to the dark basement, where the industry's penchant for the macabre is on full display, and wrap up your visit by admiring Hollywood's most famous costumes and set props on the top floor. ✉ *1660 N. Highland Ave., at Hollywood Blvd., Hollywood* ☎ *323/464–7776* ⊕ *www.the-hollywoodmuseum.com* 🖃 *$15* ⊙ *Closed Mon. and Tues.*

Hollywood RockWalk

LOCAL INTEREST | Providing equipment for countless Los Angeles bands since the 1960s, Guitar Center pays tribute to its rock-star clientele with the Hollywood RockWalk in front of the building. The concrete slabs are imprinted with the talented hands of Van Halen, Bonnie Raitt, Chuck Berry, Dick Dale, Def Leppard, Carlos Santana, KISS, and others. Two standouts are Joey Ramone's upside-down hand and Lemmy of Motörhead's "middle finger salute." The store's mini-museum displays signed sheet music and memorabilia like Bob Dylan's hat and harmonica. ✉ *Guitar Center, 7425 W. Sunset Blvd., Hollywood* ☎ *323/874–1060* ⊕ *www.rockwalk.com* 🖃 *Free.*

★ Hollywood Sign

LOCAL INTEREST | With letters 50 feet tall, Hollywood's trademark sign can be spotted from miles away. The icon, which originally read "Hollywoodland," was erected in the Hollywood Hills in 1923 to advertise a segregated housing development and was outfitted with 4,000 light bulbs. In 1949 the "land" portion of the sign was taken down. By 1973 the sign had earned landmark status, but because the letters were made of wood, its longevity came into question. A makeover project was launched and the letters were auctioned off (rocker Alice Cooper bought an "O" and singing cowboy Gene Autry sponsored an "L") to make way for a new sign made of sheet metal. Inevitably, the sign has drawn pranksters who have altered it over the years, albeit temporarily, to spell out "Hollyweed" (in the 1970s, to push for more lenient marijuana laws), "Go Navy" (before a Rose Bowl game), and "Perotwood" (during businessman Ross Perot's 1992 presidential bid). A fence and surveillance equipment have since been installed to deter intruders, but another vandal managed to pull the "Hollyweed" prank once again in 2017 after Californians voted to make recreational use of marijuana legal statewide. And while it's still very illegal to get anywhere near the sign, several area hikes will get you as close as possible for some photo ops; you can hike just over 6 miles up behind the sign via the Brush Canyon trail for epic views, especially at sunset. ⚠ **Use caution if driving up to the sign on residential streets; many cars speed around the blind corners.** ✉ *Griffith Park, Mt. Lee Dr., Hollywood* ⊕ *www.hollywoodsign.org.*

Hollywood Walk of Fame

LOCAL INTEREST | Along Hollywood Boulevard (and part of Vine Street) runs a trail of affirmations for entertainment-industry overachievers. On this mile-long stretch of sidewalk, inspired by the concrete handprints in front of TCL Chinese Theatre, names are embossed in brass, each at the center of a pink star embedded in dark gray terrazzo. They're not all screen deities; many stars commemorate people who worked in a technical field, such as sound or lighting. The first eight stars were unveiled in 1960 at the northwest corner of Highland Avenue and Hollywood Boulevard: Olive Borden, Ronald Colman, Louise Fazenda, Preston Foster, Burt Lancaster, Edward Sedgwick, Ernest Torrence, and Joanne Woodward (some of these names have stood the test of time better than others). Since then, more than 2,000 others have been immortalized, though that honor doesn't come cheap—upon selection by a special committee, the personality in question (or more likely his or her movie studio or record company) pays about $30,000 for the privilege. To aid you in spotting celebrities you're looking for, stars are identified by one of five icons: a motion-picture camera, a radio microphone, a television set, a record, or a theatrical mask. ✉ *Hollywood Blvd. and Vine St., Hollywood* ⊕ *www.walkoffame. com.*

Hollywood Wax Museum

MUSEUM | If a walk through Hollywood hasn't yielded any star-spotting, head over to this venerable icon of a museum, which has been open continuously since 1965. Get up close and personal with your favorite celebrity and experience re-created scenes from classic films, such as Katharine Hepburn and Humphrey Bogart in *The African Queen* or Tom Hanks in *Forrest Gump* , as well as the figures from the *Wizard of Oz*. There's an homage to Heath Ledger in *The Dark Knight,* alongside older icons such as John Wayne and Charlie Chaplin. Be sure to walk the red carpet with the latest Oscar stars and, if you're so inclined, creep along the dimly lit "horror chamber" where scenes from popular films of fright are reconstructed. The effect is heightened at night when fewer

You can take tours of several classic Hollywood studios, including Paramount Pictures.

visitors are around. ✉ *6767 Hollywood Blvd., Hollywood* ☎ *323/462–5991* ⊕ *www.hollywoodwaxmuseum.com* 🎟 *$30*.

Pantages Theatre

ARTS VENUE | Besides being home to the Academy Awards for a decade in the '50s, this stunning art deco–style theater near Hollywood and Vine has been playing host to many of the musical theater world's biggest and greatest productions, from the classics like *Cats*, *West Side Story*, and *Phantom of the Opera* to modern hits like *Hamilton* and *Wicked*. During your Los Angeles jaunt, see a show or two in order to really experience its splendor. While guided tours are not being offered to the public, an annual open house is available to season pass holders for an exclusive and informative tour of the theater and its history. ✉ *6233 Hollywood Blvd., Hollywood* ☎ *323/468–1770* ⊕ *www.broadwayinhollywood.com.*

★ Paramount Pictures

FILM STUDIO | With a history dating to the early 1920s, the Paramount lot was home to some of Hollywood's most luminous stars, including Mary Pickford, Rudolph Valentino, Mae West, Marlene Dietrich, and Bing Crosby. Director Cecil B. DeMille's base of operations for decades, Paramount offers probably the most authentic studio tour, giving you a real sense of the film industry's history. This is the only major studio from film's golden age left in Hollywood—all the others are now in Burbank, Universal City, or Culver City.

Memorable movies and TV shows with scenes shot here include *Sunset Boulevard*, *Forrest Gump*, and *Titanic*. Many of the *Star Trek* movies and TV series were shot entirely or in part here, and several seasons of *I Love Lucy* were shot on the portion of the lot Paramount acquired in 1967 from Lucille Ball. You can take a 2-hour studio tour or a 4½-hour VIP tour, led by guides who walk and trolley you around the back lots. As well as gleaning some gossipy history you'll spot the sets of TV and film shoots in progress. Reserve ahead for tours, which are for those ages 10 and up. ■TIP→ **You can be part of the audience for live TV tapings (tickets are free), but you must book ahead.** ☒ *5515 Melrose Ave., Hollywood* ☎ *323/956–1777* ⊕ *www.paramountstudiotour.com* ☎ *$60.*

Ripley's Believe It or Not

MUSEUM | The ticket prices may be a bit steep for these slightly faded relics of the bizarre and sometimes creepy, but where else can you see a bikini made of human hair, a sculpture of Marilyn Monroe made of shredded money, and animal freaks of nature? Whether you believe it or not, it's fun to marvel at the museum's wacky curiosities. ☒ *6780 Hollywood Blvd., Hollywood* ☎ *323/466–6335* ⊕ *www.ripleys.com/hollywood* ☎ *$25.*

TCL Chinese Theatre

ARTS VENUE | The stylized Chinese pagodas and temples of the former Grauman's Chinese Theatre have become a shrine both to stardom and the combination of glamour and flamboyance that inspire the phrase "only in Hollywood." Although you have to buy a movie ticket to appreciate the interior trappings, the courtyard is open to the public. The main theater itself is worth visiting, if only to see a film in the same setting as hundreds of celebrities who have attended big premieres here.

And then, of course, outside in front are the oh-so-famous cement hand- and footprints. This tradition is said to have begun at the theater's opening in 1927, with the premiere of Cecil B. DeMille's *King of Kings*, when actress Norma Talmadge just happened to step in wet cement. Now more than 160 celebrities have contributed imprints for posterity, including some oddball specimens, such as casts of Whoopi Goldberg's dreadlocks. ☒ *6925*

Hollywood Blvd., Hollywood ☎ *323/461–3331* ⊕ *www.tclchinesetheatres.com* ☎ *Tour $20.*

🍴 Restaurants

Hollywood has two faces; while it's a hub for tourists who come here to take photos along the Hollywood Walk of Fame, it is still in touch with its irreverent rock-and-roll roots. The result is a complex dining scene made up of cheap fast food, upscale eateries, and provocative hot spots helmed by celebrity chefs.

APL Restaurant

$$$ | STEAKHOUSE | The Hollywood dining scene tends to be pretty meat-heavy, and Adam Perry Lang's restaurant is one of the highlights of this trend. While the atmosphere is undeniably masculine, from the brown-leather seats and impressive rare whiskey selection down to the hunks of meat themselves, give it a chance, and you'll appreciate its many touches of elegance. **Known for:** perfect T-bone steak; 150-day dry-aged beef; excellent Ceasar salad. ⑤ *Average main: $30* ☒ *1680 Vine St., Hollywood* ☎ *323/416–1280* ⊕ *www.aplrestaurant.com* ◷ *Closed Sun. and Mon.*

Cactus Taqueria #1

$ | MEXICAN | FAMILY | A humble taco shack on the side of the road, Cactus offers up $3 tacos with all types of meat you could imagine, even beef tongue. They also have carne asada and chicken for the less adventurous. **Known for:** California burritos; delicious fries; excellent street-style tacos. ⑤ *Average main: $11* ☒ *950 Vine St., Hollywood* ☎ *323/464–5865* ⊕ *www.cactustaqueriainc.com.*

★ Gwen

$$$ | STEAKHOUSE | A heaven for upscale carnivores, this fine-dining restaurant serves impossibly exquisite dishes in a copper-and-marble setting. Cooking meat is more than an unceremonious,

CAPITOL RECORDS

hypermasculine endeavor here—it's an intricate, delicate art form. **Known for:** perfect steak; duck fat potatoes; strong cocktails. ⑤ *Average main: $25* ⊠ *6600 Sunset Blvd., Hollywood* ☎ *323/946–7513* ⊕ *www.gwenla.com.*

Jitlada

$$ | THAI | Los Angeles is known for wonderful holes-in-the-wall tucked inside tiny strip malls, and family-owned Jitlada is exhibit A. It's churned out delicious, spicy, southern Thai dishes since 2006. **Known for:** coco mango salad; crying tiger beef; huge menu of over 300 options. ⑤ *Average main: $20* ⊠ *5233½ W. Sunset Blvd., Hollywood* ☎ *323/667–9809* ⊕ *www.jitladala.com* ⊘ *Closed Mon.*

Luv2Eat Thai Bistro

$ | THAI | FAMILY | When it comes to Thai food, at least in Los Angeles, it's usually a rule of thumb that the more ordinary a place looks, the better the food. Such is the case of Luv2Eat Thai Bistro, whose kitschy name and food court furnishings hardly hint at the outstanding traditional Thai dishes it serves. **Known for:** jade noodles; northern Thai sausage; some very spicy menu items. ⑤ *Average main: $12* ⊠ *6660 W. Sunset Blvd., Hollywood* ☎ *323/498–5835* ⊕ *www.luv2eatthai.com.*

Marouch

$$$ | LEBANESE | Part of L.A.'s appeal is its eclectic gastronomy scene that boasts a medley of authentic cuisines from all over the world. Just take Marouch, where you can sample traditional Lebanese and Armenian plates prepared just the way they're made 7,500 miles away. Here, chef Sossi Brady has honed the art of creating comforting dishes that will make you feel at home whether you're in Hollywood, Beirut, or Yerevan. **Known for:** great hummus; wood-burning-oven-baked pita bread; delicious shawarma. ⑤ *Average main: $25* ⊠ *4905 Santa Monica Blvd., Hollywood* ☎ *323/662–9325* ⊕ *www.hollywoodmarouch.com.*

Petit Trois

$$$ | MODERN AMERICAN | With a modest, you'll-hardly-notice-it's-there exterior and a small, packed-like-sardines interior, you're likely to have to wait in line to get into Petit Trois. But the wait is worth it for the incredible classic French dishes inside. **Known for:** Big Mec double cheeseburger; trout almondine; cozy atmosphere. ⑤ *Average main: $30* ⊠ *718 N. Highland Ave., Hollywood* ☎ *323/468–8916* ⊕ *petittrois.com.*

★ Providence

$$$$ | SEAFOOD | This is widely considered one of the best seafood restaurants in the country, and chef-owner Michael Cimarusti elevates sustainably driven fine dining to an art form. The elegant space is the perfect spot to sample exquisite seafood with the chef's signature application of French technique, traditional American themes, and Asian accents. **Known for:** fresh seafood; superb chef tasting menu; exquisite dessert options. ⑤ *Average main: $150* ⊠ *5955 Melrose Ave., Hollywood* ☎ *323/460–4170* ⊕ *www.providencela.com* ⊘ *Closed Sun. and Mon. No lunch Tues.–Thurs. and Sat.*

★ Roscoe's House of Chicken and Waffles

$$ | SOUTHERN | FAMILY | Roscoe's is *the* place for down-home Southern cooking in Southern California. Just ask the patrons who drive from all over L.A. for bargain-priced fried chicken and waffles. The name of this casual eatery honors a late-night combo popularized in Harlem jazz clubs. **Known for:** simple yet famous chicken and waffles; classic soul food dishes; eggs with cheese and onions. ⑤ *Average main: $15* ⊠ *1514 N. Gower St., Hollywood* ☎ *323/466–7453* ⊕ *www.roscoeschickenandwaffles.com.*

Salt's Cure

$$ | AMERICAN | FAMILY | Not only a part of the California gastronomy scene, Salt's Cure celebrates it by keeping all its ingredients locally sourced and home-grown. The former WeHo spot comes

Local Chains Worth Indulging In

It's said that the drive-in burger joint was invented in L.A., probably to meet the demands of an ever-mobile car culture. Burger aficionados line up at all hours outside **In-N-Out Burger** (⊕ *www.in-n-out.com, multiple locations*), still a family-owned operation whose terrific made-to-order burgers are revered by Angelenos. Visitors may recognize the chain as the infamous spot where Paris Hilton got nabbed for drunk driving, but locals are more concerned with getting their burger fix off the "secret" menu, with variations like "Animal Style" (mustard-grilled patty with grilled onions and extra spread), a "4 x 4" (four burger patties and four cheese slices, for big eaters), or the bunless "Protein Style" that comes wrapped in a bib of lettuce. Go online for a list of every "secret" menu item.

Tommy's is best known for its delightfully sloppy chili burger. Visit its no-frills original location (✉ *2575 Beverly Blvd., Los Angeles* ☎ *213/389–9060*)—a culinary landmark. For rotisserie chicken that will make you forget the Colonel altogether, head to **Zankou Chicken** (✉ *5065 Sunset Blvd., Hollywood* ☎ *323/665–7845* ⊕ *www.zankouchicken.com*), a small chain noted for its golden crispy-skinned birds, potent garlic sauce, and Armenian specialties. One-of-a-kind sausage lovers will appreciate **Wurstküche** (✉ *800 E. 3rd St., Downtown* ☎ *213/457–7462* ⊕ *www.wurstkuche. com*), where the menu includes items like rattlesnake and rabbit or pheasant with *herbes de Provence*, while health nuts will devour the cuisine at **Lemonade** (✉ *9001 Beverly Blvd., West Hollywood* ☎ *310/247–2500* ⊕ *www. lemonadela.com*), which is known for its seasonally driven menu, pulled straight from L.A.'s farmers' markets.

to Hollywood to prove that despite appearances, Californians love traditional meat-based staples just as much as they love their kale salads and smoothies. **Known for:** oatmeal griddle cakes; hearty sandwiches; all California-grown ingredients. ⑤ *Average main: $15* ✉ *1155 N. Highland Ave., Hollywood* ☎ *323/465–7258* ⊕ *www.saltscure.com* ⊗ *Closed Mon. and Tues.*

Stout Burgers & Beers

$ | **BURGER** | Despite its name, Stout is more than just about beer. Though it does have an excellent craft beer selection and a practically legendary happy hour, this pub-style joint also prides itself on its heavenly burgers, homemade sauces, and (this being Los Angeles) a decent selection of vegetarian and vegan options. **Known for:** Stout protein-style burgers; secret menu; extensive beer list. ⑤ *Average main: $13* ✉ *1544 N. Cahuenga Blvd., Hollywood* ☎ *323/469–3801* ⊕ *www.stoutburgersandbeers.com.*

🛏 Hotels

Dream Hollywood

$$ | **HOTEL** | Drawing from the city's color palette of blues, whites, and oranges, this mid-century modern hotel is certainly dreamy, with a rooftop pool and floor-to-ceiling windows in guest rooms displaying epic views of Hollywood. **Pros:** lovely rooftop pool; some rooms include private balconies; bath amenities from C.O. Bigelow. **Cons:** on the pricey side; surrounding area can be sketchy at night; noise in some rooms. ⑤ *Rooms from: $300* ✉ *6417 Selma Ave., Hollywood* ☎ *323/844–6417* ⊕ *www.dreamhotels.*

com/hollywood/default-en.html ⤵ 178 rooms ☉ No meals.

★ **Hollywood Roosevelt Hotel**

$$$$ | HOTEL | Poolside cabana rooms are adorned with cow-skin rugs and marble bathrooms, while rooms in the main building accentuate the property's history at this party-centric hotel in the heart of Hollywood. **Pros:** Spare Room bowling alley on-site; pool is a popular weekend hangout; great burgers at the on-site 25 Degrees restaurant. **Cons:** reports of noise and staff attitude; stiff parking fees ($45); decor is dated in places. ⑤ *Rooms from: $419* ✉ *7000 Hollywood Blvd., Hollywood* ☎ *323/466–7000* ⊕ *www. hollywoodroosevelt.com* ⤵ *353 rooms* ☉ *No meals.*

Loews Hollywood

$$$ | HOTEL | FAMILY | Part of the massive Hollywood & Highland shopping, dining, and entertainment complex, the 20-story Loews is at the center of Hollywood's action but manages to deliver a quiet night's sleep. **Pros:** large rooms with contemporary furniture; nice pool with great views; Red Line Metro station adjacent. **Cons:** corporate feeling; very touristy; pricey parking ($50). ⑤ *Rooms from: $349* ✉ *1755 N. Highland Ave., Hollywood* ☎ *323/856–1200* ⊕ *www. loewshotels.com/en/hollywood-hotel* ⤵ *628 rooms* ☉ *No meals.*

★ **Magic Castle Hotel**

$$ | HOTEL | FAMILY | Guests at the hotel can secure advance dinner reservations and attend magic shows at the Magic Castle, a private club in a 1908 mansion next door for magicians and their admirers. **Pros:** heated pool and lush patio; central location near Hollywood & Highland; access to fun Magic Castle shows. **Cons:** strict dress code; no elevator; highly trafficked street. ⑤ *Rooms from: $250* ✉ *7025 Franklin Ave., Hollywood* ☎ *323/851–0800, 800/741–4915* ⊕ *magiccastlehotel.com* ⤵ *43 rooms* ☉ *Free breakfast.*

★ **Mama Shelter**

$ | HOTEL | Even locals adore Mama Shelter, one of Hollywood's sexiest boutique hotels, thanks to the rooftop bar populated with beautiful people lounging on love seats, simple affordable rooms with quirky amenities like Bert and Ernie masks, and a down-home lobby restaurant that serves a mean Korean-style burrito. **Pros:** delicious food and cocktails on the property; affordable rooms that don't skimp on style; foosball in lobby. **Cons:** rooms on the small side; creaky elevators; bar and restaurant often get crowded. ⑤ *Rooms from: $159* ✉ *6500 Selma Ave., Hollywood* ☎ *323/785–6600* ⊕ *www.mamashelter.com/en/los-angeles* ⤵ *70 rooms* ☉ *No meals.*

Moment Hotel

$ | HOTEL | Hollywood's best-value property housed in a former motor inn caters to young partygoers, who breeze in and out of the lobby (which doubles as a bar and breakfast lounge). **Pros:** very affordable; fun rooftop bar; free Wi-Fi. **Cons:** not the safest neighborhood for walking at night; tends to draw a partying crowd and thus noise; small-ish rooms. ⑤ *Rooms from: $180* ✉ *7370 Sunset Blvd., Hollywood* ☎ *323/822–5030* ⊕ *themomenthotel.com* ⤵ *39 rooms* ☉ *No meals.*

W Hollywood

$$$$ | HOTEL | This centrally located, ultra-modernly lit location is outfitted for the wired traveler and features a rooftop pool deck and popular on-site bars, like the Station Hollywood and the mod Living Room lobby bar. **Pros:** Metro stop outside the front door; comes with in-room party necessities, from ice to cocktail glasses; comfy beds with petal-soft duvets. **Cons:** small pool; pricey dining and valet parking; location in noisy part of Hollywood. ⑤ *Rooms from: $500* ✉ *6250 Hollywood Blvd., Hollywood* ☎ *323/798–1300, 888/625–4955* ⊕ *www.whotels.com/ hollywood* ⤵ *305 rooms* ☉ *No meals.*

◉ Nightlife

Hollywood is no longer just a tourist magnet. With the renewed interest in discovering Hollywood history, this area is once again a nightlife destination for locals and visitors alike. Its blend of glitz and grime is reflected here in the after-hours scene.

Avalon

MUSIC CLUBS | This multitasking art deco venue offers both live music and club nights. The killer sound system, cavernous space, and multiple bars make it a perfect venue for both. The club is best known for its DJs, who often spin well past the 2 am cutoff for drinks. The crowd can be a mixed bag, depending on the night, but if you're looking to dance, you likely won't be disappointed. Upstairs is **Bardot,** which hosts special events including a free Monday night showcase of up-and-coming artists. ⊠ *1735 Vine St., Hollywood* ☎ *323/462–8900* ⊕ *www. avalonhollywood.com.*

Birds

BARS/PUBS | They call it your neighborhood bar, because even if you don't live in the neighborhood you'll feel at home at this Alfred Hitchcock–themed eatery. Located in Franklin Village, a block-long stretch of bars, cafés, and bookstores, come here for pub food or a cheap poultry-centric dinner. Weekend nights mean cheap beer and well drinks, crowds spilling onto the streets, and a few rounds of oversize Jenga. ⊠ *5925 Franklin Ave., Hollywood* ☎ *323/465–0175* ⊕ *www.birdshollywood. com.*

Blue Palms Brewhouse

BREWPUBS/BEER GARDENS | Even if gastropubs are not your thing, it's still worth checking out this casual joint on Hollywood and Gower if only to get some grub after a concert at the Fonda Theatre or for the great rotating collection of more than 20 draft beers and incredible food. ⊠ *6124 Hollywood Blvd., Hollywood* ☎ *323/464–2337* ⊕ *www. bluepalmsbrewhouse.com.*

Boardner's

BARS/PUBS | Priding itself as one of the last remaining neighborhood bars in Los Angeles's ever-evolving bar scene, Boardner's has maintained its no-nonsense vibe for more than 70 years. Leave your self-importance at the door, order ice-cold beer and hearty mac and cheese, and keep an eye out for any weird apparitions—this place is known to be one of the most haunted spots in the city. ⊠ *1652 N. Cherokee Ave., Hollywood* ☎ *323/462–9621* ⊕ *www.boardners.com.*

Burgundy Room

BARS/PUBS | Around since 1919, Burgundy Room attracts a fiercely loyal crowd of locals, as well as the occasional wandering tourist. The bar is supposedly haunted (check out the Ouija boards toward the back), but that just adds to its charm. Its rock-and-roll vibe, strong drinks, and people-watching opportunities make this a worthy detour on any night out on the town. ⊠ *1621 N. Cahuenga Blvd., Hollywood* ☎ *323/465–7530.*

The Cat and Fiddle

BARS/PUBS | While shuttered for two years in the mid-2010s, the Cat and Fiddle is once again going strong at its new patio location, continuing a tradition started in 1982 by Londoner Kim Gardner and his wife, Paula. For those wanting to just grab a pint and a savory pie or to satisfy their inner anglophile, this pub is the perfect spot. ⊠ *742 N. Highland Ave., Hollywood* ☎ *323/468–3800* ⊕ *www. thecatandfiddle.com.*

★ Dirty Laundry

BARS/PUBS | Tucked away in a basement on the quiet Hudson Avenue, Dirty Laundry is a former speakeasy turned proper cocktail bar with live music and DJs spinning both fresh and throwback music. There's beer on hand, but here, cocktails are king. ⊠ *1725 Hudson Ave., Hollywood* ☎ *323/462–6531.*

The Fonda Theatre
MUSIC CLUBS | Right on the edge of the Walk of Fame, this historic venue was one of the area's first theaters when it opened in the 1920s. The Spanish Colonial–style theater now hosts some of the biggest names in indie music, but don't expect any major acts on the calendar. Drinks are pricey—so grab a cocktail on Hollywood Boulevard before the show—as is parking, which will cost you at least $20 in the adjacent lot. ⊠ *6126 Hollywood Blvd., Hollywood* ☎ *323/464–6269* ⊕ *www.fondatheatre.com.*

Frolic Room
BARS/PUBS | Once frequented by one of L.A.'s most famous sons, Charles Bukowski, the Frolic Room was also owned at one point by Howard Hughes and has served as a filming location for period flicks like *L.A. Confidential*. Despite its impressive history, its down-to-earth atmosphere and proximity to the Pantages Theatre makes it the perfect place to start off your night. ⊠ *6245 Hollywood Blvd., Hollywood* ☎ *323/462–5890.*

★ Good Times at Davey Wayne's
BARS/PUBS | It's a fridge; it's a door; it's the entrance to Davey Wayne's, a bar and lounge that pulls out all the stops to transport you back in time to the '70s. The interior is your living room; the outside is an ongoing backyard barbecue with all your friends. Come early to beat the crowds or be prepared to get up close and personal with your neighbors. ⊠ *1611 N. El Centro Ave., Hollywood* ☎ *323/498–0859* ⊕ *www.goodtimesatdaveywaynes.com.*

Harvard and Stone
MUSIC CLUBS | An interior that's one part industrial, one part mid-century modern, and one part ski lodge plays witness to the coolest live music this side of the city and serves some of the most exquisite cocktails you'll ever try in your life. Of course, if live music isn't exactly your thing, there are also dark, quiet corners where you can enjoy your drinks in peace. ⊠ *5221 Hollywood Blvd., Hollywood* ☎ *747/231–0699* ⊕ *harvardandstone.com.*

Hotel Cafe
MUSIC CLUBS | This intimate venue caters to fans of folk, indie rock, and music on the softer side. With red velvet backdrops, hardwood furnishings, and the occasional celebrity surprise performance—notably John Mayer—music lovers will not only be very happy but will receive a respite from the ordinary Hollywood experience. ⊠ *1623½ N. Cahuenga Blvd., Hollywood* ☎ *323/461–2040* ⊕ *www.hotelcafe.com.*

★ Musso and Frank Grill
BARS/PUBS | **FAMILY** | The prim and proper vibe of this old-school steak house won't appeal to those looking for a raucous night out; instead, its appeal lies in its history and sturdy drinks. Established over a century ago, its dark wood decor, red tuxedo–clad waiters, and highly skilled bartenders can easily shuttle you back to its Hollywood heyday when Marilyn Monroe, F. Scott Fitzgerald, and Greta Garbo once hung around and sipped martinis. ⊠ *6667 Hollywood Blvd., Hollywood* ☎ *323/467–7788* ⊕ *www.mussoandfrank.com.*

No Vacancy
BARS/PUBS | Though at first glance, No Vacancy might boast an air of exclusivity and pretentiousness, its relaxed interiors and welcoming staff will almost instantly make you feel like you're at a house party. You know, the kind with burlesque shows, tightrope performances, a speakeasy secret entrance, and mixologists who can pretty much whip up any drink your heart desires. ⊠ *1727 N. Hudson Ave., Hollywood* ☎ *323/465–1902* ⊕ *www.novacancyla.com.*

Pour Vous

DANCE CLUBS | It feels like you might run into F. Scott and Zelda Fitzgerald while at Pour Vous. After all, this Melrose Avenue cocktail lounge is inspired by Paris at the height of the '20s Jazz Age, from the beaux arts design elements to the black-and-white movies playing out back, where a repurposed train car offers quiet, romantic corners. Soak up those cocktails with a Nutella crepe made fresh out back. ⊠ *5574 Melrose Ave., Hollywood* ☎ *323/871–8699* ⊕ *pourvousla.com.*

Sassafras Saloon

BARS/PUBS | Put on your dancing shoes (or your cowboy boots) and step back in time. The Sassafras boasts not only an oddly cozy, Western atmosphere but plenty of opportunities to strut your moves on the dance floor. Indulge in exquisite craft mezcal, whiskey, and tequila cocktails for some liquid courage before you salsa the night away. ⊠ *1233 N. Vine St., Hollywood* ☎ *323/467–2800* ⊕ *www.sassafrassaloon.com.*

The Spare Room

PIANO BARS/LOUNGES | While your typical Hollywood crowd might be a permanent fixture at this Hollywood Roosevelt cocktail bar, it's still worth a visit for its luscious cocktails, hearty fare, and collection of classic board games. It can get a little too crowded, especially on the weekends, but if you come early, you should be able to admire its art deco appeal and perhaps enjoy a game at one of its two vintage bowling lanes. ⊠ *7000 Hollywood Blvd., Hollywood* ☎ *323/769–7296* ⊕ *www.spareroomhollywood.com.*

Three Clubs

BARS/PUBS | Cocktail bars are a dime a dozen in Hollywood, but there's something about this Vine Street joint that makes patrons keep coming back for more. Maybe it's the down-to-earth attitude, delicious no-frills cocktails, and the fact that a taco stand serving greasy grub is right next door. Come to see one of the burlesque or comedy shows for a full experience. ⊠ *1123 Vine St., Hollywood* ☎ *323/462–6441* ⊕ *www. threeclubs.com.*

★ Tropicana Pool and Cafe

BARS/PUBS | There are a few reasons to spend a bit of time at the Hollywood Roosevelt, and one of them is the Tropicana Pool and Cafe. Despite being set in the middle of Hollywood's mad dash, this surprisingly serene oasis is where California fare meets refreshing tropical cocktails. Though mostly restricted to hotel guests, visitors are welcome (at the hotel's discretion) to take advantage of its bar and kitchen service. ⊠ *Hollywood Roosevelt Hotel, 7000 Hollywood Blvd., Hollywood* ☎ *323/466–7000* ⊕ *www. thehollywoodroosevelt.com/about/ food-drink/tropicana-pool-cafe.*

The Woods

PIANO BARS/LOUNGES | Don't let the forest fairy-tale vibe—one that'll make you think that a woodsman fell in love with a tree nymph and then went on to open a bar—or the baffling strip mall location fool you. When the occasion calls for it, this little dive bar knows how to throw a party and show you a good time with the simple concoction of jukebox music, DJ spins, and signature drinks. ⊠ *1533 N. La Brea Ave., Hollywood* ☎ *323/876–6612* ⊕ *www.thewoodshollywood.com.*

🎭 Performing Arts

Fountain Theatre

THEATER | The multiple award–winning (Los Angeles Drama Critics Circle, NAACP Theater Awards, Ovation Award, to name a few) Fountain Theatre is committed to diverse theater and dance performances. Although the 80-seat venue may be intimate, it's a powerhouse at producing original plays in addition to revivals. ⊠ *5060 Fountain Ave., Hollywood* ☎ *323/663–1525* ⊕ *www.fountaintheatre.com.*

Ricardo Montalban Theatre
THEATER | Live stage and musical performances on the main stage aside, the Montalban has plenty to offer performing arts fans including small film festivals, comedy shows, and outdoor movie screenings on its rooftop. A movie-watching experience here, complete with noise-canceling headphones and comfy blankets, is a quintessentially L.A. experience. ⊠ *1615 Vine St., Hollywood* 🕾 *323/461–6999* ⊕ *www.themontalban. com.*

🛍 Shopping

Browsing Hollywood Boulevard, you'll find a mixed bag of offerings including lingerie, movie memorabilia, souvenir, and wig shops, while the crowd-heavy Hollywood & Highland complex is home to more familiar retailers and eateries.

Outside the main drag, Hollywood has a few other pockets for picking up high-end goods, including La Brea Avenue, where you'll find a handful of design-happy shops. Take a leisurely stroll as you browse upscale clothing, antiques, and furniture stores.

★ **Amoeba Records**
MUSIC STORES | Touted as the "World's Largest Independent Record Store," Amoeba is a playground for music lovers, with a knowledgeable staff and a focus on local artists. Catch free in-store appearances and signings by artists and bands that play sold-out shows at venues down the road. There's a massive and eclectic collection of vinyl records, CDs, and cassette tapes, not to mention VHS tapes, DVDs, and Blu-Ray discs. It's a paradise for both music and movie lovers. ⊠ *6200 Hollywood Blvd., Hollywood* 🕾 *323/245–6400* ⊕ *www.amoeba.com.*

Hollywood Farmers' Market
OUTDOOR/FLEA/GREEN MARKETS | Among L.A.'s many farmers' markets, the Hollywood Farmers' Market is one of the most well known. This family friendly, open-air market, which has been around for almost 30 years, is also the city's largest with more than 150 local producers and farmers touting their seasonal yields every Sunday. Start your day right and stop by to shop organic, locally grown produce, see live music, and sample some delicious California fare. ⊠ *Hollywood ✛ Ivar Ave. and Selma Ave., between Hollywood Blvd. and Sunset Blvd.* 🕾 *323/463–3171* ⊕ *www. hollywoodfarmersmarket.net.*

Hollywood & Highland Center
SHOPPING CENTERS/MALLS | If you're on the hunt for unique boutiques, look elsewhere. However, if you prefer the biggest mall retail chains America has to offer, Hollywood & Highland is a great spot for a shopping spree. The design of the complex pays tribute to the city's film legacy, with a grand staircase leading up to a pair of three-story-tall stucco elephants, a nod to the 1916 movie *Intolerance*. Pause at the entrance arch, called Babylon Court, which frames a picture-perfect view of the Hollywood sign. This place is a huge tourist magnet, so don't expect to mingle with the locals. ⊠ *6801 Hollywood Blvd., at Highland Ave., Hollywood* ⊕ *www. hollywoodandhighland.com.*

Larry Edmunds Bookshop
BOOKS/STATIONERY | Cinephiles have long descended upon this iconic 70-plus-year-old shop that in addition to stocking tons of texts about motion picture history offers film fans the opportunity to pick up scripts, posters, and photographs from Hollywood's golden era to the present. ⊠ *6644 Hollywood Blvd., Hollywood* 🕾 *323/463–3273* ⊕ *www.larryedmunds. com.*

The Record Parlour
MUSIC STORES | Vinyl records and music memorabilia abound in this hip yet modest record store–slash–music lover magnet that also touts vintage audio gear and retro jukeboxes. A visit here

is usually a multihour affair, one that involves more than just browsing through display cases, digging through wooden carts of used vinyls, and playing your picks at the listening station. ⊠ *6408 Selma Ave., Hollywood* ☎ *323/464–7757* ⊕ *therecordparlour.com.*

Space 15 Twenty

SHOPPING CENTERS/MALLS | Trendy retailer Urban Outfitters' first concept store caters to creatives by combining a more intimate shopping experience with a cultural one by way of an adjacent space that regularly hosts art exhibitions, pop-ups featuring local makers, and other interactive events. The structure is also home to other businesses including restaurants and an art gallery. ⊠ *1520 N. Cahuenga Blvd., Hollywood* ☎ *323/465–1893.*

🏃 Activities

★ Runyon Canyon Trail and Park

HIKING/WALKING | Is Runyon Canyon the city's most famous trail? To the world, it just might be, what with so many A-listers frequenting it. Many folks visiting L.A. take the trail specifically for celebrity spotting. But, if that's not something you're into, this accessible trail right in the middle of Hollywood is also a good place to hike, run, see the Hollywood sign, photograph the city skyline, or simply get a bit of fresh air. If you just happen to run into a famous face, well that's just the cherry on the cake. ⊠ *2000 N. Fuller Ave., Hollywood* ☎ *805/370–2301* ⊕ *www.nps.gov/samo/planyourvisit/runyoncanyon.htm.*

Studio City

Ventura Boulevard, the famed commercial strip, cuts through the lively neighborhood of Studio City. This area, located west of Universal City, is home to several smaller film and TV studios.

🍴 Restaurants

The dining scene here continues to grow as restaurateurs realize how many locals are looking for stylish and swanky places to eat. Japanese, Mexican, and Italian eateries can all be found in this dynamic city.

Asanebo

$$$ | **JAPANESE** | One of L.A.'s finest sushi restaurants, Asanebo is an inviting, no-frills establishment serving top-quality sushi and a wealth of innovative dishes to an A-list clientele. The affable chefs will regale you with memorable specialties such as a caviar-topped lobster, succulent seared *toro* (tuna belly), or just simple morsels of pristine fish dusted with sea salt. **Known for:** omakase (chef's choice) dinners; halibut truffle; excellent sushi. ⑤ *Average main: $30* ⊠ *11941 Ventura Blvd., Studio City* ☎ *818/760–3348* ⊕ *www.asanebo-restaurant.com/* ⊙ *Closed Mon. No lunch weekends.*

Firefly

$$$ | **AMERICAN** | One minute you're in an old library quickly converted into a lounge, the next you're in the cabana of a modest country club. Yet Firefly's eclectic design is part of its appeal, and its excellent, if a bit pricey, French-American fare will make you forget all about it. **Known for:** prix-fixe and à la carte dining; reputation as a date spot; seasonal fare. ⑤ *Average main: $30* ⊠ *11720 Ventura Blvd., Studio City* ☎ *818/762–1833* ⊕ *www.fireflystudiocity.com.*

Good Neighbor Restaurant

$ | **DINER** | Its walls may be heavy with framed photographs of film and TV stars, and folks from the biz might regularly grace its tables, but this Studio City diner is every bit as down-to-earth as your next-door neighbor, even after 40-some years. It gets pretty busy, but a plateful of that home cooking is worth the wait; or if you're in a mad dash, grab a caffeine or fruit smoothie fix from the Neighbarista.

Studio City, Universal City, Burbank, and North Hollywood

Sights ▼

1 NoHo Arts District **B1**
2 Universal Studios
  Hollywood **C3**
3 Warner Bros.
  Studios **D3**

Restaurants ▼

1 Asanebo **A4**
2 Bea Bea's **C2**
3 Café Sierra **B4**
4 Centanni Trattoria **E1**
5 Chili John's **C1**
6 Dongpo **C4**
7 Firefly **A3**
8 The Front Yard **B3**
9 Good Neighbor
  Restaurant **B4**
10 Hayat's Kitchen **B1**
11 Los Amigos **D2**
12 Miceli's **B4**
13 Mofongo's **A1**
14 Porto's Bakery **C1**
15 Rodini Park **A1**
16 Spumante
  Restaurant **A1**
17 Summer Buffalo **E1**
18 The Swingin Door
  BBQ **B1**
19 TeaPop **B2**
20 Three Broomsticks/
  Hog's Head **C3**
21 Wasabi at CityWalk **C3**

Hotels ▼

1 The Garland **B3**
2 Hotel Amarano
  Burbank **C2**
3 Sheraton Universal **B3**
4 Sportsmen's Lodge **A4**

Known for: craft-your-own omelet; cottage fries; excellent breakfast food. ⑤ *Average main: $13 ⌧ 3701 Cahuenga Blvd., Studio City ☎ 818/761–4627 ⊕ goodneighborrestaurant.com.*

Miceli's

$$ | PIZZA | FAMILY | If the charming, Italian square–inspired interior doesn't turn you into a sappy mush, then Miceli's musical servers serenading you with Italian opera will. Studio City might not be the most romantic place in L.A., but one dinner at this restaurant might make you feel like you're in a Hollywood version of Rome. **Known for:** specialty pastas; singing servers; touristy crowd. ⑤ *Average main: $21 ⌧ 3655 Cahuenga Blvd. W, Studio City ☎ 323/851–3344 ⊕ www.micelisrestaurant.com.*

Hotels

Sportsmen's Lodge

$$ | HOTEL | FAMILY | This sprawling five-story hotel, a San Fernando Valley landmark just a short jaunt over the Hollywood Hills, has an updated contemporary look highlighted by the Olympic-size pool and summer patio with an outdoor bar. **Pros:** close to Ventura Boulevard restaurants; free shuttle to Universal Hollywood; quiet garden-view rooms worth asking for. **Cons:** pricey daily self-parking fee ($25); not centrally located to other Los Angeles sights; a bit pricey for the area. ⑤ *Rooms from: $249 ⌧ 12825 Ventura Blvd., Studio City ☎ 818/769–4700, 800/821–8511 ⊕ www.sportsmenslodge. com �️ 190 rooms ⎮⍥⎮ No meals.*

Nightlife

Baked Potato

MUSIC CLUBS | Baked Potato might be a strange name to give a world-famous jazz club that's been holding performances of well-known acts (Allan Holdsworth and Michael Landau) under its roof since the '70s, but it only takes a quick peek at the menu to understand. Twenty-four different types of baked potatoes dominate its otherwise short menu, each of which come with sour cream, butter, and salad to offset all that carb intake. ⌧ *3787 Cahuenga Blvd., Studio City ☎ 818/980–1615 ⊕ www.thebakedpotato.com.*

The Fox and Hounds

BARS/PUBS | With bangers and mash, fish-and-chips, and shepherd's pie rolling out of the kitchen and 16 imported draft beers being poured into glasses, this pub is as British as can get—even if football matches share screen time with the NFL and NBA. ⌧ *11100 Ventura Blvd., Studio City ☎ 818/763–7837.*

★ Pinz Bowling Alley

BOWLING | "Bowl. Eat. Drink. Repeat" might be this bowling alley's motto, but thanks to its neon-slash-backlit lanes— each fully equipped with a touch-screen food and drink ordering system—and its very own arcade, Pinz is more than just your typical bowling experience. A few A-list names are among its loyal clientele, but you don't visit for celebrity sightings; all bells and whistles aside, it's a proper bowling alley and you come here to bowl. ⌧ *12655 Ventura Blvd., Studio City ☎ 818/769–7600 ⊕ pinzla.com.*

The Rendition Room

PIANO BARS/LOUNGES | A speakeasy cocktail lounge seems a little out of place in Studio City, especially on a middle-of-the-road commercial strip paved with quaint boutique stores, but the Rendition Room makes it work. It's a member's club with pretty laid-back rules about letting non-members in—so long as there's room, of course. Even as a tourist, you, too, can sample the Rendition's exciting cocktails, crafted by talented mixologists. ⌧ *4349 Tujunga Ave., Studio City ☎ 818/769–0905 ⊕ therenditionroom.wildapricot.org.*

Universal City

Although it has its own zip code and subway station, Universal City, over the hill from Hollywood, is simply the name for the unincorporated area of Los Angeles where Universal Studios Hollywood and CityWalk are located.

👁 Sights

★ Universal Studios Hollywood
AMUSEMENT PARK/WATER PARK | FAMILY | A theme park with classic attractions like roller coasters and thrill rides, Universal Studios also provides a tour of some beloved television and movie sets. A favorite attraction is the tram tour, during which you can duck from King Kong; see the airplane wreckage of *War of the Worlds*; ride along with the cast of the *Fast and the Furious*; and get chills looking at the house from *Psycho*.
■ **TIP→ The tram ride is usually the best place to begin your visit, because the lines become longer as the day goes on.**

Most attractions are designed to give you a thrill in one form or another, including Jurassic World—The Ride and Revenge of the Mummy along with immersive rides like the 4D Simpsons Ride, where you can actually smell Maggie Simpson's baby powder. The Wizarding World of Harry Potter, however, is the crown jewel of the park, featuring magical rides, pints of frozen butterbeer, and enough merchandise to drain you wallet faster than you can shout "Expecto Patronum." If you're in town in October, stop by for Halloween Horror Nights, featuring mazes full of monsters, murderers, and jump scares.

Geared more toward adults, CityWalk is a separate venue run by Universal Studios, where you'll find shops, restaurants, nightclubs, and movie theaters. ⊠ 100 Universal City Plaza, Universal City ☎ 800/864–8377 ⊕ www.universalstudiosholly wood.com ☎ $139.

🍴 Restaurants

Café Sierra
$$$ | SEAFOOD | FAMILY | Don't let the fact that this airy Californian and pan-Asian spot is located inside a Hilton Hotel scare you; Café Sierra has a drool-worthy seafood and prime rib buffet. Lunching here can be a splurge, but it's worth every penny. **Known for:** champagne brunch; Alaskan king crab; live jazz music. ⑤ *Average main: $30* ⊠ 555 Universal Hollywood Dr., Universal City ☎ 818/509–2030 ⊕ www.cafesierrahilton.com.

Dongpo
$$ | SICHUAN | FAMILY | Upmarket regional Chinese cuisine chain Meizhou Dongpo tries its hand at bringing its modern take on authentic Sichuanese cuisine to the area with Dongpo Kitchen, and it's exactly what the CityWalk needed to up its dining game. This bright, contemporary-meets-traditional Chinese restaurant serves delightful, affordable fare right in the middle of a sea of tourists. **Known for:** Dongpo roast duck; Sichuan dumplings; kung pao chicken. ⑤ *Average main: $20* ⊠ 1000 Universal Studios Blvd. V103, Universal City ☎ 818/358–3272 ⊕ www. citywalkhollywood.com.

Three Broomsticks/Hog's Head
$$ | BRITISH | FAMILY | While theme-park food is notoriously bad, the Three Broomsticks and Hog's Head, both at the Wizarding World of Harry Potter, are exceptions. Yes, you have to go into the park itself to grab a bite, but if you happen to be here (which, let's be honest, is probably the only reason you're in Universal City), you should wander in and feast on large helpings of traditional British fare and gulp down frozen butterbeer. **Known for:** pretty good fish-and-chips; iconic butterbeer; ultimate dining mecca for Harry Potter fans. ⑤ *Average main: $15* ⊠ Universal Studios Hollywood, 100 Universal City Plaza, Universal City ☎ 800/864–8377 ⊕ www.universalstudiosholly shollywood.com.

Wasabi at CityWalk

$$ | SUSHI | FAMILY | CityWalk is hardly the epicenter of dining in Los Angeles, but Wasabi is an enjoyable way to transport yourself to Japan. Dine on deliciously creative takes on traditional dishes under the light of traditional Japanese lamps. **Known for:** specialty rolls; beef rib eye teriyaki; garlic edamame. $ *Average main: $16* ✉ *1000 Universal City Dr., Suite 112, Universal City* ☎ *818/763–8813* ⊕ *www.wasabiatcitywalk.com.*

🛏 Hotels

Sheraton Universal

$$ | HOTEL | FAMILY | With large meeting spaces and a knowledgeable staff, this Sheraton buzzes year-round with business travelers and families, providing easy access to the free shuttle that takes guests to adjacent Universal Studios and CityWalk. **Pros:** pool area with cabanas and bar; oversize desks and office chairs in rooms; good for families and visitors to Universal Studios. **Cons:** average in-house restaurant; tourist crowd; chain hotel feel. $ *Rooms from: $250* ✉ *333 Universal Hollywood Dr., Universal City* ☎ *818/980–1212, 888/627–7184* ⊕ *www.sheratonuniversal.com* ⇩ *461 rooms* ⚬ *No meals.*

Burbank

Johnny Carson, host of *The Tonight Show*, used to ironically refer to downtown Burbank as "beautiful," but it's since become one of the area's most desirable suburbs. It's also home to Warner Bros. Studios, Disney Studios, and the Burbank Studios (formerly NBC Studios) and to Bob Hope Airport (BUR), one of the two major airports serving L.A.

👁 Sights

★ Warner Bros. Studios

FILM STUDIO | You don't need to be a big film nerd to appreciate a visit to the Warner Bros. Studios, where you can pretend to be your favorite TV or movie characters, whether at a working replica of Central Perk from *Friends* or via a Sorting Hat ceremony from the Harry Potter movies. You'll also visit backlots and soundstages to see how the magic is made.

If you're looking for an authentic behind-the-scenes look at how films and TV shows are made, head to this major studio center, one of the world's busiest. After a short film on the studio's movies and TV shows, hop aboard a tram for a ride through the sets and soundstages of such favorites as *Casablanca* and *Rebel Without a Cause*. You'll see the bungalows where Marlon Brando, Bette Davis, and other icons relaxed between shots, and the current production offices for Clint Eastwood and George Clooney. You might even spot a celeb or see a shoot in action—tours change from day to day depending on the productions taking place on the lot. ✉ *3400 W. Riverside Dr., Burbank* ☎ *818/977–8687* ⊕ *www.wbstudiotour.com* 🎟 *From $69.*

🍴 Restaurants

Home to movie and television studios, there's a quiet sophistication to this part of town. Great restaurants are tucked away in strip malls and side streets.

Bea Bea's

$ | DINER | Just because Bea Bea's is a no-nonsense kind of place, it doesn't mean the food isn't special. This diner serves breakfast food that is about as close to extraordinary as the most important meal of the day can be. **Known for:** pancakes and French toast; friendly staff; classic diner grub. $ *Average main: $13*

353 N. Pass Ave., Burbank ☎ 818/846–2327 ⊕ www.beabeas.com.

Centanni Trattoria

$$ | ITALIAN | In a city full of adventurous restaurants touting new takes on traditional dishes and swanking about with bells and whistles and stunning interiors, a run-of-the-mill-looking place like Centanni Trattoria might never make it onto the radar. But what this authentic Italian spot lacks in swagger, it more than makes up for in delicious home cooking. **Known for:** pappardelle with white truffle oil; risotto di funghi; great appetizers. ⑤ *Average main: $20* ✉ 117 N. Victory Blvd., Burbank ☎ 818/561–4643 ⊕ www.centannila.com.

Chili John's

$ | DINER | FAMILY | Hearty home-cooking may not be a big part of L.A.'s dining scene, but that doesn't mean you can't have it when you're visiting the city. Tucked in the heart of Burbank, this diner-style spot serves chili everything, from traditional chili bowls to open-faced chili burgers. **Known for:** beef chili; lemon pie; organic and locally sourced comfort food. ⑤ *Average main: $9* ✉ 2018 W. Burbank Blvd., Burbank ☎ 818/846–3611 ⊕ www.chilijohnsofca.com ⊘ Closed Sun.

Los Amigos

$$ | MEXICAN | FAMILY | If you're in the mood for good old-fashioned fun coupled with hearty Mexican fare and delicious margaritas, then you'll want to consider Los Amigos, whose legendary fruity margaritas alone are worth the drive. Pair those with something from the Platillos Mexicanos menu on karaoke night, and you're guaranteed a good time until the wee hours of the night. **Known for:** classic Mexican food; massive portions; casual dining. ⑤ *Average main: $18* ✉ 2825 W. Olive Ave., Burbank ☎ 818/842–3700 ⊕ www.losamigosbarandgrill.com.

Porto's Bakery

$ | CUBAN | FAMILY | Waiting in line at Porto's is as much a part of the experience as is indulging in one of its roasted pork sandwiches or chocolate-dipped croissants. This Cuban bakery and café has been an L.A. staple for more than 50 years, often drawing crowds during lunch. **Known for:** famous potato balls; must-try desserts; fast-moving counter service. ⑤ *Average main: $8* ✉ 3614 W. Magnolia Blvd., Burbank ☎ 818/846–9100 ⊕ www.portosbakery.com.

Summer Buffalo

$ | THAI | While there are plenty of great Thai restaurants in Los Angeles, if you're looking for something a little different, Summer Buffalo isn't just about classic Thai fare. Yes, you'll still find favorites like larb, curry, and pad Thai, but you'll also be able to sample chicken wings that come in four different sauces, including traditional *grapow*. **Known for:** city's best Thai chicken wings; drunken noodles; cozy ambience. ⑤ *Average main: $10* ✉ 449 S. Glenoaks Blvd., Burbank ☎ 818/561–4777 ⊕ www.summerbuffalo.com/burbank.

 Hotels

Hotel Amarano Burbank

$$ | HOTEL | Close to Burbank's TV and movie studios, the smartly designed Amarano feels like a Beverly Hills boutique hotel, complete with 24-hour room service, a homey on-site restaurant and lounge, and lovely rooms. **Pros:** saltwater pool; complimentary bike rentals; comfortable beds. **Cons:** street noise; away from most of the city's action; breakfast not included. ⑤ *Rooms from: $269* ✉ 322 N. Pass Ave., Burbank ☎ 818/842–8887, 888/956–1900 ⊕ www.hotelamarano.com ⇌ 132 rooms ⑩ No meals.

Laurel Canyon and Mulholland Drive 👁

The hills that separate Hollywood from the Valley are more than a symbolic dividing line between the city slickers and the suburbanites; they have a community in their own right and a reputation as a hideaway for celebrities and wealthy creatives.

The 2002 movie *Laurel Canyon* showed the lifestyle of one kind of Canyon dweller—freethinking entertainment industry movers and shakers seeking peaceful refuge in their tree-shaded homes. By day they're churning out business deals and working on projects; by night they're living it up with private parties high above the bustle of the city streets. Landslides can cause road closures in Laurel Canyon, so do some research beforehand.

Drive through Laurel Canyon and you'll pass estates and party pads dating back to the silent film era. If you have time to cruise Mulholland Drive, expect breathtaking views that show the city's serene side.

🍸 Nightlife

Flappers Comedy Club
COMEDY CLUBS | Even though this live comedy club doesn't exactly have as long a history as others in town (it opened in 2010), it's attracted an impressive list of big names like Jerry Seinfeld, Maria Bamford, and Adam Sandler thanks to its Celebrity Drop-In Tuesdays. The food and drinks are good though not great, but you're here for the laughs not the grub. ⊠ *102 E. Magnolia Blvd., Burbank* ☎ *818/845–9721* ⊕ *www.flapperscomedy.com.*

Tony's Darts Away
BARS/PUBS | Pubs serving vegan food aren't exactly a dime a dozen, but it's no surprise you can find one in Los Angeles. Tony's Darts Away is one such place, touting a predominantly vegan menu with dishes tasty enough to satisfy even the most steadfast meat lover. And craft beer lovers will be sure to appreciate the all-Californian craft beer selection. ⊠ *1710 W. Magnolia Blvd., Burbank* ☎ *818/253–1710* ⊕ *www.tonysda.com.*

🛍 Shopping

It's not a major shopping destination, but Burbank has some offbeat shops that are well worth exploring. Given its close proximity to some major studios, the area has a few hidden gems for finding postproduction castaways, like mint-condition designer and vintage clothing.

Magnolia Park Vintage
SHOPPING NEIGHBORHOODS | Melrose Avenue might be Los Angeles's most well-known vintage shopping destination, but to many locals, especially those on the Eastside, Burbank's Magnolia Park is, in many ways, better. Spanning several blocks around Magnolia Avenue, this revitalized area blends vintage, thrift, and antique shopping opportunities with the laid-back small-town vibe that Melrose lacks. Great dining spots and modern coffee shops abound, as well as foot and nail spas for a bit of pampering. ⊠ *W. Magnolia Blvd., between N. Niagara and N. Avon St., Burbank* ⊕ *www.visitmagnoliapark.com.*

North Hollywood

Originally called Lankershim after the family of ranchers and farmers who first settled here, this area took the name North Hollywood in the 1920s to capitalize on the popularity of the city just over the hill to the south. Today, the large and bustling neighborhood serves as the terminus of the Metro Red Line subway, around which the NoHo Arts District thrives.

◉ Sights

NoHo Arts District

NEIGHBORHOOD | In only a few years, North Hollywood's performance arts hub has grown from the residential home of aspiring actors who frequent a few small theaters and several chain restaurants to a completely revitalized district that boasts its own, albeit small, collection of new coffee shops and restaurants, bars serving up craft beer, and colorful street art. ✉ Lankershim and Magnolia Blvds., North Hollywood ⊕ www.nohoartsdistrict.com.

🍴 Restaurants

The Front Yard

$$$ | AMERICAN | FAMILY | Big hotel restaurants are rarely ever good, let alone adventurous with their dishes, but the Front Yard is one of the very few exceptions. The delectable fare here is served in heaps on massive plates and they pretty much let the chef experiment to his heart's content with the specials, most of which are never repeated so regulars always have something new to look forward to. **Known for:** Royale with Cheese; Valley Fried Chicken; fun weekend brunch. ⑤ Average main: $25 ✉ 4222 Vineland Ave., North Hollywood ☎ 818/255–7290 ⊕ www.thefrontyardla.com.

Hayat's Kitchen

$$ | LEBANESE | Sit down here to a table piled high with assorted hot and cold mezes, baba ghanoush, garlic fries, falafel, and kebabs piled on a bed of rice. Fresh, satisfying, and with excellent service, this reasonably priced hidden gem in the Valley is worth the trek over the hill. **Known for:** Lebanese home cooking; delicious appetizers; Kabob-shish Tawook. ⑤ Average main: $16 ✉ 11009 Burbank Blvd., Suite 117, North Hollywood ☎ 818/761–4656 ⊕ www.hayats.kitchen.

★ Mofongo's

$$ | PUERTO RICAN | Mofongo's small storefront represents one of the best and only venues to get authentic Puerto Rican food in L.A. Stop by and try the namesake dish (a delectable mash of fried plantains), but stay for the *pasteles* (cakes) and *rellenos de papa* (stuffed potatoes). **Known for:** mofongo de Pollo Guisado (fried mashed plantains with chicken stew); hard-to-find Puerto Rican food; *flan de queso* (cream cheese flan). ⑤ Average main: $14 ✉ 5757 Lankershim Blvd., North Hollywood ☎ 818/754–1051 ⊕ www.mofongosrestaurant.com.

Rodini Park

$ | MEDITERRANEAN | Nestled in the heart of the NoHo Arts District amid newly minted high-rises, Rodini Park's "build your own" concept and highly rated homemade pastries make it the place to go for a quick, fresh, and delicious take on Greek cuisine. Between the multiple protein, topping, and sauce offerings, it offers something for all palates. **Known for:** chicken shawarma; baklava cheesecake; Mount Olympus sauce. ⑤ Average main: $11 ✉ 11049 Magnolia Blvd., North Hollywood ☎ 818/358–4802 ⊕ www.rodinipark.com.

Spumante Restaurant

$$$ | ITALIAN | The family-owned Spumante Restaurant harkens back to old-school trattorias with its traditional menu,

floor-to-ceiling shelves of wine, white tablecloth settings, and excellent service. Not only are the trappings great, but the prices are reasonable and the food is plenty good, too. **Known for:** lobster ravioli; mustard chicken; classic Italian comfort food. $ *Average main: $23* ✉ *11049 Magnolia Blvd., Suite 7, North Hollywood* ☎ *818/508–7716* ⊕ *www.spumanterestaurant.com* ⊘ *Closed Sun.*

The Swingin Door BBQ

$$ | **BARBECUE** | **FAMILY** | Los Angeles is not known for barbecue so when a place like the Swingin Door does it right, it's worth taking note. Take a gander around and you'll see smokers slowly cooking all that meaty goodness, ready to be enjoyed on plastic-covered tables and doused with a variety of different hot sauces (which you can buy to take home). **Known for:** baby back ribs; assorted hot sauces; rare Tex-as-style barbecue in the city. $ *Average main: $20* ✉ *11018 Vanowen St., North Hollywood* ☎ *818/763–8996* ⊕ *bbqnorth-hollywood.wixsite.com/swingindoor* ⊘ *Closed Mon.*

TeaPop

$ | **CAFÉ** | At first glance, TeaPop may seem to be doing too many things at once, but this tea-centric café, with its art gallery–slash–industrial modern interior and picturesque patio, is a perfect spot to not only study or take a breather, but also to catch pop-up events like comedy nights and workshops. Don't let the hipster vibes turn you off—the service is fantastic and the drinks delicious. **Known for:** vintage milk tea; hipster vibes; community events. $ *Average main: $4* ✉ *5050 Vineland Ave., North Hollywood* ☎ *323/927–0429* ⊕ *teapopla.com* ⊘ *Closed Mon. and Tues.*

 Hotels

The Garland

$$ | **HOTEL** | **FAMILY** | The cool kid of the Valley with a Hollywood pedigree, this 7-acre hideaway was founded by the current hotelier's mother, actress Beverly Garland, who decked it out with a theater, restaurant, and pool to entertain her Industry friends. **Pros:** large pool and play area; private balcony or patio in each room; the Front Yard restaurant is a local fave for brunch. **Cons:** close to the freeway; bar and restaurant close early; far from other major Los Angeles sights. $ *Rooms from: $257* ✉ *4222 Vineland Ave., North Hollywood* ☎ *818/980–8000, 800/238–3759* ⊕ *www.beverlygarland.com* ⤳ *255 rooms* ⦾ *No meals.*

 Nightlife

Catcher in the Rye

PIANO BARS/LOUNGES | The theme of this bar is not specific to Holden Caulfield but rather to literature. Other odes to fictional greats can be found name-checked on the menu, including Huck Finn and Jay Gatsby. Should you have forgotten your book at home, check one out from the bar's bookshelf, or if reading's not your thing (although you might be in the wrong bar), you can grab a board game instead. ✉ *10550 Riverside Dr., North Hollywood* ☎ *818/679–9693.*

The Fifth

BARS/PUBS | Sometimes all you need is a solid dive bar and the Fifth fits the bill. Pool table? Check. Vintage arcade games? Check. Most important, cheap drinks? Absolutely. ✉ *4821 Whitsett Ave., North Hollywood* ☎ *818/856–8006* ⊕ *www.vintagebargroup.com/the-fifth.php.*

The Other Door

BARS/PUBS | The Other Door occupies a strange space, somewhere between a steampunk-themed bar, a dive bar, and a music venue with a varied calendar featuring live music, karaoke, and silent disco. It also has a pool table and a vintage photo booth on hand, in case all these diversions aren't enough to distract you. ✉ *10437 Burbank Blvd., North Hollywood* ☎ *818/508–7008* ⊕ *theotherdoorbar.com.*

🛍 Shopping

Circus Liquor

CONVENIENCE/GENERAL STORES | It might be strange to recommend a liquor store in a travel guidebook, but people come here to nab the perfect Instagram photo. There's a 32-foot neon clown sign outside, which was already L.A. famous but was made even more so by being featured in *Clueless*. And, while here, you might as well pick up some booze. ✉ *5600 Vineland Ave., North Hollywood* ☎ *818/769–1500.*

The Iliad Book Shop

BOOKS/STATIONERY | For over 30 years, Iliad not only has been selling used books but has been a set piece on a number of TV shows and movies, including *Lethal Weapon 3*. But with a collection of 125,000 books of all genres, including a solid selection of graphic novels, it's worth a visit just to peruse the aisles and find your next favorite novel. ✉ *5400 Cahuenga Blvd., North Hollywood* ☎ *818/509–2665* ⊕ *www.iliadbooks.com.*

Midcenturyla

HOUSEHOLD ITEMS/FURNITURE | The idea of going to Los Angeles to buy furniture may sound nuts, but go ahead, indulge your inner designer at Midcenturyla, a curated furniture store brimming with custom and vintage mid-century modern desks, sofas, and more. ✉ *5333 Cahuenga Blvd., North Hollywood* ☎ *818/509–3050* ⊕ *midcenturyla.com.*

Chapter 7

MID-WILSHIRE AND KOREATOWN

Updated by
Paul Feinstein

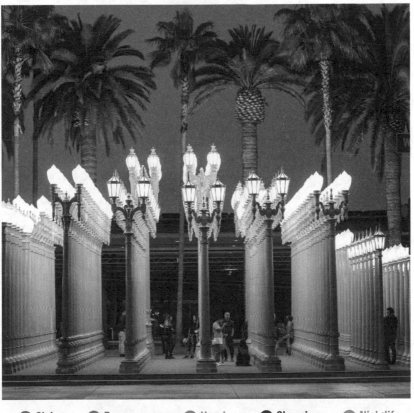

👁 Sights	🍴 Restaurants	🛏 Hotels	🛍 Shopping	🍸 Nightlife
★★★★★	★★★★☆	★★☆☆☆	★★☆☆☆	★★★☆☆

NEIGHBORHOOD SNAPSHOT

GREAT EXPERIENCES

■ **Get cultured on Miracle Mile:** Check out Museum Row, which includes LACMA, the Petersen Automotive Museum, the Academy Museum of Motion Pictures, and La Brea Tar Pits.

■ **Relax at Korean spas:** Whisk yourself away to Seoul at one of several spas in Koreatown, where you can get your scrub on or just lounge away the hours in pools and saunas.

■ **Dine on global cuisine:** Eat Oaxacan food at Guelaguetza, feast on Korean barbecue at Kobawoo House, or chow down on Ethiopian at Meals by Genet.

■ **Find the party:** Hit up the summer pool scene inside the trendy Line Hotel or wander into the Wiltern for a night of live music.

QUICK BITES

KazuNori. Dubbed "the original hand roll bar," here customers can indulge in seaweed-wrapped raw fish from a quick and easy counter. ⊠ *6245 Wilshire Blvd. #101* ⊕ *www.handrollbar.com*

Merkato. A wholly authentic Ethiopian experience, Merkato serves classics like spongy injera bread, spicy beef, and grilled fish. ⊠ *1036 ½ S. Fairfax Ave.* ⊕ *www.facebook.com/merkatoethiopianfood*

Sky's Gourmet Tacos. You'll find some of the spiciest and most succulent tacos in L.A. at Sky's. They also dish out steaming breakfast tacos and have an enormous vegan and vegetarian menu. ⊠ *5303 Pico Blvd.* ⊕ *skystacos.com*

GETTING HERE

■ Mid-Wilshire and Koreatown are in the middle of the city, meaning there isn't direct freeway access. Main thoroughfares include Wilshire, Olympic, and Pico boulevards, but to avoid traffic, try using 6th Street. Luckily, there is also direct Metro access that runs across both neighborhoods with stops at LACMA on the Westside all the way to Wilshire/Vermont on the Eastside. However you get here, remember: parking can be challenging. Side streets are heavily regulated and meters are scarce. There are some public lots, particularly in Miracle Mile, but often it's valet all the way.

PLANNING YOUR TIME

■ Take a full day to tour the Petersen Automotive, LACMA, the La Brea Tar Pits, and the Academy Museum of Motion Pictures. They're all next to each other, making travel between them easy, but check out museum websites for the most up-to-date closing days and times. LACMA is closed Wednesday. Many others close on Monday. Koreatown is the perfect evening spot to grab dinner and drinks and, schedule permitting, a show at the Wiltern.

While they're two distinctly different neighborhoods, Mid-Wilshire and Koreatown sit side by side and offer Angelenos some of the most interesting sights, sounds, and bites in the city.

Mid-Wilshire is broadly known for its wide variety of museums, but there's also a strip called Little Ethiopia, where you can find incredible cuisine. Koreatown, meanwhile, is a haven for Seoul food (pun intended) but also an area with multiethnic dining nuggets that hit the top of many restaurant lists. Once your stomach is sated, check out a Korean spa, where scrubbing and pampering can close out a perfectly long day.

Mid-Wilshire and Miracle Mile

The 1½-mile strip of Wilshire Boulevard between La Brea and Fairfax avenues was bought up by developers in the 1920s, and they created a commercial district that catered to automobile traffic. Nobody thought the venture could be successful, so the burgeoning strip became known as Miracle Mile. It was the world's first linear downtown, with building designs incorporating wide store windows to attract attention from passing cars. As L.A.'s art deco buildings have come to be appreciated, preserved, and restored over the years, the area's exemplary architecture is a highlight. The surrounding Mid-Wilshire area encompassing Miracle Mile includes the notable Petersen Automotive Museum (clad in steel racing stripe ribbons) and the years-in-the-making Academy Museum of Motion Pictures, with its massive spherical extension that beckons visitors to the many wonders of the film industry.

◉ Sights

★ Academy Museum of Motion Pictures
MUSEUM | FAMILY | The long-waited Academy Museum of Motion Pictures sits on the corner of Wilshire and Fairfax, and is highlighted by a giant spherical dome that features a 1,000-seat theater and stunning terrace with views of the Hollywood Hills. Inside, the museum has seven floors of exhibition space that delves into the history of cinema with interactive exhibits, features on award-winning story tellers, multiple theaters, and immersive experiences. Dedicated to the art and science of movies, the Academy Museum is the premier center that is a must-stop for film buffs and casual moviegoers alike. ⊠ 6067 Wilshire Blvd., Mid-Wilshire ☎ 323/930–3000 ⊕ www.academymuseum.org.

Craft and Folk Art Museum
MUSEUM | This small but important cultural landmark pioneered support for traditional folk arts. The two-story space has a global outlook, embracing social movements and long-established trends. It mounts rotating exhibitions where you might see anything from costumes of carnival celebrations around the world to handmade quilts. The courtyard area is a tranquil space often used for opening receptions. The ground-level gift shop stocks a unique collection of handcrafts, jewelry, ceramics, books, and textiles.

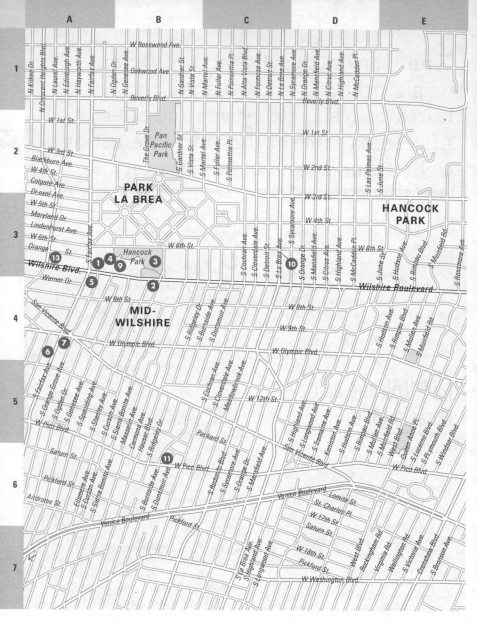

Map Legend

A	
B	
C	
D	
E	

1 W Rosewood Ave.
W Oakwood Ave.
Beverly Blvd.

W 1st St.

Pan Pacific Park

W 3rd St.
Blackburn Ave.
W 4th St.
Colgate Ave.
Drexel Ave.
W 5th St.
Maryland Dr.
Lindenhurst Ave.
W 6th St.
Orange St.

PARK LA BREA

HANCOCK PARK

Wilshire Blvd.
Warner Dr.

W 8th St.

MID-WILSHIRE

San Vicente Blvd.
W Olympic Blvd.

W 9th St.
W Olympic Blvd.

W 12th St.

W Pico Blvd.

Venice Boulevard
Lomita St.
St. Charles Pl.
W 17th St.
Saturn St.

Pickford St.
Airdrome St.

Venice Boulevard
Pickford St.
W 18th St.
Pickford St.
W Washington Blvd.

Mid-Wilshire and Koreatown

F

Clinton St.
N. Arden Blvd.
N. Lucerne Blvd.
N. Lachmont Blvd.
N. Beachwood Blvd.
H. Gower St.
N. Plymouth Blvd.
N. Windsor Blvd.
N. Irving Blvd.
N. Bronson Ave.
N. Norton Ave.

Beverly Blvd.

W. 3rd St.

W. 4th St.

S. Arden Blvd.
S. Lucerne Blvd.
S. Plymouth Blvd.
S. Windsor Blvd.
S. Lorraine Blvd.
S. Irving Blvd.
S. Norton Ave.

W. 5th St.

W. 6th St.

S. Victoria Ave.
S. Cranshaw Blvd.
S. Bronson Ave.
S. Norton Ave.
Country Club Dr.
5th Ave.
4th Ave.
Westchester Pl.

S. Van Ness Ave.

7th Ave.
6th Ave.
5th Ave.
4th Ave.
3rd Ave.
2nd Ave.

W. 17th St.

W. 18th St.

Arlington Ave.

G

Maplewood Ave.
Rosewood Ave
Elmwood Ave.

OAKWOOD

Council St.

W. 1st St.

W. 2nd St.

WILTON DISTRICT
W. 3rd St.

W. 4th St.

W. 5th St.

W. 6th St.

S. Wilton Pl.
S. Gramercy Pl.
S. Saint Andrews Pl.
S. Manhattan. Pl.

Ingraham St.

Leeward Ave.

W. 8th St.

W. 9th St.

S. Wilton Pl.
Gramercy Pl.
S. Saint Andrews Pl.
S. Manhattan. Pl.

James M Wood Blvd.

San Marino St.

W. Olympic Blvd.

W. Pico Blvd.

Venice Boulevard

W. 18th St.

W. Washington Blvd.

H

Clinton St.

N. Oxford Ave.
N. Serrano Ave.
N. Hobart Blvd.
N. Harvard Blvd.
N. Kingsley Dr.
N. Ardmore Ave.
N. Normandie Pl.

Beverly Blvd.

W. 1st St.

W. 2nd St.

S. Western Ave.
S. Oxford Ave.

S. Western Ave.
S. Serrano Ave.
S. Hobart Blvd.
S. Harvard Blvd.
S. Kingsley Dr.

(8)

(12)

Wilshire Boulevard

KOREATOWN

W. 7th St.

W. 8th St.

S. Irolo St.

James M Wood Blvd.

San Marino St.

(3)

S. Oxford Ave.
S. Hobart Blvd.
S. Harvard Blvd.
S. Kingsley Dr.
S. Ardmore Ave.
S. Irolo St.

W. Pico Blvd.

Cambridge St.

S. Ardmore Ave.

S. Oxford Ave.

S. Harvard Blvd.
S. Kingsley Dr.

I

N. Normandie Ave.

M Vermont/Beverly

Council St.

W. 1st St.

W. 3rd St.

S. Normandie Ave.
S. Mariposa Ave.
S. Alexandria Ave.
W. 4th St.

S. Kenmore Ave.

W. 5th St.

(5) (1) (2)

W. 6th St.

(2)

(1)

S. Kenmore Ave.
S. Catalina St.
S. Berendo St.

W. 7th St.

S. Normandie Ave.
S. Mariposa Ave.
Fedora St.

S. Catalina St.

S. Normandie Ave.
S. Mariposa Ave.
Fedora St.
S. Kenmore Ave.
Dewey Ave.
W. 11th St.

W. 12th St.

S. Catalina St.
S. Berendo St.

J

Mid-Wilshire and Koreatown

Vermont/Beverly

Council St.

Shatto Recreation Park

S. New Hampshire Ave.
S. Vermont Ave.

W. 5th St.

Wilshire/Vermont

M

(4)

Leeward Ave.
W. 8th St.
Francis Ave.

San Marino St.

S. New Hampshire Ave.
S. Vermont Ave.
S. Manlo Ave.
S. Westmoreland Ave.
Elden Ave.
Magnolia Ave.

W. Pico Blvd.

ALVARADO TERRACE

	KEY	
(1)	*Exploring Sights*	
(1)	*Restaurants*	
(1)	*Hotels*	
M	*Metro*	

0 —— 2,000 ft
0 —— 500 m

The museum also hosts myriad events from craft workshops and lectures to glassblowing and printmaking. ⊠ *5814 Wilshire Blvd., Mid-Wilshire* ☎ *323/937–4230* ⊕ *www.craftcontemporary.org* ⌨ *$9* ⊗ *Closed Mon.*

La Brea Tar Pits Museum

ARCHAEOLOGICAL SITE | FAMILY | Show your kids where Ice Age fossils come from by taking them to the stickiest park in town. The area formed when deposits of oil rose to the earth's surface, collected in shallow pools, and coagulated into asphalt. In the early 20th century geologists discovered that all that goo contained the largest collection of Pleistocene (Ice Age) fossils ever found at one location: more than 600 species of birds, mammals, plants, reptiles, and insects. Roughly 100 tons of fossil bones have been removed in excavations during the last 100 years, making this one of the world's most famous fossil sites. You can see most of the pits through chain link fences, and the new Excavator Tour gets you as close as possible to the action.

Pit 91 and Project 23 are ongoing excavation projects; tours are offered, and you can volunteer to help with the excavations in the summer. Several pits are scattered around Hancock Park and the surrounding neighborhood; construction in the area has often had to accommodate them, and in nearby streets and along sidewalks, little bits of tar occasionally ooze up. The museum displays fossils from the tar pits and has a glass-walled laboratory that allows visitors to view paleontologists and volunteers as they work on specimens. ■**TIP**➔ **Museum admission is free for L.A. County residents weekdays 3–5 pm.** ⊠ *5801 Wilshire Blvd., Miracle Mile* ☎ *323/934–7243* ⊕ *www. tarpits.org* ⌨ *$15; free 1st Tues. of every month (except July and Aug.) and every Tues. in Sept.*

★ Los Angeles County Museum of Art (LACMA)

MUSEUM | Los Angeles has a truly fabulous museum culture and everything that it stands for can be epitomized by the massive, eclectic, and ever-changing Los Angeles County Museum of Art. Opened at its current location in 1965, today the museum boasts the largest collection of art in the western United States with more than 135,000 pieces from 6,000 years of history across multiple buildings atop over 20 acres. Highlights include the *Urban Light* sculpture by Chris Burden (an Instagram favorite), *Levitated Mass* by Michael Heizer, and prominent works by Frida Kahlo, Wassily Kandinsky, Henri Matisse, and Claude Monet. With an illustrative permanent collection to go along with an ever-rotating array of temporary exhibits, film screenings, educational programs, and more, the museum is a beacon of culture that stands alone in the middle of the city. ■**TIP**➔ **Temporary exhibitions sometimes require tickets purchased in advance.** ⊠ *5905 Wilshire Blvd., Miracle Mile* ☎ *323/857–6000* ⊕ *www.lacma.org* ⌨ *$20* ⊗ *Closed Wed.*

Petersen Automotive Museum

MUSEUM | FAMILY | L.A. is a mecca for car lovers, which explains the popularity of this museum with a collection of more than 300 automobiles and other motorized vehicles. But you don't have to be a gearhead to appreciate the Petersen; there's plenty of fascinating history here for all to enjoy. Learn how Los Angeles grew up around its freeways, how cars evolve from the design phase to the production line, and how automobiles have influenced film and television. To see how the vehicles, many of them quite rare, are preserved and maintained, take the 90-minute tour of the basement-level Vault (young kids aren't permitted in the Vault, but they'll find plenty to keep them occupied throughout the museum). ⊠ *6060 Wilshire Blvd., Mid-Wilshire* ☎ *323/964–6331* ⊕ *www.petersen.org* ⌨ *From $17.*

Learn about the history of cars and check out rare vehicles at the Petersen Automotive Museum.

Restaurants

★ Meals by Genet

$$ | ETHIOPIAN | In a tucked-away stretch along Fairfax Avenue is Little Ethiopia, where Angelenos of all stripes flock for the African country's signatures like *tibs*, *wat*, and *kitfo*. And while there is a plethora of Ethiopian options, no one does the cuisine justice quite like Meals by Genet. **Known for:** authentic Ethiopian cuisine; jovial atmosphere; unreal tibs. ⑤ *Average main: $20* ✉ *1053 S. Fairfax Ave., Mid-Wilshire* ☎ *323/938–9304* ⊕ *www.mealsbygenetla.com* ⊗ *Closed Mon.–Wed.*

Merkato Ethiopian Restaurant and Market

$$ | ETHIOPIAN | For a wholly authentic Ethiopian experience, you can't really go wrong with Merkato. Not only does it serve the classics like spongy injera bread, spicy beef, and grilled fish, but there's also a market where you can buy Ethiopian ingredients to make your own mouthwatering cuisine at home. **Known for:** authentic Ethiopian cuisine; market

products; friendly staff. ⑤ *Average main: $15* ✉ *1036½ S. Fairfax Ave., Mid-Wilshire* ☎ *323/935–1775*.

Ray's and Stark Bar

$$ | AMERICAN | Whether you want to fill up before perusing L.A.'s best art galleries or simply grab a drink to soak in the priceless sculptures at the LACMA, Ray's and Stark Bar is the perfect complement to any museumgoer's experience. Situated just outside the main entrance of the museum, the restaurant/bar offers a variety of Americana cuisine like pizza, burgers, and pastas. **Known for:** good happy hour; fun (dog-friendly) brunch; excellent signature cocktails. ⑤ *Average main: $20* ✉ *5905 Wilshire Blvd., Miracle Mile* ☎ *323/857–6180* ⊕ *www.patina-group.com/rays-and-stark-bar* ⊗ *Closed Wed.*

★ République

$$$$ | FRENCH | FAMILY | This stunning expansive space, originally built for Charlie Chaplin back in the 1920s, serves French delicacies for breakfast, lunch, and dinner every day of the week. The scent of homemade croissants wafts through the building in the morning; steak frites can be enjoyed at night. **Known for:** French classics like escargot; unbeatable pastries; nice bar menu. ⑤ *Average main: $35* ⊠ *624 S. La Brea Ave., Beverly–La Brea* ☎ *310/362–6115* ⊕ *www.republiquela.com.*

Sky's Gourmet Tacos

$ | **MEXICAN** | If you're searching for some of the spiciest and most succulent tacos in L.A., look no further than Sky's. This quaint taco joint offers up beef, chicken, turkey, seafood, and vegan options that will leave your mouth on fire and your belly full in all the best ways possible. **Known for:** amazing tacos with a variety of fillings (including breakfast tacos); lots of spices; jovial atmosphere. ⑤ *Average main: $10* ⊠ *5303 W. Pico Blvd., Mid-Wilshire* ☎ *833/759–8226* ⊕ *www.skysgourmettacos.com.*

Uovo

$$ | **ITALIAN** | It's hard to fathom that the pasta inside this small counter restaurant is flown in weekly from Bologna. But once you take a bite of the perfect cacio e pepe, amatriciana, or tortellini with crema parmigiano, you'll become an instant believer. **Known for:** perfect pasta flown in from Italy; decadent sauces; chill atmosphere. ⑤ *Average main: $16* ⊠ *6245 Wilshire Blvd., Suite 103, Mid-Wilshire* ☎ *323/642–6386* ⊕ *www.uovo.la.*

🍸 Nightlife

★ El Rey Theater

MUSIC CLUBS | This former art deco movie house from the 1930s has been given a second life as a live music venue. Legends and rising stars grace the stage of El Rey. Everyone from the Pixies and Ringo Starr to the Jonas Brothers and Lana Del Rey have performed here. ⊠ *5515 Wilshire Blvd., Mid-Wilshire* ☎ *323/936–6400* ⊕ *www.theelrey.com.*

Koreatown

Despite its name, Koreatown is one of the most eclectic neighborhoods in all of Los Angeles, particularly when it comes to dining. Obviously, you can find drool-worthy Korean restaurants, but there are also gems like the Oaxacan eatery Guelaguetza; the knockout Japanese spot Sushi One; and the vegan burger joint Monty's Good Burger. Combine the food with the wonderful Korean spas and incredible nightlife, and you'll find a mix of everything that makes L.A. great.

🍴 Restaurants

The Boiling Crab

$$ | **SEAFOOD** | **FAMILY** | Put on your bib and prepare to get messy, because this crab shack is not for stodgy eaters. Choices of blue, Dungeness, snow, king, and southern king, are brought out in plastic bags where you can rip, tear, twist, and yank the meaty goodness out of their shells. **Known for:** giant crab legs; unfussy environment; long lines. ⑤ *Average main: $20* ⊠ *3377 Wilshire Blvd., Suite 115, Koreatown* ☎ *213/389–2722* ⊕ *www.theboilingcrab.com* Ⓜ *Wilshire/Normandie Station.*

Cassell's Hamburgers

$ | **DINER** | **FAMILY** | Since 1948, Cassell's has been grilling up some of the city's best burgers and remains on just about every top burger list in town. In-the-know burger lovers come here for the reliability of a perfectly cooked patty, a toasted bun, and fries with the right amount of crunch. **Known for:** perfectly cooked burgers and fries; no-frills diner setting; late-night eats. ⑤ *Average main: $10* ⊠ *3600 W. 6th St., Koreatown* ☎ *213/387–5502* ⊕ *www.cassellshamburgers.com* Ⓜ *Wilshire/Normandie Station.*

Guelaguetza

$$ | **MEXICAN** | **FAMILY** | A classic L.A. Mexican eatery, Guelaguetza serves the complex but not overpoweringly spicy

cooking of Oaxaca, one of Mexico's most renowned culinary capitals. Inside, you'll find a largely Spanish-speaking clientele bobbing their heads to nightly jazz and marimba while wolfing down the restaurant's specialty: the moles. **Known for:** salsa-covered chorizo; chili-marinated pork; family-owned restaurant. $ *Average main: $15* ✉ *3014 W. Olympic Blvd., Koreatown* ☎ *213/427-0608* ⊕ *www. ilovemole.com* ⊗ *Closed Mon.*

★ Kobawoo House

$$ | KOREAN | FAMILY | Nestled into a dingy strip mall, this Korean powerhouse is given away by the lines of locals waiting outside. Once inside, scents of grilled meats and kimchi immediately fill your nostrils, and soon enough, your table will be littered with sides, *kalbi* beef, *dolsot* bibimbap, *wang bosam* (cabbage wraps with boiled pork), and tall bottles of Hite beer. **Known for:** perfect kalbi beef; long lines; cheap eats. $ *Average main: $17* ✉ *698 S. Vermont Ave., Suite 109, Koreatown* ☎ *213/389-7300* ⊕ *www.kobawoo-house.com* Ⓜ *Wilshire/Vermont.*

Le Comptoir

$$$$ | FRENCH | Situated inside the Hotel Normandie in a miniscule space, Le Comptoir is a 10-seat French restaurant helmed by chef Gary Menes that features veggie-forward food in an unstuffy setting. The counter spot earned a Michelin star for its organic kitchen and intimate atmosphere that gives guests one-on-one attention from the chef who is making and plating your food right in front of you. **Known for:** eight-course tasting menu of innovative French cuisine; intimate setting; vegetarian-friendly dishes. $ *Average main: $120* ✉ *Hotel Normandie, 3606 W. 6th. St., Koreatown* ☎ *213/290-0750* ⊕ *www.lecomptoirla. com* ⊗ *Closed Mon., Wed., and Sun.* Ⓜ *Wilshire/Normandie.*

Monty's Good Burger

$ | BURGER | A 100% plant-based establishment in Koreatown shouldn't be a thing that works, but Monty's Good

Burger has the neighborhood fooled, as its Impossible Burger makes believers out of the most devout carnivores. Perfectly pressed plant-based patties come with oozing vegan cheese and fries or tots that melt in your mouth. **Known for:** plant-based burgers; epic shakes; late-night eats and long lines. $ *Average main: $11* ✉ *516 S. Western Ave., Koreatown* ☎ *213/915-0257* ⊕ *montysgood-burger.com* Ⓜ *Wilshire/Western.*

Sushi One

$$$ | JAPANESE | A large blue wave against a big white wall is meant to evoke the laid-back atmosphere of this cool, tasty, and affordable omakase sushi spot. Short-sleeved sushi chefs double as food artists when the ornate displays of toro, fresh salmon, and delectable yellowtail drop in front of you. **Known for:** ornate omakase sushi platters; crispy fried chicken; laid-back attitude. $ *Average main: $25* ✉ *3905 W. 6th St., Koreatown* ☎ *213/908-5082* ⊕ *www.instagram.com/sushione_la* ⊗ *Closed Sun.* Ⓜ *Wilshire/Western.*

🛏 Hotels

Hotel Normandie

$ | HOTEL | Originally built in 1926, this Renaissance Revival gem has been renovated to today's standards and is now a hip and not-so-pricey spot to post up in the ever-booming center of Koreatown. **Pros:** Michelin-starred French restaurant; complimentary breakfast; cheap prices. **Cons:** feels dated; tiny bathrooms; restaurant is pricey. $ *Rooms from: $190* ✉ *605 Normandie Ave., Koreatown* ☎ *213/388-8138* ⊕ *www.hotelnormandiela.com* 🛏 *92 rooms* Ⓜ *Wilshire/Normandie.*

The Line

$$ | HOTEL | This boutique hotel pays homage to its Koreatown address with dynamic dining concepts and a hidden karaoke speakeasy. **Pros:** on-site bikes to explore the area; unique decor; fun bars on-site (ask about the speakeasy).

Cons: expensive parking; lobby bar crowds public spaces; far from parts of the city you may want to explore. ⑤ *Rooms from: $250* ✉ *3515 Wilshire Blvd., Koreatown* ☎ *213/381–7411* ⊕ *www.thelinehotel.com* ⤴ *384 rooms* ⦿ *No meals* Ⓜ *Wilshire/Normandie Station.*

Nightlife

Dan Sung Sa

BARS/PUBS | Step through the curtained entrance and back in time to 1970s Korea at Dan Sung Sa, which gained wider popularity after Anthony Bourdain paid a visit. At this quirky time-capsule bar, woodblock menus feature roughly 100 small eats. You'll see much that looks familiar, but fortune favors the bold. Take a chance on corn cheese, or try the *makgeolli*: a boozy Korean rice drink you sip from a bowl. It pairs perfectly with good conversation and snacking all night long. ✉ *3317 W. 6th St., Koreatown* ☎ *213/487–9100* Ⓜ *Wilshire/Vermont.*

★ HMS Bounty

BARS/PUBS | This super-kitschy nautical-theme bar in the heart of Koreatown offers drink specials and food at prices that will make you swoon. Come for the wings, all-day breakfast specials, cheap drinks, and very eclectic crowds. ✉ *3357 Wilshire Blvd., Koreatown* ☎ *213/385–7275* ⊕ *www.thehmsbounty. com* Ⓜ *Wilshire/Normandie.*

The Prince

BARS/PUBS | *Mad Men* and *New Girl* both had multiple scenes filmed in this Old Hollywood relic, which dates back to the early 1900s. The Prince is trimmed with vintage fabric wallpaper and bedecked with a stately mahogany bar; the grand piano waits in the wings. Squire lamps punctuate red-leather booths where you can enjoy Korean fare and standard cocktails, wine, and beer. Whatever you do, get the deep-fried chicken. ✉ *3198 W. 7th St., Koreatown* ☎ *213/389–1586* Ⓜ *Wilshire/Vermont Station.*

🎭 Performing Arts

Wiltern Theater

CONCERTS | Built in 1931, this historical art deco landmark, named for its location at the intersection of Wilshire Boulevard and Western Avenue, serves mainly as a space for music (it's a top destination for touring musicians), but other live entertainment can be seen here as well, including comedy and dance. ✉ *3790 Wilshire Blvd., Los Angeles* ☎ *213/388–1400* ⊕ *www.wiltern.com* Ⓜ *Wilshire/Western.*

🏃 Activities

Aroma Spa & Sports

FITNESS/HEALTH CLUBS | It's not difficult to find amazing spa experiences throughout Koreatown. Most places will offer up standard scrubs, hot and cold baths, dry and wet saunas, and more. Aroma takes things to another level as the spa is just the centerpiece of an entire entertainment complex. Spa services include all the traditional treatments, but when you're done getting pampered, the rest of the facility includes a gym, a swimming pool, restaurants, and a state-of-the-art golf driving range. ✉ *3680 Wilshire Blvd., Koreatown* ☎ *213/387–2111* ⊕ *www. aromaresort.com* Ⓜ *Wilshire/Western.*

Wi Spa

FITNESS/HEALTH CLUBS | Koreatown is filled with endless spa experiences, but there are a few that rise above the rest. Wi Spa is a 24/7 wonderland of treatments that includes hot and cold baths, unique sauna rooms, and floors for men, women, or co-ed family spa fun. Signature sauna rooms vary from intense 231-degree thermotherapy to salt-enriched stations and specialty clay imported from Korea. Just remember, Korean spas are not for the shy at heart—you will be nude, you will get scrubbed, and you will feel like a million bucks after. ✉ *2700 Wilshire Blvd., Koreatown* ☎ *213/487–2700* ⊕ *www. wispausa.com* Ⓜ *Wilshire/Vermont.*

Chapter 8

DOWNTOWN
LOS ANGELES

Updated by
Paul Feinstein

◉ Sights	🍽 Restaurants	🛏 Hotels	🛍 Shopping	🍸 Nightlife
★★★★★	★★★★☆	★★★☆☆	★★★☆☆	★★★★★

NEIGHBORHOOD SNAPSHOT

TOP EXPERIENCES

■ **Visit Frank Gehry's Disney Concert Hall:** Be wowed by the genius architecture, and grab tickets for an L.A. Phil performance led by Gustavo Dudamel.

■ **See a Lakers or Clippers game:** Catch the action at the Staples Center and possibly rub elbows with stars like Denzel Washington and Leonardo DiCaprio.

■ **Take a historic walking tour:** The L.A. Conservancy offers several tours, such as of Olvera Street, where you can see traditional Mexican culture and shop for goods.

■ **Peruse the Last Bookstore:** This is not only one of the best bookstores in Los Angeles, it's also one of the most fantastical. Peruse the endless collection of rare and used books and LPs downstairs, then go upstairs into a labyrinth of oddities.

■ **Have a cocktail in old L.A.:** Downtown is great for drinking and even better for drinking in the history of Los Angeles. Some of the city's oldest buildings have been converted into glorious hotels with excellent bars, like the NoMad or the Freehand, while other drinking halls have been around for more than a century, like the Golden Gopher.

QUICK BITES

Cole's. One of the oldest restaurants in L.A., Cole's also lays (disputed) claim to being the originator of the French dip. There's not a lot on the menu, but what they serve is made beautifully. ⊠ *118 E. 6th St.* ⊕ *www.pouringwithheart.com/coles*

Grand Central Market. A palace of food stalls that's so overwhelming, it's almost impossible to choose a meal here. But to narrow it down, try either Ramen Hood at stall C-2 or Sticky Rice at stall C-5. ⊠ *317 S. Broadway* ⊕ *www.grandcentralmarket.com*

Philippe the Original. The other (disputed) originator of the French dip. Bottom line—when in Downtown and in want of a quick bite, eat a French dip. ⊠ *1001 N. Alameda St.* ⊕ *www.philippes.com*

GETTING HERE

■ The good news is that freeways 5, 101, 110, and 10 all get you here; the bad news is that the traffic can delay your travels. If you're coming from the Hollywood area, skip the freeways altogether and take Sunset Boulevard, which turns into César Chávez Boulevard. If you're coming from LAX, take the 105 East to the 110 North. Be warned: parking can be very expensive. It's better to rideshare or take the Metro.

PLANNING YOUR TIME

■ Visit weekdays during the day, when the area is bustling and restaurants are open for lunch. The streets are packed weekend nights, and wait times can be long at restaurants and bars. Weekday evenings tend to be much quieter and it's easy to get yourself a table or a barstool. Seeing everything in one day is possible, but it's best to spread it out over two. Plan your visits around specific areas you can walk to in one circuit.

If there's one thing Angelenos love, it's a makeover, and city planners have put the wheels in motion for a dramatic revitalization of this area in recent years. Downtown is both glamorous and gritty and is an example of Los Angeles's complexity as a whole. There's a dizzying variety of experiences not to be missed here if you're curious about the artistic, historic, ethnic, or sports-loving sides of L.A.

Downtown Los Angeles isn't just one neighborhood: it's a cluster of pedestrian-friendly enclaves where you can sample an eclectic mix of flavors, wander through world-class museums, and enjoy great live performances or sports events.

As you venture into the different neighborhoods of Downtown—**Chinatown, Little Tokyo,** and **El Pueblo de Los Angeles**—take advantage of the tastes, sounds, and sights. Eat roast duck in Chinatown, red bean cakes in Little Tokyo, or pickled cactus on Olvera Street. Spend time browsing the **Grand Central Market,** where stalls are filled with colorful locally grown produce and homemade treats from tamales and olive bread to Texan barbecue and Thai-style chicken over rice. For art lovers, the **Broad Museum** has one of the most important modern and contemporary art collections, while those who are fans of architecture should make a point to see the Gehry creation, the **Walt Disney Concert Hall,** or the massive, geometrically designed **Cathedral of Our Lady for the Angels.**

To see the glory of Broadway's golden years, look up above the storefront signs, and you'll find the marvelous architecture and theater marquees of the majestic buildings they reside in. From the late 19th century to the 1950s—before malls and freeways—**Broadway** glittered with the finest shops and the highest number of luxurious theaters in the world, making it a rich, cultural haven. Though it remains the main road through Downtown's Historic Core, the area has changed dramatically over the years. Though it once exclusively housed businesses catering to mostly Mexican and Central American immigrants, there are now trendy pockets for shopping and dining. However, you can still find the classic experience of mariachi and *banda* music blaring from electronics-store speakers between 1st and 9th streets, street-food vendors hawking sliced papaya sprinkled with chili powder, and fancy dresses for a girl's *quinceañera* (15th birthday).

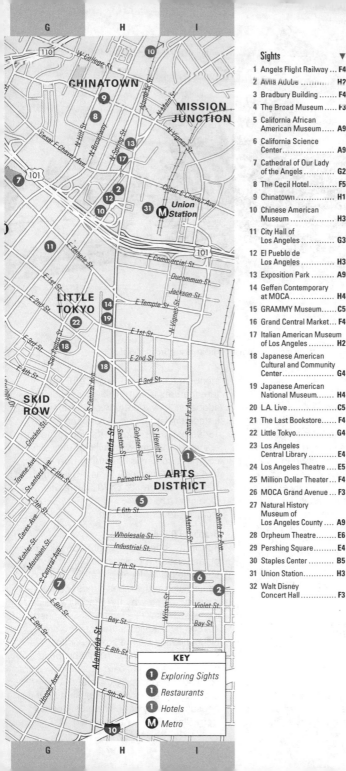

Sights ▼

1 Angels Flight Railway ... **F4**
2 Avila Adobe **H2**
3 Bradbury Building **F4**
4 The Broad Museum **F3**
5 California African American Museum..... **A9**
6 California Science Center.................... **A9**
7 Cathedral of Our Lady of the Angels **G2**
8 The Cecil Hotel.......... **F5**
9 Chinatown **H1**
10 Chinese American Museum **H3**
11 City Hall of Los Angeles **G3**
12 El Pueblo de Los Angeles **H3**
13 Exposition Park **A9**
14 Geffen Contemporary at MOCA.............. **H4**
15 GRAMMY Museum...... **C5**
16 Grand Central Market... **F4**
17 Italian American Museum of Los Angeles **H2**
18 Japanese American Cultural and Community Center.................... **G4**
19 Japanese American National Museum....... **H4**
20 L.A. Live **C5**
21 The Last Bookstore...... **F4**
22 Little Tokyo.............. **G4**
23 Los Angeles Central Library **E4**
24 Los Angeles Theatre **E5**
25 Million Dollar Theater... **F4**
26 MOCA Grand Avenue ... **F3**
27 Natural History Museum of Los Angeles County **A9**
28 Orpheum Theatre........ **E6**
29 Pershing Square......... **E4**
30 Staples Center **B5**
31 Union Station............ **H3**
32 Walt Disney Concert Hall **F3**

Restaurants ▼

1 Bavel **I6**
2 Bestia **I8**
3 Bottega Louie **D5**
4 Cole's French Dip **F5**
5 The Factory Kitchen.... **H6**
6 Guerrilla Tacos............ **I7**
7 Hayato **G7**
8 Howlin' Ray's............ **H2**
9 Langer's Delicatesen-Restaurant............... **A3**
10 Majordomo.............. **H1**
11 Original Pantry Cafe **C5**
12 Petite Peso **E5**
13 Philippe the Original ... **H2**
14 Q Sushi.................... **E5**
15 71Above................... **E4**
16 Shibumi **D5**
17 Sonoratown **E6**
18 Sushi Gen................ **H5**

Hotels ▼

1 Ace Hotel Downtown Los Angeles **D6**
2 Freehand Los Angeles **D5**
3 Hotel Figueroa **C5**
4 The Hoxton **D6**
5 InterContinental Los Angeles Downtown **D4**
6 Millennium Biltmore Hotel........................ **E4**
7 The NoMad Hotel........ **E5**
8 The Ritz-Carlton, Los Angeles **B5**
9 The Standard, Downtown LA............ **D4**
10 Westin Bonaventure Hotel and Suites **E3**

KEY

1 Exploring Sights
1 Restaurants
1 Hotels
M Metro

Tulips by Jeff Koons is just one of the many modern art exhibits at the Broad Museum.

👁 Sights

★ Angels Flight Railway
TRANSPORTATION SITE (AIRPORT/BUS/FERRY/TRAIN) | The turn-of-the-20th-century funicular, dubbed "the shortest railway in the world," operated between 1901 and 1969, when it was dismantled to make room for an urban renewal project. Almost 30 years later, Angels Flight returned with its original orange-and-black wooden cable cars hauling travelers up a 298-foot incline from Hill Street to the fountain-filled Watercourt at California Plaza. Your reward is a stellar view of the neighborhood. Tickets are $1 each way, but you can buy a souvenir round-trip ticket for $2 if you want something to take home with you. ⊠ *351 S. Hill St., between 3rd and 4th Sts., Downtown* 🕾 *213/626–1901* ⊕ *www.angelsflight.org.*

Avila Adobe
HOUSE | Built as a private home for cattle rancher Francisco Avila in 1818, this museum preserves seven of what were originally 18 rooms in the city's oldest standing residence. The graceful structure features 3-foot-thick walls made of adobe brick over cottonwood timbers, a traditional interior courtyard, and 1840s-era furnishings that bring to life an era when the city was still part of Mexico. The museum is open daily from 9 am to 4 pm and the complex is a California Historical Landmark. ⊠ *10 Olvera St., Downtown* 🕾 *213/485–6855* ⊕ *elpueblo.lacity.org* Ⓜ *Union Station.*

Bradbury Building
BUILDING | Stunning wrought-iron railings, ornate plaster moldings, pink marble staircases, a birdcage elevator, and a sky-lighted atrium that rises almost 50 feet—it's easy to see why the Bradbury Building leaves visitors awestruck. Designed in 1893 by a novice architect who drew his inspiration from a science-fiction story and a conversation with his dead brother via a Ouija board, the office building was originally the site of turn-of-the-20th-century sweatshops, but now houses a variety of businesses. Scenes from *Blade Runner*, *Chinatown*, and

500 Days of Summer were filmed here, which means there's often a barrage of tourists snapping photos. Visits are limited to the lobby and the first-floor landing. ■ TIP→ **Historic Downtown walking tours hosted by the L.A. Conservancy cost $15 and include the Bradbury Building.** ✉ *304 S. Broadway, Downtown* ☎ *213/626–1893* ⊕ *www.laconservancy.org/locations/bradbury-building* Ⓜ *Pershing Square Station.*

★ **The Broad Museum**

MUSEUM | The talk of Los Angeles's art world when it opened in 2015, this museum in an intriguing, honeycomb-looking building was created by philanthropists Eli and Edythe Broad (rhymes with "road") to showcase their stunning private collection of contemporary art, amassed over five decades and still growing. With upward of 2,000 pieces by more than 200 artists, the collection has in-depth representations of the work of such prominent names as Jean Michel Basquiat, Jeff Koons, Ed Ruscha, Cindy Sherman, Cy Twombly, Kara Walker, and Christopher Wool. The "veil and vault" design of the main building integrates gallery space and storage space (visitors can glimpse the latter through a window in the stairwell): the veil refers to the fiberglass, concrete, and steel exterior; the vault is the concrete base. Temporary exhibits and works from the permanent collection are arranged in the small first-floor rooms and in the more expansive third floor of the museum, so you can explore everything in a few hours. Next door to the Broad is a small plaza with olive trees and seating, as well as the museum restaurant, Otium. Admission to the museum is free, but book timed tickets in advance to guarantee entry. ✉ *221 S. Grand Ave., Downtown* ☎ *213/232–6200* ⊕ *www.thebroad.org* ✆ *Free* ☉ *Closed Mon.* Ⓜ *Civic Center/Grand Park Station.*

California African American Museum

MUSEUM | With more than 4,500 historical artifacts, this museum showcases contemporary art of the African diaspora. Artists represented here include Betye Saar, Charles Haywood, and June Edmonds. The museum has a research library with more than 6,000 books available for public use. ■ TIP→ **If possible, visit on a Sunday, when there's almost always a diverse lineup of speakers and performances.** ✉ *600 State Dr., Exposition Park* ☎ *213/744–7432* ⊕ *www.caamuseum.org* ✆ *Free; parking $12* ☉ *Closed Mon.* Ⓜ *Expo/Vermont Station.*

California Science Center

MUSEUM | FAMILY | You're bound to see excited kids running up to the dozens of interactive exhibits here that illustrate the prevalence of science in everyday life. Clustered in different "worlds," the center keeps young guests busy for hours. They can design their own buildings and learn how to make them earthquake-proof; watch Tess, the dramatic 50-foot animatronic star of the exhibit *Body Works,* demonstrate how the body's organs work together; and ride a bike across a trapeze wire three stories high in the air. One of the exhibits in the Air and Space section shows how astronauts Pete Conrad and Dick Gordon made it to outer space in the Gemini 11 capsule in 1966; also here is NASA's massive space shuttle *Endeavor,* located in the Samuel Oschin Pavilion, for which a timed ticket is needed to visit. The IMAX theater screens science-related large-format films. ✉ *700 Exposition Park Dr., Exposition Park* ☎ *323/724–3623* ⊕ *www.californiasciencecenter.org* ✆ *Permanent exhibits free; fees for some attractions, special exhibits, and IMAX screenings vary; parking $12* Ⓜ *Expo/Vermont.*

Cathedral of Our Lady of the Angels

RELIGIOUS SITE | A half block from Frank Gehry's curvaceous Walt Disney Concert Hall sits the austere Cathedral of Our Lady of the Angels—a spiritual draw as well as an architectural attraction. Controversy surrounded Spanish architect José Rafael Moneo's unconventional design

L.A.'s Chinatown has its share of Chinese restaurants, shops, and cultural institutions, but you'll also find a growing community of artists and galleries.

for the seat of the Archdiocese of Los Angeles. But judging from the swarms of visitors and the standing-room-only holiday masses, the church has carved out a niche for itself in Downtown L.A.

The plaza in front is glaringly bright on sunny days, though a children's play garden with bronze animals mitigates the starkness somewhat. Head underground to wander the mausoleum's mazelike white-marble corridors. Free guided tours start at the entrance fountain at 1 pm on weekdays. ■TIP→ There's plenty of underground visitors parking; the vehicle entrance is on Hill Street. ⊠ 555 W. Temple St., Downtown ☎ 213/680–5200 ⊕ www. olacathedral.org ⊠ Free Ⓜ Civic Center/ Grand Park.

The Cecil Hotel
BUILDING | Fans of the macabre will find lots to love when they learn about the history of Downtown L.A.'s most notorious lodging. Originally built in 1924, the hotel has seen many an unsavory guest, including the Night Stalker, and has been the spot of several unsolved murders, mysterious deaths, and tragic suicides. The most recent occurred only a few years ago when they found the remains of a tourist inside the hotel's water tower. That mystery (and some of the hotel's history) is explored in the popular Netflix miniseries, *Crime Scene: The Vanishing at the Cecil Hotel*. The building is currently not open as a hotel, but there are allegedly plans in the works to reopen it to guests eventually. ⊠ 640 S. Main St., Downtown Ⓜ Pershing Square.

Chinatown
NEIGHBORHOOD | Smaller than San Francisco's Chinatown, this neighborhood near Union Station still represents a slice of East Asian life. Sidewalks are usually jammed with tourists, locals, and residents hustling from shop to shop picking up goods, spices, and trinkets from small shops and miniplazas that line the street. Although some longtime establishments have closed in recent years, the area still pulses with its founding culture. During Chinese New Year, giant dragons snake

down the street. And, of course, there are the many restaurants and quick-bite cafés specializing in Chinese feasts. In recent years, a slew of hip eateries like Howlin' Ray's and Majordomo have injected the area with vibrancy.

An influx of local artists has added a spark to the neighborhood by taking up empty spaces and opening galleries along Chung King Road, a faded pedestrian passage behind the West Plaza shopping center between Hill and Yale. Also look for galleries along a little side street called Gin Ling Way on the east side of Broadway. Chinatown has its main action on North Broadway. There are several garages available for parking here that range from $5 to $10 per day. ⊠ *Bordered by the 110, 101, and 5 freeways, Downtown* ⊕ *chinatownla.com* Ⓜ *Union Station.*

Chinese American Museum

MUSEUM | Because it's in El Pueblo Plaza, you might assume that this museum features Mexican American art, but it's actually the last surviving structure of L.A.'s original Chinatown. Three floors of exhibits reveal the different cultures that have called this area home, as well as how the original residents paved the way for what is now a vibrant and varied Chinatown. Rotating exhibits feature the work of Chinese American artists. ⊠ *425 N. Los Angeles St., Downtown* ☎ *213/485–8567* ⊕ *www.camla.org* ⊠ *$3* ⊘ *Closed Mon.* Ⓜ *Union Station.*

City Hall of Los Angeles

GOVERNMENT BUILDING | This gorgeous 1928 landmark building is a TV star—it was in the opening scenes of *Dragnet* and served as the Daily Planet building in the original *Adventures of Superman*. During extensive renovations, the original Lindburg Beacon was put back in action atop the hall's 13-story tower. The revolving spotlight, inaugurated by President Calvin Coolidge from the White House via a telegraph key, was used from 1928 to 1941 to guide pilots into the Los Angeles airport. The observation deck, located on the 27th floor, is free to the public and has a stellar view of the greater Los Angeles area. ⊠ *200 N. Spring St., Downtown* ☎ *213/473–3231* ⊕ *www.lacity.org* ⊘ *Closed weekends* Ⓜ *Civic Center/Grand Park.*

★ El Pueblo de Los Angeles

NEIGHBORHOOD | The oldest section of the city, known as El Pueblo de Los Angeles, represents the rich Mexican heritage of L.A. It had a close shave with disintegration in the early 20th century, but key buildings were preserved, and eventually **Olvera Street,** the district's heart, was transformed into a Mexican American marketplace. Today vendors still sell puppets, leather goods, sandals, and woolen shawls from stalls lining the narrow street. You can find everything from salt and pepper shakers shaped like donkeys to gorgeous glassware and pottery.

At the beginning of Olvera Street is the Plaza, a Mexican-style park with plenty of benches and walkways shaded by a huge Moreton Bay fig tree. On weekends, mariachi bands and folkloric dance groups perform. Nearby places worth investigating include the historic Avila Adobe, the Chinese American Museum, the Plaza Firehouse Museum, and the America Tropical Interpretive Center. Exhibits at the Italian American Museum of Los Angeles chronicle the area's formerly heavy Italian presence. ⊠ *Avila Adobe/Olvera Street Visitors Center, 125 Paseo De La Plaza, Downtown* ☎ *213/485–6855* ⊕ *elpueblo.lacity.org* ⊠ *Free for Olvera St. and guided tours; fees at some museums.*

Exposition Park

CITY PARK | Originally developed in 1872 as an agricultural park, this 160-acre park has a lovely sunken rose garden and three museums—the California African American Museum, the California Science Center, and the Natural History Museum of Los Angeles County—as well as an IMAX theater. There's also

Olvera Street, at the heart of the city's oldest neighborhood, is the place to experience many aspects of L.A.'s Mexican American culture.

Los Angeles Memorial Coliseum where Olympic festivities were held in 1932 and 1984 and where USC games are now played. The newest addition to the park is the Banc of California Stadium, a 22,000-seat arena that's home to the LAFC soccer club. Good news for commuters: the Metro Expo Line, which connects the Westside to Downtown Los Angeles, has a stop at Exposition Park. ⚠ Note that the park and neighborhood are sketchy at night. ✉ 700 Exposition Park Dr., Exposition Park ☎ 213/744–2294 ⊕ expositionpark. ca.gov 🚗 Parking $12 Ⓜ Expo/Vermont Station.

Geffen Contemporary at MOCA

MUSEUM | The Geffen Contemporary is one of architect Frank Gehry's boldest creations. One of three MOCA branches, the 40,000 square feet of exhibition space was once used as a police car warehouse. The museum's permanent collection includes works from artists like Willem de Kooning, Franz Kline, Jackson Pollock, Mark Rothko, and Cindy Sherman. ■TIP→ Present your TAP metro card to get two-for-one admission. ✉ 152 N. Central Ave., Downtown ☎ 213/626–6222 ⊕ www.moca.org/visit/geffen-contemporary 🚗 Free; special exhibitions $18 or free every Thurs. 5–8; parking $9.

GRAMMY Museum

MUSEUM | The GRAMMY Museum brings the music industry to life. Throughout four floors and 30,000 square feet of space, the museum showcases rare footage of GRAMMY performances, plus rotating and interactive exhibits on award-winning musicians and the history of music. A 200-seat theater is great for live events that include screenings, lectures, interviews, and intimate music performances. ✉ 800 W. Olympic Blvd., Downtown ☎ 213/765–6800 ⊕ www. grammymuseum.org 🚗 $15 ⊘ Closed Tues. Ⓜ Pico.

★ Grand Central Market

MARKET | With options that include handmade white-corn tamales, warm olive bread, dried figs, Mexican fruit drinks, and much more, this mouthwatering gathering place is the city's largest and most active food market. The spot bustles nonstop with locals and visitors surveying the butcher shop's display of everything from lambs' heads to pigs' tails. Produce stalls are piled high with locally grown avocados and heirloom tomatoes. Stop by **Chiles Secos** at stall C-12 for a remarkable selection of rare chilis and spices; **Ramen Hood** at C-2, for sumptuous vegan noodles and broth; or **Sticky Rice** at stall C-5, for fantastic Thai-style chicken. Even if you don't plan on buying anything, it's a great place to browse and people-watch. ⊠ *317 S. Broadway, Downtown* ☎ *213/624–2378* ⊕ *www.grandcentralmarket.com* 🖼 *Free* Ⓜ *Pershing Square.*

Italian American Museum of Los Angeles

MUSEUM | This landmark, constructed in 1908, is noteworthy because its south wall bears an infamous mural. Famed Mexican muralist David Alfaro Siqueiros shocked his patrons in the 1930s by depicting an oppressed worker of Latin America being crucified on a cross topped by a menacing American eagle. The anti-imperialist mural was promptly whitewashed but was later restored by the Getty Museum. It can be seen on the Italian Hall building today. Today the site functions as a museum and has seven color-coded exhibits on the history of Italian Americans. The site is also home to Taste of Italy, an annual event that celebrates the Italian culinary history of Los Angeles. ⊠ *644 N. Main St., Downtown* ☎ *213/485–8432* ⊕ *iamla.org* ⊗ *Museum closed Mon.* Ⓜ *Union Station.*

Japanese American Cultural and Community Center

LOCAL INTEREST | Plenty of traditional and contemporary cultural events make this center well worth the trip. Founded in 1980, JACCC is home to a number of civic and arts organizations. Through the center's basement you reach the James Irvine Garden, a serene sunken space

where local plants mix with bamboo, Japanese wisteria, and Japanese maples. The main floor of the museum houses the George J. Doizaki Gallery, which has 2,000 square feet of exhibition space and has housed everything from national treasures of Japan to the Bugaku costumes from the Kasuga Grand Shrine in Nara. An 880-seat theater is known for any number of performing arts shows including Bunraku Puppet Theater and the Grand Kabuki of Japan. ⊠ *244 S. San Pedro St., Downtown* ☎ *213/628–2725* ⊕ *www.jaccc.org* ⊗ *Doizaki Gallery closed Mon. and Tues.; Japanese garden closed Mon.* Ⓜ *Pershing Square.*

Japanese American National Museum

MUSEUM | What was it like to grow up on a sugar plantation in Hawaii? How difficult was life for Japanese Americans interned in concentration camps during World War II? These questions are addressed by changing exhibitions at this museum in Little Tokyo that also include fun tributes to anime and Hello Kitty. Volunteer docents are on hand to share their own stories and experiences. The museum occupies its original site in a renovated 1925 Buddhist temple and an 85,000-square-foot adjacent pavilion. ■ **TIP→ Take the Metro and get $2 off general admission and a 10% discount at adjoining Chado Tea Room.** ⊠ *100 N. Central Ave., off E. 1st St., Downtown* ☎ *213/625–0414* ⊕ *www.janm.org* 🖼 *$16; free Thurs. 5–8 and all day every 3rd Thurs. of month* ⊗ *Closed Mon.* Ⓜ *Civic Center/Grand Park.*

L.A. Live

ARTS VENUE | The mammoth L.A. Live entertainment complex was opened in 2007 when there was little to do or see in this section of Downtown. Since its inception, this once creepy ghost town has become a major hub for sports, concerts, award shows, and more. The first things you'll notice as you emerge from the parking lot are the giant LED screens and sparkling lights, and the buzz of

The Los Angeles Metro

Long ago, Los Angeles had an enviable public transportation system known as the Pacific Electric Red Cars, trolleys that made it possible to get around this sprawling city without an automobile. In the mid-1900s, the last of the Red Cars disappeared, and L.A. lost itself in the car culture.

That culture is here to stay, but in recent years, a new rail system has emerged. You can now take the subway through parts of Downtown, Hollywood, Pasadena, and North Hollywood. The Red Line starts at Downtown's Union Station, then curves northwest to Hollywood and on to Universal City and North Hollywood. The Blue and Green light rail lines are designed for commuters. The Gold Line goes from Union Station up to Azusa, stopping in Pasadena. Take the Expo Line from Downtown to Santa Monica, or the Purple Line from Union Station through Koreatown and into Mid-City and its Restaurant Row. Future plans include a line that runs all the way to the Los Angeles International Airport (LAX).

The Metro Rail stations are worth exploring themselves, and you can sign up for a free docent-led **MTA Art Moves** tour (☎ 213/922–2738 ⊕ www. metro.net/about/art), which departs from the entrances to the Hollywood & Highland and Union stations. You'll receive a free day pass to ride the rails as you visit the colorful murals, sculptures, and architectural elements that illustrate themes of Los Angeles history.

The Universal City station is next to the site of the Campo de Caheunga, where Mexico relinquished control of California to the United States in 1847. The station features a time line of the area's past done in the traditional style of colorful Mexican folk art.

The North Hollywood station also celebrates local history, including native Gabrielino culture, many immigrant communities, Amelia Earhart (a local), Western wear designer Nudie, and the history of transportation in L.A. County.

There are film reels on the ceiling of the Hollywood and Vine station as well as original Paramount Pictures film projectors from the 1930s, and floor paving modeled after the yellow brick road from *The Wizard of Oz*. Imposing, glass-clad columns juxtaposed with rock formations can be seen at the Vermont and Beverly station. The old Red Car trolley makes an appearance in the Hollywood and Western station.

crowds as they head out to dinner before or after a Lakers game, movie, or live show at the Microsoft Theater. There are dozens of restaurants and eateries here, including Los Angeles favorite Katsuya, the spot for sizzling Kobe beef platters and excellent sushi (the crab rolls are not to be missed). ■ TIP→ **Park for free on weekdays from 11 am to 2 pm if you eat at one of the dozen or so restaurants here.** ✉ 800 W. Olympic Blvd., Downtown ☎ 213/763–5483 ⊕ www.lalive.com Ⓜ Pico.

★ The Last Bookstore

STORE/MALL | California's largest used and new book and record shop is a favorite for both book lovers and fans of a good photo op, thanks to elements like an archway created from curving towers of books, a peephole carved into the stacks, and an in-store vault devoted to horror texts. Aside from the awesome aesthetics, shoppers will love to get lost in the store's collection of affordable books, art, and music. ⊠ *453 S. Spring St., ground fl., Downtown* ☎ *213/488–0599* ⊕ *www. lastbookstorela.com* Ⓜ *Pershing Square.*

★ Little Tokyo

NEIGHBORHOOD | One of three official Japantowns in the country—all of which are in California—Little Tokyo is blossoming again thanks to the next generation of Japanese Americans setting up small businesses. Besides dozens of sushi bars, tempura restaurants, and karaoke bars, there's a lovely garden at the Japanese American Cultural and Community Center and a renovated 1925 Buddhist temple with an ornate entrance at the Japanese American National Museum.

On 1st Street you'll find a strip of buildings from the early 1900s. Look down when you get near San Pedro Street to see the art installation called *Omoide no Shotokyo* ("Remembering Old Little Tokyo"). Embedded in the sidewalk are brass inscriptions naming the original businesses, quoted reminiscences from residents, and steel time lines of Japanese American history up to World War II. Nisei Week (a *nisei* is a second-generation Japanese American) is celebrated every August with traditional drums, dancing, a carnival, and a huge parade. ■**TIP**➔ **Docent-led walking tours are available the last Saturday of every month starting at 10:15 am. The cost is $15 and includes entry to the Japanese American National Museum.** ⊠ *Bounded by 1st and 3rd Sts., the 101 and 110 freeways, and LA River, Downtown* ☎ *213/880–6875* ⊕ *www. visitlittletokyo.com* Ⓜ *Civic Center/Grand Park Station.*

Los Angeles Central Library

LIBRARY | The nation's third-largest public library, the handsome Los Angeles Central Library was designed in 1926 by Bertram Goodhue. Restored to their pristine condition, a pyramid tower and a torch symbolizing the "light of learning"

crown the building. The Cook rotunda on the second floor features murals by Dean Cornwell depicting the history of California, and the Tom Bradley Wing, named for a famed L.A. mayor, has a soaring eight-story atrium.

The library offers frequent special exhibits, plus a small café where you can refuel. Don't ignore the gift shop, which is loaded with unique items for readers and writers. Free docent walking tours are offered Monday through Friday at 12:30, Saturday at 11 and 2, and Sunday at 2. An Art-in-the-Garden tour is on Saturday at 12:30 pm. A self-guided tour map is also available on the library's website. ⊠ *630 W. 5th St., Downtown* ☎ *213/228–7000* ⊕ *www.lapl.org* ⊠ *Free* Ⓜ *Pershing Square.*

Los Angeles Theatre

ARTS VENUE | Built in 1931, the 2,200-seat Los Angeles Theatre opened with the premiere of Charlie Chaplin's classic *City Lights*. Full of glorious French baroque–inspired details, the six-story lobby is awe-inspiring with its dramatic staircase, enormous fountain, grandiose chandeliers, and ornate gold detailing. You can occasionally witness the old Hollywood glamour by catching a special movie screening. ⊠ *615 S. Broadway, Downtown* ☎ *213/629–2939* ⊕ *www.losangelestheatre.com* Ⓜ *Pershing Square.*

Million Dollar Theater

ARTS VENUE | The Million Dollar Theater opened in 1918 as part of Sid Grauman's famed chain of movie theaters. This Spanish baroque–style venue had the special feature of having its own organ. Film stars such as Gloria Swanson, Rudolph Valentino, and a young Judy Garland frequently made appearances. In the '40s, the venue swung with jazz and big band performers including Billie Holiday. The theater is open for special events and is worth a stop if you're walking past to inspect the lavish exterior with entertainment figures carved into the

Watts Towers 👁

Take a 20-minute drive south of Downtown and gaze upon one of the city's most stunning sights: the Watts Towers.

It took 33 years for Italian immigrant Simon Rodia to construct the Watts Towers—a massive steel structure comprising 17 interlaced mosaic-tiled spirals. Rodia settled in Los Angeles in the early 20th century and in 1921 bought a parcel of land in the Watts neighborhood of South Los Angeles. Over the next three and half decades, he single-handedly constructed the towers—without the use of construction equipment or scaffolding.

He was asked over and over a simple question: Why? And he gave a lot of different answers—it kept him away from the bottle, he didn't have a job, he just wanted to do something grand.

Rodia died in 1965, the same year the Watts riots erupted. Though much of the area was completely destroyed, the towers stood tall. They became a symbol, not only for the strength of that community, but for the enduring creativity of the entire city.

molding. ⊠ *307 S. Broadway, Downtown* ☎ *213/617–3600.*

MOCA Grand Avenue

MUSEUM | The main branch of the Museum of Contemporary Art, designed by Arata Isozaki, contains underground galleries and presents elegant exhibitions. A huge Nancy Rubins sculpture fashioned from used airplane parts graces the museum's front plaza. The museum gift shop offers apothecary items, modernist ceramics, and even toys and games for children to appease any art lover. ■TIP→ **Take advantage of the free audio tour.** ⊠ *250 S. Grand Ave., Downtown* ☎ *213/626–6222* ⊕ *www.moca.org* ✆ *General admission free; special exhibitions $18 or free Thurs. 5–8* � *Closed Tues.* Ⓜ *Civic Center/Grand Park.*

Natural History Museum of Los Angeles County

MUSEUM | FAMILY | The hot ticket at this beaux arts–style museum completed in 1913 is the Dinosaur Hall, whose more than 300 fossils include adult, juvenile, and baby skeletons of the fearsome *Tyrannosaurus rex*. The Discovery Center lets kids and curious grown-ups touch real animal pelts, and the Insect Zoo gets everyone up close and personal with the white-eyed assassin bug and other creepy crawlers. A massive hall displays dioramas of animals in their natural habitats. Also look for pre-Columbian artifacts and crafts from the South Pacific, or priceless stones in the Gem and Mineral Hall. Outdoors, the 3½-acre Nature Gardens shelter native plant and insect species and contain an expansive edible garden. ■TIP→ **Don't miss out on the Dino lab, where you can watch paleontologists unearth and clean real fossils.** ⊠ *900 W. Exposition Blvd., Exposition Park* ☎ *213/763–3466* ⊕ *www.nhm. org* ✆ *$15; free on 1st Tues. of month* Ⓜ *Expo/Vermont.*

Orpheum Theatre

ARTS VENUE | Opened in 1926, the opulent Orpheum Theatre played host to live attractions including classic comedians, burlesque dancers, jazz greats like Lena Horne, Ella Fitzgerald, and Duke Ellington, and later on rock-and-roll performers such as Little Richard. After extensive restorations, the Orpheum once again revealed a stunning white-marble lobby, majestic auditorium with fleur-de-lis panels, and two dazzling chandeliers. A thick red velvet and gold-trimmed curtain

Frank Gehry's Walt Disney Concert Hall was an instant L.A. icon.

opens at showtime, and a white Wurlitzer pipe organ (one of the last remaining organs of its kind from the silent movie era) is at the ready. The original 1926 rooftop neon sign again shines brightly, signaling a new era for this theater. Today the theater plays host to live concerts, comedy shows, and movie screenings. ⊠ 842 S. Broadway, Downtown 📠 877/677–4386 ⊕ www.laorpheum. com/events.

Pershing Square

PLAZA | FAMILY | The city's cultures come together in one of its oldest parks, named in honor of World War I general John J. Pershing. Opened in 1866, the park was renovated in the 1990s by architect Ricardo Legorreta and landscape architect Laurie Olin with faded pastel-color walls, fountains, and towers. However, most Downtown residents and architecture lovers are not fans of the design and have long lobbied for a makeover, which is perennially rumored to be unveiled. From mid-November to mid-January, an outdoor ice skating rink

attracts ice skaters and families. Every Wednesday 10–2 is the Pershing Square Farmers' Market. ⊠ 532 S. Olive St., Downtown 📠 213/847–4970 ⊕ www. laparks.org/pershingsquare ☞ Free Ⓜ Pershing Square.

Staples Center

ARTS VENUE | Home to the Lakers, the Clippers, the Sparks, and the ice hockey team Los Angeles Kings, the Staples Center is Downtown's top sports destination. It's also the preferred venue for superstars like Bruce Springsteen, Ariana Grande, and Justin Bieber. Though not open for visits except during events, the saucer-shape building is eye-catching. ⊠ 1111 S. Figueroa St., Downtown 📠 213/742–7100 ⊕ www.staplescenter. com Ⓜ Pico.

Union Station

HISTORIC SITE | Even if you don't plan on traveling by train anywhere, head here to soak up the ambience of a great rail station. Envisioned by John and Donald Parkinson, the architects who also designed the grand City Hall, the 1939 masterpiece combines Spanish Colonial Revival and art deco elements that have retained their classic warmth and quality. The waiting hall's commanding scale and enormous chandeliers have provided the backdrop for countless scenes in films, TV shows, and music videos. Recently added to the majesty are the Imperial Western Beer Company and the Streamliner, two bars that pay homage to the station's original architecture while serving homemade brews and inventive classic cocktails. ■TIP→ **Walking tours of Union Station are on Saturday at 10 and cost $15.** ✉ *800 N. Alameda St., Downtown* ⊕ *www.unionstationla.com* Ⓜ *Union Station.*

★ Walt Disney Concert Hall

CONCERTS | One of the architectural wonders of Los Angeles, the 2,265-seat hall is a sculptural monument of gleaming, curved steel designed by Frank Gehry. It's part of a complex that includes a public park, gardens, shops, and two outdoor amphitheaters, one of them atop the concert hall. The acoustically superlative venue is the home of the city's premier orchestra, the Los Angeles Philharmonic, whose music director, Gustavo Dudamel, is an international celebrity in his own right. The orchestra's season runs from late September to early June, before it heads to the Hollywood Bowl for the summer. ■TIP→ **Free 60-minute guided tours are offered on most days, and there are self-guided audio tours.** ✉ *111 S. Grand Ave., Downtown* ☎ *323/850–2000* ⊕ *www.laphil.org* 🎫 *Tours free* Ⓜ *Civic Center/Grand Park.*

🍴 Restaurants

Downtown Los Angeles is also home to L.A.'s Arts District, Financial District, Chinatown, Little Tokyo, the Theater District, and everything in between. The neighborhood, still dodgy in places, has experienced a culinary renaissance that has rippled through the area, making it a popular dining destination where people come in search of edgy and creative menus that celebrate its eclectic nature. Here you'll find plenty of cozy wine bars, quaint bistros, historical landmarks, ethnic eats, and upscale restaurants that lack pretension.

★ Bavel

$$$$ | MIDDLE EASTERN | Fans of Bestia have been lining up for stellar Mediterranean cuisine at this Arts District hot spot, which is owned by the same restaurateurs. Rose gold stools give way to marble tabletops as the open kitchen bangs out hummus and baba ghanoush spreads, along with flatbreads and lamb-neck shawarma. **Known for:** delicious Mediterranean cuisine; sceney atmosphere; great vibes. ⑤ *Average main: $40* ✉ *500 Mateo St., Downtown* ☎ *213/232–4966* ⊕ *baveldtla.com.*

Bestia

$$$$ | ITALIAN | One of the most exciting and popular Italian restaurants in L.A. is housed inside a converted warehouse in the Arts District Downtown. Exposed air ducts and brick dominate the enormous space as in-the-know eaters chow down on Alla'nduja pizza and spaghetti Rustichella with Dungeness crab. **Known for:** Alla'nduja pizza; excellent date spot; upscale modern decor. ⑤ *Average main: $35* ✉ *2121 E. 7th Pl., Downtown* ☎ *213/514–5724* ⊕ *www.bestiala.com* ☉ *No lunch.*

Bottega Louie

$$$ | ITALIAN | A Downtown dining staple, this lively Italian restaurant and gourmet market features open spaces, stark white walls, and majestic floor-to-ceiling windows. If the wait is too long at this no-reservations eatery, you can sip on Prosecco and nibble on pastries at the bar. **Known for:** mouthwatering chicken Parm; one-of-a-kind portobello fries; tartufo pizzas with black truffle mushrooms. ⑤ *Average main: $25* ✉ *700 S. Grand Ave., Downtown* ☎ *213/802–1470* ⊕ *www.bottegalouie.com* Ⓜ *7th Street/ Metro Center.*

Did You Know?

Fred Harvey opened the last of his historic Harvey House restaurants next to Union Station. Designed by architect Mary Colter, the stunning Navajo-influenced 1930s space appears in films like *The Way We Were* and can be seen during Union Station walking tours.

★ Cole's French Dip

$ | **AMERICAN** | There's a fight in Los Angeles over who created the French dip sandwich. The first contender is Cole's, whose sign on the door says it's the originator of the salty, juicy, melt-in-your-mouth meats. **Known for:** historic L.A. dining; one of the top contenders for best French dip sandwich in the country; secret speakeasy in back. ⑤ *Average main: $10 ⊠ 118 E. 6th St., Downtown* ☎ *213/622–4090* ⊕ *www.pouringwithheart.com/coles.*

The Factory Kitchen

$$$$ | **ITALIAN** | The homemade pasta here, kneaded from imported Italian flour, guarantees this place a spot on the "must eat" list. The large Arts District eatery is carved from a converted warehouse and is held up inside by towering pillars. **Known for:** focaccina calda di recco al formaggio; incredible cannoli; best pesto in the city. ⑤ *Average main: $32 ⊠ 1300 Factory Pl., Downtown* ☎ *213/996–6000* ⊕ *www.thefactorykitchen.com* ⊙ *Closed Mon.*

★ Guerrilla Tacos

$ | **MEXICAN FUSION** | What started as a food truck serving gourmet tacos has turned into a brick-and-mortar space that also has an excellent (and cheap) bar. Chefs fire up some of the most inventive tacos in the city—think sweet potato with almond chili and feta or the Baja fried cod with chipotle crema. **Known for:** gourmet tacos; cheap drinks; long lines. ⑤ *Average main: $11 ⊠ 2000 E. 7th St., Downtown* ☎ *213/375–3300* ⊕ *www.guerrillatacos.com.*

★ Hayato

$$$$ | **JAPANESE** | There's a very good reason that Michelin decided to award this elegant, peaceful restaurant one star, and it starts with chef Brandon Hayato Go's attention to detail in cooking across all Japanese techniques. Dubbed *washoku*, the chef's dishes mix simmering, frying, steaming, grilling, and sashimi styles into works of edible art that will leave your tongue, nose, and brain tingling from start to finish. **Known for:** excellent and inventive Japanese cuisine; high-quality bento boxes for weekend lunches; serene atmosphere. ⑤ *Average main: $52 ⊠ 1320 E. 7th St., Suite 126, Downtown* ☎ *213/395–0607* ⊕ *www.hayatorestaurant.com* ⊙ *No lunch weekdays.*

★ Howlin' Ray's

$$ | **SOUTHERN** | **FAMILY** | Don't let the hour-long waits deter you—if you want the best Nashville fried chicken in L.A., Howlin' Ray's is worth the effort. Right in the middle of Chinatown, this tiny chicken joint consists of a few bar seats, a few side tables, and a kitchen that sizzles as staff yell out "yes, chef" with each incoming order. **Known for:** spicy fried chicken; classic Southern sides; long waits. ⑤ *Average main: $15 ⊠ 727 N. Broadway, Suite 128, Downtown* ☎ *213/935–8399* ⊕ *www.howlinrays.com* ⊙ *Closed Sun. and Mon.* Ⓜ *Union Station.*

★ Langer's Delicatessen-Restaurant

$ | **DELI** | **FAMILY** | This James Beard Award winner not only has the look and feel of a no-frills Jewish deli from New York, it also has the food to match. The draw here is the hand-cut pastrami: lean, peppery, robust—and with a reputation for being the best in town. **Known for:** #19 aka pastrami with Swiss and coleslaw piled high on twice-baked rye; Jewish deli classics like matzo ball soup and rugelach; no-frills atmosphere. ⑤ *Average main: $13 ⊠ 704 S. Alvarado St., Downtown* ☎ *213/483–8050* ⊕ *www.langersdeli.com* ⊙ *Closed Sun. No dinner* Ⓜ *Westlake/MacArthur Park.*

★ Majordomo

$$$$ | **ECLECTIC** | You would never just stumble upon this out-of-the-way spot in Chinatown, but world-famous celeb chef David Chang likes it that way. The beautifully designed minimal space with spacious patio, an exposed-duct ceiling, and elongated wood bar has a cuisine style that defies any singular category.

Diners can sit and enjoy lunch at the Wexler's Deli counter inside Grand Central Market.

Known for: chuck short rib with raclette; rice-based drinks; hard-to-get reservations (try to eat at the bar). $ *Average main: $40* ✉ *1725 Naud St., Downtown* ☎ *323/545–4880* ⊕ *www.majordomo.la* ⊙ *Closed Mon. and Tues.*

Original Pantry Cafe

$$ | **AMERICAN** | Opened in 1924 by Dewey Logan, this classic diner claims to have never closed in the entirety of its run (COVID-19 aside) and is currently owned by former L.A. mayor Richard Riordan. Open 24-7, the diner serves American food for breakfast, lunch, and dinner, and is known for cakes, pies, steaks, and chops. **Known for:** long lines; amazing breakfast; cash-only policy. $ *Average main: $15* ✉ *877 S. Figueroa St., Downtown* ☎ *213/972–9279* ⊕ *www.pantryca-fe.com* Ⓜ *7th Street/Metro Center.*

Petite Peso

$ | **PHILIPPINE** | To quote the restaurant itself, this is "Filipino food with thoughtful ingredients," and luckily for diners, it also happens to be fantastic. The small Jewelry District spot serves up

a powerful menu of Filipino favorites, from perfect pancit and beef kare kare to crackling lumpia and assorted Filipino pastries. **Known for:** traditional Filipino dishes; excellent pastries; delicious rice bowls. $ *Average main: $10* ✉ *419 W. 7th St., Downtown* ☎ *209/438–7376* ⊕ *www.petitepeso.com* ⊙ *Closed Mon.* Ⓜ *Pershing Square.*

★ Philippe the Original

$ | **AMERICAN** | **FAMILY** | First opened in 1908, Philippe's is one of L.A.'s oldest restaurants and claims to be the originator of the French dip sandwich. While the debate continues around the city, one thing is certain: the dips made with beef, pork, ham, lamb, or turkey on a freshly baked roll stand the test of time. **Known for:** 50¢ coffee; communal tables; post–Dodgers game eats. $ *Average main: $8* ✉ *1001 N. Alameda St., Downtown* ☎ *213/628–3781* ⊕ *www.philippes.com* Ⓜ *Union Station.*

Q Sushi

$$$$ | **JAPANESE** | Every night is different at this elegant, one-Michelin-starred

omakase (chef-selected) sushi joint. It all depends on what's the freshest and what's the absolute best. **Known for:** multicourse (very expensive) omakase menu; elegant ambience; fresh bluefin tuna and Hokkaido scallops. $ *Average main: $300* ⊠ *521 W. 7th St., Downtown* ☎ *213/225–6285* ⊕ *www.qsushila.com* ☾ *Closed Sun. and Mon. No lunch Sat.* Ⓜ *7th Street/Metro Center.*

71Above

$$$$ | ECLECTIC | As its name suggests, this sky-high dining den sits on the 71st floor, 950 feet above ground level. With that elevation comes the most stunning views of any restaurant in L.A., and the food is close to matching it. **Known for:** sky-high views; fine dining with a seafood focus; classy atmosphere and loosely enforced dress code (no shorts or flip-flops). $ *Average main: $39* ⊠ *633 W. 5th St., 71st fl., Downtown* ☎ *213/712–2683* ⊕ *www.71above.com* Ⓜ *Pershing Square Station.*

Shibumi

$$$ | JAPANESE | This *kappo* (cooking and cutting) restaurant in the middle of Downtown is offering up some of the most inventive raw, steamed, grilled, and fried Japanese dishes you'll ever try. Chef David Schlosser serves you personally from the 400-year-old cypress bar. **Known for:** kappo and omakase dining with a Michelin star; actual Kobe beef; creative off-menu options (be sure to ask!). $ *Average main: $25* ⊠ *815 S. Hill St., Downtown* ☎ *323/484–8915* ⊕ *www. shibumidtla.com* ☾ *Closed Mon.* Ⓜ *7th Street/Metro Center.*

Sonoratown

$ | MEXICAN | Paying homage to the Mexican border town where owner Teo Diaz-Rodriguez Jr. grew up, Sonoratown is a Downtown L.A. joint that serves some of the best tacos in the entire city. Handmade tortillas, mesquite wood-fired carne asada, and supercheap prices have made this spot a neighborhood favorite and a must-have on any trip Downtown.

Known for: excellent Sonoran-style tacos; great prices; friendly neighborhood spot. $ *Average main: $8* ⊠ *208 E. 8th St., Downtown* ☎ *213/628–3710* ⊕ *www. sonoratown.com.*

Sushi Gen

$$ | JAPANESE | Consistently rated one of the top sushi spots in L.A., Sushi Gen continues to dole out the freshest and tastiest fish in town. Sit at the elongated bar and get to know the sushi masters while they prepare your lunch. **Known for:** chef-recommended sushi selections; limited seating; great lunch specials. $ *Average main: $20* ⊠ *422 E. 2nd St., Downtown* ☎ *213/617–0552* ⊕ *www. sushigen-dtla.com* ☾ *Closed Sun. and Mon. No lunch Sat.*

🛏 Hotels

An ongoing revitalization in Downtown, anchored around the L.A. Live complex, make this a great place to see Los Angeles in transition: think affordable accommodations rubbing elbows with business hotels, streets lined with coffeehouses, and edgy boutiques that can be explored on foot. If you're traveling alone, some parts of Downtown are better to drive rather than walk through after dark.

★ Ace Hotel Downtown Los Angeles

$$ | HOTEL | The L.A. edition of this bohemian-chic hipster haven is at once a hotel, theater, and poolside bar (called Upstairs), housed in the gorgeous Spanish Gothic–style United Artists building in the heart of Downtown. **Pros:** lively rooftop lounge/pool area; gorgeous building and views; location in the heart of Downtown. **Cons:** expensive parking rates compared to nightly rates ($36); some kinks in the service; compact rooms. $ *Rooms from: $239* ⊠ *929 S. Broadway, Downtown* ☎ *213/623–3233* ⊕ *www. acehotel.com/losangeles* ⮌ *183 rooms* ⦿ *No meals.*

★ Freehand Los Angeles

$ | HOTEL | Part hotel, part shared accommodation space, the Freehand is one of the newest hotels in Downtown Los Angeles and also one of the coolest. **Pros:** range of affordable rooms from lofts to bunk beds; active social scene; great rooftop pool and bar. **Cons:** sketchy area at night around the hotel; free lobby Wi-Fi attracts nonhotel guests; most affordable rooms are shared. $ *Rooms from: $100* ✉ *416 W. 8th St., Downtown* ☎ *213/612–0021* ⊕ *freehandhotels.com/los-angeles* ⇴ *59 shared rooms, 167 private rooms* ⦿ *No meals* Ⓜ *Pershing Square.*

Hotel Figueroa

$$ | HOTEL | The 12-story Hotel Figueroa was originally built in 1926, and touches of that originality are still seen throughout with original skylights, wood beams, and tiles. **Pros:** a short walk to L.A. Live and the convention center; great poolside bar; in-room iPads and complimentary minibar snacks. **Cons:** the area can be sketchy at night; expensive parking ($40/night); smallish pool. $ *Rooms from: $200* ✉ *939 S. Figueroa St., Downtown* ☎ *866/734–6018* ⊕ *www.hotelfigueroa. com* ⇴ *268 rooms* ⦿ *No meals* Ⓜ *Olympic/Figueroa.*

The Hoxton

$ | HOTEL | Now one of the chicest hotels in Downtown L.A., the Hoxton is an open-house hotel where the lobby is the hub of activity and thoughtful design touches permeate throughout. The historic building was once the headquarters of the L.A. Railway and now sits in an up-and-coming part of the city filled with restaurants and apartments. **Pros:** stellar restaurant; monthly event calendar; great rooftop pool. **Cons:** area can be dodgy at night; no gym; some rooms on the small side. $ *Rooms from: $160* ✉ *1060 S. Broadway, Downtown* ☎ *213/725–5900* ⊕ *www.thehoxton.com/downtown-la* ⇴ *174 rooms* ⦿ *No meals.*

InterContinental Los Angeles Downtown

$$ | HOTEL | This five-star addition to the Downtown L.A. scene impresses with views, an enormous gym, dining, and an outdoor pool. **Pros:** best views in the city; incredible restaurants and bars; top-rate service. **Cons:** too big and impersonal; busy and tricky intersection; parking is $46/night. $ *Rooms from: $300* ✉ *900 Wilshire Blvd., Downtown* ☎ *213/688–7777* ⊕ *dtla.intercontinental.com* ⇴ *889 rooms* ⦿ *No meals* Ⓜ *7th Street/Metro Center.*

Millennium Biltmore Hotel

$ | HOTEL | As the local headquarters of John F. Kennedy's 1960 presidential campaign and the location of some of the earliest Academy Awards ceremonies, this Downtown treasure, with its gilded 1923 beaux arts design, exudes ambience and history. **Pros:** 24-hour business center; tiled indoor pool and steam room; impressive history. **Cons:** pricey valet parking; standard rooms are compact; some decor is dated. $ *Rooms from: $200* ✉ *506 S. Grand Ave., Downtown* ☎ *213/624–1011, 866/866–8086* ⊕ *www. millenniumhotels.com* ⇴ *683 rooms* ⦿ *No meals* Ⓜ *Pershing Square.*

The NoMad Hotel

$$ | HOTEL | This stunningly refurbished property used to house the Bank of Italy and touches of the old bank can still be seen throughout—most notably in the lobby bathrooms that are cut out of the original vault. **Pros:** freestanding tubs; individually sourced artwork throughout; 24-hour gym. **Cons:** sketchy area at night; expensive parking ($48/night); some rooms are small. $ *Rooms from: $250* ✉ *649 S. Olive St., Downtown* ☎ *213/358–0000* ⊕ *www.thenomadhotel. com/los-angeles* ⇴ *241 rooms* ⦿ *No meals* Ⓜ *7th Street/Metro Center.*

The Ritz-Carlton, Los Angeles

$$$ | HOTEL | This citified Ritz-Carlton on the 23rd–26th floors of a 54-story tower within Downtown's L.A. Live entertainment complex features skyline views

8

Downtown Los Angeles

through expansive windows, blond woods, and smartened-up amenities such as flat-screen TVs (including one hidden in the bathroom mirror). **Pros:** designer spa; rooftop pool; daily buffet of five light meals. **Cons:** expensive valet parking ($49); corporate feel; pricey room service. $ *Rooms from: $400* ✉ *900 W. Olympic Blvd., Downtown* ☎ *213/743–8800* ⊕ *www.ritzcarlton.com* ⌘ *123 rooms* ⦿ *No meals* Ⓜ *Pico.*

The Standard, Downtown L.A.

$$ | **HOTEL** | Built in 1955 as the headquarters of Standard Oil, the building was completely revamped under the sharp eye of owner André Balazs to become a sleek, cutting-edge hotel with spacious guest rooms. **Pros:** 24/7 restaurant; rotating pop-up events; lively rooftop lounge. **Cons:** disruptive party scene on weekends and holidays; street noise; pricey valet parking. $ *Rooms from: $200* ✉ *550 S. Flower St., Downtown* ☎ *213/892–8080* ⊕ *www.standardhotels.com/la/properties/downtown-la* ⌘ *207 rooms* ⦿ *No meals* Ⓜ *7th Street/Metro Center.*

Westin Bonaventure Hotel and Suites

$$ | **HOTEL** | **FAMILY** | Step inside the futuristic lobby of L.A.'s largest hotel to be greeted by fountains, an indoor lake and track, and 12 glass elevators leading up to the historic rooms of this 35-story property. Color-coded hotel floors help newcomers navigate the hotel, which takes up an entire city block. **Pros:** spa with shiatsu massage; revolving rooftop lounge; many on-site restaurants. **Cons:** massive hotel might feel too corporate; mazelike lobby and public areas; standard rooms are on the small side. $ *Rooms from: $250* ✉ *404 S. Figueroa St., Downtown* ☎ *213/624–1000* ⊕ *westin.marriott.com* ⌘ *1358 rooms* ⦿ *No meals* Ⓜ *7th Street/Metro Center.*

✦ Nightlife

With choice music venues, upscale bars, and divier clubs, Downtown Los Angeles is high on the list of after-dark options.

BonaVista Lounge at the Westin Bonaventure

BARS/PUBS | Atop the Westin Bonaventure hotel, L.A.'s best-kept secret cocktail bar revolves 34 floors above the street. With glass walls and views of Downtown, snowcapped mountains, Hollywood, and beyond (on a clear day, you can spot the ocean), there isn't a bad seat in the house. The food is an after-thought, but the drinks are great, if slightly overpriced; but hey, you're paying for a showstopping view. ✉ *404 S. Figueroa St., Downtown* ☎ *213/612–4743* ⊕ *www.marriott.com/hotels/hotel-information/restaurant/laxbw-the-westin-bonaventure-hotel-and-suites-los-angeles* Ⓜ *7th Street/Metro Center.*

Broadway Bar

BARS/PUBS | This watering-hole-meets-dive sits in a flourishing section of Broadway (neighbors include the swank Ace Hotel). Bartenders mix creative cocktails while DJs spin tunes nightly. The two-story space includes a smoking balcony overlooking the street. The crowd is often dressed to impress. ✉ *830 S. Broadway, Downtown* ☎ *213/614–9909* ⊕ *www.broadwaybarla.com.*

Clifton's Republic

THEMED ENTERTAINMENT | Part marketplace, part bazaar of bars, part curio museum, Clifton's Republic is a wild, weird, and glorious establishment. Enter the ground floor and you'll find an indoor forest and a whole lot of grub. Upstairs is a maze of bars, dance floors, and intimate corners. ✉ *648 S. Broadway, Downtown* ☎ *213/613–0000* ⊕ *www.theneverlands.com/cliftons-republic* Ⓜ *Pershing Square.*

★ The Edison

BARS/PUBS | The glitz and glam of the Roaring '20s is alive and well in the Edison, where the decor serves as tribute to the power plant that once occupied these premises. Black-and-white silent films are projected onto the walls, and tasty nibbles and artisanal cocktails are served (in a private room, if you prefer). There's live entertainment many nights, from jazz bands to burlesque shows to magic. A dress code means no shorts, jerseys, hoodies, flip-flops, tennis shoes, or collarless shirts. ⊠ 108 W. 2nd St., Downtown ☎ 213/613–0000 ⊕ www.theneverlands.com/edison.

★ Golden Gopher

BARS/PUBS | Craft cocktails, beers on tap, an outdoor smoking patio, and retro video games—this bar in the heart of Downtown is not to be missed. With one of the oldest liquor licenses in Los Angeles (issued in 1905), the Golden Gopher is the only bar in Los Angeles with an on-site liquor store for to-go orders—just in case you want to buy another bottle before you head home. ⊠ 417 W. 8th St., Downtown ☎ 213/614–8001 ⊕ www.pouringwithheart.com/golden-gopher Ⓜ 7th Street/Metro Center.

La Cita

BARS/PUBS | This dive bar may not look like much, but it more than makes up for it with an interesting mix of barflies, urban hipsters, and reasonable drink prices. Friday and Saturday night, DJs mix Top 40 hits and a tiny dance floor packs in the crowd. For those more interested in drinking and socializing, head to the back patio where a TV plays local sports. Every day has a differently themed happy hour—hip-hop happy hour on Wednesday or rockabilly happy hour on Thursday. Specials vary from $3 Tecates to free pizza. ⊠ 336 S. Hill St., Downtown ☎ 213/687–7111 ⊕ www.lacitabar.com Ⓜ Pershing Square Station.

The Love Song Bar

BARS/PUBS | Lovers of T. S. Eliot and vinyl will find themselves instantly at home inside this cozy establishment named after Eliot's "The Love Song of J. Alfred Prufrock." When not pouring drinks, bartenders often act as DJs, playing records (the best of the '60s through the '80s) in their entirety. As it's housed inside the Regent Theater, the cozy nature of the place can be disrupted when there's a concert scheduled. For those with an appetite, fantastic food can be ordered from the pizza parlor next door—naturally, it's called Prufrock's. ⊠ 450 S. Main St., Downtown ☎ 323/284–5728 ⊕ www.spacelandpresents.com/events/the-love-song.

Redwood Bar & Grill

BARS/PUBS | If you're looking for a place with potent drinks and a good burger, this kitschy bar fits the bill perfectly. Known today as the "pirate bar" because of its nautical decor, the place dates back to the 1940s, when it was rumored to attract mobsters, politicians, and journalists due to its proximity to city hall, the Hall of Justice, and the original location of the Los Angeles Times. There's nightly music from local rock bands, though it comes with a cover charge. ⊠ 316 W. 2nd St., Downtown ☎ 213/680–2600 ⊕ www.theredwoodbar.com Ⓜ Civic Center/Grand Park.

★ Resident

MUSIC CLUBS | Catch a lineup of indie tastemakers inside this converted industrial space, or hang outdoors in the beer garden while trying bites from on-site food truck KTCHN (on cooler evenings you can congregate around the fire pits). A wide variety of draft beers and a specially curated cocktail program are available inside at the bar or at the trailer bar outside. ⊠ 428 S. Hewitt St., Downtown ☎ 213/628–7503 ⊕ www.residentdtla.com.

★ **Seven Grand**

BARS/PUBS | The hunting lodge vibe makes you feel like you need a whiskey in hand—luckily, this Downtown establishment stocks more than 700 of them. Attracting whiskey novices and connoisseurs, the bartenders here are more than willing to help you make a selection. Live jazz and blues bands play every night, so even if you're not a big drinker, there's still some appeal (although you're definitely missing out). For a more intimate setting, try the on-site **Bar Jackalope,** a bar within a bar, which has a "whiskey tasting library" specializing in Japanese varieties and seats only 18. ⊠ *515 W. 7th St., 2nd fl., Downtown* ☎ *213/614–0736* ⊕ *www.sevengrandbars.com* Ⓜ *7th Street/Metro Center.*

The Varnish

BARS/PUBS | Beeline through the dining room of Cole's to find an unassuming door that leads to this small, dimly lit bar. Wooden booths line the walls, candles flicker, and live jazz is performed Sunday through Wednesday. The bartenders take their calling to heart and shake and stir some of the finest cocktails in the city. Those who don't have a drink of choice can list their wants ("gin-based and sweet," "strong whiskey and herbaceous") and be served a custom cocktail. Be warned: patrons requiring quick drinks will want to go elsewhere—perfection takes time. ⊠ *118 E. 6th St., Downtown* ☎ *213/265–7089* ⊕ *www. pouringwithheart.com/the-varnish.*

🎭 Performing Arts

Ahmanson Theatre

THEATER | The largest of L.A.'s Center Group's three theaters, the 2,100-seat Ahmanson Theatre presents larger-scale classic revivals, dramas, musicals, and comedies like *Into the Woods,* which are either going to or coming from Broadway and the West End. The ambience is a theater lover's delight. ⊠ *135 N. Grand Ave., Downtown* ☎ *213/972–7211*

⊕ *www.musiccenter.org/visit/Our-Venues/ahmanson-theatre* Ⓜ *Civic Center/ Grand Park Station.*

★ **Dorothy Chandler Pavilion**

CONCERTS | Though half a century old, this theater maintains the glamour of its early years, richly decorated with crystal chandeliers, classical theatrical drapes, and a 24-karat gold dome. Part of the Los Angeles Music Center, this pavilion is home to the L.A. Opera though a large portion of programming is made up of dance and ballet performances as well. Ticket holders can attend free talks that take place an hour before opera performances. ■ TIP→ **Reservations for the talks aren't required, but it's wise to arrive early, as space is limited.** ⊠ *135 N. Grand Ave., Downtown* ☎ *213/972–0711* ⊕ *www. musiccenter.org/visit/Our-Venues/dorothy-chandler-pavilion* Ⓜ *Civic Center/ Grand Park.*

East West Players

THEATER | Plays at this Little Tokyo theater focus on the Asian American experience and features an Asian American cast. Its Theatre for Youth Program is a traveling production that promotes racial tolerance and understanding among students. It is also home to the David Henry Hwang Writers Institute. ⊠ *120 Judge John Aiso St., Little Tokyo* ☎ *213/625–7000* ⊕ *www. eastwestplayers.org* Ⓜ *Union Station.*

Mark Taper Forum

THEATER | Both dramas and comedies dominate the stage at the Mark Taper Forum, next door to the Ahmanson Theatre in Downtown. A showcase for new and experimental plays, quite a few shows that premiered here have gone on to Broadway and off-Broadway theaters (a number of Pulitzer Prize–winning plays have also been developed here). ⊠ *135 N. Grand Ave., Downtown* ☎ *213/628– 2772* ⊕ *www.musiccenter.org/visit/ Our-Venues/mark-taper-forum* Ⓜ *Civic Center/Grand Park.*

Continued on page 193

L.A. STORY
THE CITY'S HISTORY THROUGH ITS BARS

Los Angeles is known as a place where dreams are realized, but it is also a place where pasts are forgotten. Despite what people say about L.A.'s lack of memory, however, there are quite a few noteworthy old-school bars that pay tribute to the city's vibrant past and its famous patrons.

Collectively, these eclectic watering holes have hosted everyone from ex-presidents to rock legends to famed authors and, of course, a continual stream of countless movie stars.

The bars are located in virtually every corner of the city—from Downtown to West Hollywood to Santa Monica.

In terms of character, they run the gamut from dive to dressy and serve everything from top-shelf whisky to bargain-basement beer.

While it's their differences that have kept people coming back through the decades, they all have something in common: Each has a story to tell.

EIGHT OF L.A.'S BEST

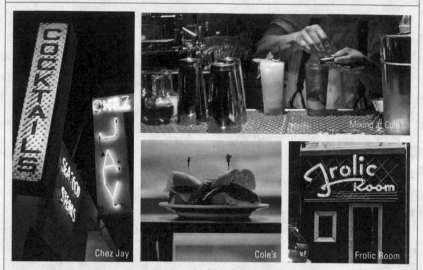

Chez Jay | Cole's | Frolic Room | Mixing at Cole's

CHEZ JAY RESTAURANT (1959)
Noteworthy for: Located down the block from the Santa Monica Pier, this steak-and-seafood joint walks the line between celebrity hangout and dive bar.
Signature drink: Martini
Celeb clientele: Members of the Rat Pack, Leonard Nimoy, Sean Penn, Julia Roberts, Renée Zellweger, Owen Wilson, Drew Barrymore
Don't miss: The little booth in the back of the restaurant, known to insiders as Table 10, is a favorite celebrity hideout.
Filmed here: A Single Man, Goliath
Join the crowd: 1657 Ocean Ave., Santa Monica, 310/395–1741

COLE'S (1908)
Noteworthy for: Found inside the Pacific Electric building, touted as Los Angeles's oldest public house, and once the epicenter of the Red Car railway network, this watering hole has its original glass lighting, penny-tile floors, and 40-foot mahogany bar.
Signature drink: Old-fashioned
Celeb clientele: The men's room boasts that Charles Bukowski and Mickey Cohen once relieved themselves here.

Don't miss: The Varnish at Cole's is an in-house speakeasy with 11 booths that can be accessed through a hidden door marked by a tiny framed picture of a cocktail glass.
Filmed here: Forrest Gump, L.A. Confidential, Mad Men
Join the crowd: 118 E. 6th St., Los Angeles, 213/622–4049

CLIFTON'S REPUBLIC (1931)
Noteworthy for: This historical cafeteria/playground featuring a giant redwood tree in the center and intimidating wildlife taxidermy throughout, serves tasty comfort food and houses three lively bars: the Monarch, the Gothic, and the Pacific Seas.
Signature drink: The Mind Eraser at the Tiki bar; El Presidio at the Monarch; the Hyperion at The Gothic Bar (careful—this one's strong).
Claim to fame: Clifton's whimsical forest-themed dining area inspired Walt Disney to create Disneyland.
Don't miss: The 40's-era Tiki Bar. Located at the top of a secret stairway, it features deliciously strong drinks, dancing

Chez Jay

Harvelle's

Dresden Restaurant

cigarette girls and the occasional appearance of a sequined mermaid.

FROLIC ROOM (1935)

Noteworthy for: This Hollywood favorite next door to the famed Pantages Theater has served actors and writers from Elizabeth Short to Charles Bukowski.

Signature drink: Cheap Budweiser ($2.75 during happy hour)

Celeb clientele: Kiefer Sutherland

Don't miss: A bowl of popcorn from the old-fashioned machine; the Hirschfeld mural depicting Marilyn Monroe, Charlie Chaplin, Louis Armstrong, Frank Sinatra, and others.

Filmed here: *L.A. Confidential, Southland*

Join the crowd: *6245 Hollywood Blvd., Los Angeles, 323/462–5890*

HARVELLE'S (1931)

Noteworthy for: Located one block off the Third Street Promenade, this dark and sexy jazz bar is said to be the oldest live music venue on the Westside.

Signature drink: The Deadly Sins martini menu offers house made mixes named after the seven sins, from Pride to Lust.

Don't miss: The Toledo Show is a pulse-quickening weekly burlesque-and-jazz performance on Sunday nights.

Join the crowd: *1432 4th St., Santa Monica, 310/395–1676.*

THE KIBITZ ROOM AT CANTER'S DELI (1961)

Noteworthy for: Adjacent to the famous Canter's Deli, which opened in 1948, this Fairfax District nightspot is definitely a dive bar, but that doesn't keep the A-listers away. Joni Mitchell, Jakob Dylan, and Fiona Apple have all played here.

Signature drink: Cheap beer

Celeb clientele: Jim Morrison, Frank Zappa, Juliette Lewis, Julia Roberts, Javier Bardem, Penélope Cruz

Don't miss: The decor is pure retro 1960s, including vinyl booths and a fall-leaf motif on the ceiling.

Filmed here: *I Ought to Be in Pictures, Entourage, Curb Your Enthusiasm,*

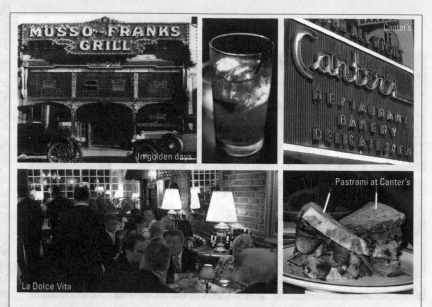

In golden days

Canter's

Pastrami at Canter's

La Dolce Vita

Sunset Strip, Enemy of the State, What's Eating Gilbert Grape
Join the crowd: *419 N. Fairfax Ave., Los Angeles, 323/651–2030.*

DOLCE VITA (1966)

Noteworthy for: Located in tony Beverly Hills, this staple for northern Italian has a classy clubhouse atmosphere, round leather booths, white tablecloths, and exposed-brick walls.
Signature drink: Martini
Celeb clientele: Members of the Rat Pack; several ex-presidents, including Ronald Reagan. The place prides itself on being a safe haven from pesky paparazzi.
Don't miss: The burgundy-hued round leather booths.
Join the crowd: *9785 Santa Monica Blvd., Los Angeles, 310/278–1845*

MUSSO & FRANK GRILL (1919)

Noteworthy for: This swanky old-timer is called the oldest bar in Hollywood. While that title may spark jealousy among some of its Tinseltown counterparts, there is no doubt that this famed grill conjures Hollywood's halcyon days with its authentic '30s-era decor—and serves a mean martini.
Signature drink: The Mean Martini
Celeb clientele: Charlie Chaplin, Greta Garbo, Ernest Hemingway, F. Scott Fitzgerald, Marilyn Monroe
Don't miss: The red tuxedo-clad waiters are famous in their own right; some have been at the restaurant for more than 40 years.
Filmed here: *Ocean's Eleven, Charlie's Angels 2, Mad Men*
Join the crowd: *6667 Hollywood Blvd., Los Angeles, 323/467–7788*

The Musso & Frank Grill

THE OLDEST RESTAURANT IN HOLLYWOOD
Since 1919

Microsoft Theater

CONCERTS | The Microsoft Theater is host to a variety of concerts and big-name awards shows—the Emmys, American Music Awards, BET Awards, and the ESPYs. This theater and the surrounding L.A. Live complex are a draw for those looking for a fun night out. The building's emphasis on acoustics and versatile seating arrangements means that all 7,100 seats are good, whether you're at an intimate acoustic concert or the People's Choice Awards. Outside, the L.A. Live complex hosts restaurants and attractions, including the GRAMMY Museum, to keep patrons entertained before and after shows (though it's open whether or not there's a performance). ⊠ *777 Chick Hearn Ct., Downtown* ☎ *213/763–6030* ⊕ *www.microsofttheater.com* Ⓜ *Pico.*

The REDCAT (Roy and Edna Disney/Cal Arts Theater)

DANCE | Located inside the Walt Disney Concert Hall, this 288-seat theater serves as a space for innovative performance and visual art in addition to film screenings and literary events. The gallery features changing art installations. Tickets are reasonably priced at $25 and under for most events. ⊠ *631 W. 2nd St., Downtown* ☎ *213/237–2800* ⊕ *www.redcat.org* Ⓜ *Civic Center/Grand Park.*

Shrine Auditorium

CONCERTS | Since opening in 1926, the auditorium has hosted nearly every major awards show at one point or another, including the Emmys and the GRAMMYs. Today, the venue and adjacent Expo Hall hosts concerts, film premieres, award shows, pageants, and special events. The Shrine's Moorish Revival–style architecture is a spectacle all its own. ⊠ *665 W. Jefferson Blvd., Downtown* ☎ *213/748–5116* ⊕ *www.shrineauditorium.com.*

🍴 Shopping

Downtown L.A. is dotted with international neighborhoods (Olvera Street, Chinatown, Koreatown, Little Tokyo) and several large, open-air shopping venues (the Fashion District, the Flower Market, Grand Central Market, the Toy District, and the Jewelry District).

It offers an urban bargain hunter's dream shopping experience if you know precisely what you're looking for (like diamonds and gems from the Jewelry District) or if you're willing to be tempted by unexpected finds (piñatas from Olvera Street, slippers from Chinatown, or lacquered chopsticks from Little Tokyo).

Fashion District

SHOPPING NEIGHBORHOODS | With the influx of emerging designers in this pocket of Downtown, it's become much more than just a wholesale market. Besides containing the plant paradise that is the Los Angeles Flower Market as well as the Fabric District and Santee Alley, the neighborhood now boasts a bevy of boutiques and cool coffee shops, thanks in part to the Row DTLA, a towering complex with curated stores, restaurants, and design spaces. ⊠ *Roughly between I–10 and 7th St., and S. Los Angeles St. and S. Central Ave., Downtown* ☎ *213/741–2661* ⊕ *www.fashiondistrict.org.*

Jewelry District

SHOPPING NEIGHBORHOODS | Filled with bargain hunters, these crowded sidewalks resemble a slice of Manhattan with nearly 5,000 individual vendors and businesses. While you can save big on everything from wedding bands to sparkling belt buckles, the neighborhood also offers several more upscale vendors for those in search of super-special pieces. ⊠ *Between Olive St. and Broadway from 5th to 8th St., Downtown* ☎ *213/928–7889* ⊕ *www.the-jewelry-district.com* Ⓜ *Pershing Square.*

★ Olvera Street

OUTDOOR/FLEA/GREEN MARKETS | FAMILY |
Known as the birthplace of Los Angeles, this redbrick walkway is lined with historic buildings and overhung with grapevines. At dozens of clapboard stalls you can browse south-of-the-border goods—leather sandals, woven blankets, and devotional candles, as well as cheap toys and souvenirs—and sample outstanding tacos. With the musicians and cafés providing the soundtrack, the area is constantly lively. Annual events include a tree-lighting ceremony and Día de los Muertos celebrations. ⊠ *Between Cesar Chavez Ave. and Arcadia St., Downtown* ⊕ *www.olvera-street.com* Ⓜ *Union Station.*

Row DTLA

SHOPPING CENTERS/MALLS | The city's newest shopping, food, and cultural destination in the venerable L.A. Arts District, Row DTLA is spread across an entire campus, with around 100 curated boutique stores like Poketo, Bodega, A+R, Flask & Field, and Tokyo Bike. Additionally, new restaurants like Rappahannock Oyster Bar and Michelin-starred Hayato seem to be popping up weekly. A weekend highlight is Smorgasburg, where every Sunday dozens of food stalls pop up in the next-door parking lot serving tasty favorites across every cuisine imaginable. ⊠ *777 Alameda St., Downtown* ☎ *213/988–8890* ⊕ *rowdtla. com.*

The Santee Alley

SHOPPING NEIGHBORHOODS | Situated in the Fashion District, the Santee Alley is known for back-alley deals on knockoffs of designer sunglasses, jewelry, handbags, shoes, and clothing. Be prepared to haggle, and don't lose sight of your wallet. Weekend crowds can be overwhelming, but there's plenty of street food to keep your energy up. ⊠ *Santee St. and Maple Ave. from Olympic Blvd. to 12th St., Downtown* ☎ *213/488–1153* ⊕ *www.fashiondistrict.org/santee-alley.*

Chapter 9

LOS FELIZ, SILVER LAKE, AND THE EASTSIDE

Updated by
Michelle Rae Uy

⊙ Sights	🍴 Restaurants	🛏 Hotels	🛍 Shopping	🍸 Nightlife
★★★☆☆	★★★★★	★★☆☆☆	★★★★☆	★★★★★

A DAY AT GRIFFITH PARK

On the trail in Griffith Park

The 4,100-acre Griffith Park (the largest municipal park and urban wilderness area in the United States) stands out as an oasis in a city covered in cement and asphalt.

On warm weekends, there are parties, barbecues, mariachi bands, and strolling vendors selling fresh fruit. Joggers, cyclists, and walkers course its roadways. There are also top attractions within the park, including the Griffith Observatory and the Los Angeles Zoo.

The park was named after Col. Griffith J. Griffith, a mining tycoon who donated 3,000 acres of land to the city for the park in 1896. It has been used as a film and television location since the early days of motion pictures. One early Hollywood producer advised, "A tree is a tree, a rock is a rock, shoot it in Griffith Park."

GETTING HERE

The park has several entrances: off Los Feliz Boulevard at Western Canyon Avenue, Vermont Avenue, Crystal Springs Drive, and Riverside Drive; from the Ventura/134 Freeway at Victory Boulevard, Zoo Drive, or Forest Lawn Drive; from the Golden State Freeway (I–5) at Los Feliz Boulevard and Zoo Drive. The park is open from 6 am to 10 pm.

TOP EXPERIENCES

Visit the Griffith Observatory. The Griffith Observatory offers breathtaking panoramic views, and the structure itself is a pristinely maintained art deco spectacle. Visit during a scheduled talk or show at the Leonard Nimoy Event Horizon Theater, look through the Zeiss Telescope on a clear night, or check out the Samuel Oschin Planetarium and its incredible dome.

The Griffith Observatory

The expansive grounds are open to the public and include a monument dedicated to James Dean; several scenes from *Rebel Without a Cause* were filmed here (if you've never seen the film, it's a definite must-watch before visiting). To see the lights of the city twinkle at night from above, stay late and head up to the Observatory Deck, open until 10 pm every evening except Monday.

Climb Mount Hollywood. There are plenty of scenic routes throughout the park, but one of the best trails is to the top of Mount Hollywood. Park at the Griffith Observatory lot and pick up the trail from there. It's an easy half-hour hike to the top. On clear days you'll be able to see all the way to the Pacific Ocean and Catalina Island. About two-thirds of the way up is Dante's View, an area with benches where you can stop for a break or snack. You'll likely cross paths with horseback riders on the way.

An up-close view of the Hollywood sign from below means hiking a little more than 6 miles round-trip from the parking lot.

Check Out the Los Angeles Zoo and Botanical Gardens. In the northeast corner of the park, the zoo's highlights include a gorilla reserve, a Sumatran tiger, a snow leopard, and an acre dedicated to one of the largest troops of chimpanzees in the United States. In addition, the zoo claims to have more flamingoes than any other zoo worldwide.

Enjoy a Bike Tour. There's a flat, family-friendly 4.7-mile path that runs along Crystal Springs Drive and Zoo Drive. Rentals are available inside the park at **Spokes n' Stuff Bike Shop** (⊠ *4730 Crystal Springs Dr., at ranger station parking lot* ☏ *323/662–6573* ⊕ *www.spokes-n-stuff.com*).

See a Concert at the Greek Theatre. The 6,100-seat **Greek Theatre** (☏ *323/665–1927* ⊕ *www.greektheatrela.com*) is an outdoor venue where top artists such as Elton John and Paul Simon have performed.

A resident of the park's zoo

NEIGHBORHOOD SNAPSHOT

TOP REASONS TO GO

■ **Hike at Griffith Park:** This is without a doubt the best place to partake in L.A.'s favorite pastime—exercising. With over 4,210 acres, it's one of the largest urban parks in the country and happens to have one of the most glorious views of the city.

■ **Stargaze at the Griffith Observatory:** Most visitors may flock to this observatory for its mesmerizing panoramas, but the more discerning travelers come for its night sky viewings and star parties.

■ **Get some culture at Barnsdall Art Park:** Architecture, art, drama, and wine all come together in one of L.A.'s best-kept secrets, where a day can be spent taking an art class, touring the appealing Frank Lloyd Wright–designed Hollyhock House, and sipping wine.

■ **Eat your way around the neighborhood:** Los Feliz is home to a host of fantastic restaurants. Indulge in Middle Eastern at Kismet, Italian at Little Dom's, and tacos at the Best Fish Taco in Ensenada.

QUICK BITES

Best Fish Taco in Ensenada. A simple, cheap, unceremonious taco stand with a selection of spicy house-made salsas—a little local treasure. ⊠ *1650 Hillhurst Ave.* ⊕ *bestfishtacoinensenada.com*

Guisados. The tacos, with handmade tortillas and braised meats, are some of the best in the city—plus each one only costs a few bucks. But you'll have to endure long lines. ⊠ *1261 Sunset Blvd.* ⊕ *www. guisados.la*

LaMill Coffee. Order up your coffee however you want it (French press, Clover, you name it) and choose from an inventive list of espresso-based drinks. ⊠ *1636 Silver Lake Blvd.* ⊕ *www.lamillcoffee. com*

GETTING HERE

■ When driving from the east, take either I–10 to I–5 heading north or State Route 134 to I–5 heading south; from the west, take I–10 to I–5 heading north or brave the U.S. 101 traffic, getting off in Hollywood then heading east. The closest Metro station is Vermont and Sunset, which puts you within walking distance of Los Feliz's most bustling streets, Vermont and Hillhurst. Metered street parking is available along Vermont and Hillhurst, while some free parking can be found on residential side streets—though pay attention to posted signs.

PLANNING YOUR TIME

■ Los Feliz is a delightfully intimate neighborhood, and it won't take long to tick off its most important highlights. However, a decent, get-your-heart-pumping hike at Griffith Park may take a couple of hours or more, and it's definitely worth spending a few more strolling around to experience all of its offerings, including Griffith Observatory. Silver Lake and Echo Park can easily take up a whole lazy day of eating, drinking, and shopping but can also be done in an afternoon.

The neighborhoods in L.A.'s Eastside are talked about with the same oh-my-god-it's-so-cool reverence by Angelenos as Brooklyn is by New Yorkers. These streets are dripping with trendiness—which will delight some and enrage others.

Almost 20 years ago, Los Feliz was the first of these rediscovered, reinvented neighborhoods, then came Silver Lake, then Echo Park. As each one became more expensive, the cool kids relocated, leaving behind their style and influence. Now Highland Park is the center of the oh-so-hip universe. But, the epicenter is constantly shifting. No doubt, by the next edition of this guide, it'll be someplace else.

Los Feliz

In the rolling hills below the stunning Griffith Observatory, Los Feliz is one of L.A.'s most affluent neighborhoods. With Hollywood just a few miles west, its winding streets are lined with mansions belonging to some of the biggest celebrities. In recent years, both Vermont and Hillhurst avenues have come alive with hip restaurants, boutiques, and theaters.

◉ Sights

Barnsdall Art Park

CITY PARK | FAMILY | The panoramic view of Hollywood alone is worth a trip to this hilltop cultural center. On the grounds you'll find the 1921 **Hollyhock House,** a masterpiece of modern design by architect Frank Lloyd Wright. It was commissioned by philanthropist Aline Barnsdall to be the centerpiece of an arts community. While Barnsdall's project didn't turn out the way she planned, the park now hosts the L.A. Municipal Art Gallery and Theatre, which provides exhibition space for visual and performance artists.

Wright dubbed this style "California Romanza" (romanza is a musical term meaning "to make one's own form"). Stylized depictions of Barnsdall's favorite flower, the hollyhock, appear throughout the house in its cement columns, roof line, and furnishings. The leaded-glass windows are expertly placed to make the most of both the surrounding gardens and the city views. On summer weekends, there are wildly popular wine tastings and outdoor movie screenings. Self-guided tours are available Thursday through Sunday from 11 to 4. ⊠ 4800 Hollywood Blvd., Los Feliz 🕾 No phone ⊕ www.barnsdall.org 🖾 Free; house tours $7 ⊗ House closed Mon.

★ Griffith Observatory

OBSERVATORY | Most visitors barely skim the surface of this gorgeous spot in the Santa Monica Mountains, but those in the know will tell you there's more to the Griffith Observatory than its sweeping views and stunning Greek Revival architecture. To start, this free-to-the-public

mountaintop observatory is home to the Samuel Oschin Planetarium, a state-of-the-art theater with an aluminum dome and a Zeiss star projector that plays a number of ticketed shows. Those spectacular shows are complemented by a couple of space-related exhibits, and several telescopes (naturally), as well as theater programs and events at the Leonard Nimoy Event Horizon Theater. For visitors who are looking to get up close and personal with the cosmos, monthly star-viewing parties with local amateur astronomers are also on hand.
■ **TIP→ For a fantastic view, come at sunset to watch the sky turn fiery shades of red with the city's skyline silhouetted.** ✉ *2800 E. Observatory Ave., Los Feliz* 📞 *213/473–0800* ⊕ *www.griffithobservatory.org* 🕑 *Closed Mon.* ☞ *Observatory grounds and parking are open daily.*

★ Griffith Park

CITY PARK | FAMILY | The country's largest municipal park, the 4,310-acre Griffith Park is a must for nature lovers, the perfect spot for respite from the hustle and bustle of the surrounding urban areas. Plants and animals native to Southern California can be found within the park's borders, including deer, coyotes, and even a reclusive mountain lion. Bronson Canyon (where the Batcave from the 1960s *Batman* TV series is located) and Crystal Springs are favorite picnic spots.

The park is named after Colonel Griffith J. Griffith, a mining tycoon who donated 3,000 acres to the city in 1896. As you might expect, the park has been used as a film and television location for at least a century. Here you'll find the Griffith Observatory, the Los Angeles Zoo, the Greek Theater, two golf courses, hiking and bridle trails, a swimming pool, a merry-go-round, and an outdoor train museum. ✉ *4730 Crystal Springs Dr., Los Feliz* 📞 *323/644–2050* ⊕ *www.laparks.org/dos/parks/griffithpk* 🎟 *Free; attractions inside park have separate admission fees.*

Vista Theatre

FILM | Around since 1923, the Vista is a single-screen gem that shows brand-new releases and features art deco fixtures and Egyptian-themed details. One of the most affordable theaters in the city, the Vista borders Los Feliz and Silver Lake, and is close to fun bars and restaurants for a pre- or postshow meal or cocktail. ✉ *4473 Sunset Blvd., Los Feliz* 📞 *323/660–6639* ⊕ *www.vintagecinemas.com/vista.*

🍴 Restaurants

This affluent hillside community has a laid-back dining scene. Wine bars, burger joints, and taco stands are among the options for a family night out.

★ The Best Fish Taco in Ensenada

$ | MEXICAN | FAMILY | In mirroring the taco stands of Ensenada, Mexico—simple, cheap, and unceremonious, with a selection of spicy homemade salsas—this little local treasure has achieved what many restaurants serving Baja tacos haven't: an authentic (and delicious) experience. **Known for:** fish-and-shrimp tacos; mango salsa; seafood shack atmosphere. ⑤ *Average main: $6* ✉ *1650 Hillhurst Ave., Los Feliz* 📞 *323/466–5552* ⊕ *www.bestfishtacoinensenada.com.*

Kismet

$$ | MEDITERRANEAN | You may feel like you're about to walk into a sauna rather than a restaurant because of its minimalist light-color wood on white paint interior, but you'll find nothing but colorful gorgeous Middle Eastern dishes here at Kismet. This James Beard nominee perfectly blends comforting Middle Eastern and Israeli cuisine with Californian flavors and plant-based flair, all served in a modern space. **Known for:** Persian crispy rice; tasty lamb meatballs; Middle Eastern classics with a Cali twist. ⑤ *Average main: $18* ✉ *4648 Hollywood Blvd., Los Feliz* 📞 *323/409–0404* ⊕ *www.kismetla.com.*

Los Feliz, Silver Lake, and the Eastside

0   1/2 mi

0   1/2 km

Griffith Park

WEST GLENDALE

GLENDALE

ADAMS SQUARE

ATWATER

LOS FELIZ

Silver Lake Reservoir

SILVER LAKE

ECHO PARK

ANGELINO HEIGHTS

Elysian Park

KOREATOWN

MacArthur Park

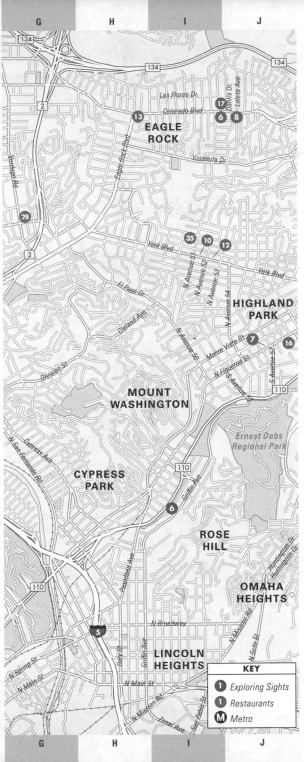

Sights ▼

1 Barnsdall Art Park................ **A5**
2 Dodger Stadium.................... **F8**
3 Elysian Park **F7**
4 Griffith Observatory **A3**
5 Griffith Park **A2**
6 Heritage Square Museum......... **I7**
7 Vista Theatre...................... **B6**

Restaurants ▼

1 Alimento **D6**
2 Atwater Village Tavern........... **D4**
3 Baracoa Cuban Cafe **D4**
4 The Best Fish Taco In
  Ensenada **B5**
5 Bon Vivant Market and Café **D4**
6 CaCao Mexicatessen **I2**
7 Cafe Birdie........................ **J4**
8 Cindy's **J2**
9 Dinosaur Coffee **B6**
10 Donut Friend........................ **I3**
11 Dune............................... **D4**
12 El Huarache Azteca **I3**
13 5 Line Tavern **H2**
14 Gingergrass **D5**
15 Kismet............................. **B5**
16 Kitchen Mouse..................... **J4**
17 Knowrealitypie.................... **I1**
18 La Pergoletta..................... **B5**
19 LaMill Coffee..................... **C7**
20 Link N Hops....................... **D4**
21 Little Dom's **B4**
22 Masa of Echo Park **D8**
23 Momed............................. **E4**
24 The Morrison...................... **C3**
25 Night + Market Song **C7**
26 Ostrich Farm...................... **E8**
27 Pine and Crane.................... **C6**
28 Polka Polish Cuisine.............. **G3**
29 Sawyer............................. **C6**
30 Sepan Chicken.................... **E4**
31 Silverlake Ramen **D8**
32 Spoon and Pork................... **C7**
33 Tacos Villa Corona................ **D4**
34 Tam O'Shanter **D3**
35 Town Pizza........................ **I3**
36 Trencher **E8**
37 Valerie Confections............... **E7**
38 Wanderlust Creamery............ **D4**
39 Wax Paper......................... **F5**

KEY

🅵 *Exploring Sights*
🅵 *Restaurants*
Ⓜ *Metro*

La Pergoletta

$$ | **ITALIAN** | Just look for the swaying Italian flag at a strip mall on Hillhurst and Melbourne, and you'll stumble into La Pergoletta, a cozy little space. Though the decor is decidedly frenzied, it still maintains a chic yet rustic quality that looks like it was cobbled together by an Italian *nonna*. **Known for:** fresh pasta you can customize; gnocchi with creamy mushroom sauce; food just like Nonna used to make. $ *Average main: $18* ✉ *1802 Hillhurst Ave., Los Feliz* ☎ *323/664–8259* ⊕ *www.lapergoletta.com.*

Little Dom's

$$ | **ITALIAN** | With a vintage bar and dapper barkeep who mixes up seasonally inspired retro cocktails, an attached Italian deli where you can pick up a pork-cheek sub, and an $18 Monday-night supper, it's not surprising that Little Dom's is a neighborhood gem. Cozy and inviting, with big leather booths you can sink into for the night, the restaurant puts a modern spin on classic Italian dishes such as *burrata* agnolotti and meatballs. **Known for:** ricotta cheese and fresh blueberry pancakes; excellent pizza margherita; fun weekend brunch. $ *Average main: $20* ✉ *2128 Hillhurst Ave., Los Feliz* ☎ *323/661–0055* ⊕ *www.littledoms.com.*

ⓨ Nightlife

While neighboring Hollywood champions nightclubs, laid-back Los Feliz favors its pubs, quirky neighborhood bars, and casual lounges. The scene is buzzing, especially on weekends, with locals dominating it. But visitors hoping to get away from the rowdiness of Hollywood are always a welcome addition.

Covell

WINE BARS—NIGHTLIFE | This laid-back spot is the embodiment of what every unpretentious wine drinker wishes a wine bar should be. It's thankfully lacking in staff who might turn up their noses should you forget to swirl the glass. But what else would you expect from a spot with repurposed furnishings and a vintage motorcycle mounted to the wall? ✉ *4628 Hollywood Blvd., Los Feliz* ☎ *323/660–4400* ⊕ *www.barcovell.com.*

Dresden Room

PIANO BARS/LOUNGES | This bar's 1940s lounge decor makes it a favorite with folks in Los Angeles. The long-running house band, Marty and Elayne, has entertained patrons for more than three decades. (They found a new generation of fans, thanks to the film *Swingers*.) Other than the entertainment, perhaps the best reason to wander in is to sip on a Blood and Sand cocktail, self-proclaimed to be "the world's most tantalizing drink." ✉ *1760 N. Vermont Ave., Los Feliz* ☎ *323/665–4294* ⊕ *www.thedresden.com.*

Tabula Rasa Bar

WINE BARS—NIGHTLIFE | This unassuming spot feels less like a wine bar and more of a neighborhood watering hole where the servers take the time to chat with customers rather than somberly educate them on the complexities of wine. But make no mistake: the wine selection is perfection and the snacks are delightful—they simply want to ensure your enjoyment of your wine rather than have you bow down at the appreciation of their knowledge. ✉ *5125 Hollywood Blvd., Los Feliz* ☎ *213/290–6309* ⊕ *www.tabularasabar.com.*

ⓧ Performing Arts

Though Los Feliz has a bit of a theater scene—mostly a spillover from Hollywood—it's home to a couple of fantastic cinemas and one of L.A.'s best live music venues: the Greek.

★ Greek Theatre

CONCERTS | With a robust lineup from May through November, acts such as Bruce Springsteen, John Legend, and Aretha

Franklin (RIP) have all graced the stage at this scenic outdoor venue. Located at the base of Griffith Park, there's usually slow preshow traffic on concert nights, but that'll give you a chance to take in the beautiful park foliage and homes in the Hollywood Hills. Paid lots are available for parking, but wear comfortable shoes and expect to walk as some lots are fairly far from the theater. Or you can park and enjoy cocktails in trendy and chic Los Feliz before a show, then walk up to the venue. ⊠ 2700 N. Vermont Ave., Los Feliz ☎ 844/524–7335 ⊕ www.lagreektheatre. com.

Vintage Los Feliz Theatre

FILM | Los Angeles has an abundance of vintage cinemas that whisk movie lovers back to the Hollywood days of yore, and the Vintage leads the small-screen charge with its three intimate theaters that showcase new releases in 4K. If you're hungry, they have a taco stand and a café serving milk tea. With a prime location on the neighborhood's busiest drag, a perfect Los Feliz evening starts with dinner, ends with drinks, and has the Vintage sandwiched in between. ⊠ 1822 N. Vermont Ave., Los Feliz ☎ 323/664–2169 ⊕ vintagecinemas.com/losfeliz.

🛍 Shopping

Stroll past the mansions on Los Feliz Boulevard before hitting the vintage shops and sophisticated boutiques with old-school tendencies—think refurbished brick and classic decor.

La La Ling

CLOTHING | FAMILY | This isn't your average kids' clothing store; La La Ling offers pieces hip enough that they could be worn by the cool parents it counts as clientele. Shoppers can expect affordable finds like Ziggy Stardust sweatshirts, rock band tees, and skinny jeans, as well as supplies for the nursery and bath time. There's also burp cloths, bibs, swaddlers, and other essentials new parents need

on the regular. ⊠ 1810 N. Vermont Ave., Los Feliz ☎ 323/664–4400 ⊕ www. lalaling.com.

Skylight Books

BOOKS/STATIONERY | A neighborhood bookstore through and through, Skylight has excellent sections devoted to kids, fiction, travel, and food; it even has a live-in cat. The space also hosts book discussion groups, panels, and author readings with hip literati. Art lovers can peruse texts on design and photography, graphic novels, and indie magazines at Skylight's annex a few doors down. ⊠ 1818 N. Vermont Ave., Los Feliz ☎ 323/660–1175 ⊕ www.skylightbooks.com.

Soap Plant/Wacko

GIFTS/SOUVENIRS | This pop-culture supermarket offers a wide range of items, including rows of books on art and design. But it's the novelty stock that makes the biggest impression, with ant farms, X-ray specs, and anime figurines for sale. An adjacent gallery space, La Luz de Jesus, focuses on underground art. ⊠ 4633 Hollywood Blvd., Los Feliz ☎ 323/663–0122 ⊕ www.soapplant.com.

Spitfire Girl

GIFTS/SOUVENIRS | When the person you're shopping for is the nontraditional type, you can count on this quirky boutique to provide unique goods including taxidermy, printed wood flasks, white magic spell kits, and cheeky socks, much of which is created by Spitfire Girl's own house label. ⊠ 1939½ Hillhurst Ave., Los Feliz ☎ 323/912–1977 ⊕ www.spitfiregirl. com.

Vamp Shoes

CLOTHING | From well-known designers to up-and-coming handcrafters who make their shoes in small batches, boutique store Vamp Shoes has a solid collection of footwear for anyone who appreciates (and who's not afraid to invest in) gorgeous, excellent-quality soles. Inventory here also includes cool bags, hosiery, jewelry, and handcrafted ceramics. ⊠ *1951 Hillhurst Ave., Los Feliz* ☎ *323/662–1150* ⊕ *www.vampshoeshop. com.*

Activities

Bronson Canyon

HIKING/WALKING | Bronson Canyon—or more popularly, Bronson Caves—is one of L.A.'s most famous filming locations, especially for western and sci-fi flicks. This section of Griffith Park, easily accessible through a trail that's less than half a mile, is a great place to visit whether you're a film buff or an exercise junkie. ⊠ *3200 Canyon Dr., Hollywood.*

Silver Lake

This hilly, mostly residential neighborhood sits southeast of Los Feliz and northwest of Echo Park. Regarded as a bohemian enclave since the 1930s, it was the site of the first large film studio built by Walt Disney. Today Silver Lake is known for cute boutiques, bougie coffeehouses, and specialty restaurants along its stretch of Sunset Boulevard.

🍴 Restaurants

With plenty of hipster appeal, the eateries of Silver Lake draw an eclectic crowd to its neighborhood hangouts.

★ Alimento

$$$ | **ITALIAN** | There's little surprise that chef Zach Pollack's soulful Italian masterpiece in Silver Lake features a lot of influences and inspirations that span the globe; the true-blue Angeleno, after all, grew up in a melting pot. Alimento's dishes are modern takes on traditional Italian cuisine, using locally sourced ingredients and varying in influences—from your classic American to Chinese and Mexican. **Known for:** chicken liver crostone; radiatori with braised pork sugo; surprising takes

on Italian classics. ⑤ *Average main: $25* ⊠ *1710 Silver Lake Blvd., Silver Lake* ☎ *323/928–2888* ⊕ *www.alimentola.com* ⊘ *Closed Mon. No lunch.*

Dinosaur Coffee

$ | **CAFÉ** | By blending geometrical shapes and horizontal lines together in an airy place with big windows, Dinosaur Coffee has utilized its space well, bringing a touch of the new into a section of Silver Lake that feels a little old. Yet it's more than just the interiors that draw people in—the coffee is excellent, as are the pastries. **Known for:** perfect oat milk latte; great cold brew; no Wi-Fi. ⑤ *Average main: $4* ⊠ *4334 W. Sunset Blvd., Silver Lake* ⊕ *dinosaurcoffee.com.*

Gingergrass

$$ | **VIETNAMESE** | **FAMILY** | With minimalist decor marked by tropical wood banquettes, Silver Lake's bohemian past and trendy present converge at Gingergrass. Traditional Vietnamese favorites emerge from the café's open kitchen, sometimes with a California twist. **Known for:** roasted pork chop with rice; seasonal curry pot pies; great desserts. ⑤ *Average main: $15* ⊠ *2396 Glendale Blvd., Silver Lake* ☎ *323/644–1600* ⊕ *www.gingergrass. com.*

LaMill Coffee

$$ | **CAFÉ** | These folks take their coffee seriously, sourcing estate-grown beans that are prepared in a variety of ways (French press or Clover, to name but two) and offering an inventive list of espresso-based drinks. To go along with the requisite coffee is a breakfast-all-day menu, as well as a proper, if select, tea selection for those who take their leaves seriously. **Known for:** Japanese iced coffee; Varlhona mocha; breakfast items served all day. ⑤ *Average main: $14* ⊠ *1636 Silver Lake Blvd., Silver Lake* ☎ *323/663–4441* ⊕ *www.lamillcoffee. com.*

★ Night + Market Song

$$ | **THAI** | There are a lot of Thai restaurants in Los Angeles, but none have quite reached the level of cult status of Night + Market Song. Tucked between a free clinic, a small clothing store, and a tax office, this second rendition of chef Kris Yenbamroong's popular WeHo restaurant might be easy to miss, but keep an eye out, as its authentic (and properly spicy) Thai dishes are practically mandatory when you're in the neighborhood. **Known for:** startled pig; khao soi; long weekend lines. $ *Average main: $15* ✉ *3322 W. Sunset Blvd., Silver Lake* ☎ *323/665–5899* ⊕ *www.nightmarketsong.com* ⊘ *Closed Tues.*

Pine and Crane

$ | **TAIWANESE** | **FAMILY** | This is not the typical Chinese restaurant you might expect; it's a fast casual, often locally sourced Taiwanese restaurant housed in a modern setting. The menu changes based on season, the wine and beer list updates constantly, and the tea menu is carefully curated. **Known for:** dan dan noodles; traditional panfried omelet; friendly staff. $ *Average main: $12* ✉ *1521 Griffith Park Blvd., Silver Lake* ☎ *323/668–1128* ⊕ *www.pineandcrane. com* ⊘ *Closed Tues.*

Sawyer

$$$ | **SEAFOOD** | Simply put, Sawyer is a stunner with its restored brick walls, beautiful hardwood floor, and tiled patio, flourished with mid-century modern furniture; it's exactly the kind of bright and airy place you'd want to start off your day in. Yet most patrons come here less for the ambience and more for the food, with a menu that leans on the healthy side but isn't afraid to indulge in the hearty stuff, touting an assortment of traditional and modern American fare. **Known for:** seafood boil; lobster roll; weekend brunch. $ *Average main: $23* ✉ *3709 Sunset Blvd., Silver Lake* ☎ *323/641–3709* ⊘ *No brunch weekdays.*

Silverlake Ramen

$$ | **RAMEN** | Now a franchise with several locations around Los Angeles (and a random one in Concord, NC), it's this original spot in the heart of the city's hipsterville that's still the best. The go-to ramen joint for Silverlake and Echo Park denizens is just the ticket if you're in dire need of some comfort food while also partaking in L.A.'s multicultural food scene. **Known for:** The Blaze, a spicy Tonkotsu ramen; crispy rice with spicy tuna; hearty Japanese fare. $ *Average main: $14* ✉ *2927 Sunset Blvd., Silver Lake* ☎ *323/660–8100* ⊕ *www.silverlakeramen.com.*

🍸 Nightlife

Most of Silver Lake's best bars can be found in one condensed area, Sunset Junction, the intersection of Sunset and Santa Monica boulevards. If you've spent your day shopping or dining here, return at night when coffee culture takes a breather and makes way for dark eclectic bars patronized by locals and L.A.'s transplant community.

Akbar

BARS/PUBS | This bar's welcoming feel is one of the reasons many people consider it their neighborhood bar, even if they don't live in the neighborhood. The crowd is friendly and inviting, and theme nights attract all sorts of folks, gay or straight. The comedy nights are favorites, as are weekends, when DJs get everyone on the dance floor. ✉ *4356 W. Sunset Blvd., Silver Lake* ☎ *323/665–6810* ⊕ *www. akbarsilverlake.com.*

Cha Cha Lounge

BARS/PUBS | If chaos and the assortment of ill-matched furnishings and decor is something you can forgive—or revel in—then this import from Seattle is a Silver Lake staple you should check out. Grab your (cheap) poison then meander through the Mexican fiesta-theme bar. Foosball tables, a photo booth, and a vending machine will give you plenty to occupy your time. ✉ *2375 Glendale Blvd., Silver Lake* ☎ *323/660–7595* ⊕ *www.chachalounge.com.*

★ 4100

BARS/PUBS | With swaths of fabric draped from the ceiling, this low-lit bar with a bohemian vibe makes it perfect for dates. Groups of locals also come through for the night, making the crowd a plentiful mix of people. The bartenders know how to pour drinks that are both tasty and potent. There's plenty of seating at the tables and stools along the central bar, which gets crowded on the weekends. ✉ *1087 Manzanita St., Silver Lake* ☎ *323/666–4460* ⊕ *www.pouringwithheart.com/4100-bar.*

The Red Lion Tavern

BREWPUBS/BEER GARDENS | You wouldn't expect old European charm in the hipster enclave of Silver Lake, but Bavarian style is served right alongside irony at the Red Lion Tavern, just as it has for more than 55 years. So, grab a schnitzel and a bratwurst and wander the many rooms chockablock with German memorabilia or head toward the beer garden for a large selection of German-only beers on draft. ✉ *2366 Glendale Blvd., Silver Lake* ☎ *323/662–5337* ⊕ *www.redliontavern.net.*

Silverlake Lounge

MUSIC CLUBS | Rock bands, burlesque performances, comedy sets, and even open-mike nights all have a home at the cross section of Sunset and Silver Lake at a little dive bar called the Silverlake Lounge. This small club with the yellow awning is a neighborhood spot—cash only, by the way—in the best way possible, with cheap drinks and local talent deserving of their time in the limelight. ✉ *2906 W. Sunset Blvd., Silver Lake* ☎ *323/663–9636* ⊕ *www.thesilverlakelounge.com.*

Thirsty Crow

BARS/PUBS | This whiskey bar serves up seasonal cocktails in a fun, rustic environment. Though small, it manages to find space for live musicians and an open-mike night on Saturday. Part of the same hospitality group as Bigfoot Lodge and Highland Park Bowl, it has a locals-only feel. As local L.A. musician Father John Misty once said, "nothing good ever happens at the goddamn Thirsty Crow," but we think you should go and see for yourself. ✉ *2939 W. Sunset Blvd., Silver Lake* ☎ *323/661–6007* ⊕ *www.thirstycrowbar.com.*

🛍 Shopping

The action here is concentrated along Sunset Boulevard, where the young and hip come to sip artisanal coffee and peruse the one-of-a-kind wares.

Mohawk General Store

CLOTHING | Filled with a brilliant combination of indie and established designers, this upscale boutique is a mainstay for the modern minimalist. Pick up the wares of local favorites Cathy Callahan and Knotwork, as well as internationally loved labels like Acne Studios, Issey Miyake, and Levi's. The Sunset Boulevard store stocks goods for men and women as well as children, plus accessories and some home goods. ✉ *4011 W. Sunset Blvd., Silver Lake* ☎ *323/669–1601* ⊕ *www.mohawkgeneralstore.com.*

Secret Headquarters

BOOKS/STATIONERY | This could be the coolest comic-book store on the planet, with a selection to satisfy both the geekiest of collectors and those more interested in artistic and literary finds. Rich wood floors and a leather chair near the front window of this intimate space mark the sophisticated setting, which features wall displays neatly organized with new comics and filing cabinets marked DC and Marvel. ✉ *3817 W. Sunset Blvd., Silver*

Lake ☎ 323/666–2228 ⊕ www.thesecret-headquarters.com.

Silver Lake Wine

WINE/SPIRITS | Boutique wineries from around the world provide this shop with the vintage bottles that fill the floor-to-ceiling racks. Looking relaxed and unassuming in jeans and T-shirts, the knowledgeable staff can steer you to the right wine or spirits for any occasion. Those who prefer to enjoy their wine in the privacy of their vacation rental or hotel will be pleased to know they also do deliveries around Silver Lake and the neighboring areas. ⊠ 2395 Glendale Blvd., Silver Lake ☎ 323/662–9024 ⊕ www.silverlakewine.com.

Yolk

GIFTS/SOUVENIRS | Stocked with a little bit of everything you'll want to get or give, this shop has a spot-on selection of fresh designer goods. Look for unique kids toys and furnishings, exquisite home accessories, stationery, and handcrafted items from Californian artisans. ⊠ 1626 Silver Lake Blvd., Silver Lake ☎ 323/660–4315 ⊕ www.shopyolk.com.

Echo Park

Silver Lake's edgier older cousin and neighbor, Echo Park is centered on a beautifully restored lakefront park (you can even rent a paddleboat and experience the lake in all its glory). The first residential neighborhood northwest of Downtown Los Angeles, Echo Park has long been under (deserved) scrutiny for gentrification, along with Highland Park and Silver Lake. This predominantly Latino and Mexican neighborhood has experienced an influx of young artists and industry hopefuls in recent years, as well as rent hikes, but it's not devoid of diversity or character. Film buffs take note: it was one of the principal locations of Roman Polanski's film *Chinatown*.

◉ Sights

★ Dodger Stadium

SPORTS VENUE | **FAMILY** | Home of the Dodgers since 1962, Dodger Stadium is the third-oldest baseball stadium still in use and has had quite the history in baseball, including Sandy Koufax's perfect game in 1965 and Kirk Gibson's 1988 World Series home run. Not only has it played host to the Dodgers' ups and downs and World Series runs, it's also been the venue for some of the biggest performers in the world, including the Beatles, Madonna, and Beyoncé. The stadium can be tough to get into on game day, so consider getting dropped off in the park and walking up. Alternately, you can arrive early, as locals tend not to roll up until the third inning. If you have the opportunity to take in a Friday night game, make sure to stick around for the fireworks show that follows—if you're patient, you can even wait in line and watch it from the field. ⊠ 1000 Vin Scully Ave., Echo Park ☎ 866/363–4377 ⊕ dodgers.mlb.com/la/ballpark.

Elysian Park

HIKING/WALKING | **FAMILY** | Though not Los Angeles's biggest park—that honor belongs to Griffith Park—Elysian comes in second, and also has the honor of being the city's oldest. It's also home to one of L.A.'s busiest and most beloved attractions, Dodger Stadium, the home field to the Los Angeles Dodgers. For this reason, baseball fans flock to this 600-acre park for tailgate parties. The rest of the time, however, Elysian Park serves as the Echo Park residents' backyard, thanks to its network of hiking trails, picnic spaces, and public playgrounds. ⊠ 929 Academy Rd., Echo Park ⊕ www.laparks.org/park/elysian.

🍴 Restaurants

Echo Park's diversity manifests in its gastronomic scene. While vegan and Mexican restaurants are plentiful, there are other offerings to round out the selection and satisfy every taste bud, from French and Italian to Filipino and Thai.

Masa of Echo Park

$$ | PIZZA | FAMILY | While Masa of Echo Park does do excellent "bistro pizzas," as the restaurant calls them, it's mostly known for the delectable deep-dish pies that may just be the best you'll find this side of Chicago. Be prepared though—it can take a while to get seated and up to 45 minutes to get that deep dish you ordered, so it might be best to call ahead. **Known for:** vegan menu options; family-style dining; Italian classics. $ *Average main: $20* ✉ *1800 W. Sunset Blvd., Echo Park* ☎ *213/989–1558* ⊕ *www.masaofechopark.com.*

Ostrich Farm

$$ | MODERN AMERICAN | The husband and wife team at the helm of Ostrich Farm are proud to serve the neighborhood that they both love and live in. They've even turned a tiny plot of land into a garden to add a true farm-to-table aspect to their already sustainable concept with hints of European cooking. **Known for:** fried chicken; bacon-wrapped meat loaf; weekend brunch. $ *Average main: $18* ✉ *1525 W. Sunset Blvd., Echo Park* ☎ *213/537–0657* ⊕ *www.ostrichfarmla.com* ۩ *Closed Mon. and Tues.*

Spoon and Pork

$$ | PHILIPPINE | In a city where food trucks can be successful enough to have their own brick-and-mortar spaces, and where Filipino food has quickly become a craze, it's no surprise that Spoon and Pork has found its rightful place in the neighborhood. With a name that cleverly plays on the traditional Filipino way of eating (using both spoon and fork), this modern Filipino food spot is the perfect introduction to the cuisine. **Known for:** adobo pork belly; lechon kawali; Filipino comfort food. $ *Average main: $14* ✉ *3131 W. Sunset Blvd., Echo Park* ☎ *323/922–6061* ⊕ *www.spoonandpork.com* ۩ *Closed Mon.*

Trencher

$ | AMERICAN | The simple brick-and-wood interiors and friendly, always-up-for-a-conversation staff at Trencher are just the kind of homey welcome travelers need when visiting a big city like L.A. Hot sandwiches are the staple here, and are best enjoyed with a side of animal-style fries. **Known for:** fried chicken banh mi; The Coupe sandwich (fried chicken with jalapeno pickle slaw and siracha aioli); intimate setting. $ *Average main: $13* ✉ *1305 Portia St., Echo Park* ☎ *323/604–9621* ⊕ *www.trencherla.com* ۩ *Closed Mon. and Tues.*

Valerie Confections

$ | CAFÉ | Most cafés treat tea as an afterthought, but at Valerie Confections, it's the main event. Different varieties of tea take over half the menu and many of the morsels advertised only serve to complement the tea. **Known for:** home-made chocolates; petit fours; excellent tea. $ *Average main: $12* ✉ *1665 Echo Park Ave., Echo Park* ☎ *213/250–9365* ⊕ *valerieconfections.com.*

Wax Paper

$$ | DELI | While Wax Paper has a few outdoor tables set up for dining, this tiny sandwich place in Frogtown is tailor-made for to-go orders. The modest selection of brilliantly prepared sandwiches are made with fresh ingredients and named after NPR hosts; they're best enjoyed along the river or at a park nearby. **Known for:** creative to-go sandwiches; Kai Ryssdal tuna sandwich; friendly, low-key atmosphere. $ *Average main: $14* ✉ *2902 Knox Ave., Echo Park* ☎ *No phone* ⊕ *www.waxpaperco.com* ۩ *Closed Mon.*

⊙ Nightlife

See an up-and-coming local band, bring your own records to the bar, or impress a date in this eclectic neighborhood that manages to maintain its cultural authenticity more so than its neighbor, Silver Lake.

★ The Echo

MUSIC CLUBS | Echo Park is peppered with music venues, but if you want to be in the heart of the neighborhood's live music scene, you should head to the Echo. With a full bar and recurring theme nights, the spot hosts cutting-edge music from both up-and-coming local and touring acts as well as well-known bands. ☒ *1822 Sunset Blvd., Echoplex entrance at 1154 Glendale Blvd., Echo Park* ☎ *No phone* ⊕ *www.spacelandpresents.com.*

El Prado

BARS/PUBS | A small selection of constantly rotating wine and beer ensures you'll get to try something new and interesting each time you visit. A record player serves as the main source of music—while the idea may seem twee, it's the heart of a popular Tuesday night record club, where patrons bring in their own vinyl. ☒ *1805 W. Sunset Blvd., Echo Park* ⊕ *www.elpradobar.com.*

★ Mohawk Bend

BARS/PUBS | There are plenty of reasons to stop by Mohawk Bend: 72 craft beers on tap, a wide range of California-only liquor, a vegetarian and vegan-friendly menu that includes tailored-to-your-wants pizza, and a buffalo cauliflower that—rumor has it—started the whole trend. There might be a long line to get into this 100-year-old former theater in the evenings, but it's worth it. ☒ *2141 Sunset Blvd., Echo Park* ☎ *213/483–2337* ⊕ *mohawk.la.*

The Semi-Tropic

PIANO BARS/LOUNGES | This is a bar that feels more like a café—a place with an atmosphere perfect for studying or relaxing over a cold drink. It has a full menu that boasts everything from Moroccan spiced popcorn to heartier meatballs and garlic bread. Once evening hits, it comes

alive with DJs spinning vinyl, music showcases, and hip locals indulging in craft beer, tropical cocktails, and fine wines. ☒ *1412 Glendale Blvd., Echo Park* ☎ *213/568–3827* ⊕ *www.thesemitropic. com.*

★ 1642

BARS/PUBS | This romantically lit hole-in-the-wall is easy to miss, but you should aim to check it out if you're a discerning wine connoisseur or looking to experience the best of California's microbreweries. Perfect for first dates, come here to experiment with craft beers or to warm up with wine while listening to some live old-time fiddle tunes. ☒ *1642 W. Temple St., Echo Park* ☎ *213/989–6836* ⊕ *www.1642bar.com.*

Sunset Beer Company

BARS/PUBS | When you first walk into this spot, you'll find a retail beer shop stocked with an incredibly wide selection with a focus on Californian and Belgian beers, all reasonably priced and available individually. What makes this place unique is the adjoining tasting room where they'll pour whatever you get from the store for a small corkage fee. Be sure to grab a seat at the sofa chairs and a board game to play with friends. ☒ *1498 W. Sunset Blvd. Suite 3, Echo Park* ☎ *213/481–2337* ⊕ *www.sunsetbeerco.com.*

Tilda

WINE BARS—NIGHTLIFE | Tucked into Echo Park's more residential area where its only other commercial companions are a cactus shop, a tiny neighborhood market, a juice store, and a vegan restaurant, Tilda may not be at the center of the city's buzzing nightlife scene. But wine connoisseurs would agree that it's the perfect place to sample California natural wines. Pair your favorites with the wine bar's modest selection of simple fare. ☒ *1507 Echo Park Ave., Echo Park* ☎ *213/995–6090* ⊕ *www.tildawine.com.*

🛍 Shopping

With a bit more edge than neighboring Silver Lake, this increasingly cool area has an artsy, do-it-yourself appeal. Secondhand stores squeeze in alongside vegan restaurants, hip dive bars, and friendly boutiques stocked with clothes by local designers.

Esqueleto

JEWELRY/ACCESSORIES | There's a touch of the macabre on display at Esqueleto, but what do you expect from a jewelry boutique with a name that means "skeleton" in Spanish? That doesn't mean the light, airy, contemporary shop is stereotypically Goth in style. Both its design and the inventory it stocks are perfectly polished and selected with a discerningly artistic eye. With a mix of excellent vintage finds and emerging designers, the shop has become a go-to destination for alternative brides' engagement rings and wedding bands. ⊠ *1928 W. Sunset Blvd., Echo Park* ☎ *213/947–3508* ⊕ *www. shopesqueleto.com.*

Stories Books and Café

BOOKS/STATIONERY | With an off-the-beaten-path collection of new and used literature, a café catering to freelancers and free thinkers, and a back patio that showcases singer-songwriters, Stories Books and Café is an authentic reflection of Echo Park. Readings, signings, and other events are a regular occurrence. ⊠ *1716 Sunset Blvd., Echo Park* ☎ *213/413–3733* ⊕ *www.storiesla.com.*

Time Travel Mart

SPECIALTY STORES | **FAMILY** | You probably won't find anything useful in the Time Travel Mart and that's exactly the point. From dinosaur eggs to robot milk, this is a store that touts the absurdly hilarious—all of which should bring back memories of your childhood and maybe a little bit of joy. That's because the store holds a secret: it's really a fundraiser for the nonprofit 826LA, which tutors neighborhood kids in the back section. So even when you're buying something unnecessary but absolutely wonderful, remember it's for a noble and worthy cause. ⊠ *1714 W. Sunset Blvd., Echo Park* ☎ *213/413–3388* ⊕ *826la.org/store.*

Atwater Village

Alongside nearby Glassell Park and Cypress Park, Atwater Village is one of the seven neighborhoods that make up the Northeast Los Angeles region, christened NELA by some locals. While it mostly mirrors the former two neighborhoods' predominantly residential status, it also swaggers with Los Feliz's upmarket hip vibe. The main thoroughfares of Glendale and Los Feliz boulevards are paved with neighborhood bars, elevated restaurants, and independent coffee shops, not to mention smart boutique shops touting artisanal goods.

🍴 Restaurants

Quality trumps quantity in Atwater Village. Expect modest yet eclectic menus stuffed with epicurean delights. Dropping by on a Sunday gives you the option to shop for fresh produce at the farmers' market.

Atwater Village Tavern

$ | **AMERICAN** | There's no denying that part of the reason why this charming rectangular joint on Glendale Boulevard has effortlessly established itself as a regular fixture in the neighborhood is its incredible pub food. The fried shrimp tacos, Baja-style, are to die for, but when you toss in happy hour deals like $7 margarita Tuesday, $7 whiskey Wednesday, and $7 cuba libre Thursday, you'll realize this place isn't too shabby as a bar either. **Known for:** fried fish-and-shrimp tacos; daily drink specials; low-key vibe. ⑤ *Average main: $12* ⊠ *3216 Glendale Blvd., Atwater Village* ☎ *323/644–0605* ⊕ *www. atwatervillagetavern.com.*

Baracoa Cuban Cafe

$$ | CUBAN | FAMILY | As far as Cuban food goes in Los Angeles, Baracoa's cozy café, whose interiors loosely resemble an old colonial Spanish square, is perhaps not the most popular, but it's definitely one of the best. This is the kind of nonfancy, home-cooked food that makes you feel good inside, with lovely desserts to boot. **Known for:** bistec de palomilla; pechuga de pollo; small, intimate setting. ⑤ *Average main: $15 ⊠ 3175 Glendale Blvd., Atwater Village* ☎ *323/665–9590.*

Bon Vivant Market and Café

$$$ | AMERICAN | The extensive and eclectic breakfast, lunch, and dinner menus here, coupled with the fantastic cocktail menu and charming little marketplace, are sure to please any visitor. Patrons tend to adopt a slow pace, staggering orders of coffee, luscious crepes, small plates, and delicious entrées, all while adopting a laissez-faire attitude. **Known for:** cheese and fruit boards; classic American fare; partially open-air setting. ⑤ *Average main: $26 ⊠ 3155 Glendale Blvd., Atwater Village* ☎ *323/284–8013* ⊕ *www.bonvivantmarketcafe.com.*

Dune

$ | MEDITERRANEAN | FAMILY | Simple, small, and understated, it's easy to miss the best falafel spot in town. Hearty Middle Eastern falafel and chicken shawarma are piled on homemade flatbread. **Known for:** organic green-herb falafel sandwich; fried chicken shawarma; simple yet friendly atmosphere. ⑤ *Average main: $12 ⊠ 3143 Glendale Blvd., Atwater Village* ☎ *323/486–7073* ⊕ *www.dunekitchen. com.*

Link N Hops

$ | HOT DOG | Almost just your typical sports bar, there are a couple of things that elevate Link N Hops above its competitors, like excellent hot dog sandwiches and 24 craft beers on tap. And about those signature links: there are more than 20, some of which are made with more exotic ingredients like rattlesnake and alligator, not to mention a choice of toppings. **Known for:** Atwater knackwurst; smoked Portuguese Hawaiian sausage; happy hour specials. ⑤ *Average main: $10 ⊠ 3111 Glendale Blvd., Atwater Village* ☎ *323/426–9049* ⊕ *linknhops.com.*

Momed

$$$ | MIDDLE EASTERN | The perfect pairing of simplicity and complexity, Momed serves Mediterranean fare that is comforting yet upscale. The welcoming atmosphere is just as perfect for a romantic date night as it is for a more boisterous brunch with friends. **Known for:** excellent Atlantic salmon; short rib tagine; fun weekend brunch. ⑤ *Average main: $27 ⊠ 3245 Casitas Ave., Atwater Village* ☎ *323/522–3488* ⊕ *www. atmomed.com* ☾ *Closed Mon.*

The Morrison

$$ | BURGER | FAMILY | A friendly neighborhood Scottish pub, the Morrison comes with a bit of an upmarket flair, a kids' menu, and believe it or not, dishes for your canine friends. And, since this is L.A., it serves a damn fine brunch. **Known for:** bacon bourbonator burger; cheese fries with bacon jam; eclectic whiskey menu. ⑤ *Average main: $17 ⊠ 3179 Los Feliz Blvd., Atwater Village* ☎ *323/667– 1839* ⊕ *www.morrisonrestaurant.com.*

Sepan Chicken

$ | MIDDLE EASTERN | Despite appearances (it looks like a fast-food chicken shack), Sepan Chicken serves one of the best rotisserie chickens in town, or at least this side of Hollywood. Pop in for an order to go because, frankly, it's not the coziest place to dine in. **Known for:** cheap Middle Eastern dishes; lule kebab; chicken shawarma. ⑤ *Average main: $10 ⊠ 3324 Glendale Blvd., Atwater Village* ☎ *323/669–0616* ⊕ *sepan-chicken.com.*

Tacos Villa Corona

$ | MEXICAN | You likely won't notice this cramped little spot on Glendale Boulevard unless there's a line or you're a fan of the late, great Anthony Bourdain, who was a big fan. About that line—it's almost always there, especially weekend mornings, when Tacos Villa Corona caters to the hungover crowd. **Known for:** chorizo and potato burrito; breakfast burritos; long lines. Ⓢ *Average main: $4* ⊠ *3185 Glendale Blvd., Atwater Village* ☎ *323/661–3458.*

Tam O'Shanter

$$$$ | IRISH | It's a bit of a specific recognition, but Tam O'Shanter is the oldest restaurant run by the same family in the same location in Los Angeles, operating for more than 90 years in its Tudor-style spot—that alone makes this place a worthy addition to any Atwater Village visit. Then there's their delicious food whose $30 prices are completely worth it, not to mention the fact that, once upon a time, it was Walt Disney's favorite restaurant. **Known for:** Tam O'Shanter cut of steak; interesting history; Scotch flights. Ⓢ *Average main: $32* ⊠ *2980 Los Feliz Blvd., Atwater Village* ☎ *323/664–0228* ⊕ *www. lawrysonline.com/tam-oshanter.*

Wanderlust Creamery

$ | AMERICAN | FAMILY | This ice-cream shop showcases the flavors of the globe in artisanal frozen delights. Every single ice cream is light, creamy, and made with 100% organic milk. **Known for:** mango sticky rice vegan ice cream; ube malted crunch; seasonal flavors. Ⓢ *Average main: $5* ⊠ *3134 Glendale Blvd., Atwater Village* ☎ *818/774–9888* ⊕ *www.wanderlustcreamery.com.*

Nightlife

★ Bigfoot Lodge

BARS/PUBS | Don't be turned off by the glaring log cabin theme (which is intensified by signature cocktails called Scout's Honor and Roasted Marshmallow). Bigfoot Lodge is beloved by Eastside denizens, and despite appearances, it's every bit a low-key, unpretentious neighborhood bar that specializes in shots

and beer and welcomes the occasional tourist that happens to stumble inside. ⊠ *3172 Los Feliz Blvd., Atwater Village* ☎ *323/662–9227* ⊕ *www.bigfootlodge. com.*

Golden Road Brewing

BREWPUBS/BEER GARDENS | Sustainability and support of local community has always been a big part of this L.A. brewery's ethos, but more important, so is making great food and, of course, excellent beer. With several core brands, as well as a few specialty and seasonal brands, this is a must-stop for any craft beer lover vacationing in the City of Angels. ⊠ *5410 W. San Fernando Rd., Atwater Village* ☎ *213/373–4677* ⊕ *goldenroad.la/atwater.*

★ Moonlight Rollerway Skating Rink

SPORTS VENUE | It seems like every night there's a hubbub at Moonlight Rollerway, whether it's skating to *Purple Rain* for a Prince tribute night, a tricky mannequin challenge, or a Harry Potter–themed skate night. If you're looking for a quick throwback to your childhood or a simple break from life, this is just the ticket. This vintage roller rink also offers affordable lessons, in case you're rusty and need a crash course. ⊠ *5110 San Fernando Rd., Atwater Village* ☎ *818/241–3630* ⊕ *moonlightrollerway.com.*

The Roost

BARS/PUBS | Forget all your misconceptions about dive bars and walk into the Roost, whose comforting elements—a jukebox that comes fully loaded with Tom Petty, Springsteen, and the Allman Brothers Band, cozy leather booths, dimmed lights, and decent hearty food—will make you feel like you've flown back to your hometown for the holidays. The cocktails aren't too shabby either, but do bring cash. ⊠ *3100 Los Feliz Blvd., Atwater Village* ☎ *323/664–7272.*

Verdugo Bar

BARS/PUBS | It's hard to decide whether the best thing about this place is its selection of 16 craft beers on tap and menu of "to-go" beer or the large beer garden furnished with picnic tables. Be warned, this place can get crowded, but it's worth it, especially on a hot sunny day (so pretty much every day). ⊠ *3408 Verdugo Rd., Atwater Village* ☎ *323/257–3408* ⊕ *www.verdugobar.com.*

🛍 Shopping

Atwater Village partakes in the tradition of independent boutique shops boasting a bright, modern look and touting artisanal and locally made goods from small businesses. It's a small neighborhood, so shopping till you drop may be out of the question, but you can definitely knock off a good couple of hours popping in for a bit of retail therapy.

Potted

FLOWERS | There's something comforting about Potted, like you've just walked into your parents' sunroom or a woodland fairy's home. This is a garden full of colors, nooks and crannies to tuck yourself into, and treasures of the botanic kind waiting to be discovered. It's every plant lover's paradise, but even those who wouldn't consider themselves to be plant fiends will be tempted to spend a fortune here. ⊠ *3158 Los Feliz Blvd., Atwater Village* ☎ *323/665–3801* ⊕ *pottedstore.com.*

Treehaus

CLOTHING | The beauty of Treehaus isn't that it's an independent boutique—Los Angeles has plenty of those—but that it carries a great assortment of retail pieces, from women's and children's clothing to accessories and home goods, all in a cozy rectangular space. ⊠ *3153 Glendale Blvd., Atwater Village* ☎ *323/230–6776* ⊕ *www.treehausla.com.*

Highland Park

In the early 20th century, Highland Park was a bastion for artists who erected numerous Arts and Crafts movement houses. It evolved into a largely immigrant community in the middle of the century and in the last few years has become a hybrid of its history. Local business owners have revived beautiful, historic buildings and turned them into exciting new restaurants, shops, and watering holes that pay ode to the area's past. These stand side by side with longtime establishments that serve up some of the best, and most authentic, tacos in town.

👁 Sights

Heritage Square Museum

MUSEUM | Looking like a prop street set up by a film studio, Heritage Square resembles a row of bright dollhouses in the modest Highland Park neighborhood. Five 19th-century residences, a train station, a church, a carriage barn, and a 1909 boxcar that was originally part of the Southern Pacific Railroad, all built between the Civil War and World War I, were moved to this small park from various locations in Southern California to save them from the wrecking ball. The latest addition, a re-creation of a World War I–era drugstore, has a vintage soda fountain and traditional products. Docents dressed in period costume lead visitors through the lavish homes, giving an informative picture of Los Angeles in the early 1900s. Don't miss the unique 1893 Octagon House, one of just a handful of its kind built in California. ⊠ *3800 Homer St., Highland Park* ☎ *323/225–2700* ⊕ *www.heritagesquare. org* ⊠ *$10* ☉ *Closed Tues.–Thurs. and federal holiday Mon.*

🍴 Restaurants

Highland Park's gastronomic experiences tout an eclectic mix of culinary creations serving Mexican, vegan, Polish, and a whole lot of delicious donuts, all punctuated by independent coffee shops. A day along Figueroa, its main strip, will certainly be an epicurean adventure.

CaCao Mexicatessen

$$ | MEXICAN | Opened by local Christie Lujan in 2009, CaCao Mexicatessen was one of the first places in town to showcase the creative potential of the street-style taco, offering options such as sea urchin and pork crackling as fillings. With handmade tortillas and a serious commitment to the flavors of Mexico, CaCao has embedded itself as one of the go-to places for Mexican food in Northeast L.A. **Known for:** duck carnitas taco; Korean short rib tacos; modern Mexican cuisine. ⑤ *Average main: $14* ✉ *1576 Colorado Blvd., Highland Park* ☎ *323/478–2791* ⊕ *www.cacaodeli.com* ☉ *Closed Mon.*

Cafe Birdie

$$ | MEDITERRANEAN | This spacious 1920s-style spot along a quickly revitalizing stretch of Figueroa has established itself as a neighborhood bistro frequented by Highland Park residents, as well as folks from nearby neighborhoods. The eclectic menu skillfully blends elements of European, Southern, and Japanese cuisines, tying them together with a fresh California flair and a gorgeous interior inspired by a fictional meeting-of-two-souls narrative. **Known for:** square pies; seasonal cocktails; modern, airy spot. ⑤ *Average main: $19* ✉ *5631 N. Figueroa St., Highland Park* ☎ *323/739–6928* ⊕ *www.cafebirdiela.com.*

Cindy's

$$ | DINER | FAMILY | The husband-and-wife team that took over Cindy's never set out to create a trendy space for hipsters looking for their next artisanal fix; they just wanted to make great, accessible food. That's exactly what they've done, and by doing so they've established a neighborhood restaurant with reasonable prices and back-to-basics food that just so happens to look retro cool. **Known for:** brisket hash; barbecue cheeseburger with "cowboy candy"; retro diner–style space. ⑤ *Average main: $14* ✉ *1500 Colorado Blvd., Highland Park* ☎ *323/257–7375* ⊕ *cindyseaglerock.com.*

★ Donut Friend

$ | BAKERY | When this music-influenced doughnut shop first opened on York Boulevard in the early days of Highland Park's renaissance, there wasn't much there, and its arrival helped shape the now bustling strip and its vegan inclinations. Donut Friend had evolved into a destination in its own right, touting both a signature and limited menu of purely vegan doughnuts—which also happen to be inspired by the pop punk and emo music scene. **Known for:** fun flavors like Green Teagan and Sara (with matcha tea glaze); all vegan ingredients; make-your-own doughnut option. ⑤ *Average main: $4* ✉ *5107 York Blvd., Highland Park* ☎ *213/908–2745* ⊕ *www.donutfriend.com.*

El Huarache Azteca

$ | MEXICAN | FAMILY | While you definitely should try the flat shoe-shaped dish El Huarache Azteca is named after—think somewhere between a flatbread and a tostada—you cannot go wrong with any of the other options at this family restaurant that's been a fixture in the area for the last couple of decades. Just be aware there's often a wait for the food to come out. **Known for:** no-frills Mexican dishes; agua fresca; super huarache. ⑤ *Average main: $10* ✉ *5225 York Blvd., Highland Park* ☎ *323/478–9572* ⊕ *elhuaracheazte-calive.com.*

5 Line Tavern

$$ | BURGER | This would be just another neighborhood spot in a neighborhood full of neighborhood spots, were it not for its

50 beers on tap, long list of delectable pizzas, burgers, and sandwiches, and a full and diverse bar that has everything from a jalapeño margarita to an 18-year-aged Glenfiddich. If that's not enough incentive, there's a speakeasy hiding in the back. **Known for:** tasty chicken wings; large selection of beers; football game crowd. ⑤ *Average main: $16* ✉ *2136 Colorado Blvd., Highland Park* ☎ *323/474–6218* ⊕ *www.5linetavern.com.*

Kitchen Mouse

$ | DINER | Born out of the owner's need for more kitchen space for her growing production catering business, Kitchen Mouse has blossomed into a wildly popular neighborhood restaurant with a cozy rustic-meets-modern look and an inspired, mostly organic vegan-vegetarian menu. The food is bright with vibrant flavors. **Known for:** Morning Glory Bowl; oat corn and buckwheat pancakes; excellent breakfast and brunch. ⑤ *Average main: $11* ✉ *5904 N. Figueroa St., Highland Park* ☎ *323/259–9555* ⊕ *www.kitchen-mousela.com.*

★ Knowrealitypie

$ | BAKERY | The award-winning Knowre-alitypie, hidden in a shop the size of a large walk-in closet, serves homemade pies every Friday through Saturday and only stays open until it sells out, which it often does. So hurry on down to partake in a rotating menu of seasonal savory and sweet pies, turnovers, and other pastries while supplies last. **Known for:** triple cherry Cabernet pie; caramel mango passion pie; small space that only stays open until they sell out. ⑤ *Average main: $6* ✉ *5106 Townsend Ave., Highland Park* ☎ *916/799–5772* ⊕ *www.knowrealitypie. com* ☉ *Closed Mon.–Thurs.*

Polka Polish Cuisine

$$ | POLISH | There's a coziness in Polka Polish Cuisine that can only be matched by a grandmother's living room. The food here, traditional Polish fare, also has that same comfort. **Known for:** hearty Polish

comfort food; traditional pierogi and kielbasa; mom-and-pop ambience. ⑤ *Average main: $20* ✉ *4112 Verdugo Rd., Highland Park* ☎ *323/255–7887* ⊕ *www. polkarestaurant.com* ☉ *Closed Mon. and Tues.*

Town Pizza

$$ | PIZZA | The red building situated on the corner of York and North Avenue 51 houses a pizzeria that's as quirky and hip as the neighborhood it inhabits. Pizza purists, however, may cringe at some of the toppings, which include beets, corn, and mole. **Known for:** vegan topping options; creative pizzas like Town Mole (mole and roast pork); trendy atmosphere. ⑤ *Average main: $20* ✉ *5101 York Blvd., Highland Park* ☎ *323/344–8696* ⊕ *www.townla.com.*

🍸 Nightlife

Block Party

BARS/PUBS | This spot fills the beer garden need in Highland Park, and it does it very well with a large shuffleboard and a Wii hooked up to a projector, along with plenty of picnic tables where you can chug (or nurse) beer and wine. The selection, from small-batch and craft vendors, is on point; the more adventurous may want to grab a *michelada* and *paleta* combo. ✉ *5052 York Blvd., Highland Park* ☎ *323/741–2747* ⊕ *www.blockpartyhlp. com.*

The Hermosillo

BARS/PUBS | This is the kind of laid-back pub every neighborhood should have, with an excellent selection of locally focused draft beer on tap, a rotating wine list, and mouthwatering food. To add to its allure, award-winning Highland Park Brewery got its start in the pub's back storage room and is still featured prominently on the menu. ✉ *5125 York Blvd., Highland Park* ☎ *323/739–6459* ⊕ *thehermosillo.com.*

★ Highland Park Bowl

BARS/PUBS | FAMILY | Once an ambitious restoration project, Highland Park Bowl now serves as a massive throwback to its Prohibition Era roots as an alcohol-prescribing doctor's office and drugstore with its own bowling alley. That bowling alley remains, complete with the original pin machine. The hooch-pushing doctor and druggist, however, are long gone. But now there's an Italian restaurant that serves excellent pizza made from scratch using a mother dough brought all the way from Italy. ✉ *5621 N. Figueroa St., Highland Park* ☎ *323/257–2695* ⊕ *www.highlandparkbowl.com.*

La Cuevita

PIANO BARS/LOUNGES | Everyone could use a little more mezcal and tequila in their lives, and La Cuevita has a lot of it, often in its collection of tasty cocktails. This Mexico-themed bar—complete with free Taco Tuesdays, a dark red interior, and a picture of a bandito overlooking the patrons—has one of the cheapest happy hours in L.A., making it the perfect place to start your evening. ✉ *5922 N. Figueroa St., Highland Park* ☎ *323/255–6871.*

The York

BARS/PUBS | Since 2007, before Highland Park became trendy, the York has been holding its own as the ultimate neighborhood bar. It's not just that the aesthetic gives off that neighborhood vibe (think exposed brick and chalkboard menus), but the craft beers on tap are great, and the pub food is delicious—the cheddar burger and the fish-and-chips are favorites. ✉ *5018 York Blvd., Highland Park* ☎ *323/255–9675* ⊕ *www.theyorkonyork.com.*

👜 Shopping

Figueroa Boulevard isn't buzzing only with bars and restaurants but also with ample opportunities for retail therapy. Small style outposts pave this street, as well as the connecting York Boulevard, with adorable gift shops, record stores, and spots to satisfy your vintage shopping itch.

Galco's Soda Pop Stop

FOOD/CANDY | FAMILY | A local fixture in Highland Park for decades, Galco's is in some ways a trip down memory lane, carrying more than 600 sodas—most of which harken back to the days when soda was a regional affair—and options from all over the world. They also have a collection of retro candies, a soda creation station with more than 100 syrups to choose from, and a selection of alcohol that would put most liquor stores to shame. ✉ *5702 York Blvd., Highland Park* ☎ *323/255–7115* ⊕ *sodapopstop.com.*

Permanent Records

MUSIC STORES | Part of the vinyl resurgence since 2013, Permanent Records stocks new and used vinyl for every musical taste and does it without any snobbery. The record store, which often has in-store performances, also runs its own label that focuses on local bands, limited-edition runs, and reissues. ✉ *1906 Cypress Ave., Highland Park* ☎ *323/332–2312* ⊕ *www.permanentrecordsla.com.*

TOPO by Kitchen Mouse

FOOD/CANDY | Adjacent to its sister establishment, Kitchen Mouse, is this charming little market stop for all your pastry, grab 'n' go nourishment, and catering needs, complete with a small shop that touts adorable home and gift items. It's a must-stop after you've had your vegan fix at the restaurant. ✉ *5906 N. Figueroa St., Highland Park* ☎ *323/259–9555* ⊕ *www.kitchenmousela.com/market.*

Chapter 10

PASADENA

Updated by
Candice Yacono

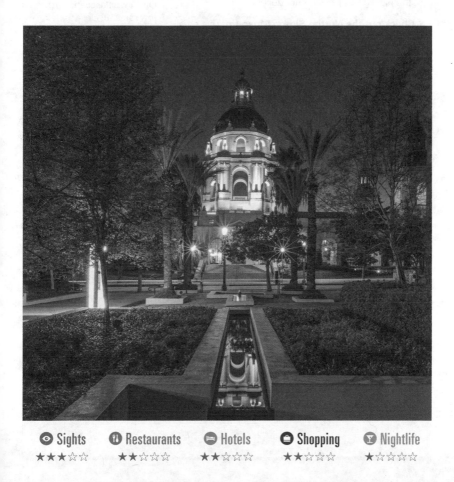

👁 Sights   🍴 Restaurants   🛏 Hotels   💼 Shopping   🍸 Nightlife
★★★☆☆   ★★☆☆☆   ★★☆☆☆   ★★☆☆☆   ★☆☆☆☆

NEIGHBORHOOD SNAPSHOT

TOP EXPERIENCES

■ **Visit the Huntington Library:** In addition to a collection of 18th-century British art, this library has 4 million manuscripts and 700,000 books, including the Gutenberg Bible.

■ **Walk through the Huntington's Botanical Gardens:** Set aside a couple of hours to enjoy the expansive lawns and stately trees surrounding the Huntington Library.

■ **See American craftsmanship at the Gamble House:** The teak staircase and cabinetry are just a few of the highlights at this home, built in 1908.

■ **Check out the Norton Simon Museum:** This small museum's fine collection features works by Renoir, Degas, Gauguin, and others

■ **Hang out in Old Town Pasadena:** Spend the afternoon walking around this 12-block historic town filled with cafés, restaurants, and shops.

QUICK BITES

Lêberry Bakery & Donut. If you've been hesitant to try vegan or gluten-free baked goods, the heavenly doughnuts, pies, cakes, cinnamon rolls, and more at this Black and Asian American family-owned shop—all made from quality ingredients—will turn your world upside down. ⊠ *445 E. Colorado Blvd.* ⊕ *leberrybakery.com*

Pie 'n Burger. This small and charming diner does two things really well: pie and burgers. Most seats are counter-style, with a griddle searing up patties. Burgers are pretty simple but the pies are killer. ⊠ *913 E. California Blvd.* ⊕ *www.pienburger.com*

The Raymond 1886. Carved out of an old cottage, head to the patio (especially for happy hour) as chefs dish out everything from microfarmed oysters and truffle polenta to seared salmon and mac and cheese. ⊠ *1250 S. Fair Oaks Ave.* ⊕ *www.theraymond.com*

GETTING HERE

■ To reach Pasadena from Downtown Los Angeles, drive north on the Pasadena Freeway (I–110). From Hollywood and the San Fernando Valley, use the Ventura Freeway (Highway 134, east), which cuts through Glendale, skirting the foothills, before arriving in Pasadena. There are several city parking lots located in Old Town Pasadena with low rates, all close to Colorado Boulevard, the main drag. On-street parking here is also widely available with few restrictions.

PLANNING YOUR TIME

■ The Huntington Library should command most of your time. Just be sure to keep the summer heat in mind when you visit—the gardens are more pleasant during the cooler morning hours. A stop at the beautiful Gamble House shouldn't take more than an hour, leaving plenty of time for an afternoon visit to the Norton Simon Museum, one of the area's best spots to enjoy world-class art. Unless you're planning on seeing a game or hitting the flea market, you will probably want to skip the Rose Bowl. Head to Old Pasadena in the evening, when the wide boulevards and leafy side streets come to life.

Although seemingly absorbed into the general Los Angeles sprawl, Pasadena is a separate and distinct city. It's best known for the Tournament of Roses, or more commonly, the Rose Bowl, seen around the world every New Year's Day. But the city has sites worth seeing year-round—from gorgeous Craftsman homes to exceptional museums, particularly the Norton Simon and the Huntington Library, Art Museum, and Botanical Gardens. Note that the Huntington and the Old Mill reside in San Marino, a well-heeled, 4-square-mile residential area just over the Pasadena line.

First-time visitors to L.A. only here for a short time might find it hard to get out to Pasadena. However, if you've had your fill of city life and are looking for a nearby escape that feels much farther away than it is, with open space and fresher air, it's the perfect trip.

Start at the **Botanical Gardens,** then spend the afternoon strolling around **Old Town Pasadena,** with shops and restaurants filling its 19th-century brick buildings. Art and architecture lovers shouldn't miss the city's top sight, the **Norton Simon Museum,** most noted for its excellent collection of Degas, as well as works by Rembrandt, Goya, and Picasso. The **Gamble House** is an immense three-story house and one of the country's shining examples of American Arts and Crafts bungalow architecture. The thing that might surprise you most about visiting Pasadena is that even the drive here—on the freeway, though not during rush hour—is a scenic one. The Pasadena Freeway follows the curves of an *arroyo* (dry creek), lined with old sycamore trees. It was the main road north during the early days of Los Angeles, when horses and buggies made their way through the countryside to the small town of Pasadena. In 1939 the road became the Arroyo Seco Parkway, the first freeway in Los Angeles.

Pasadena

The Japanese Garden at the Huntington Botanical Gardens features an authentic ceremonial teahouse built in Kyoto in the 1960s.

⊙ Sights

Castle Green

HISTORIC SITE | One block south of Colorado Boulevard stands the onetime social center of Pasadena's elite. This Moorish building is the only remaining section of a turn-of-the-20th-century hotel complex. Today the often-filmed tower (see *The Sting*, *Edward Scissorhands*, *The Last Samurai*, and *The Prestige*) is residential. The building is not open to the public on a daily basis, but it does organize two tours a year in June and December. ⊠ *99 S. Raymond Ave., Pasadena* ☎ *626/793–0359* ⊕ *www.castlegreen.com* ✉ *Tours from $30.*

Descanso Gardens

GARDEN | Getting its name from the Spanish word for "rest," this 160-acre oasis is a respite from city life, shaded by massive oak trees. Known for being a smaller, mellower version of the nearby Huntington, Descanso Gardens features denser foliage, quaint dirt paths, and some hilly climbs that can make for good exercise. It's the perfect place to come in search of wonderful scents—between the lilacs, the acres of roses, and the forest of California redwoods, pines, and junipers, you can enjoy all sorts of fragrances. A forest of California live oak trees makes a dramatic backdrop for thousands of camellias and azaleas and the breathtaking 5-acre International Rosarium holding 1,700 varieties of antique and modern roses. A small train ride draws families on weekends. There are also a child's train, a gift shop, a historic home, and a café. ⊠ *1418 Descanso Dr., La Cañada/Flintridge* ☎ *818/949–4200* ⊕ *www.descansogardens.org* ✉ *$15; often free 3rd Tues. of month.*

Fenyes Mansion

HOUSE | With its elegant dark-wood paneling and floors, curved staircases, and a theatrical stage in the parlor, it's easy to envision how this 1907 mansion along Pasadena's Millionaire's Row once served as gathering place for the city's elite (it also housed the Finnish consulate until 1965). Most rooms on the ground and second floors are still fitted with original furniture; you can peek into these roped-off spaces, now home to mannequins dressed in period clothing, to get a sense of what life was like a century ago. You can visit the mansion (on a 90-minute tour), the adjacent Finnish Folk Art Museum, and the Historical Center Gallery, which has rotating exhibits dedicated to the art and culture of Pasadena. ⊠ *470 W. Walnut St., Pasadena* ☎ *626/577–1660* ⊕ *www.pasadenahistory.org* ☛ *From $9* ⊘ *Closed Mon. and Tues.*

The Gamble House

HOUSE | Built by Charles and Henry Greene in 1908, this American Arts and Crafts bungalow illustrates the incredible craftsmanship that went into early L.A. architecture. The term "bungalow" can be misleading, since the Gamble House is a huge three-story home. To wealthy Easterners such as the Gambles (as in Procter & Gamble), this type of vacation home seemed informal compared with their mansions back home. Admirers swoon over the teak staircase and cabinetry, the Greene and Greene–designed furniture, and an Emil Lange glass door. The dark exterior has broad eaves, with sleeping porches on the second floor. An hour-long, docent-led tour of the Gamble's interior will draw your eye to the exquisite details. For those who want to see more of the Greene and Greene homes, there are guided walks around the historic Arroyo Terrace neighborhood. Advance tickets are highly recommended. ■TIP→ **Film buffs might recognize this as Doc Brown's house from** *Back to the Future.* ⊠ *4 Westmoreland Pl., Pasadena* ☎ *626/793–3334* ⊕ *gamblehouse.org* ☛ *$15* ⊘ *Closed Mon.*

★ **Huntington Library, Art Museum, and Botanical Gardens**

MUSEUM | If you have time for just one stop in the Pasadena area, be sure to see this sprawling estate built for railroad tycoon Henry E. Huntington in the early 1900s. Henry and his wife, Arabella (who was also his aunt by marriage), voraciously collected rare books and manuscripts, botanical specimens, and 18th-century British art. The institution they established became one of the most extraordinary cultural complexes in the world.

The library contains more than 700,000 books and 4 million manuscripts, including one of the world's biggest history of science collections and a Gutenberg Bible.

Don't resist being lured outside into the 130-acre Botanical Gardens, which extend out from the main building. The 10-acre Desert Garden has one of the world's largest groups of mature cacti and other succulents (visit on a cool morning or late afternoon). The Shakespeare Garden, meanwhile, blooms with plants mentioned in Shakespeare's works. The Japanese Garden features an authentic ceremonial teahouse built in Kyoto in the 1960s. A waterfall flows from the teahouse to the ponds below. In the Rose Garden Tea Room, afternoon tea is served (reserve in advance). The Chinese Garden, which is among the largest outside China, sinews around waveless pools.

The Bing Children's Garden lets tiny tots explore the ancient elements of water, fire, air, and earth. A 1¼-hour guided tour of the Botanical Gardens is led by docents at posted times, and a free brochure with a map and property highlights is available in the entrance pavilion. Tickets for the monthly free admission day are snapped up within minutes, so plan carefully. ⊠ *1151 Oxford Rd., San Marino* ☎ *626/405–2100* ⊕ *www.huntington.org* ☛ *From $25; free admission 1st Thurs. of every month with advance ticket* ⊘ *Closed Tues.*

Los Angeles County Arboretum and Botanic Garden

GARDEN | Wander through a re-created tropical forest, a South African landscape, or the Australian outback at this arboretum. One highlight is the tropical greenhouse, with carnivorous-looking orchids and a pond full of brilliantly colored goldfish. The house and stables of the eccentric real-estate pioneer Lucky Baldwin are well preserved and worth a visit. Kids will love the many peacocks and waterfowl that roam the property. The most recent addition is a water-harvesting farm, where tall stalks of rainbow corn and vines of passion fruit grow in abundance. ✉ *301 N. Baldwin Ave., Arcadia* ☎ *626/821–3222* ⊕ *www.arboretum. org* ☑ *$15; free 3rd Tues. of month with advance ticket.*

★ Norton Simon Museum

MUSEUM | As seen in the New Year's Day Tournament of Roses Parade, this low-profile brown building is one of the finest midsize museums anywhere, with a collection that spans more than 2,000 years of Western and Asian art. It all began in the 1950s when Norton Simon (Hunt-Wesson Foods, McCalls Corporation, and Canada Dry) started collecting works by Degas, Renoir, Gauguin, and Cézanne. His collection grew to include works by old masters and impressionists, modern works from Europe, and Indian and Southeast Asian art. Today the museum is richest in works by Rembrandt, Picasso, and, most of all, Degas.

Head down to the bottom floor to see temporary exhibits and phenomenal Southeast Asian and Indian sculptures and artifacts, where pieces like a Ban Chiang blackware vessel date back to well before 1000 BC. Don't miss a living artwork outdoors: the garden, conceived by noted Southern California landscape designer Nancy Goslee Power. The tranquil pond was inspired by Monet's gardens at Giverny. ✉ *411 W. Colorado Blvd., Pasadena* ☎ *626/449–6840* ⊕ *www.nortonsimon.org* ☑ *$15; free 1st Fri. of month 5–8* ☾ *Closed Tues.*

The Old Mill (El Molino Viejo)

BUILDING | Built in 1816 as a gristmill for the San Gabriel Mission, the mill is the state's oldest commercial building and one of the last remaining examples in Southern California of Spanish Mission architecture. The thick adobe walls and textured ceiling rafters give the interior a sense of quiet strength. Be sure to step into the back room, now a gallery with rotating quarterly exhibits. Outside, a chipped section of the mill's exterior reveals the layers of brick, ground seashell paste, and ox blood used to hold the structure together. The surrounding gardens are reason enough to visit, with a flower-decked arbor and old sycamores and oaks. In summer the Capitol Ensemble performs in the garden. ✉ *1120 Old Mill Rd., San Marino* ☎ *626/449–5458* ⊕ *www.old-mill.org* ☑ *Free* ☾ *Closed Mon.*

Old Town Pasadena

NEIGHBORHOOD | This 22-block historic district contains a vibrant mix of restored 19th-century brick buildings interspersed with contemporary architecture. Chain stores have muscled in, but there are still some homegrown shops, plenty of tempting cafés and restaurants, and a bustling beer scene. In recent years, a vibrant Asian food scene has popped up in the vicinity as well. In the evening and on weekends, the streets are packed with people. Old Town's main action takes place on Colorado Boulevard between Pasadena Avenue and Arroyo Parkway. ✉ *Pasadena* ☎ *626/356–9725* ⊕ *www.oldpasadena.org.*

★ Rose Bowl and Flea Market

MARKET | With an enormous rose on its exterior, this 90,000-plus-seat stadium is home to the UCLA Bruins and the annual Rose Bowl Game on New Year's Day, and also regularly sees performances

from the biggest recording artists in the world. Set at the bottom of a wide arroyo in Brookside Park, the facility is closed except during games, concerts, and special events like its famed Flea Market, a Southern California institution. The massively popular and eclectic event, which happens the second Sunday of each month (rain or shine), deservedly draws crowds that come to find deals from more than 2,500 vendors on goods including mid-century and antique furniture, vintage clothing, pop culture collectibles, books, and music. Food and drink options are on hand to keep shoppers satiated, parking is free, and general admission is just $9, but VIP/ early-bird options are available for a little extra. Crowds tend to peak mid-day. Bring cash to avoid an inevitable line at the ATM, and feel free to try your hand at haggling. ⊠ *1001 Rose Bowl Dr., Pasadena* ☎ *626/577–3100* ⊕ *www.rosebowlstadium.com.*

Tournament House (Wrigley Mansion)

HOUSE | Chewing gum magnate William Wrigley purchased this white Italian Renaissance–style house in 1914. When his wife died in 1958, Wrigley donated the house to the city of Pasadena under the stipulation that it be used as the headquarters for the Tournament of Roses. The mansion features a green tile roof and manicured rose garden with 1,500 varieties. The interior provides a glimpse of the area's over-the-top style in the early 20th century. Tours of the house are every Thursday from 2 to 3 from February to August; fans of the Rose Parade can see the various crowns and tiaras worn by former Rose Queens, plus trophies and memorabilia. ⊠ *391 S. Orange Grove Blvd., Pasadena* ☎ *626/449–4100* ⊕ *www.visitpasadena.com/businesses/tournament-house* ⊠ *Free.*

🍴 Restaurants

With the revitalization of Old Town Pasadena, more people are discovering the beauty of Rose City. They mingle at bistros, upscale eateries, and taco trucks, but are also discovering the newer innovative dining spots that are giving Pasadena a hipper feel.

The Arbour Pasadena

$$$ | **MODERN AMERICAN** | This farm-to-table eatery uses all local ingredients to whip up creative cuisine in a chic environment. Savory musts include the bacon tart with béchamel, as well as the outstanding Mediterranean sea bass. **Known for:** farm-to-table cuisine; chic atmosphere; mezcal margarita. ⑤ *Average main: $30* ⊠ *527 S. Lake Ave., Suite 120, Pasadena* ☎ *626/396–4925* ⊕ *www.thearbourpasadena.com.*

Pie 'n Burger

$$ | **DINER** | Since 1963, this small and charming diner has done two things really well—pies and burgers. Most seats are counter-style, with a griddle searing up patties. **Known for:** simple burgers; enormous pie slices; retro-style decor. ⑤ *Average main: $14* ⊠ *913 E. California Blvd., Pasadena* ☎ *626/795–1123* ⊕ *pienburger.com.*

The Raymond 1886

$$$ | **MODERN AMERICAN** | The coolest kid on the Pasadena block, the Raymond 1886 is carved out of an old cottage, and has an expansive patio with long wooden tables and hanging lights. Chefs dish out everything from a burrata-and-pear pairing to pork loin Milanese and tots with eel sauce. **Known for:** solid happy hour; great bar food; expansive patio. ⑤ *Average main: $30* ⊠ *1250 S. Fair Oaks Ave., Pasadena* ☎ *626/441–3136* ⊕ *theraymond.com* ⊗ *Closed Mon.*

★ Union

$$$ | ITALIAN | There's a Michelin-quality Italian restaurant hiding in plain sight in Pasadena. The small and homey space where Northern Italy meets California is typically filled to the brim as diners await heaven-sent wild mushrooms with G&T polenta or the squid-ink *lumache* (shell pasta) with Maine lobster. **Known for:** superb wine list; excellent Italian food with a California twist; buzzy yet intimate atmosphere. ⑤ *Average main: $31* ☒ *37 E. Union St., Pasadena* ☎ *626/795–5841* ⊕ *www.unionpasadena.com* ☽ *No lunch.*

🎭 Performing Arts

A Noise Within

THEATER | Named for one of Shakespeare's stage directions in *Hamlet*, A Noise Within is the Los Angeles area's preeminent place to see classic theater. The Bard's own works are told alongside those of Oscar Wilde and the Greek tragedies, often with a twist. The company boasts fierce talent among its revolving repertory of resident actors, many of whom also work in Hollywood. Audience members are never more than eight rows away from its platform stage, creating a sense of intimacy for all in attendance. ☒ *3352 E. Foothill Blvd., Pasadena* ☎ *626/356–3100* ⊕ *www. anoisewithin.org.*

Fremont Centre Theatre

THEATER | This theater centers on original material and world premieres with professional actors year-round. The small venue is known for its dedication to diversity and its inclusive atmosphere, with "talkbacks" (Q&As between actors and audience members) after certain shows. Ray Bradbury regularly produced shows here for five years before his death in 2012, including a stage adaptation of *Fahrenheit 451.* ☒ *1000 Fremont Ave., South Pasadena* ☎ *626/441–5977* ⊕ *www.fremontcentretheatre.com.*

The Pasadena Playhouse

THEATER | Exceptional plays and musicals, occasionally featuring known TV and movie actors, are what this theater is mostly known for—that and it's an historical landmark that's been operating as a theater since 1925. The 650-seat playhouse also holds the title of official state theater of California. Tours of the venue are available by appointment. ☒ *39 S. El Molino Ave., Pasadena* ☎ *626/356–7529* ⊕ *www.pasadenaplayhouse.org.*

🛍 Shopping

The stretch of Colorado Boulevard between Pasadena Avenue and Arroyo Parkway, known as Old Town, is a popular pedestrian shopping destination, where retailers such as Crate & Barrel, H&M, and Tiffany and Co. rub elbows with clothing resale shops, dog treat bakeries, and gelaterias. A few blocks east on Colorado, the open-air "urban village" known as Paseo Colorado mixes residential, retail, dining, and entertainment spaces along Colorado Boulevard between Los Robles and Marengo avenues. Enter on Colorado or Marengo for free parking.

Elisa B

CLOTHING | This small but well-edited shop stocks casual wear from established basics brands like Michael Stars and Heartloom alongside high-end designer finds by labels including Rachel Comey and A.L.C. ☒ *16 E. Holly St., Pasadena* ☎ *626/397–4770* ⊕ *www.elisab.com.*

Gold Bug

GIFTS/SOUVENIRS | Antiques, sculptures, animal specimens, crystals, and other unique oddities for the eccentric giftees on your list are all found inside this offbeat boutique located just around the corner from bustling Colorado Boulevard, but the main draw here is the jewelry. Funky, whimsical finds like a black beaded bracelet with a diamond-flecked snake-head clasp or a fur-and-chain-mail cuff are stocked alongside more minimal (yet still nature-inspired) pieces, all of which are created by independent designers and made of fine materials like gold or silver and semiprecious stones. ⚠ **No photos allowed inside.** ✉ *34 E. Union St., Pasadena* ☎ *626/744–9963* ⊕ *www.goldbugpasadena.com.*

Ten Thousand Villages

GIFTS/SOUVENIRS | At Pasadena's favorite fair-trade retailer, many of the shop workers are volunteers, which helps to maximize profits for the stable of artisans from more than 30 countries who produce eye-catching and unique home decor, accessories, gifts, art, and more here. Enticing options include an indigo Nepalese robe, intricately cut metal wall hangings of birds and trees made in Haiti from oil drum lids, or one-of-a-kind Bangladeshi dog beds crafted from upcycled saris. ✉ *567 S. Lake Ave., Pasadena* ☎ *626/229–9892* ⊕ *www.tenthousandvillages.com/pasadena.*

Vroman's Bookstore

BOOKS/STATIONERY | Southern California's oldest and largest independent bookseller is justly famous for its great service. A newsstand, café, and stationery store add to the appeal, and it's a favorite with locals for its on-trend, eclectic gift selection. A regular rotation of events including trivia night, kids' story time, author meet-and-greets, crafting sessions, discussions, and more get the community actively involved. ✉ *695 E. Colorado Blvd., Pasadena* ☎ *626/449–5320* ⊕ *www.vromansbookstore.com.*

Chapter 11

MALIBU AND THE BEACHES

Updated by
Candice Yacono

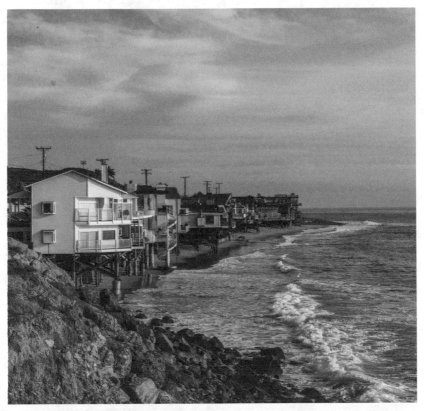

👁 Sights	🍴 Restaurants	🛏 Hotels	🛍 Shopping	🍸 Nightlife
★★★★☆	★★★★☆	★★★☆☆	★★★☆☆	★★★☆☆

NEIGHBORHOOD SNAPSHOT

TOP EXPERIENCES

■ **Watch the sunset over the Pacific in Malibu:** Whether you watch it cliffside or parked on a beach blanket, the view will stay fixed in your mind as a trip highlight.

■ **Have a bonfire at Dockweiler Beach:** Bonfires are pretty much illegal in L.A., except at Dockweiler. Pick up a grill and have a barbecue, or just toast marshmallows.

■ **Explore the Getty Villa:** Pretend you're a Roman patrician at this sprawling museum and garden complex, designed to replicate an authentic villa unearthed near Pompeii.

■ **Step back in time on the *Queen Mary*:** Experience the golden age of sea travel without the seasickness by stepping aboard this art deco masterpiece reminiscent of a pre-iceberg *Titanic*.

QUICK BITES

Churros Pier Bakery. If you find yourself ambling the Redondo Beach Pier and think you know what a churro is, make a pit stop here to be educated. And if you also love coffee and ice cream, try the churro affogato. ⊠ *100 Fishermans Wharf, Redondo Beach*

John's Garden Fresh Health Store. Assemble a beach picnic like a true Malibu denizen at this humble deli where sandwiches include the Surfer Princess (turkey and avocado, naturally). You can also choose from smoothies and juices, salads, açaí bowls, snacks, drinks, and more. ⊠ *3835 Cross Creek Rd., Malibu* ⊕ *www.johnsgardenmalibu.com*

Long Beach Creamery. For some literal local flavor, it doesn't get fresher than this jewel of an ice-cream shop, where the organic ingredients come from local farmers and small businesses; flavors include Love Potion, Midnight Oolong, and LB Crack. ⊠ *222 E. Broadway Ave., Long Beach* ⊕ *www.longbeach-creamery.com*

GETTING HERE

■ From Downtown, the easiest way to get to Malibu is by taking the Santa Monica Freeway (I–10) due west. Once you reach the end of the freeway, I–10 runs into the Pacific Coast Highway. Head north on the PCH to pass through Pacific Palisades into Malibu. Driving along the coast is a quintessential L.A. experience—but so is sitting in beach traffic. Avoid driving to Malibu during rush hour when traffic along the PCH moves at a snail's pace.

■ Public parking is usually available at the beaches, though fees can range anywhere from $8 to $20. While public transportation options are slim, MTA buses do run from Downtown along Pico, Olympic, Santa Monica, Sunset, and Wilshire boulevards to the coast. The Metro E (or Expo) Line also runs to Downtown Santa Monica. From there, the 534 bus whisks you along the coast into Malibu.

■ To reach Downtown Long Beach and attractions like the *Queen Mary*, take the I–110 Freeway south. Via public transportation, take the Metro A (or Blue) line south. For the South Bay, a car or Uber is your best bet; no Metro line goes straight to its coast, though the C (Green) line will get you to the general area.

The beaches and coastal areas of Los Angeles are an iconic symbol of the region's casual friendliness and endless optimism, and the local love for them is as much a trope as it is a reality.

Angelenos are known for working hard and playing hard, and the coast is where they come to play. Getting some sand on the floor of your car is a rite of passage here. Like its most ardent fans, this stretch of the Pacific is best known for its beauty: cosmetically enhanced in some areas and ruggedly pristine in others. From the hillside mansions of Malibu, where even the air is rarified, to the cultural dynamism of Long Beach, the gently arching coastline tells an L.A. story all its own as it transitions from ultrarich to bohemian to working class. Through it all, the sand remains the center of the action.

Malibu

North of Santa Monica, up the Pacific Coast Highway, past rockslides, roller-bladers, and cliffside estates, Malibu is home to blockbuster names like Spielberg, Hanks, and Streisand. This ecologically fragile 23-mile stretch of coastline is a world of its own, with its slopes slipping dramatically into the ocean. But Malibu is constantly reinventing itself, and the devastating 2018 Woolsey Fire has forced it to reinvent once more.

In the public imagination Malibu is synonymous with beaches and wealth—but in the past couple of years there's been some friction between these two signature elements. Some property owners, such as billionaire music producer David Geffen, have come under attack for

blocking public access to the beaches in front of their homes. All beaches are technically public, though; if you stay below the mean high-tide mark you're in the clear.

◉ Sights

Adamson House and Malibu Lagoon Museum

HOUSE | With spectacular views of Surfrider Beach and lush garden grounds, this Moorish Spanish–style house epitomizes all the reasons to live in Malibu. It was built in 1929 by the Rindge family, who owned much of the Malibu area in the early part of the 20th century. The Rindges had an enviable Malibu lifestyle, decades before the area was trendy. In the 1920s, Malibu was quite isolated; in fact all visitors and some of the supplies arrived by boat at the nearby Malibu Pier. (The town becomes isolated today whenever rockslides close the highway.) The house, covered with magnificent tile work in rich blues, greens, yellows, and oranges from the now-defunct Malibu Potteries, is right on the beach—high chain link fences keep out curious beachgoers. Even an outside dog bathtub near the servants' door is a tiled gem. Docent-led tours provide insights on family life here as well as the history of Malibu and its real estate. Signs posted around the grounds outside direct you on a self-guided tour, but you can't go inside the house without a guide. Guided tours take place on Friday and Saturday at 11 am. There's

The Getty Villa is a gorgeous setting for a spectacular collection of ancient art.

pay parking in the adjacent county lot or in the lot at PCH and Cross Creek Road. ⊠ *23200 Pacific Coast Hwy., Malibu* ☎ *310/456–8432* ⊕ *www.adamsonhouse. org* ⊠ *$7* ⊙ *Check website for closing times.*

Dan Blocker Beach (*Corral Beach*)
BEACH—SIGHT | The narrow stretch of fine sand and rocks here make this little beach great for walking, light swimming, kayaking, and scuba diving rather than large gatherings. Clustered boulders create cozy spots for couples and picnickers, and because of the limited parking available along the PCH and the short hike necessary to reach the beach, it's rarely crowded. Originally owned by the star of the *Bonanza* TV series, the beach was donated to the state after Dan Blocker (who played Hoss) died in 1972. Locals still know this as Corral Beach. From the parking lot, walk a short distance up PCH in either direction to access the beach. **Amenities:** lifeguards; toilets. **Best for:** solitude; walking; swimming; snorkeling. ⊠ *26000 Pacific Coast Hwy., at Corral Canyon Rd., Malibu* ☎ *310/305–9503* ⊕ *beaches.lacounty.gov/ dan-blocker-beach.*

★ **Getty Villa Malibu**
HOUSE | Feeding off the cultures of ancient Rome, Greece, and Etruria, the villa exhibits astounding antiquities, though on a first visit even they take a backseat to their environment. This megamansion sits on some of the most valuable coastal property in the world. Modeled after the Villa dei Papiri in Herculaneum, a Roman estate owned by Julius Caesar's father-in-law that was covered in ash when Mt. Vesuvius erupted, the Getty Villa includes beautifully manicured gardens, reflecting pools, and statuary. The structures blend thoughtfully into the rolling terrain and significantly improve the public spaces, such as the outdoor amphitheater, gift store, café, and entry arcade. Talks, concerts, and educational programs are offered at an indoor theater. ■ **TIP→ An advance timed entry ticket is required for admission. Tickets are free and may be ordered**

from the museum's website or by phone.
✉ *17985 Pacific Coast Hwy., Pacific Palisades* ☎ *310/440–7300* ⊕ *www.getty. edu* ☞ *Free, tickets required; parking $20* ⊘ *Closed Tues.*

Las Tunas Beach

BEACH—SIGHT | This small, rarely crowded beach, the southernmost in Malibu, is known for its groins (metal gates constructed in 1929 to protect against erosion) and has good swimming, diving, and fishing conditions and a rocky coastline that wraps elegantly around the Pacific Coast Highway. Watch out for high tides and parking along the PCH. **Amenities:** lifeguards; food and drink. **Best for:** solitude; swimming. ✉ *19444 Pacific Coast Hwy., Malibu* ☎ *310/305–9545* ⊕ *beaches.lacounty.gov/las-tunas-beach.*

Leo Carrillo State Park

BEACH—SIGHT | **FAMILY** | On the very edge of Ventura County, this narrow beach is better for exploring than for sunning or swimming (watch that strong undertow!). If you do plan to swim, stay north of lifeguard towers 2, 4, and 5, but be sure to ask lifeguards about water conditions when you arrive. On your own or with a ranger, venture down at low tide to examine the tide pools among the rocks. Sequit Point, a promontory dividing the northwest and southeast halves of the beach, creates secret coves, sea tunnels, and boulders on which you can perch and fish. Generally, anglers stick to the northwest end of the beach; experienced surfers brave the rocks to the southeast. Campgrounds are set back from the beach; campsites must be reserved well in advance. Tide pools make this a great place for exploration. **Amenities:** parking; lifeguards (seasonally); toilets; showers. **Best for:** sunset; surfing; swimming; walking; windsurfing. ✉ *35000 Pacific Coast Hwy., Malibu* ☎ *310/457–8143* ⊕ *parks. ca.gov/?page_id=616.*

Malibu Lagoon State Beach

BEACH—SIGHT | Bird-watchers, take note: in this 5-acre marshy area near Malibu Beach Inn you can spot egrets, blue herons, avocets, and gulls. (You need to stay on the boardwalks so as not to disturb their habitats.) The path leads out to a rocky stretch of Surfrider Beach and makes for a pleasant stroll. The sand is soft, clean, and white, and you're also likely to spot a variety of marine life. Look for the signs to help identify these sometimes exotic-looking creatures. The lagoon is particularly enjoyable in the early morning and at sunset—and even more so now, thanks to a restoration effort that improved the lagoon's scent. The parking lot has limited hours, but street-side parking is usually available at off-peak times. An on-site museum reveals local history, and close by are shops and a theater. **Amenities:** parking (fee); lifeguards; toilets; showers. **Best for:** sunset; walking. ✉ *23200 Pacific Coast Hwy., Malibu* ☎ *310/457–8143* ⊕ *www. parks.ca.gov/?page_id=835* ☞ *Parking $12.*

Malibu Pier

MARINA | **FAMILY** | This rustically chic 780-foot fishing dock is a great place to drink in the sunset, take in some coastal views, or watch local fishermen reel up a catch. Some tours also leave from here. A pier has jutted out on this spot since the early 1900s; storms destroyed the last one in 1995, and it was rebuilt in 2001. Over the years, private developers have worked with the state to refurbish the pier, which now yields a gift shop, water-sport rentals, a jeweler housed in a vintage Airstream trailer, and a wonderful farm-to-table restaurant with stunning views and locations at both ends of the pier. ✉ *Pacific Coast Hwy. at Cross Creek Rd., Malibu* ⊕ *www.malibupier.com.*

Malibu

Sights ▶

1 Adamson House and
Malibu Lagoon
Museum.................E2
2 Dan Blocker Beach......D2
3 Getty Villa Malibu.......G1
4 Las Tunas Beach.......F2
5 Leo Carrillo
State Park.............A1

6 Malibu Lagoon
State Beach.............E2
7 Malibu Pier..............E2
8 Malibu Surfrider Beach...E2
9 Nicholas Canyon
County Beach............A2
10 Robert H. Meyer
Memorial State
Beach...................B2

11 Topanga State
Beach......................G2
12 Topanga State Park......G1
13 Westward Beach–
Point Dume...............C2
14 Zuma Beach Park.........C2

Restaurants ▶

1 Mastro's Ocean Club.....G2
2 Nobu Malibu.............E2
3 Reel Inn.................G2
4 The Sunset
Restaurant and Bar.......C2

Hotels ▶

1 Malibu Beach Inn.........E2

KEY

1 Exploring Sights

1 Restaurants

1 Hotels

PACIFIC OCEAN

Malibu Surfrider Beach

BEACH—SIGHT | Steady 3- to 5-foot waves make this beach, just west of Malibu Pier, a surfing paradise. Water runoff from Malibu Canyon forms a natural lagoon that's a sanctuary for 250 species of birds). Bird-watch, play volleyball, or take a walk on one of the nature trails, which are perfect for romantic sunset strolls. Guided tours of the surrounding wetlands are available seasonally. **Amenities:** parking (fee); lifeguards; toilets; food and drink; showers. **Best for:** sunset; surfing; swimming; windsurfing. ⊠ *23050 Pacific Coast Hwy., Malibu* ☎ *310/457–8143* ⊕ *www.beaches.lacounty.gov/malibu-surfrider-beach* 🅿 *$12 parking.*

Nicholas Canyon County Beach

BEACH—SIGHT | Sandier and less private than most of the rocky beaches surrounding it, this little beach is great for picnics. You can sit at a picnic table high up on a bluff overlooking the ocean or cast out a fishing line. Surfers call it Zero Beach because the waves take the shape of a hollow tube when winter swells peel off the reef. This site also hosts a 4-acre traditional Chumash village, which replicates a day in the life of the Chumash people, including their homes, canoes, handicrafts, and ceremonies. Request a guided tour in advance. **Amenities:** parking (fee); lifeguards; toilets; showers. **Best for:** solitude; surfing; walking; windsurfing. ⊠ *33805 Pacific Coast Hwy., Malibu* ☎ *310/305–9503* ⊕ *www.beaches.lacounty.gov/nicholas-canyon-beach.*

★ Robert H. Meyer Memorial State Beach

BEACH—SIGHT | Part of Malibu's most beautiful coastal area, this beach is made up of three minibeaches—El Pescador, La Piedra, and El Matador—each with the same spectacular view. Scramble down the steps to the rocky coves via steep, steep stairways; all food and water needs to be toted in, as there are no services. Portable toilets at the trailhead are the only restrooms. "El Mat" has a series of caves, Piedra some nifty rock formations, and Pescador a secluded feel, but they're all picturesque and fairly private. ⚠ **Keep track of the incoming tide so you won't get trapped between those otherwise scenic boulders. Amenities:** parking (fee); toilets. **Best for:** snorkeling; solitude; sunset; surfing; walking; windsurfing. ⊠ *32350, 32700, and 32900 Pacific Coast Hwy., Malibu* ☎ *818/880–0363* ⊕ *www.parks.ca.gov/?page_id=633.*

Topanga State Beach

BEACH—SIGHT | The beginning of miles of public beach, Topanga has good surfing at the western end, the mouth of the canyon, but is not an ideal swimming spot. Close to a busy section of PCH and rather narrow, the beach here is more lively, as groups of teenagers often zip over Topanga Canyon Boulevard from the Valley. There are swing sets on-site, as well as spots for fishing. **Amenities:** parking (fee); lifeguards; toilets; food and drink; showers. **Best for:** surfing. ⊠ *18700 block of Pacific Coast Hwy., Malibu* ☎ *310/305–9503* ⊕ *beaches.lacounty.gov/topanga-beach.*

Topanga State Park

NATIONAL/STATE PARK | Boasting more than 14,000 acres of open space and 36 miles of celebrity-studded trails, Topanga State Park is many Malibu residents' extended backyard. The Trippet Ranch entrance gives you several trail options including a ½-mile nature loop, a 7-mile round-trip excursion to the Parker Mesa Overlook—breathtaking on a clear day—or a 10-mile trek to the Will Rogers park. (Exit U.S. 101 onto Topanga Canyon Boulevard in Woodland Hills and head south until you can turn left onto Entrada; if going north on PCH, turn onto Topanga Canyon Boulevard—a bit past Sunset Boulevard—and go north until you can turn right onto Entrada.) ⊠ *20829 Entrada Rd., Malibu* ☎ *310/574–2488* ⊕ *www.parks.ca.gov/?page_id=629* 🅿 *Parking $10.*

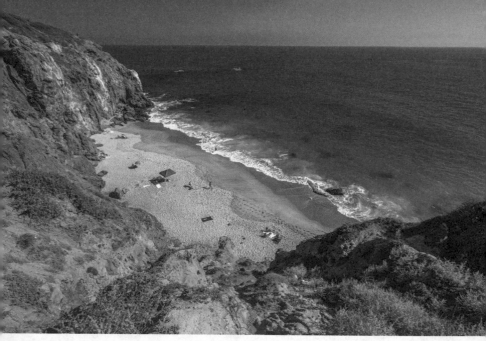

Around Point Dume, you'll find beautiful sandy coves.

Westward Beach–Point Dume

BEACH—SIGHT | This famed promontory is a Malibu pilgrimage for any visitor to the area. Go tide pooling, fishing, snorkeling, or bird-watching (prime time is late winter to early spring). Hike to the top of the sandstone cliffs at Point Dume to whale-watch—their migrations can be seen between December and April—and take in dramatic coastal views. Westward is a favorite surfing beach, but the steep surf isn't for novices. The Sunset restaurant is between Westward and Point Dume (at 6800 Westward Beach Road). Otherwise, bring your own food, since the nearest concession is a long hike away. **Amenities:** parking (fee); lifeguards; toilets; food and drink; showers. **Best for:** surfing; walking. ✉ *71030 Westward Beach Rd., Malibu* ☎ *310/305–9503* 🚗 *Parking $14.*

Zuma Beach Park

BEACH—SIGHT | This 2-mile stretch of white sand, usually dotted with tanning teenagers, has it all, from fishing and kitesurfing to swings and volleyball courts. Beachgoers looking for quiet or privacy should head elsewhere. Stay alert in the water: the surf is rough and inconsistent and riptides can surprise even experienced swimmers. **Amenities:** parking; lifeguards; toilets; food and drink; showers. **Best for:** partiers; sunset; swimming; walking. ✉ *30000 Pacific Coast Hwy., Malibu* ☎ *310/305–9522* ⊕ *www.zuma-beach.com* 🚗 *Parking $10.*

🍽 Restaurants

The beauty of the coastline makes every meal here taste like the best you've ever had. Here you'll find quaint family spots and extravagant hot spots.

Mastro's Ocean Club

$$$$ | STEAKHOUSE | This steak house not only features the best views of the beach, it's also a great place to scope out A-listers. You may be paying for the ambience, but mouthwatering Wagyu steaks, Dungeness crab, and lobster mashed potatoes just seem to taste better when the ocean is nipping at your feet. **Known for:** lively weekend brunch; live jazz nightly; reservations needed in advance. $ *Average main: $50* ⊠ *18412 Pacific Coast Hwy., Malibu* ☎ *310/454–4357* ⊕ *www.mastrosrestaurants.com.*

Nobu Malibu

$$$$ | **JAPANESE** | At famous chef-restaurateur Nobu Matsuhisa's coastal outpost, super-chic clientele sails in for morsels of the world's finest fish. It's hard not to be seduced by the oceanfront property, and stellar sushi and ingenious specialties match the upscale setting. **Known for:** exotic fish; A-list celebrity chef; bento box Valrhona chocolate soufflé. $ *Average main: $35* ⊠ *22706 Pacific Coast Hwy., Malibu* ☎ *310/317–9140* ⊕ *www. noburestaurants.com.*

Reel Inn

$$ | **SEAFOOD** | **FAMILY** | Escape the glitz and glamour at this decades-old, down-home Malibu institution. Long wooden tables and booths are often filled with fish-loving families chowing down on mahimahi sandwiches and freshly caught swordfish. **Known for:** easy-to-miss spot on the PCH; fresh catches; dog-friendly patio. $ *Average main: $17* ⊠ *18661 Pacific Coast Hwy., Malibu* ☎ *310/456–8221* ⊕ *www.reelinnmalibu.com.*

★ The Sunset Restaurant and Bar

$$ | **AMERICAN** | This local secret is as close to the beach—Zuma Beach, in this case—as you can get for a meal without getting sand in your drink. Stop in for a cocktail at the friendly bar, a light meal of grilled fish tacos, or one of the unique salads. **Known for:** close to the beach, off-the-beaten path location; beautiful views; good happy hour. $ *Average main: $15* ⊠ *Off Pacific Coast Hwy., just north of Zuma Beach, 6800 Westward Beach Rd., Malibu* ☎ *310/589–1007* ⊕ *www. thesunsetrestaurant.com.*

🛏 Hotels

Malibu Beach Inn

$$$$ | **B&B/INN** | Set right on exclusive Carbon Beach in a stretch known as Billionaire's Beach, Malibu's hideaway for the super-rich remains the room to nab along the coast, with an ultrachic look thanks to designer Waldo Fernandez and an upscale restaurant and wine bar perched over the Pacific. **Pros:** views of the ocean from your private balcony; world-class chocolate chip cookies at reception; ultimate beachside luxury. **Cons:** millionaire's travel budget required; some in-room noise from PCH; no pool, gym, or hot tub. $ *Rooms from: $749* ⊠ *22878 Pacific Coast Hwy., Malibu* ☎ *310/456–6444* ⊕ *www.malibubeach-inn.com* ⇆ *47 rooms* ❏ *No meals.*

🍸 Nightlife

Duke's Barefoot Bar

BARS/PUBS | **FAMILY** | With a clear view of the horizon from almost everywhere, a sunset drink at Duke's Barefoot Bar is how many beachgoers like to end their day. The entertainment is in keeping with the bar's theme, with Hawaiian dancers as well as live music on Friday night by Hawaiian artists. The menu features island favorites like *poke* tacos, macadamia-crusted fish, and kalua pork and a Sunday brunch buffet from 10 to 2. Just don't expect beach-bum prices, unless you stop by the happy hour weekday events like Taco Tuesday (bargain-priced fish, kalua pork, or grilled chicken tacos and beers). ⊠ *21150 Pacific Coast Hwy., Malibu* ☎ *310/317–0777* ⊕ *www.dukes-malibu.com.*

Moonshadows

BARS/PUBS | This outdoor lounge attracts customers with its modern look and views of the ocean. Think dark woods, cabana-style draperies, and ambient lighting in the Blue Lounge, open late on weekends. DJs are constantly spinning

Malibu is surrounded by the ocean on one side, and the Santa Monica Mountains on the other.

lounge music in the background, and there's never a cover charge. Sunday afternoons perfectly blend the laid-back ambience with good vibes. Try a sunset dinner or the lobster roll and dessert lineup. ⊠ *20356 Pacific Coast Hwy., Malibu* ☎ *310/456–3010* ⊕ *www.moonshadows-malibu.com.*

🎭 Performing Arts

Will Geer Theatricum Botanicum
THEATER | FAMILY | This open-air theater puts on classic as well as new and relevant plays from June to October, along with several off-season events and Family Fundays. The gardens have sitting areas for picnics before the show and they encourage you to "Play and Stay" in the Topanga area by pairing your theater experience with a hike in the local hills or a trip to one of the area's unique restaurants beforehand; the company also hosts dinner (and a show) on certain nights. ■ **TIP→ Select weekends are great for families, with special shows performed**

with children in mind. ⊠ *1419 N. Topanga Canyon Blvd., Topanga* ☎ *310/455–3723* ⊕ *www.theatricum.com.*

🛍 Shopping

★ Malibu Country Mart
SHOPPING CENTERS/MALLS | Stop by this outdoor outpost for the ultimate Malibu lifestyle experience, complete with browsing designer clothing (Rubin & Chapelle, Ron Herman, or Madison) and eclectic California housewares and gifts (Malibu Colony Company), picking up body-boosting wellness goodies at SunLife Organics, and finishing the day off with dinner at long-standing eatery Tra di Noi, reputed to be a favorite of Barbra Streisand. If you can squeeze in a workout, there's a Pure Barre and a 5 Point Yoga to choose from, plus tarot readings at metaphysical outpost Malibu Shaman. Then reward yourself for your good health habits by stopping at K Chocolatier by Diane Krön for some of her famed truffles, derived from a Hungarian family

recipe. ⊠ *3835 Cross Creek Rd., Malibu* ☎ *310/456–7300* ⊕ *www.malibucountry-mart.com.*

Malibu Lumber Yard

SHOPPING CENTERS/MALLS | Emblematic Malibu lifestyle stores in this shopping complex just down the street from the Malibu Country Mart include James Perse, Maxfield, and too-chic Intermix. The playground with a large aquarium and alfresco dining area make this an ideal weekend destination for families. Café Habana, a fresh import from Nolita and Brooklyn, brings pan-Cuban cuisine and a Shephard Fairey patio mural to the mix. ⊠ *3939 Cross Creek Rd., Malibu* ⊕ *www.themalibulumberyard.com.*

Pacific Palisades

Stunning ocean views, glamorous homes, and dusty canyons define this affluent area snug between Santa Monica and Malibu. Although there is a downtown village of sorts south of Sunset Boulevard, natural terrain is the main draw here, luring visitors to hiking trails or the Palisades' winding roads.

◉ Sights

Self-Realization Fellowship Lake Shrine

GARDEN | A quintessential (and free) L.A. experience, the nondenominational Lake Shrine temple and meditation garden was founded by guru Paramahansa Yogananda's Self-Realization Fellowship, a nonprofit spiritual organization headquartered in Los Angeles that promotes traditional yoga and meditation. The gardens, lakes, trails, windmill, and other structures are enjoyed by practitioners, locals, celebrities, and office workers alike as a place to step out of the rat race and into tranquillity for a few minutes. ⊠ *17190 Sunset Blvd., Pacific Palisades* ☎ *310/454–4114* ⊕ *www.lakeshrine.org* ⊗ *Closed Mon. and Tues.*

Will Rogers State Beach

BEACH—SIGHT | This clean, sandy, 3-mile beach, with a dozen volleyball nets, gymnastics equipment, and a playground for kids, is an all-around favorite. The surf is gentle, perfect for swimmers and beginning surfers, and crowds are frequently smaller than in other spots along the shore. However, it's best to avoid the beach after a storm, when untreated water flows from storm drains into the sea. **Amenities:** parking; lifeguards; toilets; food and drink; showers. **Best for:** sunset; swimming; walking. ⊠ *17700 PCH, 2 miles north of Santa Monica Pier, Pacific Palisades* ☎ *310/305–9503* ⊕ *www.parks.ca.gov* ⊠ *Parking from $4.*

Will Rogers State Historic Park and Museum

HISTORIC SITE | A humorist, actor, and rambling cowboy, Will Rogers lived on this site in the 1920s and 1930s. His ranch house, a folksy blend of Navajo rugs and Mission-style furniture, has become a museum of Rogers memorabilia. A short film shown in the visitor center highlights Rogers's roping technique and homey words of wisdom. Open for docent-led tours Thursday through Sunday, the ranch house features Rogers's stuffed practice calf and the high ceiling he raised so he could practice his famed roping style indoors.

Rogers was a polo enthusiast, and in the 1930s his front-yard polo field attracted such friends as Douglas Fairbanks Sr. for weekend games. Today the park's broad lawns are excellent for picnicking, and there are miles of eucalyptus-lined trails for hiking, as well as a horseback riding concession. Free weekend games are scheduled from May through October, weather permitting.

Also part of the park is **Inspiration Point Trail.** Who knows how many of Will Rogers's famed witticisms came to him while he and his wife hiked or rode horses along this trail from their ranch? The point is on a detour off the lovely 2-mile loop, which you can join near the riding stables beyond the parking lot. The panorama is one of L.A.'s widest and most wow-inducing, from the peaks of the San Gabriel Mountains in the east and the Oz-like cluster of Downtown skyscrapers to Catalina Island looming off the coast to the southwest. If you're looking for a longer trip, the top of the loop meets up with the 65-mile Backbone Trail, which connects to Topanga State Park. ⊠ *1501 Will Rogers State Park Rd., Pacific Palisades* ☎ *310/454–8212* ⊕ *www.parks. ca.gov/?page_id=626* 🖅 *Free; parking $12.*

El Segundo

Just south of LAX, you'll find this quaint, sleepy beach community. Originally an oil town—Standard Oil set up its second refinery in El Segundo (hence the name, which means "the second" in Spanish)— now it's full of families, out wandering the cute residential streets.

◉ Sights

Dockweiler Beach

BEACH—SIGHT | Is there a dreamier way to top off your day at the beach than a bonfire at twilight? In L.A., where beach bonfires are largely illegal, you can have that along Dockweiler's 3.7-mile stretch. Here, lighting up isn't just permitted, it's practically encouraged, thanks to fire pits peppered throughout. It's probably for this reason that the beach is almost always a scene where young twenty- and thirty-somethings are roasting jumbo marshmallows on long, makeshift skewers as they guzzle beer in red cups. ⊠ *12001 Vista Del Mar, Playa del Rey* ☎ *310/322–4951.*

🛏 Hotels

Sheraton Gateway Los Angeles

$$ | HOTEL | LAX's swanky hotel just had some serious work done to its already sleek look, yet the appeal is in more than just the style; in-transit visitors love the 24-hour room service, pool (with private cabana rentals) and hot tub, fitness center, and airport shuttle, making this the perfect option for an early-morning flight. **Pros:** significantly lower weekend rates; free LAX shuttle; good on-site restaurant, Costero California Bar and Bistro with a craft beer menu. **Cons:** convenient to airport but not much else; chain hotel feel; on the expensive side for an airport hotel. ⑤ *Rooms from: $279* ⊠ *6101 W. Century Blvd., Los Angeles International Airport* ☎ *310/642–1111, 800/325–3535* ⊕ *www.sheratonlosangeles.com* ⇥ *803 rooms* �‖ *No meals.*

Manhattan Beach

Chic boutiques, multimillion-dollar homes, and some of the best restaurants in Los Angeles dot the hilly downtown streets of this tiny community. While the glamour and exclusivity are palpable, with attractive residents making deals over cocktails, this is still a beach town. Annual volleyball and surfing tournaments, crisp ocean breezes, and a very clean walking and biking path invite all visitors.

◉ Sights

Manhattan Beach

BEACH—SIGHT | A wide, sandy strip with good swimming and rows of volleyball courts, Manhattan Beach is the preferred destination of fit, tanned young professionals. There are also such amenities as a bike path, a playground, a bait shop, fishing equipment for rent, and a sizable fishing pier. It's also the perfect place to unwind during a long layover at LAX. **Amenities:** parking (fee); lifeguards; toilets; food and drink; showers. **Best for:** swimming; walking. ⊠ *Manhattan Beach Blvd. at N. Ocean Dr., Manhattan Beach* ☎ *310/372-2166* ⊕ *beaches.lacounty.gov/manhattan-beach* ⊠ *Metered parking; long- and short-term lots.*

🛏 Hotels

Ayres Hotel

$$ | HOTEL | The rates may be relatively modest, but the style here is grand, with the hotel resembling a stone-clad château, but don't let that "French countryside" feel fool you: it's close to I-405 and in close proximity to LAX and the beaches. **Pros:** free Wi-Fi; lower weekend rates; great on-site restaurant. **Cons:** requires a drive to the ocean; not in the most

centrally located neighborhood to other L.A. sights; rooms could use an update. ⑤ *Rooms from: $209* ⊠ *14400 Hindry Ave., Manhattan Beach* ☎ *310/536-0400, 800/675-3550* ⊕ *www.ayreshotels.com/ayres-hotel-manhattan-beach-hawthorne* ⤴ *173 rooms* ❙◎❙ *No meals.*

shade

$$$$ | HOTEL | Super-contemporary design makes this hotel, rooftop pool, and Skydeck feel like an adults-only playground, and it's just a short walk to the shoreline, the local pier, and Manhattan Beach's lively downtown. **Pros:** fun freebies like cake pops and bike use; passes to Equinox gym; cool amenities like "chromatherapy" lighting and in-room martini shaker. **Cons:** sharp-edged furniture; recommended for adults or older kids only; small dipping pool.

Did You Know?

Manhattan Beach (along with Hermosa Beach and Redondo Beach) make up the Beach Cities, which feature over two miles of stunning coastline.

⑤ *Rooms from: $449* ✉ *1221 N. Valley Dr., Manhattan Beach* ☎ *310/546–4995, 866/742–3377* ⊕ *www.shadehotel.com* ⇄ *38 rooms* ⭘⭕ *Free breakfast.*

Hermosa Beach

This energetic beach city boasts some of the priciest real estate in the country. But down by the sand, the vibe is decidedly casual, with plenty of pubs and ambling young couples. Volleyball courts line the wide beach, drawing many amateur and pro tournaments. The walkable 330-yard pier features dramatic views of the coastline winding southward.

◉ Sights

Hermosa Beach
BEACH—SIGHT | South of Manhattan Beach, Hermosa Beach has all the amenities of its neighbor but attracts a rowdier crowd. Swimming takes a backseat to the volleyball games and parties on the pier and bustling boardwalk, but the water here is consistently clean and inviting. **Amenities:** parking (fee); lifeguards; toilets; food and drink; showers. **Best for:** partiers; surfing; swimming. ✉ *1201 The Strand, Hermosa Ave. at 33rd St., Hermosa Beach* ☎ *310/372–2166* ⊕ *beaches.lacounty.gov/hermosa-beach/* ⛱ *Parking (metered) at 11th St. and Hermosa Ave., and 13th St. and Hermosa Ave.*

Restaurants

Baran's 2239
$$ | **CONTEMPORARY** | This gem of a restaurant, tucked into an unassuming strip mall, has taken Hermosa Beach and L.A. at large by storm; even the foccacia bread has a cult following. Diners love the revolving seasonal menu, with its eclectic mix of European, Mexican, and Asian influences reminiscent of the city's own diverse makeup. **Known for:** clever,

rotating seasonal menu; hip California modern farmhouse vibe; "secret" breakfast burrito that locals swear by. ⑤ *Average main: $22* ✉ *502 Pacific Coast Hwy., Hermosa Beach* ☎ *424/247–8468* ⊕ *www.barans2239.com* ⊘ *Closed Mon. and Tues.*

🛏 Hotels

★ Beach House Hotel at Hermosa
$$$ | **HOTEL** | **FAMILY** | Bordering the Strand (SoCal's famous bike path on the beach), Beach House looks like a New England sea cottage from a century ago but has contemporary amenities in its bright studio suites. **Pros:** in-room massages available; enjoy delicious muffins and coffee (and more) in the breakfast room; oceanfront rooms and sunset views. **Cons:** noise from the busy Strand, especially on weekends; no pool; continental breakfast only. ⑤ *Rooms from: $349* ✉ *1300 The Strand, Hermosa Beach* ☎ *310/374–3001, 888/895–4559* ⊕ *www.beach-house.com* ⇄ *96 suites* ⭘⭕ *Free breakfast.*

🍸 Nightlife

The Comedy and Magic Club
COMEDY CLUBS | With Los Angeles being Los Angeles, a disproportionate amount of comedians call the city home, from the would-be to the been-there-done-that. The decades-old Comedy and Magic Club attracts them all. One popular engagement is when 10 up-and-coming comedians perform, one right after the other, in a sort of comic brinksmanship. Other nights might see the occasional magician or an icon of the field like Jay Leno or Bob Saget, there to keep their timing fresh and try out new material for adoring crowds. Stiff drinks and decent entrees and appetizers reward those who arrive early for the best seats, but try grabbing a meal nearby before arriving 30 to 60 minutes prior to the show (budget a little more time for someone

like Leno, who's a regular but still draws crowds). ⊠ *1018 Hermosa Ave., Hermosa Beach* ☎ *310/372–1193* ⊕ *www.comedyandmagicclub.com* ✉ *From $20.*

Redondo Beach

With its worn-in pier and cozy beach, Redondo is a refreshingly unglamorous counterpoint to neighboring beach cities. This was the first port in Los Angeles County in the early 1890s, before business shifted south to San Pedro Harbor, and the community still retains a working-class persona. The best way to soak up the scene these days is with a stroll along the sprawling pier, which features shops, casual restaurants, a live-fish market, and fantastic sunset views.

◉ Sights

Redondo Beach
BEACH—SIGHT | The pier here marks the starting point of this wide, busy beach along a heavily developed shoreline community. Restaurants and shops flourish along the pier, excursion boats and privately owned crafts depart from launching ramps, and a reef formed by a sunken ship creates prime fishing and snorkeling conditions. If you're adventurous, you might try to kayak out to the buoys and hobnob with pelicans and sea lions. A series of free rock and jazz concerts takes place at the pier every summer. **Amenities:** parking; lifeguards; food and drink; toilets; showers; water sports. **Best for:** snorkeling; sunset; swimming; walking. ⊠ *Torrance Blvd. at Catalina Ave., Redondo Beach* ☎ *310/372–2166* ⊕ *www.redondopier.com.*

⌷ Hotels

The Portofino Hotel & Yacht Club
$$$ | **HOTEL** | **FAMILY** | Open your balcony door and listen to the calls of seabirds

and sea lions from ocean- and channel-side rooms here (earplugs are provided for humbugs); marina-side rooms overlook sailboats and docks. **Pros:** bike or walk to beach from the hotel's private peninsula; excellent Baleen restaurant overlooking the harbor; complimentary beach cruiser rentals. **Cons:** higher rates in summer and for ocean-view rooms; restaurant may be noisy due to the adjacent bar; sea lions may be too enthusiastic for some ocean-view room guests. ⑤ *Rooms from: $369* ⊠ *260 Portofino Way, Redondo Beach* ☎ *310/379–8481, 800/468–4292* ⊕ *www.hotelportofino.com* ⌂ *166 rooms* ⦿ *No meals.*

★ **Terranea**
$$$$ | **RESORT** | **FAMILY** | The Pacific Ocean and Catalina Island are within view at Terranea, L.A.'s only full-service oceanfront resort straddling 102 terraced acres at land's end on the scenic Palos Verdes Peninsula. Its location gives it the feel of a retreat. **Pros:** kid-friendly amenities and pool slide; blissful oceanfront spa; four saline pools and hot tubs. **Cons:** pricey on-site dining; with resort fee and parking, this luxury becomes very expensive; nearby beach is more rocky than sandy. ⑤ *Rooms from: $475* ⊠ *100 Terranea Way, Rancho Palos Verdes* ☎ *310/265–2800* ⊕ *www.terranea.com* ⌂ *582 rooms* ⦿ *No meals.*

Long Beach and San Pedro

About 25 miles southeast of Los Angeles, via I–110 south.

A beguiling blend of big city and eclectic small town, Long Beach has metamorphosed in recent years into a full-fledged tourist destination with a wide range of attractions rivaling many major cities. The biggest draw is the *Queen Mary,* a 1930s luxury ocean liner frozen in time in its

On the historic *Queen Mary*, you can get a drink in the first-class lounge, have afternoon tea, and go on a ghost tour.

permanent home, where tours, special events, and even floating hotel rooms draw visitors from around the world. The Aquarium of the Pacific is a hit with families; kids can't get enough of its sharks, penguins, sea lions, and more. Add in a variety of museums, restaurants, and outdoor recreation experiences ("Long Beach" isn't a misnomer), and you have all you need for an epic trip.

Nearby San Pedro is still very much a working port, but it houses another kind of floating attraction: the Battleship USS *Iowa*, which served in three wars and now lets visitors stand in the mess hall and wonder what life was like for its crew.

◉ Sights

★ Aquarium of the Pacific

ZOO | **FAMILY** | Sea lions, zebra sharks, and penguins—this aquarium focuses on creatures of the Pacific Ocean and is home to more than 12,000 animals.

The main exhibits include large tanks of sharks, stingrays, and ethereal sea dragons, which the aquarium has successfully bred in captivity. The museum's first major expansion in years, Pacific Visions, features a 29,000-square-foot multisensory experience in which attendees can immerse themselves in humankind's relationship with the natural world through video projections, soundscapes, tactile exhibits, a touchscreen wall, interactive game tables, rumbling theater seats, and more. For a nonaquatic experience, head to Lorikeet Forest, a walk-in aviary full of the friendliest parrots from Australia. Buy a cup of nectar and smile as you become a human bird perch.
If you're a true animal lover, book an up-close-and-personal Animal Encounters Tour (extra fee) to learn about and assist in the care and feeding of sharks, penguins, and other aquarium residents; or find out how the aquarium functions with the extensive Behind the Scenes Tour (extra fee). Certified divers can book a supervised dive in the aquarium's Tropical

Reef Habitat (extra fee) and kids go wild for frequent overnight camp experiences in the aquarium. Twice-daily whale-watching trips on Harbor Breeze Cruises depart from the dock adjacent to the aquarium; summer sightings of blue whales are an unforgettable thrill. ⊠ *100 Aquarium Way, Long Beach* ☎ *562/590–3100* ⊕ *www. aquariumofpacific.org* ⊠ *$30.*

Battleship USS *Iowa* Museum

HISTORIC SITE | **FAMILY** | For those seeking a more rough-hewn alternative or counterpoint to the genteel *Queen Mary*, the battleship USS *Iowa* in nearby San Pedro lets visitors of all ages clamber through hatches, peer through portholes, and climb into the seat of an antiaircraft gun, envisioning the past. The *Iowa*, the only such tourable battleship on the West Coast, was commissioned in 1943 as the lead of its class and served in World War II, Korea, and the Cold War. Volunteer "crew members," many of whom once served on the ship, happily offer their personal stories to kids and adults alike.

■**TIP**➔ **You're bound to be hungry after such an intrepid expedition. While most people would return to Long Beach or L.A., the nearby pedestrian-friendly, old-timey Downtown San Pedro strip, which centers on 6th and 7th streets, boasts some outstanding dining options, from a British pub to killer Mediterranean and Italian options.** ⊠ *250 S. Harbor Blvd., San Pedro* ☎ *877/446–9261* ⊕ *www.pacificbattleship.com* ⊠ *$20.*

★ ***Queen Mary***

HISTORIC SITE | **FAMILY** | Though berthed, the *Queen Mary* is an impressive example of 20th-century cruise ship opulence and sadly the last of its kind. The beautifully preserved art deco–style ocean liner was launched in 1936 and made 1,001 transatlantic crossings before finally berthing in Long Beach in 1967.

Take one of several daily themed tours such as the informative Glory Days

historical walk, a traipse into the boiler rooms on the Steam and Steel Tour, or the downright spooky Haunted Encounters tour. (Spirits have reportedly been spotted in the pool and engine room.) You can add ongoing theatrical performances by illusionist Aiden Sinclair, a Winston Churchill exhibit, a 4-D documentary experience, a wine tasting room, and a daily British-style high tea. Holidays and special events are celebrated onboard as well, from a haunted Halloween experience to an annual Scottish festival. Stay for dinner at one of the ship's restaurants, listen to live jazz or order a cocktail in the Observation Bar (the sumptuous original first-class lounge), or even spend the night in one of the 347 wood-paneled cabins. The ship's neighbor, a geodesic dome originally built to house Howard Hughes's *Spruce Goose* aircraft, now serves as a terminal for Carnival Cruise Lines, making the *Queen Mary* the perfect pit stop before or after a cruise. Anchored next to the *Queen* is the *Scorpion,* a Russian submarine you can tour for a look at Cold War history. ⊠ *1126 Queens Hwy., Long Beach* ☎ *877/342–0738* ⊕ *www.queenmary.com* ☉ *Tours from $16.*

🛏 Hotels

★ **Hyatt Centric the Pike Long Beach**

$ | **HOTEL** | **FAMILY** | A boutique hotel with a playful nautical theme throughout, the highlight here is the rooftop pool and bar that offers panoramic views of the harbor. **Pros:** great location; rooftop offers views, a swimming pool, and a lounge; modern rooms. **Cons:** parking is at mall next-door; some rooms view a parking structure; no sit-down restaurant on-site. ⑤ *Rooms from: $150* ⊠ *285 Bay St., Long Beach* ☎ *562/432–1234* ⊕ *www. hyatt.com* ⊅ *138 rooms* ⧓*No meals.*

★ Queen Mary Hotel

$ | HOTEL | FAMILY | Experience the golden age of transatlantic travel without the seasickness: 1936 art deco–style reigns on the *Queen Mary,* from the ship's mahogany paneling to its nickel-plated doors to the majestic Grand Salon. **Pros:** walkable, historic teakwood Promenade deck; views from Long Beach out to the Pacific; meticulous art deco detailing. **Cons:** spotty service; vintage soundproofing makes for a sometimes challenging night's sleep; mandatory facility fee. ⑤ *Rooms from: $129 ⊠ 1126 Queens Hwy., Long Beach* ☎ *562/435–3511, 877/342–0742* ⊕ *www.queenmary.com* ⇌ *347 staterooms* ‖◯‖ *No meals.*

Renaissance Long Beach Hotel

$$ | HOTEL | Set in the heart of Long Beach's business district, directly across from the Long Beach Convention Center's side entrance, the Renaissance caters primarily to convention goers and business types. **Pros:** easy walk to Convention Center; near Shoreline Village dining and Aquarium of the Pacific; lively lobby bar. **Cons:** rooms facing south have best views; definite corporate vibe; Wi-Fi extra cost. ⑤ *Rooms from: $229 ⊠ 111 E. Ocean Blvd., Long Beach* ☎ *562/437–5900, 800/228–9898* ⊕ *www.marriott.com* ⇌ *374 rooms.*

The Varden

$ | B&B/INN | Constructed in 1929 to house a wealthy Long Beach man's mistress, circus performer Dolly Varden, this small, historic, European-style hotel on the Metro line in downtown Long Beach now caters to worldly budget travelers. **Pros:** great value; discount passes to Gold's Gym across the street; complimentary continental breakfast and evening reception. **Cons:** no resort services; small rooms; no elevator. ⑤ *Rooms from: $129 ⊠ 335 Pacific Ave., Long Beach* ☎ *562/432–8950* ⊕ *www.thevardenhotel.com* ⇌ *35 rooms* ‖◯‖ *Free breakfast.*

Chapter 12

DISNEYLAND AND ORANGE COUNTY

WITH KNOTT'S BERRY FARM AND CATALINA ISLAND

Updated by
Jill Weinlein

⊙ Sights	🍴 Restaurants	🛏 Hotels	🛍 Shopping	🍸 Nightlife
★★★★★	★★★★☆	★★★★★	★☆☆☆☆	★☆☆☆☆

WELCOME TO DISNEYLAND AND ORANGE COUNTY

TOP REASONS TO GO

★ **Disneyland:** Walking down Main Street, U.S.A., with Sleeping Beauty Castle straight ahead, you really will feel like you're in one of the happiest places on Earth.

★ **Beautiful beaches:** Surf, swim, kayak, paddleboard, or just relax on some of the state's most breathtaking stretches of coastline. Calm coves offer clear water for snorkeling and scuba diving.

★ **Santa Catalina Island:** Just 22 miles from the mainland, Santa Catalina Island is the only inhabited island of the Channel Islands chain. A fast and easy cruise away on a high-speed catamaran, once there you can explore the Mediterranean-inspired small town of Avalon, dive or snorkel through the state's first underwater park, or explore the unspoiled beauty of the island's wild interior.

★ **Family fun:** Ride roller coasters, eat ice cream and frozen chocolate-dipped bananas, bike on oceanfront paths, fish off ocean piers, or rent a Duffy boat and cruise around the calm harbors.

1 Disneyland Resort. Once a humble vision of Walt Disney's, Southern California's top family and tourist destination has grown to become a megaresort, with more attractions spilling over into Disney's California Adventure. There's plenty here to entertain kids and adults alike.

2 Knott's Berry Farm. Amusement park lovers will enjoy this Buena Park attraction, with thrill rides, the *Peanuts* gang, and lots of fried chicken and boysenberry pie.

3 The Coast. The O.C.'s beach spots like Newport Harbor and Laguna Beach offer an array of water activities, spectacular gardens, and some of the most luxurious oceanfront resorts in the country.

4 Catalina Island. This unspoiled island paradise—with its pocket-size town, Avalon, and large nature preserve—is just off the Orange County coast.

With its tropical flowers and palm trees, the stretch of coast between Seal Beach and San Clemente is often called the Southern California Riviera. Upscale Newport Beach and artsy Laguna are the stars, but lesser-known gems on the glistening coast—such as Corona del Mar and Dana Point—are also worth visiting. Offshore, meanwhile, lies picturesque Catalina Island, an unspoiled paradise and a favorite for tourists, boaters, divers, and backpacking campers alike.

Few of the citrus groves that gave Orange County its name remain. This region south and east of Los Angeles is now ruled by tourism and high-tech business rather than agriculture. Despite a building boom that began in the 1990s, the area is still a place to find wilderness trails, canyons, greenbelts, and natural environs. Just offshore is a deep-water wilderness that's possible to explore via daily whale-watching excursions.

Planning

Getting Here and Around

AIR
Orange County's main facility is John Wayne Airport Orange County (SNA), which is served by six major domestic airlines and one commuter line. Long Beach Airport (LGB) is served by four airlines, including its major player, Jet-Blue. It's roughly 20 to 30 minutes by car from Anaheim.

Super Shuttle and Prime Time Airport Shuttle provide transportation from John Wayne and LAX to the Disneyland area of Anaheim. Round-trip fares average about $28 per person from John Wayne and $34 to $80 from LAX.

BUS
The Orange County Transportation Authority will take you virtually anywhere in the county, but it will take time; OCTA buses go from Knott's Berry Farm and Disneyland to Newport Beach. Bus 1 travels along the coast; Buses 701 and 721 provide express service to Los Angeles. Anaheim offers Anaheim Resort Transportation (ART) service that connects hotels to Disneyland Resort, downtown Anaheim, Buena Park, and the Metrolink train center. Rides are $3 each way.

CONTACTS Anaheim Resort Transportation.
✉ 2099 S. State College Blvd., Suite 600,
Anaheim ☎ 714/563–5287 ⊕ rideart.org.
Orange County Transportation Authority.
☎ 714/636–7433 ⊕ www.octa.net.

CAR

The San Diego Freeway (Interstate 405),
the coastal route, and the Santa Ana
Freeway (Interstate 5), the inland route,
run north–south through Orange County.
South of Laguna, Interstate 405 merges
into Interstate 5 (called the San Diego
Freeway south from this point). A toll
road, Highway 73, runs 15 miles from
Newport Beach to San Juan Capistrano;
it costs $6.22–$8.48 (lower rates are for
weekends and off-peak hours) and is usually less jammed than the regular freeways. Do your best to avoid all Orange
County freeways during rush hours (6–9
am and 3:30–6:30 pm). Highway 55 leads
to Newport Beach. The Pacific Coast
Highway (Highway 1) allows easy access
to beach communities and is the most
scenic route but expect it to be crowded,
especially on summer weekends and
holidays.

FERRY

There are two ferries that service
Catalina Island; Catalina Express runs
multiple departures daily from San Pedro,
Long Beach, and Dana Point. From
each port, it takes about 90 minutes to
reach the island. The Catalina Flyer runs
from Newport Beach to Avalon in about
75 minutes. Reservations are strongly
advised for summer months and weekends. During the winter months, ferry
crossings are not as frequent.

TRAIN

Amtrak makes daily stops in Orange
County at all major towns. Metrolink is a
weekday commuter train that runs to and
from Los Angeles and Orange County.

CONTACTS Amtrak. ✉ 2626 E. Katella
Ave., Anaheim ☎ 800/872–7245 ⊕ www.
amtrak.com. **Metrolink.** ✉ 800 N.

Alameda St., Los Angeles ☎ 800/371–
5465 ⊕ www.metrolinktrains.com.

Restaurants

Guests dining at restaurants in Orange
County generally wear beach casual,
although at top resorts and fine dining
venues, guests usually choose to dress
up. Of course, there's also a swath of
casual places along the beachfronts—
seafood takeout, taquerias, burger
joints—that won't mind if you wear
shorts and flip-flops. Reservations are
recommended for the nicest restaurants.

Many places don't serve past 11 pm, and
locals tend to eat early. Remember that
according to California law, smoking is
prohibited in all enclosed areas.

Hotels

Along the coast there are remarkable
luxury resorts; if you can't afford a stay,
pop in for the view at Laguna Beach's
Montage Mosiac Tile pool or the always
welcoming Ritz-Carlton at Dana Point. For
a taste of the O.C. glam life, the Resort
at Pelican Hills is an idyllic place for
lunch, brunch or dinner at its Coliseum
Grill overlooking the world's largest
circular pool and the ocean beyond. For a
nautical experience, enjoy lunch or dinner
next to multimillion-dollar yachts secured
in Newport Bay at the Balboa Bay Resort.

As a rule, lodging prices tend to rise the
closer the hotels are to the beach. If
you're looking for value, consider a hotel
that's inland along the Interstate 405
freeway corridor.

In most cases, you can take advantage
of some of the facilities of the high-end
resorts, such as restaurants and spas,
even if you aren't an overnight guest.

*Restaurant and hotel reviews have been
shortened. For full information, visit
Fodors.com. Prices in the restaurant*

12

Disneyland and Orange County PLANNING

reviews are the average cost of a main course at dinner or, if dinner is not served, at lunch. Prices in the hotel reviews are the lowest cost of a standard double room in high season.

What It Costs in U.S. Dollars

$	$$	$$$	$$$$
RESTAURANTS			
under $20	$20–$30	$31–$40	over $40
HOTELS			
under $200	$200–$300	$301–$400	over $400

Visitor Information

Visit Anaheim is an excellent resource for both leisure and business travelers and can provide materials on many area attractions. Kiosks at the Anaheim Convention Center act as a digital concierge and allow visitors to plan itineraries and buy tickets to area attractions.

The Orange County Visitors Association's website is also a useful source of information.

CONTACTS Orange County Visitors Association. ⊕ www.travelcostamesa. com/visittheoc . **Visit Anaheim.** ✉ 2099 S. State College Blvd., Suite 600, Anaheim ☎ 714/765–2800 ⊕ www.visitanaheim. org.

Disneyland Resort

26 miles southeast of Los Angeles, via I–5.

The snowcapped Matterhorn, the centerpiece of Disneyland, punctuates the skyline of Anaheim. Since 1955, when Walt Disney chose this once-quiet farming community for the site of his first amusement park, Disneyland has attracted more than 650 million visitors and tens of thousands of workers, and Anaheim has been their host. Today, there are more than 60 attractions and adventures in the park's nine themed lands: Fantasyland, Adventureland, Tomorrowland, Frontierland, Main Street U.S.A., New Orleans Square, Critter Country, Mickey's Toontown, and Star Wars: Galaxy's Edge.

The resort is a sprawling complex that includes Disney's two amusement parks (Disneyland and Disney's California Adventure); three hotels; and Downtown Disney, a shopping, dining, and entertainment promenade. Anaheim's tourist center includes Angel Stadium of Anaheim, home of baseball's Los Angeles Angels of Anaheim; the Honda Center (formerly the Arrowhead Pond), which hosts concerts and the Anaheim Ducks hockey team; and the enormous Anaheim Convention Center.

GETTING THERE

Disney is about a 30-mile drive from either LAX or Downtown. From LAX, follow Sepulveda Boulevard south to the Interstate 105 freeway and drive east 16 miles to the Interstate 605 north exit. Exit at the Santa Ana Freeway (Interstate 5) and continue south for 12 miles to the Disneyland Drive exit. Follow signs to the resort. From Downtown, follow Interstate 5 south 28 miles and exit at Disneyland Drive. **Disneyland Resort Express** (☎ 800/828–6699) offers daily nonstop bus service between LAX, John Wayne Airport, and Anaheim. Reservations are not required. The cost is $30 one-way from LAX, and $20 from John Wayne Airport.

SAVING TIME AND MONEY

If you plan to visit for more than a day, you can save money by buying multiday Park Hopper tickets that grant same-day "hopping" privileges between Disneyland and Disney's California Adventure. You get a discount on the multiple-day passes if you buy online through the Disneyland website.

Single-day admission prices vary by date. A one-day Park Hopper pass costs $147–$185 for anyone 10 or older, $141–$177 for kids ages three to nine. Admission to either park (but not both) is $97–$135 for adults or $91–$127 for kids three to nine; kids two and under are free.

In addition to tickets, parking is $20–$35 (unless your hotel has a shuttle or is within walking distance), and meals in the parks and at Downtown Disney range from $15 to $75 per person.

Disneyland

★ Disneyland

AMUSEMENT PARK/WATER PARK | FAMILY | An imaginative original, Disneyland was an unproven concept when it opened in 1955, but Walt Disney himself could never have predicted the park's success and its beloved place in the hearts of Southern Californians. It is the only one of the parks to have been overseen by Walt himself, has a genuine historic feel, and occupies a unique place in the Disney legend. Expertly run, with perfectly maintained grounds and a helpful staff ("cast members" in the Disney lexicon), the park offers plenty of fun experiences that you won't find anywhere else: you can visit a galaxy far, far away in the *Star Wars* land; cruise to a world of pirates in search of Jack Sparrow from the *Pirates of the Caribbean* series; and take a ride to Storybook Land, with its miniature replicas of animated Disney scenes from classics such as *Frozen* and *Alice in Wonderland*. Beloved Disney characters appear for autographs and photos throughout the day; times and places are posted at the entrances and on the Disneyland mobile app. Live shows, parades, strolling musicians, fireworks (on weekends and during the summer and holidays), and endless creative snack choices add to the carnival atmosphere. You can also meet some of the animated icons at one of the character meals ·

served at the three Disney hotels (open to the public, but reservations are needed). Belongings can be stored in lockers just off Main Street while stroller rentals, wheelchairs, and Electric Conveyance Vehicles (ECV) are at the entrance gate as convenient options for families with mobility challenges. The park's popularity means there are always crowds, especially during the holidays and summer months, so take advantage of the Disney FastPass Service to spend less time waiting in lines. Also be sure to make dining reservations at least three weeks before your visit to guarantee a table without a wait. ⊠ *Disneyland Park, 1313 S. Disneyland Dr., between Ball Rd. and Katella Ave., Anaheim* ☎ *714/781–4636 guest information* ⊕ *disneyland.disney. go.com* ✉ *From $97; parking $20.*

PARK NEIGHBORHOODS
Neighborhoods for Disneyland are arranged in geographic order.

MAIN STREET, U.S.A.
Walt's hometown of Marceline, Missouri, was the inspiration behind this romanticized image of small-town America, circa 1900. The sidewalks are lined with a penny arcade and shops that sell everything from tradeable pins to Disney-themed clothing, an endless supply of sugar confections, and a photo shop that offers souvenirs created via Disney's PhotoPass (on-site photographers capture memorable moments digitally—you can access them in person or online via the Disneyland app). Main Street opens half an hour before the rest of the park, so it's a good place to explore if you're getting an early start to beat the crowds (it's also open an hour after the other attractions close, so you may want to save your shopping for the end of the day).

Step into city hall to receive a complimentary button showcasing whatever you're celebrating (your first visit, a birthday, a marriage, or just Disney in general); throughout the day, Disney cast members will congratulate you

5

San Diego Freeway

MICKEY'S TOONTOWN

Minnie's House
Mickey's House
Chip 'n Dale Treehouse
Gadget's Go Coaster
Donald's Boat
Goofy's Playhouse
Roger Rabbit's Car Toon Spin

Millennium Falcon: Smugglers Run

Star Wars: Galaxy's Edge

Star Wars: Rise of the Resistance

Fantasyland Theatre

It's A Small World

FANTASYLAND

Dumbo the Flying Elephant
Casey Jr. Circus Train
Storybook Land Canal Boats
Peter Pan's Flight
Mad Tea Party
Mr. Toad's Wild Ride
Alice in Wonderland

DISNEYLAND PARK

King Arthur Carousel

Rivers of America

FRONTIERLAND

Big Thunder Mountain RR

Pinocchio's Daring Journey
Snow White's Scary Adventures

Matterhorn Bobsleds

Finding Nemo's Submarine Voyage

Autopia

The Many Adventures of Winnie the Pooh

Canoes

Tom Sawyer Island

Fantasy Faire

Plaza Garden Stage

Buzz Lightyear Astro Blasters

Star Wars Launch Bay

CRITTER COUNTRY

Sailing Ship Columbia

Mark Twain Riverboat

Shootin' Exposition

Central Plaza

Astro Orbiter

Star Wars: Path of the Jedi

Splash Mountain

Rafts

Golden Horseshoe Stage

Star Tours- The Adventure Continues

Haunted Mansion

Enchanted Tiki Room

TOMORROWLAND

Pirates of the Caribbean

Jungle Cruise

Space Mountain

NEW ORLEANS SQUARE

Tarzan's Treehouse

ADVENTURE-LAND

Main Street Cinema

Indiana Jones Adventure

MAIN STREET, U.S.A.

Disneyland Railroad

House of Blues Stage

DOWNTOWN DISNEY

AMC Theaters

LEGO Imagination Center

Red Car Trolley

Monsters Inc. Mike & Sulley to the Rescue

Soarin' Around the World

Hollywood Backlot Stage

HOLLYWOOD LAND

Disneyland Hotel

Parking

Grand Californian Hotel

Sunset Showcase Theatre

Turtle Talk with Crush

Frozen

SUNSHINE PLAZA

Disney Junior

Disney Animation

Paradise Pier Hotel

Grizzly River Run

GRIZZLY PEAK

BUENA VISTA STREET

Web Slingers: A Spiderman Adventure

Avengers

Guardians of the Galaxy- Mission:BREAKOUT!

Redwood Creek Challenge Trail

Little Mermaid- Ariel's Undersea Adventure

Wine Country Trattoria

The Bakery Tour

DISNEY CALIFORNIA ADVENTURE

Goofy's Sky School

Jumpin' Jellyfish

PARADISE GARDENS PARK

Golden Zephyr

Silly Symphony Swings

PACIFIC WHARF

Luigi's Rollickin' Roadsters

Harbor Boulevard

PIXAR PIER

Pixar Pal-A-Round

Lamplight Lounge

Radiator Springs Racers

CARS LAND

Toy Story Midway Mania!

California Screamin'

Games of the Boardwalk

King Triton's Carousel

Incredicoaster

Disneyland Drive

Parking

KEY

👫 *Restrooms*

├─┤ *Rail Line*

⊂⊃ *Monorail*

Disneyland

Katella Avenue

with friendly smiles and well wishes. **Main Street Cinema** offers a cool respite from the crowds and six classic Disney animated shorts, including *Steamboat Willie*. There's rarely a wait to enter. Grab a cappuccino and fresh-made pastry at the Jolly Holiday bakery to jump-start your visit. Board the **Disneyland Railroad,** an authentic steam-powered train located at the entrance that makes stops in the park's different lands. Or the 18-minute scenic round-trip will also give you unique views of Star Wars: Galaxy's Edge, Autopia, Splash Mountain, the Grand Canyon, and Rivers of America.

NEW ORLEANS SQUARE

This minireplica of the French Quarter in New Orleans, with narrow streets, hidden courtyards, and live street performances, is home to two iconic attractions and the Cajun-inspired Blue Bayou restaurant. The **Pirates of the Caribbean** ride now features Jack Sparrow and the cursed Captain Barbossa of the blockbuster series, plus enhanced special effects and battle scenes (complete with cannonball explosions). Nearby **Haunted Mansion** continues to spook guests with its stretching walls and "doombuggy" rides (there's now an expanded storyline for the beating-heart bride). The *Nightmare Before Christmas* holiday overlay is an annual tradition that starts in the fall and extends throughout the holidays. This is a good area to eat; you can get a nonalcoholic mint julep and Mickey Mouse–shaped beignets; a Monte Cristo sandwich at Cafe Orleans; or corn chowder in a sourdough bread bowl, po-boy sandwiches, and jambalaya at the French Market Restaurant. Food carts offer everything from just-popped popcorn to churros and even fresh fruit.

FRONTIERLAND

Between Adventureland and Fantasyland, Frontierland transports you to the wild, wild West with its rustic buildings, shooting gallery, foot-stompin' dance hall, and singing birds in the Enchanted Tiki Room.

The marquee attraction, **Big Thunder Mountain Railroad,** is a relatively tame roller coaster ride (no steep descents) that takes the form of a runaway mine car as it rumbles and turns through desert canyons and an old mining town. Tour the Rivers of America on the 19th-century **Mark Twain Riverboat,** which takes you on a 14-minute paddleboat cruise around Tom Sawyer Island, or the **Sailing Ship Columbia,** a full-scale replica of a merchant ship that once sailed the globe (usually limited to weekends). From here, you can also ride a motorized raft over to Pirate's Lair on **Tom Sawyer Island,** where you can explore pirate-themed caves, go on a treasure hunt, and climb a fort. Dine outside at the River Belle Terrace for Southern culinary favorites including Mickey Mouse pancakes for breakfast, barbecued ribs and fried chicken sandwich for lunch, and a healthier barbecued tofu for dinner. Or take a seat on the festive Mexican terrace at Rancho del Zocalo for a trio of street tacos, fire-grilled citrus-marinated chicken, and creamy flan for dessert.

CRITTER COUNTRY

Iconic Splash Mountain is the biggest draw to this down-home country-themed area, but you can also take a peek through Winnie the Pooh's Hundred-Acre Wood and paddle the Rivers of America on Davy Crockett's Explorer Canoes. The patio of the popular Hungry Bear Restaurant has great views of Tom Sawyer's Island, and beyond is a galaxy far, far away: the Star Wars: Galaxy's Edge section of the park.

STAR WARS: GALAXY'S EDGE

This 14-acre expansive land has guests step into the planet Batuu, designed from architectural locations in Morocco, Turkey, and Israel. At the **Star Wars: Rise of the Resistance** ride, you will accept a mission from the Resistance to fight against the First Order; to ride, guests need to obtain a timed boarding group on the Disneyland app or at the park's main

Best Tips for Disneyland

Download the Disneyland mobile app. You can do a lot with this app so it's a no-brainer to download if you have a smartphone. It provides a ticket barcode to skip long ticket lines; you can view maps of both parks and get access to FastPass tickets via the digital MAXPASS; learn about shows and attraction wait times, character visits, and parade times; view restaurant menus and make dining reservations; preorder and pay for contactless pickup at both parks; and download and share Disney PhotoPass photos.

Buy entry tickets in advance. Lines at ticket booths can take more than an hour on busy days. Save time by buying in advance. Nearby hotels sell park admission tickets; you can also buy them through Disney's website and the Disneyland app. Seek out package deals offered through AAA and discount Disneyland Park Hopper tickets at Costco.

Come midweek. Weekends (especially during the summer, Halloween, and winter holidays) are often the busiest times to visit. A rainy winter weekday is often the least crowded time to check out the parks.

Plan your times to hit the most popular rides. Get to the park as early as possible, even before the gates open, and make a beeline for the top rides before the crowds reach a critical mass. Later in the evening the parks thin out and you can catch a special show or parade. Save the quieter attractions for midafternoon.

Use FastPass. These passes allow you to reserve your place in line at some of the most popular attractions (only one at a time). Distribution machines are posted near the entrances of each attraction. Show the barcode on your Disneyland app or feed in your park admission ticket, and you'll receive a pass with a printed time frame (up to one to four hours later) during which you can return to wait in a much shorter line or walk right onto the ride.

Avoid peak mealtime crowds. Outside food and beverages in nonglass containers are allowed inside the parks, but dining at one of the park's many theme restaurants can be an experience to remember. For any sit-down establishment, be sure to make dining reservations in advance or wait until after 2 pm to avoid a long wait. If you just need a quick recharge, Disney carts offer creative snacks including popcorn in souvenir buckets, Mickey Mouse–shaped pretzels, Rice Crispies treats, cake pops, and ice cream.

If you want to eat at the **Blue Bayou** in Disneyland's New Orleans Square or Carthay Circle at Disney California Adventure, you can make a reservation up to 60 days in advance of your visit online or via the Disneyland app. It's always a good idea to bring water, juice boxes, and snacks for little ones.

Check the daily events schedule online, on the Disneyland app, or at the park entrance. During parades, fireworks, and other special events, sections of the parks are filled with crowds. This distraction can work in your favor to take advantage of shorter lines at dining venues and rides. It also can work against you in maneuvering around a section of the park so plan ahead.

entrance. You can also take a thrilling interactive ride on **Millennium Falcon: Smugglers Run,** where you will soar into hyperspace and be assigned to be a pilot, engineer, or gunner on a smuggling mission.

The Build-a-Droid Workshop is stocked with colorful parts, chips, and tech items. Starting at $99.99, you will receive a basket and blueprint to build your droid. Another treasure to purchase and take home is a hand-built lightsaber at Savi's Workshop.

For dining, popular Oga's Cantina is good for coffee, all-day light snacks, and unique cocktails for grown-ups. Galactic food and drink options can be found at the Milk Stand, where guests can sample Batuu's legendary blue and green beverages, similar to what Luke Skywalker drank in the movies.

ADVENTURELAND
Modeled after the lands of Africa, Polynesia, and Arabia, this tiny tropical paradise is worth braving the crowds that flock here for the ambience and better-than-average food. Sing along with the animatronic birds and tiki gods in the **Enchanted Tiki Room,** sail the rivers of the world with joke-cracking skippers on **Jungle Cruise,** and climb the *Disneyodendron semperflorens* (the always-blooming Disney tree) to **Tarzan's Treehouse,** where you can walk through scenes, some interactive, from the 1999 animated film. Cap off the visit with a wild jeep ride at **Indiana Jones Adventure,** where the special effects and decipherable hieroglyphics distract you while you're waiting in line. There's a single-rider option for a quicker ride. The skewers (some vegetarian options available) at Bengal Barbecue and pineapple whip at Tiki Juice Bar are some of the best fast-food options in the park.

FANTASYLAND
Sleeping Beauty Castle marks the entrance to Fantasyland, a visual wonderland of princesses, spinning teacups, flying elephants, and other classic storybook characters. Rides, and shops such as the princess-themed Bibbidi Bobbidi Boutique, take precedence over restaurants in this area of the park, but outdoor carts sell everything from churros to turkey legs. Tots love the **King Arthur Carousel, Casey Jr. Circus Train,** and **Storybook Land Canal Boats.** This is also home to **Mr. Toad's Wild Ride, Peter Pan's Flight, Snow White's Enchanted Wish,** and **Pinocchio's Daring Journey,** all classic movie-theater-dark rides that immerse riders in Disney fairy tales. Keep an eye out for the Abominable Snowman when he pops up on the **Matterhorn Bobsleds,** a roller coaster that twists and turns up and around on a made-to-scale model of the real Swiss mountain. Anchoring the east end of Fantasyland is **It's a Small World,** a smorgasbord of dancing animatronic dolls, cuckoo clock–covered walls, and variations of the song everyone knows, or soon *will* know, by heart. Beloved Disney characters like Ariel from *The Little Mermaid* are also part of the mix. Fantasy Faire is a fairy tale–style village that collects all the Disney princesses together. Each has her own reception nook in the Royal Hall. Condensed retellings of *Tangled* and *Beauty and the Beast* take place at the Royal Theatre.

MICKEY'S TOONTOWN
Geared toward small kids, this lopsided cartoonlike downtown, complete with cars and trolleys that invite interactive exploring, is where Mickey, Donald, Goofy, and other classic Disney characters hang their hats. One of the most popular attractions is **Roger Rabbit's Car Toon Spin,** a twisting, turning cab ride through the Toontown of *Who Framed Roger Rabbit?* You can also walk through **Mickey's House** to meet and be photographed with the famous mouse, take a low-key ride on **Gadget's Go Coaster,** or bounce around the fenced-in playground in front of **Goofy's Playhouse.** For food, you can enjoy pizza at Daisy's Diner, hot dogs

at Pluto's Dog House, and sweet treats at Clarabelle's.

TOMORROWLAND

This popular section of the park continues to tinker with its future, adding and enhancing rides regularly. *Star Wars*–themed attractions can't be missed, like the immersive, 3-D **Star Tours—The Adventures Continue,** where you can join the Rebellion in a galaxy far, far away. **Finding Nemo's Submarine Voyage** updates the old Submarine Voyage ride with the exploits of Nemo, Dory, Marlin, and other characters from the Disney-Pixar film. Try to visit this popular ride early in the day if you can, and be prepared for a wait. The interactive **Buzz Lightyear Astro Blasters** lets you zap your neighbors with laser beams and compete for the highest score. Hurtle through the cosmos on **Space Mountain** or check out mainstays like the futuristic **Astro Orbiter** rockets, **Star Wars Launch Bay,** which showcases costumes, models, and props from the franchise, and **Star Wars, Path of the Jedi,** which catches viewers up on all the movies with a quick 12-minute film. Put the pedal to the metal while driving a flashy coupe through winding roads at **Autotopia,** powered by Honda. Disneyland Monorail and Disneyland Railroad both have stations here. There's also a video arcade and dancing water fountain that makes a perfect playground for kids on hot summer days. The Jedi Training Academy spotlights future Luke Skywalkers in the crowd.

Besides the nine lands, the daily live-action shows and parades are always crowd pleasers. ■TIP➜ **Arrive early to secure a good view; if there are two shows scheduled for the day, the second one tends to be less crowded. A fireworks display lights up weekends and most summer evenings.** Brochures with maps, available at the entrance, list show and parade times.

Disney California Adventure

★ **Disney California Adventure**
AMUSEMENT PARK/WATER PARK | FAMILY | The sprawling Disney California Adventure, adjacent to Disneyland (their entrances face each other), pays tribute to the Golden State with multiple theme areas that re-create vintage architectural styles and embrace several hit Pixar films via engaging attractions. Visitors enter through the art deco–style Buena Vista Street, past shops and a helpful information booth that advises wait times on attractions. The 12-acre *Cars* Land features Radiator Springs Racers, a speedy trip in six-passenger speedsters through scenes featured in the blockbuster hit. (FastPass tickets for the ride run out early most days, but there is a single rider line to experience the thrills quicker). Other popular attractions include the World of Color, a nighttime water-effects show and Toy Story Midway Mania!, an interactive adventure ride hosted by Woody and Buzz Lightyear. At night the park takes on neon hues as glowing signs light up Route 66 in Cars Land and Pixar Pal-A-Round, a giant Ferris wheel on the Pixar Pier. Cocktails, beer, and wine are available; craft beers and premium wines from California are poured. Live nightly entertainment also features a 1930s jazz troupe that arrives in a vintage jalopy. Some rides have a minimum height limit of 40 inches. Opened in 2021, the Avengers Campus is a land for a new generation of superheroes, focusing on the characters of the Marvel Cinemetic Universe. On Web-Slingers: A Spider-man Adventure, guests of all ages can help wrangle Spider-bots while wearing 3-D glasses; the free-falling Guardians of the Galaxy—Mission: BREAKOUT! is more for teens and adults. ✉ *1313 S. Disneyland Dr., between Ball Rd. and Katella Ave., Anaheim* ☎ *714/781–4636* ⊕ *disneyland.disney.go.com* 🎫 *From $97; parking $20.*

PARK NEIGHBORHOODS
BUENA VISTA STREET

California Adventure's grand entryway re-creates the lost 1920s Los Angeles that Walt Disney encountered when he moved to the Golden State. There's a **Red Car trolley** (modeled after Los Angeles's bygone streetcar line); hop on for the brief ride to Hollywood Land. Buena Vista Street is also home to a Starbucks outlet—within the Fiddler, Fifer and Practical Café—and the upscale Carthay Circle Restaurant and Lounge, which serves modern craft cocktails and beer. The comfy booths of the Carthay Circle restaurant on the second floor feel like a relaxing world away from the theme park outside. Keep an eye out for Officer Blue; he is known to give guests a citation to take home as a unique souvenir.

GRIZZLY PEAK

This woodsy land celebrates the great outdoors. Test your skills on the **Redwood Creek Challenge Trail,** a challenging trek across net ladders and suspension bridges. **Grizzly River Run** mimics the river rapids of the Sierra Nevadas; be prepared to get soaked.

Soarin' Around the World is a spectacular simulated hang-gliding ride over internationally known landmarks like Switzerland's Matterhorn and India's Taj Mahal.

HOLLYWOOD LAND

With a main street modeled after Hollywood Boulevard, a fake sky backdrop, and real soundstages, this area celebrates California's film industry. **Disney Animation** gives you an insider's look at how animators create characters. **Turtle Talk with Crush** lets kids have an unscripted chat with a computer-animated Crush, the sea turtle from *Finding Nemo.* The Hyperion Theater hosts **Frozen,** a 45-minute live performance from a Broadway-size cast with terrific visual effects. ■TIP→ **Plan on getting in line about half an hour in advance; the show is worth the wait.** On the film-inspired ride **Monsters, Inc. Mike & Sulley to the Rescue,** visitors climb into taxis and travel the streets of Monstropolis on a mission to safely return Boo to her bedroom.

CARS LAND

Amble down Route 66, the main thoroughfare of Cars Land, and discover a pitch-perfect re-creation of the vintage highway. Quick eats are found at the Cozy Cone Motel (in a teepee-shaped motor court) while Flo's V8 café serves hearty comfort food. Start your day at Radiator Springs Racers, the park's most popular attraction, where waits can be two hours or longer. Strap into a nifty sports car and meet the characters of Pixar's *Cars*; the ride ends in a speedy auto race through the red rocks and desert of Radiator Springs. ■TIP→ **To bypass the line, there's a single-rider option for Radiator Springs Racers.**

PACIFIC WHARF

In the midst of the California Adventure you'll find 10 different dining options, from light snacks to full-service restaurants. The Wine Country Trattoria is a great place for Italian specialties; relax outside on the restaurant's terrace for a casual bite while sipping a California-made craft beer or wine. Mexican cuisine and potent margaritas are available at the Cocina Cucamonga Mexican Grill and Rita's Baja Blenders, and Lucky Fortune Cookery serves Chinese stir-fry dishes.

PARADISE GARDENS PARK

The far corner of California Adventure is a mix of floating, zigzagging, and flying rides: soar via the **Silly Symphony Swings**; **Goofy's Sky School** rollicks and rolls through a cartoon-inspired landscape; and the sleek retro-style gondolas of the **Golden Zephyr** mimic 1920s movies and their sci-fi adventures. Journey through Ariel's colorful world on **The Little Mermaid—Ariel's Undersea Adventure.** The best views of the nighttime music, water, and light show, **World of Color,** are from the paths along Paradise Bay. FastPass tickets are available. Or for a guaranteed spot, book dinner at the Wine Country Trattoria that includes a ticket to a viewing area to catch all the show's stunning visuals.

PIXAR PIER

This section re-creates the glory days of California's seaside piers, themed with Pixar film characters. If you're looking for thrills, join The Incredibles family on the **Incredicoaster** as the fast-moving roller coaster takes its riders from 0 to 55 mph in about four seconds and proceeds through scream tunnels, steeply angled drops, and a 360-degree loop. **Pixar Pal-A-Round,** a giant Ferris wheel, provides a good view of the grounds, though some cars spin and sway for more kicks. There are also carnival games, an aquatic-themed carousel, and **Toy Story Midway Mania!,** an interactive ride where you can take aim at a series of cartoon targets. Soft-serve ice cream, turkey legs, hot dogs, and churros are readily available for quick snacking. At the **Lamplight Lounge** adults can chill out and overlook the action while sipping on craft cocktails.

OTHER ATTRACTIONS
Anaheim GardenWalk

PROMENADE | FAMILY | This popular dining, shopping, and entertainment outdoor complex offers 10 eateries, a bowling lounge, an escape room, and an Art on the Walk showcasing local artists and nonprofit organizations. Monthly and seasonal pop-up events are displayed on the website. ⊠ *400 W. Disney Way, Anaheim* ☎ *562/695–1513* ⊕ *www.anaheimgarden-walk.com.*

Downtown Disney District

AMUSEMENT PARK/WATER PARK | FAMILY The Downtown Disney District is a 20-acre promenade of dining, shopping, and entertainment that connects the resort's hotels and theme parks. Get refreshed at the bar or dining room at **Splitsville,** a mid-century modern–style bowling alley serving American comfort food. At **Ralph Brennan's Jazz Kitchen** you can dig into New Orleans–style food and

music. Enjoy a cold beer at Ballast Point Brewery and gourmet burger at Black Tap Craft Burgers. Save room for sweets: **Salt and Straw** has gourmet ice cream while **Sprinkles** offers ultrarich cupcakes. Disney merchandise and artwork is showcased at the brightly lit **World of Disney** store. Deck your home and garden with Disney decorative items at **HOME**; they even have a Disney Tails & Pet Collection for your four-legged friends. At the megasize **LEGO Store** there are bigger than life LEGO creations, hands-on demonstrations and space to play with the latest LEGO creations. All visitors must pass through a security checkpoint and metal detectors before entering. ⊠ *1580 Disneyland Dr., Anaheim* ☎ *714/781–4565* ⊕ *disneyland.disney. go.com/downtown-disney* ⊠ *Free.*

🍴 Restaurants

Anaheim White House

$$$$ | ITALIAN | FAMILY | Although a massive fire gutted the Anaheim White House in 2017, owner and executive chef Bruno Serato rebuilt and expanded the local landmark known for its specialty pastas. The 1909-built original mansion was the inspiration for the complete renovation, and Serato added olive trees and a courtyard outside and Italian frescoes and mosaics inside. **Known for:** classic Mediterranean cuisine; popular salmon chocolat (salmon with white chocolate mashed potatoes); friendly chef who is a pillar of the community. ⑤ *Average main: $40* ⊠ *887 S. Anaheim Blvd., Anaheim* ☎ *714/772–1381* ⊕ *www.anaheimwhite-house.com* ⊙ *Closed Mon. and Tues.*

Catal Restaurant and Uva Bar and Cafe

$$ | MEDITERRANEAN | This relaxed bi-level Mediterranean spot offers more than 30 wines by the glass, craft beers, and craft cocktails that pair well with the Spanish-influenced dishes. Upstairs, Catal's menu has tapas, a variety of flavorful paellas, and charcuterie. **Known for:** gourmet burgers; good happy hour; outdoor

terrace with Disneyland fireworks views. $ *Average main: $30* ✉ *Downtown Disney District, 1580 S. Disneyland Dr., Suite 103, Anaheim* ☎ *714/774–4442* ⊕ *www.patinagroup.com.*

Napa Rose

$$$$ | **AMERICAN** | Done up in a handsome Craftsman style, Napa Rose's rich seasonal cuisine is matched with an extensive wine list, with 1,500 labels and 80 available by the glass. For a look into the open kitchen, sit at the counter and watch the chefs as they whip up such signature dishes as grilled diver scallops and chanterelles, and lamb pot roast topped with a pomegranate mint glaze. **Known for:** excellent wine list; kid-friendly options; gorgeous dining room. $ *Average main: $50* ✉ *Disney's Grand Californian Hotel, 1600 S. Disneyland Dr., Anaheim* ☎ *714/300–7170, 714/781–3463 reservations* ⊕ *disneyland.disney.go.com/grand-californian-hotel/napa-rose.*

 ## Hotels

Anaheim Fairfield Inn by Marriott

$$ | **HOTEL** | **FAMILY** | Attentive service and a great location just across the street from Disneyland's entrance makes this high-rise hotel a big draw for families. **Pros:** across the street from Disneyland; Disney-themed guest rooms; reasonable rates for the area. **Cons:** some rooms have just parking lot views; lack of green space; can be noisy when guests return from parks. $ *Rooms from: $225* ✉ *1460 S. Harbor Blvd., Anaheim* ☎ *714/772–6777* ⊕ *www.marriott.com* ➷ *467 rooms* ⦿ *No meals.*

Anaheim Marriott

$ | **RESORT** | This busy two-tower hotel is well equipped for business travelers, and has nice amenities for vacationers. **Pros:** balconies in all rooms; large pool and deck area; offers shuttle to Disneyland. **Cons:** most rooms only have a shower; popular with conventioneers who often take over the place; no Disney-themed

guest rooms. $ *Rooms from: $159* ✉ *700 W. Convention Way, Anaheim* ☎ *714/750–8000, 888/236–2427* ⊕ *www.marriott.com* ➷ *1030 rooms* ⦿ *No meals.*

Desert Palms Hotel and Suites

$ | **HOTEL** | **FAMILY** | This hotel midway between Disneyland and the Anaheim Convention Center is a great value, with some one-bedroom suites that can accommodate groups of six or more. **Pros:** large lobby that welcomes with Disney decor; variety of special rates; free Wi-Fi. **Cons:** drab exterior fronts busy Katella Avenue; small pool gets limited sun; some noise issues. $ *Rooms from: $125* ✉ *631 W. Katella Ave., Anaheim* ☎ *714/535–1133, 888/521–6420* ⊕ *www.desertpalmshotel.com* ➷ *195 rooms* ⦿ *No meals.*

★ Disney's Grand Californian Hotel and Spa

$$$$ | **RESORT** | **FAMILY** | The most opulent of Disneyland's three hotels, the Craftsman-style Grand Californian offers views of Disney California Adventure and Downtown Disney. **Pros:** gorgeous lobby; family-friendly with three beautiful pools; direct access to California Adventure. **Cons:** very expensive; standard rooms are on the small side; waits to dine at on-site restaurants. $ *Rooms from: $625* ✉ *1600 S. Disneyland Dr., Anaheim* ☎ *714/635–2300* ⊕ *disneyland.disney.go.com/grand-californian-hotel* ➷ *1019 rooms* ⦿ *No meals.*

Doubletree Suites by Hilton Hotel Anaheim Resort-Convention Center

$ | **HOTEL** | This busy hotel near the Anaheim Convention Center and a 20-minute walk from Disneyland caters to business travelers and vacationers alike. **Pros:** huge suites; walking distance to a variety of restaurants; chocolate chip cookies at check-in. **Cons:** a bit far from Disneyland; pool area is small; daily parking fee. $ *Rooms from: $153* ✉ *2085 S. Harbor Blvd., Anaheim* ☎ *714/750–3000, 800/215–7316* ⊕ *doubletreeanaheim.com* ➷ *252 rooms* ⦿ *No meals.*

Hilton Anaheim

$ | HOTEL | FAMILY | Next to the Anaheim Convention Center, this busy Hilton is the third-largest hotel in Southern California, with a restaurant and food court, hopping lobby lounge with communal tables, a full-service gym, and its own Starbucks. **Pros:** 15-minute walk to Disneyland; fast-casual dining options; some rooms have views of the park fireworks. **Cons:** huge size can be daunting; fee to use health club; megasize parking lot. $ *Rooms from: $159* ⊠ *777 Convention Way, Anaheim* ☎ *714/750–4321, 800/445–8667* ⊕ *www.hiltonanaheimhotel.com* ⇱ *1572 rooms* ⊙ *No meals.*

Hyatt Regency Orange County

$ | HOTEL | FAMILY | This Disney-friendly hotel sells park tickets in the lobby and offers a free shuttle to Disneyland. **Pros:** large suites for families; modern rooms in coastal colors; two pools, one kid-friendly and one with adult-only hours. **Cons:** North Tower rooms are dated in decor and furniture; parking is $28 a day; a little more than 1 mile from Disneyland Parks. $ *Rooms from: $199* ⊠ *11199 Harbor Blvd., Anaheim* ☎ *714/750–1234* ⊕ *www.hyatt.com* ⇱ *653 rooms* ⊙ *No meals.*

★ JW Marriott, Anaheim Resort

$$ | RESORT | FAMILY | The first luxury hotel in the area to open outside the Disneyland Resorts and the first JW Marriott in Orange County, this resort pays homage to the agricultural history of the region with unique architectural elements. **Pros:** gorgeous artwork throughout; great fireworks views; luxury amenities. **Cons:** popular event space for conventions and big gatherings; no Disneyland-themed rooms; valet parking only ($40 a day). $ *Rooms from: $225* ⊠ *1775 S. Clementine St., Anaheim* ☎ *714/294–7800* ⊕ *www.marriott.com* ⇱ *468 rooms* ⊙ *No meals.*

Majestic Garden Hotel

$ | HOTEL | FAMILY | If you're hoping to escape from the commercial atmosphere of the hotels near Disneyland and California Adventure, consider this sprawling replica of an English Tudor estate. **Pros:** large, attractive lobby; spacious rooms with comfortable beds; shuttle to the theme parks. **Cons:** confusing layout; hotel sits close to a busy freeway; small bathrooms. $ *Rooms from: $150* ⊠ *900 S. Disneyland Dr., Anaheim* ☎ *714/778–1700, 844/227–8535* ⊕ *www.majesticgardenhotel.com* ⇱ *489 rooms* ⊙ *No meals.*

🏃 Activities

Anaheim Ducks

HOCKEY | FAMILY | The National Hockey League's Anaheim Ducks, winners of the 2007 Stanley Cup, play at Honda Center. ⊠ *Honda Center, 2695 E. Katella Ave., Anaheim* ☎ *877/945–3946* ⊕ *nhl.com/ducks.*

Los Angeles Angels of Anaheim

BASEBALL/SOFTBALL | FAMILY | Professional baseball's Los Angeles Angels of Anaheim have called Anaheim and Angel Stadium home since 1966. An "Outfield Extravaganza" celebrates great plays on the field, with fireworks and a geyser exploding over a model evoking the California coast. ⊠ *Angel Stadium, 2000 E. Gene Autry Way, Anaheim* ☎ *714/426–4357* ⊕ *www.angels.com* Ⓜ *Metrolink Angels Express.*

Knott's Berry Farm

25 miles south of Los Angeles, via I-5, in Buena Park.

Once an actual farm, Knott's Berry Farm now offers a non-Disney theme park option for anyone with a love of roller coasters and boysenberries.

Knott's Berry Farm

AMUSEMENT PARK/WATER PARK | FAMILY | The land where the boysenberry was invented (by crossing raspberry, blackberry, and loganberry bushes) is now occupied by a popular amusement park.

In 1934, Cordelia Knott began serving chicken dinners on her wedding china to supplement her family's income. The dinners and her boysenberry pies proved more profitable than her husband Walter's farm, so the two moved first into the restaurant business and then into the entertainment business. The park is now a 160-acre complex with close to 40 rides, dozens of restaurants and shops, arcade games, live shows, and a brick-by-brick replica of Philadelphia's Independence Hall. Take a step back into the 1880s while walking through Knott's Old West Ghost Town. Ride on a horse-drawn stagecoach or board a steam engine to start your journey into the park; just keep your valuables close to you, as bandits might enter your train car and put on quite a show. Camp Snoopy has plenty to keep small children occupied as they explore 15 kid-friendly attractions. The park is also known for its awesome thrill rides in the Boardwalk area, including the zooming HangTime that pauses dramatically then drops nearly 15 stories, and the Xcelerator that goes from zero to 80 mph in 2.3 seconds.

And, yes you can still get that boysenberry pie, as well as boysenberry soft serve ice cream, jam, juice, you name it. There's even a Boysenberry Food Festival once a year. In the fall, part of the park is turned into Knott's Scary Farm, a popular activity for teens and adults. Buy adult tickets online for a discount; FastLane wristbands give you quicker access to the most popular rides. Nearby Knott's Soak City is open during the summer for guests who want to float on the lazy river, go down waterslides, and swim in the wave pool. ✉ 8039 Beach Blvd., Buena Park ✛ Between La Palma Ave. and Crescent St., 2 blocks south of Hwy. 91 ☎ 714/220–5200 ⊕ www.knotts.com 🎫 $82.

Park Neighborhoods

THE BOARDWALK

Not-for-the-squeamish thrill rides and skill-based games dominate the scene at the **Boardwalk.** Roller coasters—Coast Rider, Surfside Glider, and Pacific Scrambler—surround a pond that keeps things cooler on hot days. **HangTime** towers 150 feet above the boardwalk as coaster cars hang, invert and drop the equivalent of 15 stories. The boardwalk is also home to a string of test-your-skill games that are fun to watch whether you're playing or not, and Johnny Rockets, the park's all-American diner.

CAMP SNOOPY

It can be gridlock on weekends, but kids love this miniature High Sierra wonderland where the *Peanuts* gang hangs out. Tykes can push and pump their own mini-mining cars on **Huff and Puff,** soar around via **Charlie Brown's Kite Flyer,** and hop aboard **Woodstock's Airmail,** a kids' version of the park's Supreme Scream ride. Most of the rides here are geared toward kids only, leaving parents to cheer them on from the sidelines. **Sierra Sidewinder,** a roller coaster near the entrance of Camp Snoopy, is aimed at older children, with spinning saucer-type vehicles that go a maximum speed of 37 mph.

FIESTA VILLAGE

Over in **Fiesta Village** are two more musts for adrenaline junkies: **Montezooma's Revenge,** a roller coaster that goes from 0 to 55 mph in less than five seconds, and **Jaguar!,** a three-minute long coaster, which simulates the motions of a cat stalking its prey, twisting, spiraling, and speeding up and slowing down as it takes you on its stomach-dropping course through a Mayan temple. There's also **Hat Dance,** a version of the spinning teacups but with sombreros, and a 100-year-old **Dentzel carousel,** complete with an antique organ and menagerie of hand-carved animals. In a nod to history, there are restored scale models of the

California Missions at Fiesta Village's southern entrance.

GHOST TOWN

Clusters of authentic old buildings relocated from their original mining-town sites mark this section of the park. You can stroll down the street, stop and chat with a blacksmith, pan for gold (for a fee), crack open a geode, check out the chalkboard of a circa-1879 one-room schoolhouse, and ride an original Butterfield stagecoach. Looming over it all is **GhostRider,** Orange County's first wooden roller coaster. Traveling up to 56 mph and reaching 118 feet at its highest point, the park's biggest attraction is riddled with sudden dips and curves, subjecting riders to forces up to three times that of gravity. On the Western-themed **Silver Bullet,** riders are sent to a height of 146 feet and then back down 109 feet. Riders spiral, corkscrew, fly into a cobra roll, and experience overbanked curves. The **Calico Mine** ride descends into a replica of a working gold mine complete with 50 animatronic figures. The **Timber Mountain Log Ride** is a visitor favorite: the flume ride tours through pioneer scenes before splashing down. Also found here is the **Pony Express,** a roller coaster that lets riders saddle up on packs of "horses" tethered to platforms that take off on a series of hairpin turns and travel up to 38 mph. Take a step inside the **Western Trails Museum,** a dusty old gem full of Old West memorabilia and rural Americana, plus menus from the original chicken restaurant and an impressive antique button collection. **Calico Railroad** departs regularly from Ghost Town station for a round-trip tour of the park (bandit holdups notwithstanding). You can order a boysenberry soft serve ice cream cone nearby afterward.

This section is also home to **Big Foot Rapids,** a splash-fest of white-water river rafting over towering cliffs, cascading waterfalls, and wild rapids. Don't miss the visually stunning show at **Mystery Lodge,** which tells the story of Native Americans in the Pacific Northwest with lights, music, and special effects.

INDIAN TRAILS

Celebrate Native American traditions through interactive exhibits like tepees and daily dance and storytelling performances.

Knott's Soak City Waterpark is directly across from the main park on 13 acres next to Independence Hall. It has a dozen major water rides; **Pacific Spin** is an oversize waterslide that drops riders 75 feet into a catch pool. There's also a children's pool, a 750,000-gallon wave pool, and a fun house. Soak City's season runs mid-May to mid-September. It's open daily after Memorial Day, weekends only after Labor Day, and then closes for the season.

🍴 Restaurants

★ Mrs. Knott's Chicken Dinner Restaurant

$$ | **AMERICAN** | **FAMILY** | Cordelia Knott's fried chicken and boysenberry pies drew crowds so big that Knott's Berry Farm was built to keep the hungry customers occupied while they waited. The restaurant's current incarnation (outside the park's entrance) still serves crispy fried chicken, along with fluffy handmade biscuits, mashed potatoes, and Mrs. Knott's signature chilled cherry-rhubarb compote. **Known for:** famous fried chicken; long waits especially on weekends; pies and desserts. ⑤ *Average main: $22 ⊠ Knott's Berry Farm Marketplace, 8039 Beach Blvd., Buena Park ☎ 714/220–5200 ⊕ www. knotts.com/california-marketplace/ mrs-knott-s-chicken-dinner-restaurant.*

🛏 Hotels

Knott's Berry Farm Hotel

$ | **HOTEL** | **FAMILY** | This convenient low-rise hotel is run by the park and sits right on park grounds surrounded by graceful

12

Disneyland and Orange County | KNOTT'S BERRY FARM

palm trees. **Pros:** easy access to Knott's Berry Farm; tennis court; decent on-site dining. **Cons:** lobby and hallways can be noisy; can hear the nearby roller coaster; dated room decor. ⑤ *Rooms from: $129* ✉ *7675 Crescent Ave., Buena Park* ☎ *714/995–1111, 866/752–2444* ⊕ *www. knotts.com/knotts-berry-farm-hotel* ⌇ *320 rooms* ⦿ *No meals.*

The Coast

Running along the Orange County coastline is scenic Pacific Coast Highway (Highway 1, known locally as the PCH). Older beachfront settlements, with their modest bungalow-style homes, are joined by posh gated communities. The pricey land between Newport Beach and Laguna Beach is where novelist Dean Koontz, those infamous Real Housewives of Bravo, and a slew of finance moguls live.

Though the coastline is rapidly being filled in, there are still a few stretches of beautiful, protected open land. And at many places along the way you can catch an idealized glimpse of the Southern California lifestyle: surfers hitting the beach, boards under their arms.

Huntington Beach

40 miles southeast of Los Angeles.

Once a sleepy residential town with little more than a string of rugged surf shops, Huntington Beach has transformed itself into a resort destination,commonly referred to as Surf City U.S.A. The town's appeal is its broad white-sand beaches with often-towering waves, complemented by a lively pier, shops, and restaurants on Main Street, and a growing collection of resort hotels.

A draw for sports fans and partiers of all stripes is the U.S. Open professional surf competition, which brings a festive atmosphere to town annually in late July. There's even a Surfing Walk of Fame, with plaques set in the sidewalk around the intersection of PCH and Main Street.

ESSENTIALS
Visit Huntington Beach

✉ *301 Main St., Suite 212* ☎ *714/969–3492, 800/729–6232* ⊕ *www.surfcityusa. com.*

◉ Sights

Bolsa Chica Ecological Reserve

NATURE PRESERVE | FAMILY | Wildlife lovers and bird-watchers flock to Bolsa Chica Ecological Reserve, which has a 1,445-acre salt marsh where 302 bird species—including great blue herons, snowy and great egrets, and brown pelicans—have been spotted. Throughout the reserve are trails for bird-watching, including a comfortable 1½-mile loop. There are two entrances off the Pacific Coast Highway: one close to the Interpretive Center and a second one 1 mile south on Warner Avenue, opposite Bolsa Chica State Beach. Each parking lot connects to 4 miles of walking and hiking trails with scenic overlooks. ✉ *Bolsa Chica Wetlands Interpretive Center, 3842 Warner Ave.* ☎ *714/846–1114* ⊕ *www. bolsachica.org* ⌁ *Free.*

Bolsa Chica State Beach

BEACH—SIGHT | FAMILY | In the northern section of the city, Bolsa Chica State Beach is usually less crowded than its southern neighbors. The sand is somewhat gritty and not the cleanest, but swells make it a hot surfing spot. Picnic sites can be reserved in advance. Fire pits attract beachgoers most nights. **Amenities:** food and drink; lifeguards; parking; showers; toilets. **Best for:** sunset; surfing; swimming; walking; RV camping. ✉ *Pacific Coast Hwy., between Seapoint St. and Warner Ave.* ☎ *714/846–3460* ⊕ *www.parks.ca.gov* ⌁ *$15 parking.*

The Orange County Coast

Catalina Island
see detail map

Cleveland National Forest

San Diego County

Camp Pendleton Marine Corps Base

Trabuco Canyon
Rancho Santa Margarita
Coto de Caza
Las Flores
Ladera Ranch
Mission Viejo
San Juan Capistrano
San Clemente
San Capistrano Beach
Dana Point

Laguna Hills
Aliso Viejo
Laguna Niguel
Monarch Bay
South Laguna

ORANGE COUNTY
Lake Forest
Laguna Woods
Laguna Coast Wilderness Park
Roger's Gardens
Crystal Cove State Park
Laguna Beach

Orange
North Tustin
Tustin
Irvine
John Wayne Orange County Airport
Fashion Island
Corona del Mar
Balboa Island and Peninsula
Newport Beach
Newport Beach Pier

Anaheim
Disneyland Resort
Garden Grove
Westminster
Midway City
Santa Ana
Fountain Valley
Costa Mesa
International Surfing Museum
Huntington State Beach
Huntington Beach Pier
Huntington Beach

Stanton
Los Alamitos Army Airfield
Bolsa Chica Ecological Reserve
Bolsa Chica State Beach
Pacific Coast Hwy (PCH)

Signal Hill
Long Beach Airport
Seal Beach
Seal Beach NWS
Seal Beach NWR
Sunset Beach
Rossmoor

Long Beach
San Pedro
Lomita
Rolling Hills Estates
Rancho Palos Verdes

PACIFIC OCEAN

FERRY TO CATALINA ISLAND (1hr 30 min)

FERRY TO CATALINA ISLAND (1hr 10 min)

FERRY TO CATALINA ISLAND (1hr 20 min)

CATALINA ISLAND
Avalon

Lively Huntington Beach is a center for surfing on the coast.

Huntington Beach Pier

MARINA | FAMILY | This municipal pier stretches 1,856 feet out to sea, past the powerful waves that gave Huntington Beach the title of "Surf City U.S.A." Well above the waves, it's a prime vantage point to watch the dozens of surfers in the water below. On the pier you'll find a snack shop and a shop where you can buy fishing rod rentals, tackle, and bait to fish off the pier. ✉ *Pacific Coast Hwy.* ⊕ *www.surfcityusa.com.*

Huntington City Beach

BEACH—SIGHT | FAMILY | Stretching for 3½ miles from Bolsa Chica State Beach to Huntington State Beach, Huntington City Beach is most crowded around the pier; amateur and professional surfers brave the waves daily. Fire pits, numerous concession stands, an area for dogs, and well-raked white sand make this a popular beach come summertime. **Amenities:** food and drink; lifeguards; parking; showers; toilets. **Best for:** sunset; surfing; swimming; walking. ✉ *Pacific Coast Hwy., from Beach Blvd. to Seapoint St.*

☎ *714/536–5281, 714/536–9303 surf report* ⊕ *www.huntingtonbeachca.gov/ residents/beach_info* ✉ *Parking from $15.*

Huntington State Beach

BEACH—SIGHT | FAMILY | This state beach also has 200 fire pits, so it's popular day and night. There are changing rooms, concession stands, lifeguards, Wi-Fi access, and ample parking. An 8.5-mile bike path connects Hunnington to Bolsa Chica State Beach. Picnic areas can be reserved in advance for a fee depending on location; otherwise it's first come, first served. On hot days, expect crowds at this broad, soft sandy beach. **Amenities:** food and drink; lifeguards; parking; showers; toilets. **Best for:** sunset; surfing; swimming; walking; surf fishing. ✉ *Pacific Coast Hwy., from Beach Blvd. south to Santa Ana River* ☎ *714/536–1454* ⊕ *www.parks.ca.gov/?page_id=643* ✉ *$15 parking.*

International Surfing Museum

MUSEUM | FAMILY | Just up Main Street from Huntington Pier, the International

Surfing Museum pays tribute to the sport's greats with an impressive collection of surfboards and related memorabilia. Exhibits are designed to encourage kids to study and to surf. ⊠ *411 Olive Ave.* ☎ *714/465–4350* ⊕ *www.surfingmuseum.org* ☜ *$3, under 18 free* ☾ *Closed Mon.*

Restaurants

Duke's

$$$$ | SEAFOOD | FAMILY | Freshly caught seafood reigns supreme at this homage to surfing legend Duke Kahanamoku; it's also a prime people-watching spot right at the beginning of Huntington Beach Pier. Choose from several fish-of-the-day selections—many topped with Hawaiian ingredients—and shellfish like lobster, king crab, and shrimp. **Known for:** Hawaiian-style decor; gorgeous sunset views; mai tai cocktails. ⑤ *Average main: $45* ⊠ *317 Pacific Coast Hwy.* ☎ *714/374–6446* ⊕ *www.dukeshuntington.com.*

Wahoo's Fish Taco

$ | MEXICAN FUSION | FAMILY | Proximity to the ocean makes this eatery's seafood-filled tacos and burritos taste even better. The healthy fast-food chain—tagged with dozens of surf stickers—brought Baja's fish tacos north of the border to quick success. **Known for:** organic ingredients; Hawaiian onion ring burrito; casual beachy ambience. ⑤ *Average main: $12* ⊠ *120 Main St.* ☎ *714/536–2050* ⊕ *www.wahoos.com.*

🛏 Hotels

Hyatt Regency Huntington Beach Resort and Spa

$$$ | RESORT | FAMILY | The Spanish design of this sprawling property incorporates arched courtyards, beautiful tiled fountains, and fire pits, all a nod to California's Mission period. **Pros:** close to beach; variety of pool areas; family-friendly vibe. **Cons:** some partial ocean-view rooms; resort and daily valet fees; some rooms

can hear the traffic on PCH. ⑤ *Rooms from: $360* ⊠ *21500 Pacific Coast Hwy.* ☎ *714/698–1234* ⊕ *www.hyatt.com* ⇨ *517 rooms* ⑩ *No meals.*

Kimpton Shorebreak Resort

$$ | HOTEL | FAMILY | This surfer-style Kimpton hotel is not only across the street from the beach, but it's the closest hotel to the Huntington Beach Pier and Main Street. **Pros:** proximity to beach and shops; free surfboard storage; quiet rooms despite central location. **Cons:** $35 valet parking fee; courtyard rooms have uninspiring alley views; additional resort fee to receive best perks. ⑤ *Rooms from: $250* ⊠ *500 Pacific Coast Hwy.* ☎ *714/861–4470, 877/212–8597* ⊕ *www. shorebreakhotel.com* ⇨ *157 rooms* ⑩ *No meals.*

Pasea Hotel & Spa

$$$ | RESORT | FAMILY | Painted in shades of sea blue, the contemporary-styled Pasea is a rarity along the O.C. coast: at eight stories, almost every room has an ocean view and all have balconies to take in the fresh breezes. **Pros:** excellent ocean views; beach butlers to provide everything for a beach day; supercomfortable beds. **Cons:** pool can get crowded; $40 valet parking fee; noise issues from nearby bars at Pacific City. ⑤ *Rooms from: $350* ⊠ *21080 Pacific Coast Hwy.* ☎ *866/478–9702* ⊕ *www. meritagecollection.com/pasea-hotel* ⇨ *250 rooms* ⑩ *No meals.*

The Waterfront Beach Resort, a Hilton Hotel

$$ | RESORT | FAMILY | This two-tower resort offers a variety of amenities for families, couples, and business travelers alike. **Pros:** quick walk to beach and pier; fun surf decor; oceanfront views from rooms. **Cons:** different towers have different vibes; valet parking only for $42; crowded pool and deck during summer. ⑤ *Rooms from: $239* ⊠ *21100 Pacific Coast Hwy.* ☎ *714/845–8000, 855/271–3617* ⊕ *www.waterfrontresort. com* ⇨ *437 rooms* ⑩ *No meals.*

🛍 Shopping

HSS Main St

SPORTING GOODS | FAMILY | The largest surf-gear source in town is Huntington Surf and Sport, right across from Huntington Pier. Staffed by true surf enthusiasts, it's also one of the only surf shops with a coffee counter inside. Surfboard rentals are $15 an hour or $50 all day while soft top boards are $18 per hour or $30 a day. They also rent bodyboards and wetsuits. ⊠ *300 Pacific Coast Hwy.* ☎ *714/841–4000* ⊕ *www.hsssurf.com.*

🏃 Activities

Corky Carroll's Surf School

SURFING | FAMILY | This surf school organizes lessons, weeklong workshops, and international surf camps at Bolsa Chica State Beach. They also provide hard and soft top boards and wetsuits to rent during your lesson. ⊠ *Bolsa Chica State Beach, Lifeguard Tower 18* ☎ *714/969–3959* ⊕ *www.surfschool.net.*

Dwight's Beach Concession

BICYCLING | FAMILY | You can rent surrey or cruiser bikes, wet suits, surfboards, bodyboards, umbrellas, and beach chairs at Dwight's, one block south of Huntington Pier. They also serve casual beach food, including their world-famous cheese strips. ⊠ *201 Pacific Coast Hwy.* ☎ *714/536–8083* ⊕ *www.dwightsbeach-concession.com.*

Zack's HB

BICYCLING | FAMILY | This place offers beach equipment, surfing lessons and boards, wet suits, and bicycles. Food like hamburgers, corn dogs, fish and chips, grilled mahimahi, and Mexican favorites are sold here, too. ⊠ *405 Pacific Coast Hwy., at Main St.* ☎ *714/536–0215* ⊕ *www.zackssurfcity.com.*

Newport Beach

6 miles south of Huntington Beach.

Newport Beach has evolved from a simple seaside village to an icon of chic coastal living. Its ritzy reputation comes from megayachts bobbing in the harbor, boutiques that rival those in Beverly Hills, and spectacular homes overlooking the ocean.

The city boasts some of the cleanest beaches in Southern California; inland Newport Beach's concentration of high-rise office buildings, shopping centers, and luxury hotels drives the economy. But on the city's Balboa Peninsula, you can still catch a glimpse of a more humble, down-to-earth town scattered with taco spots, tackle shops, and sailor bars.

VISITOR AND TOUR INFORMATION Visit Newport Beach Concierge. ⊠ *Atrium Court at Fashion Island, 1600 Newport Center Dr.* ☎ *949/719–6100* ⊕ *www.newport-beachandco.com.*

👁 Sights

★ Balboa Island

BEACH—SIGHT | FAMILY | This sliver of terra firma in Newport Harbor boasts quaint streets tightly packed with impossibly charming multimillion-dollar cottages. The island's main drag, Marine Avenue, is lined with equally picturesque cafés, frozen chocolate banana shops, and apparel stores. Rent a bike and pedal around on the car-free bike path and boardwalk encircling much of the island for an easy and scenic ramble. Be sure to visit the free Balboa Island Museum, too.

To get here, you can either park your car on the mainland side of the PCH in Newport Beach and walk or bike over the bridge onto Marine Avenue, or take the Balboa Island Ferry, the country's longest-running auto ferry. The one-way fare is $1.25 for an adult pedestrian; $1.50 for an adult with a bike; and $2.25

Newport Beach is another popular place in the O.C. to catch waves.

to take your car on board. ✉ *Marine Ave.* ☎ *949/719–6100* ⊕ *www.visitnewport-beach.com.*

Balboa Peninsula

BEACH—SIGHT | FAMILY | Newport's best beaches are on Balboa Peninsula, where many jetties pave the way to ideal swimming areas. The most intense spot for bodysurfing in Orange County, and arguably on the West Coast, known as the **Wedge,** is at the south end of the peninsula. It was created by accident in the 1930s when the Federal Works Progress Administration built a jetty to protect Newport Harbor. ■**TIP➔ Rip currents and punishing waves mean it's strictly for the pros—but it sure is fun to watch an experienced local ride it.** ✉ *Newport Beach* ⊕ *www.visitnewportbeach.com/beaches-and-parks/the-wedge.*

★ Newport Harbor

BEACH—SIGHT | FAMILY | Sheltering nearly 16,000 small boats, Newport Harbor may seduce even those who don't own a yacht. Spend an afternoon exploring the charming avenues and surrounding alleys or take California's longest-running auto ferry across to Balboa Island, popular with pedestrians, bicyclists, and automobiles. Several grassy areas on the primarily residential Lido Isle have views of the water. To truly experience the harbor, rent a kayak or an electric Duffy boat for a pleasant picnic cruise or try stand-up paddleboarding to explore the sheltered waters. ✉ *Pacific Coast Hwy.* ⊕ *www.balboaislandferry.com.*

Newport Beach Pier

BEACH—SIGHT | FAMILY | Jutting out into the ocean near 21st Street, Newport Pier is a popular fishing spot. Below is 5 miles of sandy beach for sunbathing, surfing, and walking along the beach. Street parking is difficult, so grab the first space you find and be prepared to walk. Early on Wednesday–Sunday morning you're likely to encounter dory fishermen hawking their predawn catches, as they've done for generations. On weekends the area is alive with kids of all ages on in-line skates, skateboards, and bikes dodging pedestrians and whizzing past fast-food joints and classic dive bars. Skate, bike, and surfboard rental shops are nearby. ⊠ *70 Newport Pier* ☎ *949/644–3309* ⊕ *www.visitnewportbeach.com.*

Sculpture Exhibition in Civic Center Park
PUBLIC ART | FAMILY | This outdoor museum is a favorite walking spot for locals and visitors. Look for the array of meaningful and whimsical public art sculptures on a hillside looking out toward the Pacific Ocean. Families love "Bunnyhenge," a collection of 14 white bunny statues arranged in a circle. ⊠ *1000 Avocado Ave.* ☎ *949/717–3802* ⊕ *www.newportbeach-ca.gov.*

🍴 Restaurants

Basilic Restaurant
$$$ | BRASSERIE | This intimate French-Swiss bistro adds a touch of old-world elegance to Balboa Island with its white linen and flower-topped tables. Chef Bernard Althaus grows the herbs used in his classic French dishes. **Known for:** French classics; fine wine; old-school ambience. ⑤ *Average main: $32* ⊠ *217 Marine Ave., Balboa Island* ☎ *949/673–0570* ⊕ *www.basilicrestaurant.com* ⊘ *Closed Sun. and Mon.*

★ Bear Flag Fish Co.
$ | SEAFOOD | FAMILY | Expect long lines in summer at this indoor/outdoor dining spot serving up the freshest local fish (swordfish, sea bass, halibut, and tuna) and a wide range of creative seafood dishes (the Hawaiian-style *poke* salad with ahi tuna is a local favorite). Order at the counter, which doubles as a seafood market, and sit inside the airy dining room or outside on a grand patio. **Known for:** freshest seafood thanks to restaurant's own fishing boat; fish tacos with homemade hot sauce; craft beers. ⑤ *Average main: $15* ⊠ *Newport Peninsula, 3421 Via Lido* ☎ *949/673–3474* ⊕ *www.bearflagfishco.com.*

Bluewater Grill
$$$ | SEAFOOD | FAMILY | On the site of an old sportfishing dock, this popular spot offers a variety of seafood, from Idaho trout amandine and lemon pepper mahimahi to lobster, pan-seared scallops, and chipotle-blackened swordfish. There's a tranquil bay view from either the dining room, which is adorned with early-1900s fishing photos, or the waterfront patio. **Known for:** boat and harbor views; happy hour specials; daily-changing menu of fresh fish. ⑤ *Average main: $35* ⊠ *Lido Peninsula, 630 Lido Park Dr.* ☎ *949/675–3474* ⊕ *www.bluewatergrill.com.*

The Cannery
$$$ | SEAFOOD | This 1920s cannery building still teems with fish, but now they go into dishes on the eclectic Pacific Rim menu rather than being packed into crates. Settle in at the sushi bar, in the dining room, or on the patio before choosing between sashimi, freshly shucked oysters, or cilantro-marinated fish tacos. **Known for:** waterfront views; seafood specialties; craft cocktails. ⑤ *Average main: $37* ⊠ *3010 Lafayette Rd.* ☎ *949/566–0060* ⊕ *www.cannerynewport.com* ⊘ *Closed Mon. and Tues.*

Gulfstream
$$$ | SEAFOOD | FAMILY | Established in 1999, this on-trend restaurant has an open kitchen, comfortable booths, and outdoor seating. The patio is a fantastic place to hang out to enjoy a shrimp cocktail and glass of wine. **Known for:** oysters on the half shell; local hangout; outdoor patio. ⑤ *Average main: $35* ⊠ *850 Avocado Ave.* ☎ *949/718–0188* ⊕ *www.gulfstreamrestaurant.com.*

🛏 Hotels

Balboa Bay Resort
$$$ | RESORT | FAMILY | Sharing the same frontage as the private Balboa Bay Club that long ago hosted Humphrey Bogart, Lauren Bacall, and Ronald Reagan, this waterfront resort has one of the

best bay views around, especially at its lively gastropub. **Pros:** exquisite bayfront views; comfortable beds; two popular restaurants for locals and visitors. **Cons:** swimming pool in the middle of the resort has no views; $35 nightly hospitality fee; some rooms don't face the bay. ⑤ *Rooms from: $339* ✉ *1221 W. Coast Hwy.* ☎ *949/645–5000* ⊕ *www. balboabayresort.com* ⇨ *159 rooms* ⊗ *No meals.*

Fashion Island Hotel

$$ | RESORT | FAMILY | Across a palm tree–lined boulevard from stylish Fashion Island, this 20-story tower caters to business types during the week and leisure travelers on weekends. **Pros:** lively lounge scene; large tropical heated pool; great location. **Cons:** steep valet parking prices; some rooms have views of mall parking; destination fee added to price. ⑤ *Rooms from: $295* ✉ *690 Newport Center Dr.* ☎ *949/759–0808, 877/591–9145* ⊕ *www. fashionislandhotel.com* ⇨ *295 rooms* ⊗ *No meals.*

Hyatt Regency Newport Beach

$$ | RESORT | FAMILY | The best aspect of this beloved resort-style Newport hotel is its lushly landscaped acres: 26 of them, all overlooking the Back Bay. The casually elegant architecture, spread over the generous grounds, will appeal to travelers weary of high-rise hotels. **Pros:** high-quality linens; centrally located for shopping; numerous sport activities offered. **Cons:** $30 self-parking is far from main property; 10-minute drive to beach; $30 daily resort fee. ⑤ *Rooms from: $235* ✉ *1107 Jamboree Rd.* ☎ *949/729–1234* ⊕ *www.hyatt.com* ⇨ *410 rooms* ⊗ *No meals.*

★ Lido House, Autograph Collection

$$$ | RESORT | FAMILY | This Marriott Autograph Collection resort is located at the gateway of the exclusive Lido Island and three blocks from the beach. **Pros:** large hot tub and pool deck; lively hotel bar; free bikes to cruise the nearby boardwalk. **Cons:** pricey restaurant; $35

resort fee; $43 valet parking. ⑤ *Rooms from: $325* ✉ *3300 Newport Blvd., Balboa Island* ☎ *949/524–8500* ⊕ *www. lidohousehotel.com* ⇨ *130 rooms, 5 cottages* ⊗ *No meals.*

Newport Beach Hotel

$$$$ | B&B/INN | FAMILY | At this charming boutique hotel just steps from the beach and Newport Beach Pier, some of the coastal-themed guest rooms have ocean views, all have complimentary Wi-Fi, and most offer a whirlpool bathtub and shower. **Pros:** beach and oceanview guest rooms; in a lively area near restaurants; steps to the pier and beach. **Cons:** some rooms are small; not all rooms have views; parking is $25 a day. ⑤ *Rooms from: $425* ✉ *2306 W. Oceanfront* ☎ *949/673–7030* ⊕ *www. thenewportbeachhotel.com* ⇨ *15 rooms* ⊗ *Free breakfast.*

Newport Beach Marriott Hotel and Spa

$$ | RESORT | FAMILY | This centrally located property is across the street from the popular Fashion Island shopping and dining complex. **Pros:** million-dollar views of Orange County and beyond; large spa; central location across from Fashion Island. **Cons:** sprawling floor plan; smaller bathrooms; valet parking $36 a day. ⑤ *Rooms from: $229* ✉ *900 Newport Center Dr.* ☎ *949/640–4000* ⊕ *www.marriott.com* ⇨ *523 rooms* ⊗ *No meals.*

🛍 Shopping

★ Fashion Island

STORE/MALL | Shake the sand out of your shoes to head inland to the ritzy Fashion Island outdoor mall, a cluster of archways and courtyards complete with koi pond, fountains, and a mix of high-end shopping and chain dining. It has the luxe department stores Neiman Marcus, Nordstrom, and Bloomingdale's, plus expensive boutiques like Trina Turk, Kate Spade, and Michael Stars. ✉ *401 Newport Center Dr., between Jamboree and MacArthur Blvds., off PCH*

A whimbrel hunts for mussels at Crystal Cove State Park.

☎ *949/721–2000, 855/658–8527* ⊕ *www. fashionisland.com.*

🏃 Activities

BOAT RENTALS
Balboa Boat Rentals
BOATING | FAMILY | You can tour the waterways surrounding Lido and Balboa isles on six-person power motorboats ($85 an hour), and electric Duffy boats ($95 to $115 an hour for 8 to 12 people) at Balboa Boat Rentals. ✉ *510 E. Edgewater Ave., Balboa Island* ☎ *855/690–0794* ⊕ *www. boats4rent.com.*

BOAT TOURS
Catalina Flyer
TOUR—SPORTS | FAMILY | At Balboa Pavilion, the *Catalina Flyer* operates a 90-minute round-trip passage daily to Catalina Island for $70. Reservations are required; check the schedule for times, as crossings may be rescheduled due to weather or annual maintenance. All day parking is $27 a day in a nearby Newport Beach lot. Payment is made at self-serve pay stations. ✉ *400 Main St., Balboa Island* ☎ *949/673–5245* ⊕ *www. catalinainfo.com.*

Hornblower Cruises and Events
TOUR—SPORTS | This operator books two-hour harbor cruises, Sunday brunch cruises, and three-hour weekend dinner cruises with dancing. The trips traverse the mostly placid and scenic waters of Newport Harbor. ✉ *2431 W. Coast Hwy.* ☎ *949/646–0155* ⊕ *www.hornblower. com.*

FISHING
Davey's Locker
FISHING | FAMILY | In addition to a complete tackle shop, Davey's Locker offers two-hour whale-watching cruises starting at $28, half-day sportfishing trips starting at $34; and overnight fishing excursions starting at $149. ✉ *Balboa Pavilion, 400 Main St., Balboa Island* ☎ *949/673–1434* ⊕ *www.daveyslocker.com.*

Corona del Mar

2 miles south of Newport Beach.

A small jewel on the Pacific Coast, Corona del Mar (known by locals as "CDM") has exceptional beaches that some say resemble their majestic Northern California counterparts. South of CDM is an area referred to as the Newport Coast or Crystal Cove—whatever you call it, it's another dazzling spot on the California Riviera.

◉ Sights

Corona del Mar State Beach

BEACH—SIGHT | FAMILY | This beach is actually made up of two beaches, Little Corona and Big Corona, separated by a cliff. Both have soft, golden-hue sand. Facilities include fire pits and volleyball courts. Two colorful reefs (and the fact that it's off-limits to boats) make Corona del Mar great for snorkelers and beachcombers. Parking in the lot is pricey, but you can often find a spot on the street on weekdays. **Amenities:** lifeguards; parking; showers; toilets. **Best for:** snorkeling; sunset; swimming. ✉ *3100 Ocean Blvd., Corona del Mar* ☎ *949/644–3151* ⊕ *www. parks.ca.gov.*

★ Crystal Cove State Park

BEACH—SIGHT | FAMILY | Midway between Corona del Mar and Laguna, Crystal Cove State Park is a favorite of local beachgoers and wilderness trekkers. It encompasses a 3.2-mile stretch of unspoiled beach and has some of the best tide-pooling in Southern California. Here you can see starfish, crabs, and sea anemones near the rocks. The park's 2,400 acres of backcountry are ideal for hiking and mountain biking, but stay on the trails to preserve the beauty. The Moro Campground offers campsites with picnic tables, including spots designated for RVs and trailers. The Crystal Cove Historic District holds a collection of historic cottages (24 of which are available for overnight rental), decorated and furnished to reflect the 1935 to 1955 beach culture that flourished here. On the sand above the high tide line and on a bluff above the beach, the cottages offer a funky look at beach life in times past. ✉ *8471 N. Coast Hwy., Laguna Beach* ☎ *949/494–3539* ⊕ *www.crystalcovestatepark.org* 🅿 *$15 parking.*

Roger's Gardens

GARDEN | FAMILY | One of the largest retail gardens in Southern California, Roger's showcases some of the best holiday decorations during Halloween and Christmas. An on-site Farmhouse at Roger's Gardens restaurant is popular with visitors and locals, who enjoy the locally sourced menu items while overlooking the bucolic gardens. ✉ *2301 San Joaquin Hills Rd.* ☎ *949/640–5800* ⊕ *www.rogersgardens.com.*

Sherman Library and Gardens

GARDEN | FAMILY | This 2½-acre botanical garden and library specializes in the history of the Pacific Southwest. You can wander among cactus gardens, rose gardens, a cool fern garden, and a tropical conservatory. There's a good gift shop, too. Café Jardin serves lunch on weekdays and Sunday brunch. ✉ *2647 E. Pacific Coast Hwy.* ☎ *949/673–2261* ⊕ *www.thesherman.org* 🅿 *$5.*

Store

HISTORIC SITE | Located among the Crystal Cove Cottages in the area's Historic District, Store carries fine art works by local plein air artists, as well as seaglass and ocean-themed jewelry, children's toys, snacks, and beach apparel. ✉ *State Park Historic District, Newport Coast* ☎ *949/376–6200* ⊕ *www.crystalcove.org/ visit/things-to-do/store-gallery.*

🍴 Restaurants

The Beachcomber Cafe at Crystal Cove

$$ | SEAFOOD | Beach culture flourishes in this Crystal Cove Historic District's restaurant, thanks to its umbrella-laden deck

just a few steps above the white sand. This is where you can sip a really good mai tai at the Bootlegger Bar, while waiting for your chance to sample ahi tacos, Maine lobster pasta, or blue crab–stuffed salmon. **Known for:** beachside cocktails; fresh seafood; big crowds and long waits (try to make a reservation in advance). $ *Average main: $25* ✉ *15 Crystal Cove* ☎ *949/376–6900* ⊕ *www.thebeachcombercafe.com.*

Shake Shack at Crystal Cove

$ | **DINER** | **FAMILY** | This Southern California landmark sitting on a bluff off the PCH is the perfect spot to get a quick breakfast or to sample a tasty Cove burger with a side of fries or cole slaw for lunch or dinner. The menu also includes a vegan Impossible burger, hot dogs, and fish-and-chips. **Known for:** over 30 different shake flavors; casual ocean-view dining; small parking lot with 30 minute limit. $ *Average main: $15* ✉ *7703 E. Coast Hwy., Newport Coast* ☎ *949/464–0100* ⊕ *www.crystalcoveshakeshack.com.*

🛏 Hotels

The Resort at Pelican Hill

$$$$ | **RESORT** | **FAMILY** | Built on a protected coastal enclave across the PCH and Crystal Cove State Park, this upscale Italian Renaissance–style resort has a dramatic domed rotunda, antique olive jars, and Tuscan columns and pilasters in the lobby. **Pros:** ocean-view paradise for golfers; spectacular swimming pool (the largest of its kind in the world); great spa and dining options. **Cons:** one of the most expensive resorts in Orange County; swimming pool can get very crowded during the holidays; pricey resort fee. $ *Rooms from: $795* ✉ *22701 Pelican Hill Rd. S, Newport Coast* ☎ *949/612–0332, 888/507–6427* ⊕ *www.pelicanhill.com* ⤴ *204 rooms, 128 villas* ❄ *No meals.*

🛍 Shopping

Crystal Cove Promenade

STORE/MALL | **FAMILY** | Adding to Orange County's overwhelming supply of high-end shopping and dining is Crystal Cove Promenade, which might be described as the toniest strip mall in America. The mix of well-known storefronts, unique boutiques, and popular restaurants of this Mediterranean-inspired center are lined up across the street from Crystal Cove State Park, with the shimmering Pacific waters in plain view. ✉ *7845–8085 E. Coast Hwy., Newport Beach* ☎ *949/494–1239* ⊕ *www.shopirvinecompany.com.*

Laguna Beach

10 miles south of Newport Beach on PCH, 60 miles south of Los Angeles, I–5 south to Hwy. 133, which turns into Laguna Canyon Rd.

Driving in along Laguna Canyon Road from the Interstate 405 freeway gives you the chance to cruise through a gorgeous coastal canyon, large stretches of which remain undeveloped, before arriving at a glistening wedge of ocean. There are 30 coves and beaches to visit, all with some of the cleanest water in Southern California. During the summer, there's a convenient and free trolley service through town that cruises from North Laguna to Main Beach and all the way to the Ritz Carlton Laguna Niguel.

Laguna's welcome mat is legendary. On the corner of Forest and Park avenues is a gate proclaiming, "This gate hangs well and hinders none, refresh and rest, then travel on." A gay community has long been established here; art galleries dot the village streets, and there's usually someone daubing up a plein air on the bluff in Heisler Park. Along the Pacific Coast Highway you'll find dozens of clothing boutiques, jewelry stores, and cafés.

Laguna Beach Visitors Center. ✉ *381 Forest Ave.* ☏ *949/497–9229, 800/877–1115* ⊕ *www.visitlagunabeach.com.*

◉ Sights

Festival of Arts and Pageant of the Masters
FESTIVAL | An outdoor amphitheater near the mouth of the canyon hosts the annual Pageant of the Masters, Laguna's signature event. Local participants arrange tableaux vivants, in which live models and carefully orchestrated backgrounds merge in striking mimicry of classical and contemporary paintings. The pageant is part of the **Festival of Arts,** held in July and August; tickets are in high demand, so plan ahead. ✉ *650 Laguna Canyon Rd.* ☏ *949/497–6582, 800/487–3378* ⊕ *www.foapom.com.*

Heisler Park
CITY PARK | FAMILY | One of the most picturesque parks in Laguna Beach, Heisler Park offers plenty of chances for fun and relaxation. Picnic Beach has picnic tables overlooking palm trees and panoramic ocean views while stairs lead down to Diver's Cove for snorkeling, scuba diving, and tidepool exploring. Take the paved walking path along the cliff all the way to Laguna's Main Beach. There are public restrooms and outdoor showers. This is also a popular area for plein-air artists to set up an easel and chair and paint for hours. ✉ *400 Cliff Dr.* ⊕ *www.visitlagunabeach.com.*

Laguna Art Museum
MUSEUM | This museum displays work by California artists from all time periods, representing scenery in Laguna, and life and history of the Golden State in general. Special exhibits change quarterly. ✉ *307 Cliff Dr.* ☏ *949/494 8971* ⊕ *www.lagunaartmuseum.org* ⚏ *$7* ◷ *Closed Wed.*

Laguna Coast Wilderness Park
HIKING/WALKING | FAMILY | With easy, moderate, and difficult trails spread over 7,000 acres of canyon to coastal territory, Laguna Coast Wilderness Park is a hiker's paradise. The 40 miles of trails offer expansive views and are also popular with mountain bikers. Trails open daily at 7 am and stay open until sunset, weather permitting. No dogs are allowed in the park. ✉ *18751 Laguna Canyon Rd.* ☏ *949/923–2235* ⊕ *www.ocparks.com/parks/lagunac* ⚏ *$3 parking.*

⏱ Beaches

★ **Main Beach Park**
BEACH—SIGHT | FAMILY | Centrally located in the main town of Laguna Beach near multiple dining venues, art galleries, and shops, Main Beach Park has a fitting name. Walk along this soft-sand beach to Bird Rock and explore nearby tide pools or sit on one of the benches and watch people bodysurfing, playing beach volleyball, or scrambling around two half-basketball courts. The beach also has a children's play area with climbing equipment. Most of Laguna's hotels are within a short (but hilly) walk. **Amenities:** lifeguards; toilets; showers. **Best for:** sunrise, sunset; swimming. ✉ *Broadway at S. Coast Hwy.* ⊕ *www.visitlagunabeach.com.*

1,000 Steps Beach
BEACH—SIGHT | FAMILY | Off South Coast Highway at 9th Street, 1,000 Steps Beach isn't too hard to find and actually only has 207 steps. It's one of the many coves in Laguna Beach offering a long stretch of soft sand, waves, and dramatic rock formations. Sea caves and tide pools enhance the already beautiful natural spot. Walking back up to your car, you will feel like you got a good workout. **Amenities:** showers. **Best for:** snorkeling; surfing; swimming. ✉ *S. Coast Hwy., at 9th St.* ⊕ *www.visitlagunabeach.com.*

Wood's Cove
BEACH—SIGHT | FAMILY | Off South Coast Highway, Wood's Cove is especially quiet during the week. Big rock formations

Looking for shells on Laguna Beach, one of the nicest stretches of sand in Southern California.

hide lurking crabs. This is a prime scuba-diving spot, and at high tide much of the beach is underwater. Climbing the steps to leave, you can see a Tudor-style mansion that was once home to Bette Davis. Street parking is free yet limited. **Amenities:** none. **Best for:** snorkeling; scuba diving; sunset. ⊠ *Diamond St. and Ocean Way* ⊕ *www.visitlagunabeach. com.*

🍴 Restaurants

The Cliff

$$$ | SEAFOOD | FAMILY | Walk through the quaint Laguna Beach artist village to get to the Cliff and its 180-degree views of Main Beach and the Pacific coastline. The multilevel dining patios serve hearty breakfasts and coastal seafood for lunch and dinner. **Known for:** some of Laguna Beach's best ocean-view dining; reservations necessary; splurge-worthy seafood towers. ⑤ *Average main: $35* ⊠ *577 S. Coast Hwy.* ☎ *949/494–1956* ⊕ *www. thecliffrestaurant.com.*

Gelato Paradiso

$ | EUROPEAN | Each morning this gelato shop makes fresh small batches of artisanal gelatos and dairy-free sorbettos in a variety of appealing flavors. Located in back of the charming Peppertree Lane shopping center, there is a small outdoor patio where people gather to enjoy the authentic Italian gelato after a day at the beach or to cap off an evening. **Known for:** authentic Italian gelato; fruit flavors; patio gathering spot. ⑤ *Average main: $6* ⊠ *Peppertree Lane , 448 S. Coast Hwy.* ☎ *949/464–9255* ⊕ *www.gelatoparadiso. com.*

★ Las Brisas

$$ | MEXICAN FUSION | FAMILY | Located in what used to be the Victor Hugo Inn, Las Brisas is now a Laguna Beach landmark restaurant. Sit on the expansive patio to take in the spectacular coastline views while enjoying signature margaritas and coastal Mexican cuisine with a California twist. **Known for:** fresh seafood; panoramic coastal views; reservations a must. ⑤ *Average main: $30* ⊠ *361 Cliff Dr.*

☎ *949/497–5434* ⊕ *www.lasbrisaslagu-nabeach.com.*

The Rooftop Lounge
$$ | AMERICAN | Another popular sunset cocktail and light dinner venue in South Laguna for its views. Located at the top of La Casa del Camino, be sure to make a reservation to sit at a front row table to watch the sun lower behind Catalina Island. **Known for:** spectacular sunset views; craft cocktails; burgers, pasta, salads and sandwiches. ⑤ *Average main: $30* ✉ *1289 S. Coast Hwy.* ☎ *949/497–2446* ⊕ *www.rooftoplagunabeach.com.*

Sapphire
$$ | INTERNATIONAL | FAMILY | This Laguna Beach establishment set in a historic Craftsman-style building is part gourmet pantry (a must-stop for your every picnic need) and part global dining adventure. Enjoy comfort cuisine from around the world paired with an eclectic wine and beer list. **Known for:** sapphire salad; weekend brunch; pet-friendly patio. ⑤ *Average main: $30* ✉ *The Old Pottery Place, 1200 S. Coast Hwy.* ☎ *949/715–9888* ⊕ *www.sapphirelagunabeach.com.*

★ Studio
$$$$ | MODERN AMERICAN | In a nod to Laguna's art history, Studio has house-made specialties that entice the eye as well as the palate. The restaurant occupies its own Craftsman-style bungalow, atop a 50-foot bluff overlooking Treasure Island Park and the Pacific coastline. **Known for:** chef's creative tasting menu; great spot for special occasions; California coastal dishes with a French flair. ⑤ *Average main: $75* ✉ *30801 S. Coast Hwy.* ☎ *949/715–6030* ⊕ *www.studiolagunabeach.com* ☾ *No lunch.*

Taco Loco
$ | MEXICAN | FAMILY | This may look like a fast-food taco stand, and the hemp blackened burgers and brownies on the menu may make you think the kitchen's *really* laid-back, but the quality of the food here equals that in many higher-price

restaurants. Some Mexican standards get a seafood twist, like swordfish, calamari, and shrimp tacos. **Known for:** vegetarian tacos; sidewalk seating; surfer clientele. ⑤ *Average main: $16* ✉ *640 S. Coast Hwy.* ☎ *949/497–1635* ⊕ *www.lagunabeachmexicanfood.com.*

Urth Caffe
$$ | BAKERY | FAMILY | A local favorite for organic heirloom coffee and hand-blended fine organic teas, Urth is also the place to go for health-conscious breakfast dishes like an egg white and spinach breakfast panini. Sit outside on the charming garden patio looking out toward the Laguna Art Museum across the street. **Known for:** health-conscious cuisine; organic coffee and tea; long lines on the patio during peak hours and weekends. ⑤ *Average main: $20* ✉ *308 N. Pacific Coast Hwy.* ☎ *949/376–8888* ⊕ *www.urthcaffe.com/laguna-beach.*

Zinc Café and Market
$ | AMERICAN | FAMILY | Families flock to this small Laguna Beach institution for reasonably priced breakfast and lunch options. Try the signature quiches or poached egg dishes in the morning, or swing by later in the day for healthy salads, homemade soups, quesadillas, or pizzettes. **Known for:** gourmet pastries, some gluten-free; avocado toast; busy outdoor patio. ⑤ *Average main: $18* ✉ *350 Ocean Ave.* ☎ *949/494–6302* ⊕ *www.zinccafe.com* ☾ *No dinner Nov.–Apr.*

🛏 Hotels

Inn at Laguna Beach
$$$ | HOTEL | FAMILY | This golden local landmark is stacked neatly on the hillside at the north end of Laguna's Main Beach and it's one of the few hotels in the area set almost on the sand. **Pros:** rooftop with fabulous ocean views; beach essentials provided; beachfront location. **Cons:** ocean-view rooms are pricey; tiny hot tub; some rooms are dark and small.

⑤ *Rooms from: $379* ⊠ *211 N. Coast Hwy.* ☎ *949/497–9722, 800/544–4479* ⊕ *www.innatlagunabeach.com* ⇘ *70 rooms* ⦿| *No meals.*

La Casa del Camino

$$ | **HOTEL** | The look is Old California at the 1929-built La Casa del Camino, with dark woods, arched doors, wrought iron, and a beautiful tiled fireplace in the lobby. **Pros:** breathtaking views from rooftop lounge; modern decor; steps to the beach. **Cons:** some rooms face the highway; pipes can be noisy; some rooms are small. ⑤ *Rooms from: $225* ⊠ *1289 S. Coast Hwy.* ☎ *949/497–6029, 855/634–5736* ⊕ *www.lacasadelcamino. com* ⇘ *36 rooms* ⦿| *Free breakfast.*

★ Montage Laguna Beach

$$$$ | **RESORT** | **FAMILY** | Built on a picturesque coastal bluff above the Pacific Ocean and Treasure Island Beach, this elegant Craftsmen-style resort features 30 acres of grassy lawns, soft sand beaches, and a marine sanctuary. **Pros:** picturesque coastal location; stunning tiled mosaic swimming pool; residential style villas with sweeping ocean views. **Cons:** one of the area's priciest resorts, especially during holidays or summer weekends; $60 valet parking; $42 daily resort fee. ⑤ *Rooms from: $895* ⊠ *30801 S. Coast Hwy.* ☎ *949/715–6000, 866/271–6953* ⊕ *www.montagehotels.com/lagunabeach* ⇘ *258 rooms* ⦿| *No meals.*

★ Surf and Sand Resort

$$$$ | **RESORT** | **FAMILY** | One mile south of downtown, on an exquisite stretch of beach with thundering waves and gorgeous rocks, this is a getaway for those who want a boutique hotel experience without all the formalities. **Pros:** easy sandy beach access; intimate boutique resort; good restaurant with wonderful views. **Cons:** pricey valet parking; surf can be loud; no air-conditioning (but overhead fans help). ⑤ *Rooms from: $450* ⊠ *1555 S. Coast Hwy.* ☎ *877/741–5908* ⊕ *www. surfandsandresort.com* ⇘ *167 rooms* ⦿| *No meals.*

⬤ Shopping

Coast Highway, Forest and Ocean avenues, and Glenneyre Street are full of art galleries, fine jewelry stores, souvenir shops, and clothing boutiques.

Adam Neeley Fine Art Jewelry

JEWELRY/ACCESSORIES | Be prepared to be dazzled at Adam Neeley Fine Art Jewelry, where artisan proprietor Adam Neeley creates one-of-a-kind modern pieces. ⊠ *352 N. Coast Hwy.* ☎ *949/715–0953* ⊕ *www.adamneeley.com.*

Art for the Soul

CRAFTS | A riot of color, Art for the Soul has hand-painted furniture, crafts, and unusual whimsical gifts. ⊠ *272 Forest Ave.* ☎ *949/675–1791* ⊕ *www.ra4ts.com.*

Candy Baron

FOOD/CANDY | **FAMILY** | Get your sugar fix at the time-warped Candy Baron, filled with old-fashioned goodies like gumdrops, licorice, bull's-eyes, sugar-free candies, and more than 50 flavors of saltwater taffy. ⊠ *231 Forest Ave.* ☎ *949/497–7508* ⊕ *www.thecandybaron.com.*

La Rue du Chocolat

FOOD/CANDY | Located off the PCH in the quaint Peppertree Lane boutique shopping center, this sophisticated chocolate and truffle shop sells handcrafted seasonal chocolates, chocolate-covered strawberries, and creative holiday treats. ⊠ *Peppertree La., 448 S. Coast Hwy., Suite B* ☎ *949/494–2372* ⊕ *www.laruedu-chocolat.com.*

San Juan Capistrano

5 miles north of Dana Point, 60 miles north of San Diego.

San Juan Capistrano is best known for its historic mission, where the swallows traditionally return each year, migrating from their winter haven in Argentina, but these days they are more likely to choose other local sites for nesting. St. Joseph's

Mission San Juan Capistrano was founded in 1776.

Day, March 19, launches a week of fowl festivities. Charming antiques stores, which range from pricey to cheap, line Camino Capistrano.

GETTING HERE AND AROUND

If you arrive by train, which is far more romantic and restful than battling freeway traffic, you'll be dropped off across from the mission at the San Juan Capistrano depot. With its appealing brick café and preserved Santa Fe cars, the depot retains much of the magic of early American railroads. If driving, park near Ortega and Camino Capistrano, the city's main streets.

◉ Sights

★ Los Rios Historic District

NEIGHBORHOOD | FAMILY | Take a walk back in time on the oldest residential street in Southern California, where houses date back to 1790. The Silvas Adobe is a typical example of the dozen or more one-room adobes in the area. Mission San Juan Capistrano was the first Californian

mission to allow workers to live outside the mission grounds. On the street you'll also find the Historical Society Museum and the ZOOMARS petting zoo for families. Shopping and dining options abound. ✉ 31831 Los Rios St. ☎ 949/493–8444 ⊕ www.nps.gov.

★ Mission San Juan Capistrano

RELIGIOUS SITE | FAMILY | Founded in 1776 by Father Junípero Serra (consecrated as St. Serra), Mission San Juan Capistrano was one of two Roman Catholic outposts between Los Angeles and San Diego. The Great Stone Church, begun in 1797, is the largest structure created by the Spanish in California. After extensive retrofitting, the golden-hued interiors are open to visitors who may feel they are touring among ruins in Italy rather than the O.C. Many of the mission's adobe buildings have been restored to illustrate mission life, with exhibits of an olive millstone, tallow ovens, tanning vats, metalworking furnaces, and the padres' living quarters. The beautiful gardens, with their fountains and koi pond, are a lovely spot in which to wander. The bougainvillea-covered Serra Chapel is believed to be the oldest church still standing in California and is the only building remaining in which St. Serra actually led Mass. Enter via a small gift shop in the gatehouse. ✉ *26801 Ortega Hwy.* ☎ *949/234–1300* ⊕ *www.missionsjc.com* 🎫 *$14.*

San Juan Capistrano Library

LIBRARY | FAMILY | Near Mission San Juan Capistrano is the San Juan Capistrano Library, a postmodern structure built in 1983. Architect Michael Graves combined classical and Mission styles to striking effect. Its courtyard has secluded places for reading. ✉ *31495 El Camino Real* ☎ *949/493–1752* ⊕ *ocpl.org/libloc/sjc* 🕐 *Closed Sun. and Mon.*

🍴 Restaurants

Cedar Creek Inn

$$ | AMERICAN | FAMILY | Just across the street from Mission San Juan Capistrano, this restaurant has a patio that's perfect for a late lunch or a romantic dinner. The menu is fairly straightforward, dishes are tasty, and portions are substantial—try the Cobb salad or a burger at lunch, or splurge on the prime rib for dinner. **Known for:** gluten-free and vegetarian options; rich desserts; comfortable seating. ⑤ *Average main: $30* ✉ *26860 Ortega Hwy.* ☎ *949/240–2229* ⊕ *www. cedarcreekinn.com.*

L'Hirondelle

$$$ | FRENCH | Locals have romanced at cozy tables for decades at this delightful restaurant directly across from the San Juan Capistrano Mission. Such classic dishes as beef bourguignon and a New York strip in a black-peppercorn-and-brandy sauce are the hallmarks of this French and Belgian restaurant, whose name means "the little swallow." The extensive wine list is matched by an impressive selection of Belgian beers. **Known for:** popular Sunday brunch; traditional French and Belgian cuisine; good Belgian beer

selection. ⑤ *Average main: $39* ✉ *31631 Camino Capistrano* ☎ *949/661–0425* ⊕ *www.lhirondellesjc.com* 🕐 *Closed Mon.*

The Ramos House Cafe

$$$ | AMERICAN | It may be worth hopping the Amtrak to San Juan Capistrano just for the chance to have breakfast or lunch at one of Orange County's most beloved restaurants, located in a historic board-and-batten home dating back to 1881. This café sits practically on the railroad tracks across from the depot—nab a table on the patio and dig into a hearty breakfast featuring seasonal items, such as the smoked bacon scramble with wilted rocket and apple fried potatoes. **Known for:** Southern specialties; weekend brunch; historic setting. ⑤ *Average main: $35* ✉ *31752 Los Rios St.* ☎ *949/443–1342* ⊕ *www.ramoshouse.com* 🕐 *Closed Wed. No dinner.*

🛏 Hotels

★ Inn at the Mission San Juan Capistrano

$$$ | HOTEL | FAMILY | This family-friendly hacienda-style boutique hotel is located across the street from the famed San Juan Capistrano Mission, and the property incorporates this history by featuring glass mission bell lighting fixtures and equestrian decor and art. **Pros:** great location next to the mission; terrific culinary program; luxury rooms and suites. **Cons:** guests may hear freeway noise; beach is just less than 3 miles away; expensive parking. ⑤ *Rooms from: $350* ✉ *31692 El Camino Real* ☎ *949/503–5700* ⊕ *www. marriott.com* ⬑ *135 rooms* ⑩ *No meals.*

★ Ritz-Carlton, Laguna Niguel

$$$$ | RESORT | FAMILY | Combine the Ritz-Carlton's top-tier level of service with an unparalleled view of the Pacific, and you're in the lap of luxury at this resort. **Pros:** beautiful grounds and views; luxurious bedding; sophisticated service. **Cons:** some rooms are small for the price; in-house dining prices are high;

$50 resort fee. $ *Rooms from: $685* ⊠ *1 Ritz-Carlton Dr., Dana Point* ☎ *949/240–2000, 800/542–8680* ⊕ *www.ritzcarlton. com/en/hotels/california/laguna-niguel* ⤴ *396 rooms* ❑ *No meals.*

ⓨ Nightlife

Swallow's Inn

BARS/PUBS | Across the way from Mission San Juan Capistrano you may spot a line of Harleys in front of the down-home and downright funky Swallow's Inn. Despite a somewhat tough look, it attracts all kinds—bikers, surfers, modern-day cowboys, grandparents—for a drink, a casual bite, karaoke nights, and some rowdy live country music. ⊠ *31786 Camino Capistrano* ☎ *949/493–3188* ⊕ *www. swallowsinn.com.*

Catalina Island

Just 22 miles out from the L.A. coastline, across from Newport Beach and Long Beach, Catalina has virtually unspoiled mountains, canyons, coves, and beaches; best of all, it gives you a glimpse of what undeveloped Southern California once looked like.

Water sports are a big draw, as divers and snorkelers come for the exceptionally clear water surrounding the island. Kayakers are attracted to the calm cove waters and thrill seekers book the eco-themed zipline that traverses a wooded canyon. The main town, Avalon, is a charming, old-fashioned beach community, where yachts and pleasure boats bob in the crescent bay. Wander beyond the main drag and find brightly painted little bungalows fronting the sidewalks; golf carts are the preferred mode of transport.

In 1919, William Wrigley Jr., the chewing-gum magnate, purchased a controlling interest in the company developing Catalina Island, whose most famous landmark, the Casino, was built in 1929

under his orders. Because he owned the Chicago Cubs baseball team, Wrigley made Catalina the team's spring training site, an arrangement that lasted until 1951.

In 1975, the Catalina Island Conservancy, a nonprofit foundation, acquired about 88% of the island to help preserve the area's natural flora and fauna, including the bald eagle and the Catalina Island fox. These days the conservancy is restoring the rugged interior country with plantings of native grasses and trees. The organization helps oversee the interior's 50 miles of bike trails and 165 miles of hiking trails and helps protect the island's 60 endemic species. Along the coast you might spot oddities like electric perch, saltwater goldfish, and flying fish.

GETTING HERE AND AROUND
FERRY TRAVEL

Two companies offer ferry service to Catalina Island. The boats have both indoor and outdoor seating and snack bars. Excessive baggage is not allowed, and there are extra fees for bicycles and surfboards. The waters around Catalina can get rough, so if you're prone to seasickness, come prepared. Winter, holiday, and weekend schedules vary, so reservations are strongly recommended.

Catalina Express makes an hour-long run from Long Beach or San Pedro to Avalon and a 90-minute run from Dana Point to Avalon with some stops at Two Harbors. Round-trip fares begin at $73.50, with discounts for seniors and kids. On busy days, a $15 upgrade to the Commodore Lounge, when available, is worth it. Service from Newport Beach to Avalon is available through the *Catalina Flyer*. The boat leaves from Balboa Pavilion at 9 am (in season), takes 75 minutes to reach the island, and costs $70 round-trip. The return boat leaves Catalina at 4:30 pm. Reservations are required for the *Catalina Flyer* and recommended for all weekend and summer trips. ■**TIP→ Keep an eye**

out for dolphins, which sometimes swim alongside the ferries.

FERRY CONTACTS Catalina Express. ✉ *320 Golden Shore, Long Beach* ☎ *562/485–3200* ⊕ *www.catalinaexpress.com.* **Catalina Flyer.** ✉ *Balboa Pier, 400 Main St., Newport Beach* ☎ *949/673–5245* ⊕ *www.catalinainfo.com.*

GOLF CARTS

Golf carts constitute the island's main form of transportation for sightseeing in the area; however, some parts of town are off-limits, as is the island's interior. Drivers 21 and over with valid driver's license can rent them along Avalon's Crescent Avenue and Pebbly Beach Road for about $50 per hour with a $50 deposit, payable via cash only.

GOLF CART RENTALS Island Rentals. ✉ *125 Pebbly Beach Rd., Avalon* ☎ *310/510–1456* ⊕ *www.catalinagolfcartrentals.com.*

TIMING

Although Catalina can be seen in one thrilling day, several inviting hotels make it worth extending your stay for one or more nights. A short itinerary might include breakfast on the pier, a tour of the interior, a snorkeling excursion at Casino Point, or beach day at the Descanso Beach Club and a romantic waterfront dinner in Avalon.

After late October, rooms are much easier to find on short notice, rates drop dramatically, and many hotels offer packages that include transportation from the mainland and/or sightseeing tours. January to March you have a good chance of spotting migrating gray whales on the ferry crossing.

TOURS

Santa Catalina Island Company runs both land tours and ocean tours, including the *Flying Fish* boat trip (summer evenings only); a comprehensive inland motor tour; a tour of Skyline Drive; several Casino tours; a scenic tour of Avalon;

a glass-bottom-boat tour; an undersea tour on a semisubmersible vessel; an eco-themed zipline tour that traverses a scenic canyon, a speedy Ocean Runner expedition that searches for all manner of sea creatures and a fast Cyclone boat tour that takes you to the less populated center of the island, Two Harbors. Reservations are highly recommended for the inland tours. Tours cost $22 to $130. There are ticket booths on the Green Pleasure Pier, in the plaza, and at the boat landing. Catalina Adventure Tours, which has booths at the boat landing and on the pier, also arranges excursions at comparable prices.

The Catalina Island Conservancy organizes custom ecotours and hikes of the interior. Naturalist guides drive open jeeps through some gorgeously untrammeled parts of the island. Tours start at $70 per person for a two-hour trip (two-person minimum). The tours run year-round.

CONTACTS Catalina Adventure Tours. ✉ *302 Pebbly Beach Rd., Avalon* ☎ *562/432–8828* ⊕ *www.catalinaadventuretours.com.* **Catalina Island Conservancy.** ✉ *708 Crescent Ave., Avalon* ☎ *310/510–2595* ⊕ *www.catalinaconservancy.org.* **Santa Catalina Island Company.** ☎ *877/778–8322* ⊕ *www.visitcatalinaisland.com.*

Avalon

A 1- to 2-hour ferry ride from Long Beach, Newport Beach, or San Pedro.

Avalon, Catalina's only real town, extends from the shore of its natural harbor to the surrounding hillsides. Its resident population is about 3,800, but it swells with tourists on summer weekends. Most of the city's activity, however, is centered on the pedestrian mall on Crescent Avenue, and most sights are easily reached on foot. Private cars are restricted and rental cars aren't allowed, but taxis, trams, and shuttles can take you anywhere you need

to go. Bicycles, electric bikes, and golf carts can be rented from shops along Crescent Avenue.

◉ Sights

★ Casino
BUILDING | Built in 1929, this circular white structure is one of the finest examples of art deco architecture anywhere. Its Spanish-inspired floors and murals gleam with brilliant marine blue and sea foam green Catalina tiles. In this case, *casino,* the Italian word for "gathering place," has nothing to do with gambling. The circular ballroom once famously hosted 1940s big bands and is still used for gala events. The Santa Catalina Island Company leads two narrated walking tours of the Casino. ⊠ *1 Casino Way* ☎ *310/510–0179* ⊕ *www. visitcatalinaisland.com.*

Casino Point Dive Park
BEACH—SIGHT | **FAMILY** | In front of the Casino are the crystal clear waters of the Casino Point Dive Park, a protected marine preserve where moray eels, bat rays, spiny lobsters, harbor seals, and the bright orange Garibaldi (California's state marine fish) cruise around kelp forests and along the sandy bottom. No need to don a wet suit: the brilliantly orange Garibaldi, can sometimes be viewed from the seawall. It's a terrific site for scuba diving, with some shallow areas suitable for snorkeling. Equipment can be rented on and near the pier. The shallow waters of Lover's Cove, east of the boat landing, are also good for snorkeling. ⊠ *1 Casino Way* ⊕ *www.divingcatalina.com.*

Catalina Island Museum
MUSEUM | **FAMILY** | The exterior of the Catalina Island Museum is a nod to Catalina Island's developer William Wrigley Jr.—it's modeled after Wrigley Field in Chicago. Inside the interactive museum visitors can learn about the island's history from the native Chumash people to its role in Hollywood history and beyond. Two galleries host traveling exhibitions.

Catalina's Bison ◉

Zane Grey, the writer who put the Western novel on the map, spent a lot of time on Catalina, and his influence is still evident in a peculiar way. As the story goes, when the movie version of Grey's book *The Vanishing American* was filmed here in 1924, American bison were ferried across from the mainland to give the land that western plains look. After the crew packed up and left, the buffalo stayed, and a small herd of about 150 still remains, grazing the interior.

The view from the outside terrace takes in lovely Avalon and its picturesque harbor. A small gift shop offers Catalina-themed souvenirs and reproductions of the island's signature colorful Catalina pottery tiles. ⊠ *217 Metropole Ave.* ☎ *310/510–2414* ⊕ *www.catalinamuseum.org* ▨ *$17* ⊘ *Closed Mon. and Tues.*

Green Pleasure Pier
LOCAL INTEREST | **FAMILY** | Head to the Green Pleasure Pier for a good vantage point of Avalon. On the pier you can find the visitor information, snack stands, and scads of squawking seagulls. It's also the landing where visiting cruise-ship passengers catch tenders back out to their ship. ⊠ *1 Green Pleasure Pier* ⊕ *www. lovecatalina.com.*

Wrigley Memorial and Botanic Garden
GARDEN | **FAMILY** | Two miles south of the bay is Wrigley Memorial and Botanic Garden, home to many plants native only to Southern California and the Channel Islands. Today there are five different sections where you can see Catalina ironwood, wild tomato, and rare Catalina mahogany. The Wrigley family

commissioned the garden as well as the monument, which has a grand staircase and a Spanish-style mausoleum inlaid with colorful Catalina tile. Wrigley Jr. was once buried here but his remains were moved to Glendale, CA, during World War II. ⊠ *Avalon Canyon Rd.* ☎ *310/510–2897* ⊕ *www.catalinaconservancy.org* 🖾 *$8.*

🍴 Restaurants

Bluewater Grill

$$ | SEAFOOD | FAMILY | Overlooking the ferry landing and the entire harbor, the open-to-the-salt-air Bluewater Grill offers freshly caught fish, savory chowders, and all manner of shellfish. If they're on the menu, don't miss the swordfish steak, the lobster roll, or the sand dabs. **Known for:** fresh local fish; handcrafted cocktails; overwater harbor views. ⑤ *Average main: $30* ⊠ *306 Crescent Ave.* ☎ *310/510–3474* ⊕ *www.bluewatergrill.com.*

Descanso Beach Club

$ | AMERICAN | FAMILY | Set on an expansive deck overlooking the water, Descanso Beach Club serves a wide range of favorites: grilled burgers, street tacos, clam chowder, salads, and layered nachos are all part of the selection. Watch the harbor seals frolic just offshore while sipping the island's supersweet signature cocktail, the Buffalo Milk, a mix of fruit liqueurs, vodka, and whipped cream. **Known for:** tropical beach vibe; scenic views; chic cabana rentals. ⑤ *Average main: $12* ⊠ *Descanso Beach, 1 Descanso Ave.* ☎ *310/510–7410* ⊕ *www.visitcatalinaisland.com.*

★ Eric's on the Pier

$ | AMERICAN | This little snack bar has been an Avalon family–run institution since the 1920s. It's a good place to people-watch while drinking a draft beer and munching on a breakfast burrito, fish-and-chips, or signature buffalo burger. **Known for:** comfort foods; quick eats; beachside location. ⑤ *Average main: $15* ⊠ *2 Green Pier* ☎ *310/510–0894* ⊕ *www.lovecatalina.com/listing/erics-on-the-pier/23.*

The Lobster Trap

$$ | SEAFOOD | Seafood rules at the Lobster Trap—the restaurant's owner has his own boat and fishes for the catch of the day and, in season, spiny lobster. Ceviche is a great starter, always fresh and brightly flavored. **Known for:** locally caught seafood; convivial atmosphere; locals' hangout. ⑤ *Average main: $25* ⊠ *128 Catalina St.* ☎ *310/510–8585* ⊕ *catalinalobstertrap.com.*

Steve's Steakhouse and Seafood

$$$ | STEAKHOUSE | FAMILY | Within spitting distance of the bay, this second-floor restaurant keeps hungry diners happy with sizzling steaks and slow-cooked baby back ribs. There's also ample seafood, such as locally caught swordfish and shrimp. **Known for:** friendly staff; water views; steak and seafood dinners. ⑤ *Average main: $32* ⊠ *417 Crescent Ave.* ☎ *310/510–0333* ⊕ *www.stevessteakhouse.com.*

🏨 Hotels

Aurora Hotel

$$ | HOTEL | In a town dominated by historic properties, the Aurora is refreshingly contemporary, with a hip attitude and sleek furnishings. **Pros:** trendy design; quiet location off main drag; close to restaurants. **Cons:** standard rooms are small; no elevator; two-night minimum stay required. ⑤ *Rooms from: $279* ⊠ *137 Marilla Ave.* ☎ *310/510–0454* ⊕ *www.auroracatalina.com* 🛏 *18 rooms* �“❘ *Free breakfast.*

Bellanca Hotel

$$ | HOTEL | One of the closest boutique hotels to the Catalina Casino, this European-style hotel creates an intimate feel with brick courtyards and serene suites. **Pros:** romantic setting; close to beach; expansive sundeck with comfortable lounge furniture. **Cons:** ground-floor rooms can hear golf carts drive by; some rooms are on the small side; no elevator. $ *Rooms from: $299* ✉ *111 Crescent Ave.* ☎ *310/510–0555, 888/510–0555* ⊕ *www.bellancahotel.com* 🛏 *35 rooms* ❍ *No meals.*

★ Hotel Atwater

$$ | **HOTEL** | **FAMILY** | Just one block from the beach in the center of Avalon, Hotel Atwater originally opened in 1920 and was recently redesigned to honor Helen Atwater's (daugher-in-law of famed local William Wrigley) impeccable sense of style and deep love for Catalina Island. **Pros:** unique and historical decor; central location; nice amenities. **Cons:** some rooms have street noise; certain rooms on the small side; not on the beach. $ *Rooms from: $269* ✉ *125 Sumner Ave.* ☎ *310/510–1789* ⊕ *www.visitcatalinaisland.com* 🛏 *95 rooms* ❍ *No meals.*

Hotel Mac Rae

$ | **HOTEL** | Family-owned for more than a century, the fourth generation now operates this boutique hotel right on Crescent Avenue, with a few rooms overlooking the beach and Avalon Bay. One of the best-priced hotels next to the beach, guests receive a complimentary continental breakfast; beach towels; Internet access; and after checkout luggage storage and shower facility to use after spending a day at the beach and before boarding a return boat home. **Pros:** great value for location; spectacular beachfront views; free breakfast. **Cons:** no elevator and hotel is on the second floor; basic rooms and furniture; restaurants and bars below can mean noise in the evening. $ *Rooms from: $150* ✉ *409 Crescent Ave.* ☎ *310/510–0246* ⊕ *www.HotelMacRae.com* 🛏 *26 rooms* ❍ *Free breakfast.*

Hotel Vista del Mar

$$ | **HOTEL** | **FAMILY** | On the bay-facing Crescent Avenue, this third-floor property is steps from the beach, where complimentary towels, chairs, and umbrellas await guests. **Pros:** comfortable beds; central location; in-room fireplace. **Cons:** no restaurant or spa facilities; few rooms with ocean views; no elevator. $ *Rooms from: $235* ✉ *417 Crescent Ave.* ☎ *310/510–1452, 800/601–3836* ⊕ *www.hotel-vistadelmar.com* 🛏 *14 rooms* ❍ *Free breakfast.*

Mt. Ada

$$$$ | **B&B/INN** | If you stay in the 1921 mansion where Wrigley Jr. once lived, you can enjoy all the comforts of a millionaire's home—at a millionaire's prices. **Pros:** a step back in timeless charm; all-inclusive services, including complimentary shuttle from ferry dock; incredible canyon, bay, and ocean views. **Cons:** some rooms and bathrooms are small; a far walk into town; expensive. $ *Rooms from: $600* ✉ *398 Wrigley Rd.* ☎ *310/510–7330* ⊕ *www.visitcatalinaisland.com* 🛏 *6 rooms* ❍ *All-inclusive.*

Pavilion Hotel

$$ | **HOTEL** | **FAMILY** | This mid-century modern–style hotel is Avalon's most citified spot, though just a few steps from the sand. **Pros:** steps from the beach and harbor; plush bedding; chic decor. **Cons:** no pool; rooms near stairs can be noisy; no elevator. $ *Rooms from: $275* ✉ *513 Crescent Ave.* ☎ *310/510–1788* ⊕ *www.visitcatalinaisland.com* 🛏 *71 rooms* ❍ *No meals.*

★ Zane Grey Pueblo

$$$$ | **HOTEL** | The prolific best-selling Western novelist Zane Grey built his home as a retreat to take in the views of Avalon while writing over 100 books; his home was turned into this quaint boutique hotel in 1939. **Pros:** breathtaking views; complimentary continental breakfast; heated swimming pool with ocean views. **Cons:** three-story addition has no elevator; a hike up a hill from town; bell tower chimes can be loud for some people. $ *Rooms from: $400* ✉ *199 Chimes Tower Rd.* ☎ *310/510–0966* ⊕ *www.zanegreyhotel.com* 🛏 *17 rooms* ❍ *Free breakfast.*

🏃 Activities

BICYCLING
Brown's Bikes
BICYCLING | FAMILY | Look for rentals on Crescent Avenue and Pebbly Beach Road, where Brown's Bikes is located. Beach cruisers start at $25 per day, mountain bikes are $30 per day, and electric bikes are $50 for a day rental, and a good choice for Catalina's hills. ✉ *107 Pebbly Beach Rd.* ☎ *310/510–0986* ⊕ *www.catalinabiking.com.*

DIVING AND SNORKELING
The Casino Point Underwater Park, with its handful of wrecks and ample sea life, is best suited for diving. Lover's Cove is better for snorkeling (but you'll share the area with glass-bottom boats). Both are protected marine preserves.

Catalina Divers Supply
SCUBA DIVING | Head to Catalina Divers Supply to rent equipment, sign up for guided scuba and snorkel tours, and attend certification classes. It also has an outpost at the Dive Park at Casino Point and one on the Green Pleasure Pier. Both offer gear rental and tank air fills. ✉ *1 Casino Way* ☎ *310/510–0330* ⊕ *www. catalinadiverssupply.com.*

HIKING
Catalina Island Conservancy
HIKING/WALKING | FAMILY | Permits from the Catalina Island Conservancy are required for hiking into Santa Catalina Island's rugged interior, where there are more than 165 miles of trails of all levels to explore. If you plan to backpack overnight, you'll need a camping reservation. The interior is dry and desertlike; bring plenty of water, sunblock, a hat, and all necessary supplies. The permits are free or you can make a donation to the Conservancy. You don't need a permit for shorter hikes, such as the 20-minute one from Avalon to the Wrigley Botanical Garden. It's also possible to hike between Avalon and Two Harbors, starting at the Hogsback Gate, above Avalon, but the 28-mile journey has an elevation gain of 3,000 feet and is not for the weak. ■TIP→ **For a pleasant 4-mile hike out of Avalon, take Avalon Canyon Road to the Wrigley Botanical Garden and follow the trail to Lone Pine. At the top there's an amazing view of the Palisades cliffs and, beyond them, the sea.** ✉ *708 Crescent Ave.* ☎ *310/510–2595* ⊕ *www.catalina-conservancy.org.*

Index

Photo Credits

Front Cover: Jon Arnold Images Ltd / Alamy Stock Photo [Description: The Broad, a contemporary art museum built in 2015 in Los Angeles.]. **Back cover, from left to right:** TierneyMJ/Shutterstock, Boarding1Now/iStockphoto, Cameron Venti/Shutterstock. **Spine:** JingleBeeZ Photo Gallery/Shutterstock. **Interior, from left to right:** 4nadia/iStockphoto (1). choness/iStockphoto (2). ames sf/Flickr, [CC BY-SA 2.0] (5). **Chapter 1: Experience Los Angeles:** Jill Krueger (6-7). Courtesy of Walt Disney Concert Hall (8). Marco Rubino (9). Visit Santa Monica (9). Matt Marriott/Courtesy of Los Angeles Tourism (10). Walter Cicchetti/Shutterstock (10). Courtesy of Los Angeles County Museum of Art (10). Hamilton Pytluk/Universal Studios Hollywood (10). Lux Blue/shutterstock (11). Mike Kelley/Courtesy The Broad (11). Julia-Bogdanova/Shutterstock (12). Courtesy of Los Angeles Tourism (12). Courtesy of Los Angeles Tourism (12). Carl Yu (12). Ershov_Maks/iStockphoto (13). Briana Edwards/Paramount studios (14). Kevinleestudio7 | Dreamstime.com (14). Courtesy of Los Angeles Tourism (14). egdigital/iStockphoto (14). OLOS/shutterstock (15). Courtesy of Griffith Observatory (15). www.nicholasnicholas.com (20). Suzanne Pratt/Shutterstock (21). Kim.jihoon/shutterstock (22). Jon Bilous - Dreamstime.com (22). Rosana Scapinello/Dreamstime (22). DavidMSchrader/Dreamstime (22). Lucky-photographer/Shutterstock (23). divanov/shutterstock.com (24). Jill Krueger (24). Donald Riddle Images (24). Lisa Bronitt/Shutterstock (24). Sean Pavone/shutterstock (25). www.nicholasnicholas.com (26). Pinz Bowling Center (26). The Hollywood Roosevelt (26). The Grove (26). ROB STARK (27). Henry Hargreaves (27). Catch Hospitality Group (27). Chateau Mormont (27). Tina Whatcott (28). Courtesy of Cole's French Dip (29). Jill Krueger (30). Mitchblatt/Dreamstime (31). **Chapter 3: Santa Monica and Venice with Brentwood and Sawtelle Japantown:** Appalachianviews | Dreamstime.com (57). Asterixvs | Dreamstime.com (62). Ingus Kruklitis/iStockphoto (64). ViewApart/iStockphoto (71). arkantostock | Dreamstime.com (72). Naki Kouyioumtzis / age fotostock (74). ames sf/Flickr, [CC BY-SA 2.0] (75). Pygmy Warrior/Flickr, [CC BY-SA 2.0] (75). alonzoD/Flickr, [CC BY-SA 2.0] (75). Anton J. Geisser / age fotostock (75). Wolterk | Dreamstime.com (78). Biker x days/Shutterstock. (81). **Chapter 4: Beverly Hills with Culver City:** Andrew Zarivny/Shutterstock (83). gregobagel/iStockphoto (88). Scott Leigh/iStockphoto (90-91). Stella Levi/iStockphoto (96). Wolterk/iStockphoto (99). **Chapter 5: West Hollywood and Fairfax:** Michael Gordon/Shutterstock. (101). Heeb Christian / age fotostock (108). stevelyon/Flickr, [CC BY-SA 2.0] (109). Neil Emmerson / age fotostock (109). Kjetil Ree/Wikimedia Commons (110). IK's World Trip/Flickr, [CC BY-SA 2.0] (110). Hyatt (111). Stepan Mazurov/Flickr, [CC BY-SA 2.0] (111). mertxe iturrioz/Flickr, [CC BY-SA 2.0] (111). Mike Simpson/iStockphoto (112). **viv**/Flickr, [CC BY-SA 2.0] (112). 4kclips/Shutterstock. (116). Justin Higuchi (119). ChrisGoldNY/Flickr (123). **Chapter 6: Hollywood and the Studios:** Sepavo | Dreamstime.com (125). Chicco7 | Dreamstime.com (132). Gary Bembridge/Flickr, [CC BY 2.0] (134). Davel5957 (136). DAVID SPRAGUE (147). **Chapter 7: Mid-Wilshire and Koreatown:** Michael Gordon/Shutterstock. (155). Steve Cukrov/Shutterstock. (161). **Chapter 8: Downtown Los Angeles:** Eddie Hernandez Photography (165). Biansho | Dreamstime.com (170). Merkuri2 | Dreamstime.com (172). Usataro | Dreamstime.com (174). f11photo/Shutterstock. (179). Lilyling1982 | Dreamstime.com (181). Jakob N. Layman (183). michael balderas/iStockphoto (189). Trujillo Paumie (189). tannazie/Flickr, [CC BY-SA 2.0] (190). Tamsin Slater/Flickr, [CC BY-SA 2.0] (190). Atomazul | Dreamstime.com (190). Trujillo Paumie (190). Chez Jay (191). Meg Butler (191). bORjAmATiC/Flickr, [CC BY-SA 2.0] (191). Trujillo Paumie (191). rawkblog.blogspot.com/flickr, [CC BY-SA 2.0] (192). arnold | inuyaki/flickr, [CC BY-SA 2.0] (192). Never Cool in School / Leslie Kalohi/Flickr, [CC BY-SA 2.0] (192). Howard Wise (192). **Chapter 9: Los Feliz, Silver Lake, and the Eastside:** yhelfman/Shutterstock. (195). David Livingston/iStockphoto (196). Clinton Steeds/Flickr, [CC BY-SA 2.0] (197). wolfsavard/Flickr, [CC BY-SA 2.0] (197). Meinzahn/iStockphoto (200). **Chapter 10: Pasadena:** Kit Leong/Shutterstock. (219). James Casil/Shutterstock. (224). wikipedia.org (227). **Chapter 11: Malibu and the Beaches:** Nick Fox/Shutterstock. (231). Mark Roger Bailey/Shutterstock. (234). Benny Marty/Shutterstock. (238). Andy Konieczny/Shutterstock. (240). Kirk Wester/Shutterstock. (244-245) Rigucci/Shutterstock. (248). **Chapter 12: Disneyland and Orange County With Knott's Berry Farm and Catalina Island:** Jon Bilous/Shutterstock. (251). www.ericcastro.biz/Flickr, [CC BY-SA 2.0] (262). Ashley Hadzopoulos/Shutterstock. (272). KKfotostock/dreamstime. (275). www.rwongphoto.com / Alamy (278). Brett Shoaf/Artistic Visuals Photography (282). Alessandro Campagnolo/Shutterstock. (285). Steve Heap 2017 (290). **About Our Writers:** All photos are courtesy of the writers.

*Every effort has been made to trace the copyright holders, and we apologize in advance for any accidental errors. We would be happy to apply the corrections in the following edition of this publication.

Notes

Fodor's LOS ANGELES

Publisher: Stephen Horowitz, *General Manager*

Editorial: Douglas Stallings, *Editorial Director*; Jill Fergus, Amanda Sadlowski, Caroline Trefler, *Senior Editors*; Kayla Becker, Alexis Kelly, *Editors*

Design: Tina Malaney, *Director of Design and Production*; Jessica Gonzalez, *Graphic Designer*; Mariana Tabares, *Design & Production Intern*

Production: Jennifer DePrima, *Editorial Production Manager*; Elyse Rozelle, *Senior Production Editor*; Monica White, *Production Editor*

Maps: Rebecca Baer, *Senior Map Editor*; David Lindroth, Mark Stroud (Moon Street Cartography), *Cartographers*

Photography: Viviane Teles, *Senior Photo Editor*; Namrata Aggarwal, Ashok Kumar, *Photo Editors*; Rebecca Rimmer, *Photo Intern*

Business & Operations: Chuck Hoover, *Chief Marketing Officer*; Robert Ames, *Group General Manager*; Devin Duckworth, *Director of Print Publishing*; Victor Bernal, *Business Analyst*

Public Relations and Marketing: Joe Ewaskiw, *Senior Director of Communications & Public Relations*

Fodors.com: Jeremy Tarr, *Editorial Director*; Rachael Levitt, *Managing Editor*

Technology: Jon Atkinson, *Director of Technology*; Rudresh Teotia, *Lead Developer*; Jacob Ashpis, *Content Operations Manager*

Writers: Paul Feinstein, Michelle Rae Uy, Jill Weinlein, Candice Yacono

Editor: Amanda Sadlowski

Production Editor: Monica White

29th Edition

ISBN 978-1-64097-406-7

ISSN 1095–3914

Library of Congress Control Number 2018966977

All details in this book are based on information supplied to us at press time. Always confirm information when it matters, especially if you're making a detour to visit a specific place. Fodor's expressly disclaims any liability, loss, or risk, personal or otherwise, that is incurred as a consequence of the use of any of the contents of this book.

SPECIAL SALES
This book is available at special discounts for bulk purchases for sales promotions or premiums. For more information, e-mail SpecialMarkets@fodors.com.

PRINTED IN CANADA

10 9 8 7 6 5 4 3 2 1

About Our Writers

Paul Feinstein is an international-al travel writer based in Los Angeles. He has written countless guides, reviews, and articles in cities around the world, including Bangkok, Barcelona, Florence, Stockholm, the French countryside, and Tokyo. An avid traveler, Paul has been to nearly 60 countries, lived in Israel, and is particularly obsessed with Italy and Japan. This edition, he updated the Experience, Travel Smart, Beverly Hills, West Hollywood, Mid-Wilshire and Koreatown, and Downtown Los Angeles chapters.

Michelle Rae Uy loves travel, adores photography, and is obsessed with animals. When she isn't off on a new adventure, she is seen at home cuddling with her cats and devouring films, often with a snack or two on hand. More important, in relation to this guidebook, she is a freelance travel and tech writer based in Los Angeles. She updated Hollywood and the Studios and Los Feliz and the Eastside chapters this edition.

Los Angeles-based freelance writer **Jill Weinlein** writes a weekly restaurant news and reviews column in the *Beverly Press and Park LaBrea News*. Her travel reviews are also featured in JustLuxe and *Luxe Beat* Travel. In addition, she has a monthly travel column in *Not Born Yesterday* and maintains her own "Dine and Travel" blog. While updating the Disneyland and Orange County chapter, she discovered some new hotels, restaurants, gardens, and outdoor activities that are featured in this book.

Orange County native **Candice Yacono** is a writer, editor, and designer for clients world-wide, including the *Los Angeles Times*, *Coast Magazine*, and the U.S. Department of State. She never learned to ride a bike, so she overcompensates today with cars, trains, and planes. When she's traveling, you can usually find her at the local ruins, library, or cat café. At home she's an MA and MFA fellow at Chapman University, where she studies English and creative writing. She updated Santa Monica and Venice, Pasadena, and Malibu and the Beaches.